Humanity's Law

Humanity's Law

Ruti Teitel

OXFORD
UNIVERSITY PRESS

OXFORD
UNIVERSITY PRESS

Oxford University Press, Inc., publishes works that further
Oxford University's objective of excellence
in research, scholarship, and education.

Oxford   New York

Auckland   Cape Town   Dar es Salaam   Hong Kong   Karachi
Kuala Lumpur   Madrid   Melbourne   Mexico City   Nairobi
New Delhi   Shanghai   Taipei   Toronto

With offices in

Argentina   Austria   Brazil   Chile   Czech Republic   France   Greece
Guatemala   Hungary   Italy   Japan   Poland   Portugal   Singapore
South Korea   Switzerland   Thailand   Turkey   Ukraine   Vietnam

Published by Oxford University Press, Inc.
198 Madison Avenue, New York, NY 10016

www.oup.com

Library of Congress Cataloging-in-Publication Data
Teitel, Ruti G.
Humanity's law / Ruti Teitel.
p.   cm.
Includes bibliographical references and index.
ISBN-13: 978-0-19-537091-1 (hardcover : alk. paper)
ISBN-10: 0-19-537091-0 (hardcover : alk. paper)
1. Human rights.   2. International law.
3. Humanitarian law.   I. Title.
K3240.T45 2011
341.4'8—dc22   2011006038

Printed in the United States of America
on acid-free paper

For Rob

CONTENTS

PREFACE

We are living in a time of destabilizing political and legal changes. Often, it seems difficult to know whether we are at war or at peace; to determine what sort of conflict is at stake in a given situation; and, relatedly, to decide how best to address the conflict and to protect the persons, peoples, and/or states that it threatens. While both the end of polarized relations and the advent of globalization have their appeal, the renewed engagement has frequently seemed to mean that we see the possibility of intervention, but that hope is too often thwarted. Yet the closer we look, the more one can see that this situation has too frequently been viewed from a twentieth-century, state-centered perspective. Recently, there have been profound changes in the nature of interstate relations and conflict—all of which have pointed in the direction of the paradigm shift toward humanity law and, to some extent, away from interstate international law, that is identified here.

After I finished my first book *Transitional Justice*, which explored legal and political responses to the transitions characterizing the end of the twentieth century, it became apparent that—despite lurches toward liberal democratic peace—conflict and violence not only were here to stay, but in some regard were ever more conspicuous, at least insofar as they were having a vivid impact on civilians. Indeed, it seemed that it was precisely during fragile transitions—that is, moments of weakness—that states were at their most vulnerable.

Another puzzle that arose was that of the role of law, and why legal mechanisms and solutions seemed to proliferate. How could this development best be explained? It was clear that the lens we were using—which viewed situations from a state-centric perspective—lacked sufficient explanatory power. But why might that be? The law's role seemed problematic, given the changes we had witnessed in the nature of the violence. It was necessary to ask: To what extent is the law addressing the real sources of conflict? What sort of law should properly be applied to twenty-first-century conflicts?

Other changes, too, are under way, leading us to ask: Exactly who is the current subject in foreign affairs today? And, in a concededly globalizing politics, what exactly might be the role of actors beyond the state? Large numbers of civilians were being affected by conflict, and accordingly, it was vital to examine the role of a human-centered (not state-centered) politics and law in the search for legitimacy. Compounded vulnerabilities speak to other identities, which in turn illuminated the extraordinary rise in ethnic conflict. These persistent questions gave rise to the exploration here into the conditions for, the status of, and the changing role for law. They have led me to postulate that we are witnessing at least a partial change of legal regime, departing from the preexisting interstate regime and moving toward a regime I term "humanity law"—that is, the law of persons and peoples.

Pursuing a project of this sort necessitated taking an interdisciplinary perspective, as it involved exploring some of the legal developments in relation to (and as enmeshed in) politics and conflict. In this journey, I have been fortunate to have support and feedback from numerous workshops, colloquia, and institutions. Early ideas were presented at the Centre National de la Recherche Scientifique (CNRS) Colloque on World Civility, Ethical Norms and Transnational Diffusion (October 2002); Yale Law School, Globalization Seminar (May 2003); University of Essex Centre for Theoretical Studies in the Humanities and Social Sciences Seminar (October 2003) and its International Law Seminar in November 2005; and the University of Tel Aviv, Law and History Colloquium (April 2004), as well as the University's law-school-faculty workshop. Ideas were further developed through the London School of Economics Centre for the Study of Global Governance, International Law Seminar (November 2005). Moreover, ideas about the direction of global justice evolved at Hebrew University, in a short course on that subject at the law school, where I guest-taught in the summer of 2007.

Portions of chapter 4, on justice and war, were presented at my alma mater, Cornell Law School, at its Conference on Global Justice, in remarks responding to "Just War and the Noncombatant Defense" (April 2006), which were published as "Wages of Just War," in the Cornell Law School symposium issue (*Cornell International Law Journal* 39 [2006]). In the fall of 2006, I was grateful for the support of the University of Connecticut's Human Rights Institute, where I was given a visiting Gladstein Chair for Human Rights, as a result of which I gave three university-wide talks. These began with an overarching view of the project, "For Humanity: The Emerging Shift in the Rule of Law in Global Politics," and ended with a presentation on the evolution of the law toward a humanity law regime at the University of Connecticut Faculty Workshop (November 2006).

Over the next year, various chapters of this book benefited from workshops at American University, Washington College of Law; Georgetown Law School's Constitutional Law Colloquium; Harvard Law School's International Law Colloquium workshop series; and the Columbia Law School Associates Series, where I presented at its international law seminar. Chapter 3 benefited from discussions at Columbia University's Associates-in-Law Workshop Series (February 2007); and a Fall Speaker series where I presented "Humanity's Law: Regulating a World of Conflict" hosted by Columbia Law School's Center for Global Legal Problems (October 2007).

In my last sabbatical, 2007–2008, I am grateful to Yale Law School for support in the way of an Orville H. Schell, Jr. Center for International Human Rights Fellowship, and for the feedback of students and faculty in the Schell Human Rights workshop, where I presented parts of this book (specifically, chapter 3). That spring, I was a visiting professor at Fordham Law School, where the Faculty Workshop offered a most hospitable environment to present parts of the book, particularly chapter 5. During that sabbatical, I was invited to teach at Columbia University, in the Politics Department, and benefited from presenting at the Columbia University Politics Speaker Series on November 7, 2008. I am also grateful to Fordham University Law School for discussions of chapter 3 that occurred in March 2008. Moreover, ideas on humanity law as the basis for interpretation, as discussed in chapter 7, benefited from presentation at Fordham Law School's International Law and International Relations Theory Colloquium, as well as from part of an international law conference on interpretation and the Constitution, which would later be published in Fordham Law School's Symposium Issue, "International Law and the Constitution: Terms of Engagement" (2008). My discussion of the area of applied humanity law in the global antiterror campaign benefited from a presentation at Oxford University's Roundtable entitled "Human Rights and the War on Terror," convened by David Rodin in November 2008. Chapter 4 benefited from a presentation at Georgetown International Human Rights Colloquium in January 2008, and a presentation at Temple Law School's International Law Workshop in April 2008. I am grateful for exchanges relating to humanity law at London School of Economics over the last years in my capacity as visiting professor in Global Governance.

My home institution, New York Law School, has been very supportive, through its summer grant research assistance program and the Ernst C. Stiefel Chair, which for some years now has supported my research. Having had a chance to get to know the late Ernst Stiefel and his dynamic view of international law, I believe that he would have liked this book. I am very grateful to the New York Law School law library staff, and particularly to Ms. Camille Broussard and Margaret Butler. I also owe an enormous debt to my terrific research assistants at New York Law School, without whom this book would not have been possible—most recently Luna Droubi, who somehow balanced this with her editorial role on the Law Review, Aman Shareef, as well as my former research assistants over the last three years: Sandra Dubow, Diane Bradshaw, Eric Grossmann, Theresa Loken, and William Vidal. I would also like to convey my gratitude and admiration to Human Rights Watch for their excellent research reports. In this project, as always, my assistant Stan Schwartz has been invaluable in word processing and other assistance.

Many friends and colleagues have been helpful: I owe thanks especially to my editor at Oxford, David McBride, who saw a spark in this project, and to three anonymous reviewers, all of whom pushed me in important directions. I would also like to express my appreciation for the helpful comments of Bill Alford, Michael Dorf, Michael Doyle, Martin Flaherty, Ryan Goodman, Aeyal Gross, Tom Lee, Joanne Mariner, Jeremy Paul, Iavor Rangelov, Anthony Sebok, Jack Snyder, Peter Spiro, Simon Teitel, Mark Tushnet, and Richard Wilson. To my family, many thanks for the distraction that is their humanity. Most of all, I am indebted to Rob Howse for his deep thinking and profound solidarity on this project.

Humanity's Law

CHAPTER 1

Introduction

Every Man, as Man has a Right to claim the Aid of other Men, in Necessity. And every Person is obliged to give it to him, if in his Power by the Laws of Humanity.
      Hugo Grotius, *The Rights of War and Peace, book 2, chapter 25 (1853)*

[A]n evaluation of international right and wrong, which heretofore existed only in the heart of mankind, has now been written into the books of men as the Law of Humanity. This law is not restricted to events of war. It envisages the protection of humanity at all times.
      Opinion and judgment of the tribunal of the *Einsatzgruppen case (1948)*

When we read the charter today, we are more than ever conscious that its aim is to protect individual human beings, not to protect those who abuse them.
      Kofi A. Annan, *"Two Concepts of Sovereignty" (1999)*

To brush aside America's responsibility as a leader and—more profoundly—our responsibilities to our fellow human beings under such circumstances would have been a betrayal of who we are. Some nations may be able to turn a blind eye to atrocities in other countries. The United States of America is different. And as President, I refused to wait for the images of slaughter and mass graves before taking action.
      Barack Obama, *Remarks on Libya (March 28, 2011)*

The end of the Cold War gave rise to hopes for a new peace, to be cemented by multilateral institutions and inspired by universal law. But, in short order, the collapse of communism released a wave of political violence. There followed a range of interventions and engagements undertaken in the name of "humanity"—from Kosovo to Darfur, to Afghanistan and Iraq. We have been confronted with new kinds of conflicts. The obsolescence or inadequacy of long-standing devices and doctrines—such as nuclear deterrence, spheres of influence, and "containment" approaches—to effectively manage conflict has become increasingly apparent. From the Balkans to Africa to the Middle East, we see a rising number of weak and failed states and increasing political fragmentation, civil strife, displacement, and migration, and we witness the plight of peoples whose very survival is under threat. Terrorism and religious extremism add to the pervasive sense of volatility and existential insecurity.

This history has created the context for a transformation in the relationship of law to violence in global politics. The normative foundations of the international legal order have shifted from an emphasis on state security—that is, security as defined by borders, statehood, territory, and so on—to a focus on human security: the security of persons and peoples.[1] In an unstable and insecure world, the law of humanity—a framework that spans the law of war, international human rights law, and international criminal justice—reshapes the discourse of international relations.

Courts, tribunals, other international bodies, and political actors draw from the various elements of the framework, in assessing the rights and wrongs of conflict; determining whether and how to intervene; and imposing accountability and responsibility on both state and nonstate actors. In interpreting and elaborating the law of humanity, courts, tribunals, and other agents have had to address tensions between, and gaps within, the different traditional doctrinal sources of humanity law. In so doing, they have expanded rights and responsibilities to encompass wider and wider circles of conduct, and additional actors within conflicts. At the same time, they have also increased the legal responsibilities of states, even for the behavior of nonstate actors the Bosnian Serb militias, for example, in the case of *Tadic*, while exhibiting less deference to the traditional sovereign prerogatives of states, where doing so would interfere with the overriding goal of protecting persons and peoples.

All this engages the sources, content, institutions, and agents of international law. The law of war has traditionally included both *jus in bello*—which addresses the manner in which war is waged—and *jus ad bellum*, which sets the legal rules that determine whether going to war is permissible in the first place. *Jus ad bellum* has mostly been codified in the UN Charter, which bans the use of force by states against other states, except in self-defense or with the authorization of the Security Council.[2] *Jus in bello* is codified to a significant extent in the postwar Geneva Conventions and Additional Protocol, substantial parts of which are now regarded as customary international law, binding on the entire community of states.

Among the most important norms set out in Common Article 3 of the 1949 Geneva Conventions are the prohibitions on murder, torture, and cruel treatment. The targeting of civilians is prohibited; the principle of proportionality requires the avoidance of excessive force, demanding that it be proportionate to a legitimate military objective; and humane standards of treatment for prisoners of war are set forth. Additional Protocol 1 to the Geneva Conventions pertains to civil wars and is also widely considered to be operative as "customary international law." Protocol 1, Article 48 formulates the basic rule relating to the protection of civilians—a treaty formulation of the customary rule of discrimination, aimed at ensuring respect for, and protection of, the civilian population and civilian objects. These duties primarily fall upon the signatory states, while the most serious are now enforced by international criminal tribunals.

Next, there is human rights law. The international law of human rights engages states in peacetime, primarily to protect certain individual and group rights of those who reside in their territory. But as the International Court of Justice has opined, its application extends to armed conflict as well, subject to relevant limits.

This body of law is usually said to have its source in the postwar Universal Declaration of Human Rights. Many of the rights in the Declaration have been elaborated in the International Covenant on Civil and Political Rights, a multilateral instrument that is binding on the majority of the world's states, and that is enforced via an elaborate institutional apparatus for monitoring compliance and hearing complaints. The Covenant on Economic, Social and Cultural Rights has been more controversial, especially during the Cold War, when East-West ideological tensions were reflected in differing views on the meaning—and in some cases, on the very legitimacy—of the Covenant on Economic, Social and Cultural Rights. (The United States is still not fully bound as a party to this covenant.) Now, increasingly, as will be seen, these kinds of rights are the subject of litigation and decisionmaking in the Inter-American and European regimes and tribunals among others.

Finally, also informing the humanity law framework is the law of international criminal justice, which is closely associated with international humanitarian law, as it has evolved since the end of the last world war. Under the law of international criminal justice, enforcement focuses on individuals. This approach may be seen as beginning with the landmark International Military Tribunal at Nuremberg, and drawing from the law of war. It is central to the Torture Convention, and to the charters of the ad hoc international criminal tribunals that were constituted after genocides in Europe and Africa. This approach also characterizes the proceedings of the permanent International Criminal Court (ICC), and encompasses the concept of "universal jurisdiction," as well as widespread norms that universally prohibit the most egregious of offenses, such as torture and slavery ("jus cogens"). Such norms allow—and, indeed, may even require—the prosecution of offenders by any state that is able to do so.

This book maps the rise of humanity law, and considers how that body of law is shaped by, and is reshaping, each of the three international legal regimes just discussed. While the book does not espouse a formal fusion of rules or doctrines, I argue that humanity law provides a framework that both legal and political actors employ in today's world, as they confront the challenges of conflict and of insecurity. This framework is most evidently at work in the jurisprudence of the tribunals—international, regional, and domestic—that are charged with applying a diverse range of legal materials to particular disputes, disputes that often span issues of internal and international conflict and security. Thus, throughout this book, I will discuss and analyze this jurisprudence. Most international legal scholarship focuses on individual regimes or tribunals, as if they operated in a relatively self-contained way. But under that approach, it is easy to miss the evolution of a jurisprudence that is being generated by a normative and interpretive framework that operates across these divides, and connects the mandates and decisions of diverse tribunals and institutions.

I explore the humanity law phenomenon by looking to its historical roots, its contemporary tendencies, and its effect on the discourse of international relations. By opting for this approach, I am seeking to elucidate the new dilemmas of engagement in global politics, and the increasing overlap and interconnection between the law of war and the law of peace; between international and other levels of legal order (domestic, regional, even subnational); and between and among the regimes regulating the public and private spheres.

Today, when violent conflict is conspicuous and pervasive in parts of the world, the law of war is expanding alongside the parameters of contemporary transnational conflict.[3] Heightened violence, particularly across state borders, coincides with the ascendance of a humanity-driven discourse in politics.[4] I will elucidate the tension between the ascendant rule of law and the management of the use of force, by exploring the changed law of humanity and its impact on the traditional law of war and human rights law.

The shift in the role of law in managing conflict reflects a changed political consciousness—and the change at issue goes to the very values and principles associated with legality itself. The law and discourse of humanity law are penetrating the sphere of foreign policy decisionmaking, as can be seen in the increasing frequency with which situations of conflict that have hit a political impasse are being referred to court—as has occurred, for example, in the Balkans, Sierra Leone, Darfur, Lebanon, and most recently Libya.

Moreover, as we will see, this framework informs our analysis of globalization and the current economic crisis—raising the vital question "What do we owe each other?" The "responsibility to protect" ("RtoP") means, in the first instance, the duty of the state to protect its citizens against the worst sorts of political violence, such as ethnic cleansing and genocide. But even absent those extreme circumstances, that duty still points to a shared responsibility. The kinds of legal norms that are often assumed to be epiphenomenal (that is, functioning largely outside a given situation, and retrospectively) in politics—for instance, the norms imposed by the laws of war regarding limits on harm to civilians—are now invoked prospectively, to justify military interventions, such as those that have occurred in Kosovo, Afghanistan, Iraq, and recently Libya. The North Atlantic Treaty Organization sought to justify its bombing of Kosovo and Serbia by making the following statement before the World Court, in which the very purpose of armed intervention is argued in legal terms: "To safeguard... essential values which also rank as *jus cogens*. Are the right to life, physical integrity, the prohibition of torture, are these not norms with the status of *jus cogens*?"[5] Similar justifications to limit political violence against solutions appear in the Security Council's resolution legalizing the intervention in Libya: "[a]uthoriz[ing] Member States... to take all necessary measures,... to protect civilians and civilian populated areas under threat of attack."[6]

The extent to which this new (or transformed) language of justification is actually altering states' perceptions of their interests, and changing the underlying determinants of state behavior is, of course, a matter for further social-scientific investigation and debate. But the first step to take here is to properly *define and understand* the grammar and syntax, as it were, of the new language of justification; its origins; and how it has developed in response to changing political realities.

The interstate system is challenged by the claims of new subjects such as persons and peoples, organized along affiliative ties (such as race, religion, and ethnicity) that extend beyond the state and even beyond nationality. These claims range from demands for secession and sovereignty to assertions of novel rights, to claims for protection, assistance, and accountability for past wrongs, both individual- and group-based. We also see the interstate system facilitating both the civil and the criminal accountability of nonstate actors, while making a strong statement about the universal reach of the rule of law, and the universalizable content of the core humanity law norms.

These developments have gone hand in hand with the rise of nonstate actors in international law as bearers of both rights and duties, and the interconnected tendency toward judicialization. Here, one thinks of the emergence of international criminal law processes and institutions, as well as the prevailing regional courts, and how they are being shaped by individuals' involvement in adjudication, and also of the appellate jurisprudence of the World Trade Organization—a legal system that formally remains within the classic interstate model yet is unable in its lawmaking to resist the shift to non-state-centric subjectivity, as seen by its judge-made decisions entertaining amicus submissions from nonstate actors and in its decision to open hearings to the public.[7]

What might explain the appeal of the new humanitarianism? To what extent does it play to the longing for universalism in a divisive and skeptical age? Is it perhaps addressing the failure of traditional state-based processes and institutions to cope with, and adjust to, changed political realities?

THE PARADIGM SHIFT

At issue is the extended reach of legality. This extension takes as a departure point classic conceptions of state sovereignty and state interests, and moves toward the incorporation of humanitarian concerns (such as concerns for the protection of the rights to life of persons and peoples) as a crucial element in the justification of state action. Under the classic state-sovereignty-based approach, states were largely unconstrained in terms of what they did within their own borders (except for the minimus standards relating to the treatment of aliens—the law of diplomatic protection). And externally, apart from jus cogens, states were constrained only by norms to which they had consented, either by explicit agreement (as in the case of conventional law), or by state practice and *opinio juris* (as in the case of customary law). As it developed with the UN Charter, this system contemplated only very limited justifications for the use of force: Force could be justified only by the need for the maintenance or reestablishment of international peace and security, and *only* where authorized or coordinated *multilaterally* (through the Security Council). Accordingly, Article 2(4) of the UN Charter provides as follows: "All Members shall refrain in their international relations from the threat or use of force against the territorial integrity or political independence of any state."

The UN Charter did recognize one exception: the "inherent" right of self-defense. For, Article 51 provides that, "nothing...shall impair the inherent right of individual or collective self-defence if an armed attack occurs." At least until the Security Council had been able to act, the right to self-defense may be exercised *unilaterally* or through other collective institutions (such as NATO, etc.). Of course, as conceded by the 1990s-era UN Secretary-General Kofi Annan, in reality, this "old orthodoxy" was never absolute. The UN Charter, after all, was issued in the name of "the peoples," not the governments, of the United Nations. As Annan has commented, the Charter's aim was not only to preserve international peace but also "to reaffirm faith in fundamental human rights, in the dignity and worth of the human person"; thus, Annan observed, "The Charter protects the sovereignty of peoples. It was never meant as a license for governments to trample on human rights and human dignity."[8]

Over the last decade, humanitarianism's meaning for the international legal system has been hotly contested. For some, humanitarianism has become a source of resistance to economic globalization. Yet humanitarian law is actually redefining the struggle for justice in terms that focus not on the preservation of state autonomy against the global legal order, but on the effects of law on persons and peoples, and on our evolving understandings of human security. In Annan's words,

> state sovereignty, in its most basic sense, is being redefined—not least by the forces of globalisation and international co-operation. States are now widely understood to be instruments at the service of their peoples, and not vice versa. At the same time individual sovereignty—by which I mean the fundamental freedom of each individual, enshrined in the charter of the UN and subsequent international treaties—has been enhanced by a renewed and spreading consciousness of individual rights. When we read the Charter today, we are more than ever conscious that its aim is to protect individual human beings, not to protect those who abuse them.[9]

For centuries, international law worked hand-in-glove with statism to reinforce modern nation-building. The commitment to self-determination as set out in Declaration on Principles of International Law Concerning Friendly Relations and Co-operation among States was qualified by the sanctity of borders, and the persistence of the traditional doctrine of recognition, which looked to facts such as control of territory (as embodied in the Montevideo Convention). From the basic understanding of security that is spelled out in the UN Charter and through to the baseline of state responsibility, and even to the understandings of rights in the international sphere, the state-centered vision still held sway. But that vision is now in the process of being transformed and relativized by a normative order that is grounded in the protection of humanity. Drawing from the postwar moment, as Justice Robert H. Jackson declared at Nuremberg, it has become clear that "humanity need not supplicate for a Tribunal in which to proclaim its rights.... *Humanity can assert itself by law. It has taken on the robe of authority.*"[10]

Of course, sovereignty is in no way disappearing, but it is losing its traditional status of primacy in the legal ordering that governs matters that occur beyond the level of the individual state. Sovereignty is no longer a self-evident foundation for international law. This shift is driving the move from the state-centric normative discourse of global politics—which had prevailed until recently—to a far-ranging, transnational discourse in which references to changed subjectivity have consequences. That new discourse is constructed more along humanity law lines.

Debates about the legality and legitimacy of the use of force by states increasingly center on the rights and claims of persons and peoples rather than on the interests and prerogatives of states as such. More and more, humanity law is being extended beyond situations that involve protected persons in interstate conflict to situations that occur outside international conflict, under both national and international supervision. Examples of such situations include interventions or protracted occupations, or involve the "war on terror."

Humanitarian commitments have been broadened and deepened by treaties providing for new forms of conflict regulation of a humanitarian nature, such as the Landmines Convention, and by certain UN Security Council processes and resolutions. Humanitarian enforcement has also been furthered by new regional or international judiciaries, such as the International Criminal Court (ICC), that are invested with various new supervisory and adjudicatory powers. Yet because the ICC lacks certain enforcement resources (such as a police force), the ICC must depend on state and interstate cooperation to bring the accused before the court, detain suspects, acquire evidence, and so forth. Security Council actions are now not just operating on the state but also—and increasingly—targeting individuals and holding them responsible. This dynamic can be seen especially in the war on terror, where sanctions have been imposed on identified individuals who are alleged to have some involvement in terror.

More institutions are invested with juridical law enforcement powers that are meant to allow them to protect humanity law–related rights and duties. Among these institutions are international and regional tribunals—for example, the European Court of Human Rights, the Inter-American Court of Human Rights, the ICC, and the Inter-American Commission on Human Rights. Meanwhile, domestic courts, too, consider humanity law claims involving violations of the law of nations, under customary law and doctrines of "extraterritorial" or universal jurisdiction. For example, the UK House of Lords accepted that Spain had jurisdiction to try deposed former Chilean dictator Augusto Pinochet for violations of *jus cogens* prohibitions of, and protections against, torture so long as the conduct was seen as criminal under the UK law at the time. Such developments reframe and reconceptualize the meaning of accountability in the international realm, enabling a move away from the state and its collective responsibility, through the reconception of the law in terms of the primacy of individual responsibility. This reconceptualization is creating alternative and potentially independent paths to conflict resolution, occurring often without explicit state consent while arguably also, over time, building a sense of shared global community.

INTERNATIONAL CRISES REFLECT THE SHIFT

The 1648 Westphalia Peace Treaty allowed states to acknowledge each other's exclusive authority, and created a defining split between international and domestic law, relegating interstate conflict to the orbit of international law. This "classic" international law was rarely enforced or interpreted by courts and tribunals. Instead, it usually elaborated by a small circle of academic commentators and "foreign office" legal advisers. Classic international law was often regarded as autonomous—that is, entirely separate from any nation's domestic law—though some constitutional traditions, such as that of the United States, incorporated elements of international law, as discussed by David Golove.[11]

Thus, in the words of the International Criminal Tribunal for the Former Yugoslavia (ICTY) in *Prosecutor v. Dusko Tadic*, the tribunal held that "a state-sovereignty-oriented approach have [*sic*] been gradually supplanted by a human-being-oriented approach.... Why protect civilians from belligerent violence or ban rape, torture or the wanton destruction of hospitals, churches... as well as proscribe weapons causing unnecessary suffering when two sovereign States are engaged in war, and yet refrain from enacting the same bans or providing the same protection when armed violence has erupted 'only' within the territory of a sovereign State."[12]

In present political conditions, there is a growing gap between the older bases of legality and contemporary understandings of legitimacy, which are informed by an evolving norm of humanity law. For example, "emerging slowly but... surely is an international norm against the violent repression of minorities that will and must take precedence over concerns of State sovereignty."[13] The new understanding of legitimacy is reflected in a reshaped legal order, staked out in terms of interests in humanity. The relationship between this new, altered legal order and the subsisting traditional order of interstate relations, embodied by sources such as the UN Charter's rules on use of force, remains tense and unresolved.

The international community's failure to respond to the Rwandan genocide, coming on the heels of Bosnia, prompted a marked shift in expectations about the protection of humanity. In particular, there emerged a strong demand to protect humanity rights, even if state sovereignty had to be compromised—as, for example, through military intervention. In the words of then Secretary-General Annan, "it has cast in stark relief the dilemma of what has been called humanitarian intervention: on one side, the question of the legitimacy of an action taken by a regional organization without a UN mandate; on the other, the universally recognized imperative of effectively halting gross and systematic violations of human rights with grave humanitarian consequences."[14]

When ethnic persecution returned to the heart of Europe, it eventually led to NATO military action, including the bombing of Serbia's capital, Belgrade, on the basis of the need to enforce humanity rights. The long-standing prohibition on the use of force except in self-defense or with the Security Council's approval was jettisoned in favor of a claim to the right to wage a "just war" in the name of humanity. More generally, responses to contemporary foreign affairs crises involving weak states and large-scale human rights violations display the limits of the classic view of international legality, which has been premised on state sovereignty and territorial integrity. In the case of NATO's bombing of Kosovo and Serbia, a subsequent investigation by the UN-appointed Independent Commission of Experts concluded that the NATO military intervention was "illegal but legitimate." The Commission concluded that the intervention was illegal because it lacked prior approval from the UN Security Council. Yet in the Commission's eyes, the intervention was still justified because all diplomatic avenues had been exhausted, and because the intervention had the effect of liberating the majority population of Kosovo from a long period of oppression under Serbian rule.[15]

Hence, for many in the international community, the effort to put a decisive end to "ethnic cleansing" in Kosovo was thought to be justified *morally*, even if not *legally*, as an otherwise unauthorized NATO intervention. Now, the way has been paved for a "duty of protection" to be invoked, regarding the possibility of intervention in places like Darfur and, as was recently seen in the first Security Council authorized humanitarian intervention in Libya, taken up at chapter 4. The recognition of a responsibility for the protection of others is also seen in the emerging "human security" focus of a range of political and legal fora and actors—for example, in the United Nations, and in the Human Security Commission and Report, where appeals to justice increasingly are being framed and justified in humanity law terms.

Various post-9/11 political developments have accelerated the rise of the humanity-centered regime. Fear of terrorism, coupled with the concern about the proliferation of weapons of mass destruction, has heightened anxiety regarding the potential for humanitarian disaster on a global scale.

In an increasingly interdependent world, few discernable lines demarcate interstate interests in security from interests that are based simply on our common humanity. As former U.S. president Bill Clinton put it, "philosophers and theologians have talked for millennia about how we are interdependent because of our shared humanity. Politicians have taken it seriously at least since the end of World War II, the dropping of the bomb, and the establishment of the United Nations. But now it is a reality that no ordinary citizen of the world anywhere can escape."[16]

THE DILEMMAS OF GLOBAL ENGAGEMENT
AND HUMANITARIAN INTERVENTION

As noted, the humanity law framework reconceives security in terms of the protection and preservation of persons and peoples. Once the relevant subjects and goals in the international realm are reconceived in this way, the meaning and challenges of security in both war and peacetime become blurred. Contemporary conflict is complex: There are a large number of situations where humanity rights are at stake that cannot easily be classified as either a state of war in the classic sense or a state of peace or normal legality. Under classical international law, the state enjoyed a monopoly on the use of violence within its territory—a precept that informed the traditional view of revolutionary and secessionist movements, and that has its source in the early modern political thought that created the grounding of classical liberalism, going back to Hobbes, and others. But that precept becomes highly problematic when the law is made in the name not of states but of humanity; and when the law supports claims not only for universal human rights but also the self-determination of peoples. Such claims have spurred a demand for forceful intervention in "humanity's" name, not in the name of the state.

Meanwhile, too, the trend toward the legalization of conflict has arguably marginalized, or even displaced, elements of normative political and diplomatic discourse. Hence, we can see, for example, in the Middle East, that the political claims underlying violent conflict in the last war in Lebanon and the intervention in Gaza have now taken second stage to competing claims concerning humanity law violations. Genuine political and ideological conflict reemerges, but as a conflict over humanity's multiple meanings and, in particular, over what rights pertain to peoples. Such a contest, however, occurs among diffuse actors, in many sites at once. Present political conditions pose a real challenge to the universal realization of human security, and put into question the degree to which humanity rights are protectable on a transnational basis.

In the chapters that follow, I seek to articulate and elucidate the implications of a humanity-centered global turn. The new "humanity law" translates into a changed language for policymaking, and describes the transformation of international normative order: its constitutive principles, processes, and values. The book confronts and seeks to discern both order in and tension among a rich, interrelated set of legal materials and phenomena—including multilateral treaties and conventions; the foreign-relations-related decisions of domestic courts; the writings of international legal scholars; the advocacy of NGOs and popular movements; the rulings of international courts and tribunals; debates about legality in diplomatic and political fora (such as the UN Security Council); and even, to some extent, in the media and in domestic politics. This is a greatly expanded juridical-philosophical landscape, where, as I shall show, arguments, doctrines, and interpretations shift with great speed from one site to another, and from one level of political or social ordering to another. Tracing the logic that governs these movements—a logic that is susceptible, to a significant extent, I argue, to a "humanity law" interpretation—is a major goal of this book.

A ROADMAP

Chapter 2 addresses the genesis and evolution of humanity law. At each stage or moment of its development, humanity law has been sharpened by the particulars of its political conditions and structures. In this chapter, I also explore affinities with earlier periods—for example, the older law of empire and the premodern "just war" tradition.

This genealogy elucidates the normative force of humanitarianism, and its potential for transnational diffusion. This value is apt to transcend national and cultural differences. Yet the prospect of universalizing humanity law's extension across state borders can come into genuine tension with political realities relating to the maintenance of the interstate system. The problem of humanitarian intervention arises today within the context of post–Cold War global realities that, unlike their historical counterparts, are distinguished by interconnection—yet lack of integration. This situation points to the relevance, and importance, of humanity law as a transnational juridical framework. Despite its universalizing appeal, humanity law is inevitably particular, and associated with the distinctive politics of the time and place: Neither progress nor return, here is a multi-layered, normative framework that best captures the tension, and constitutes the principles, that are apt to guide the present global order.

Chapter 3 articulates the book's central claim, concerning a paradigm shift in the rule of law. It aims to delineate the salient dimensions of the proposed legal framework, by identifying humanity law's discursive and constitutive roles in global politics and economic concerns. Humanity-centered law constitutes a leading contemporary discourse. Reaching beyond the state and the prevailing international system, it offers a new basis for legitimation and interpretation—first, of many traditionally diffuse and diverse legal norms and doctrines and structures in international law, and second (more tentatively but equally importantly), of political actions and claims. This capacious discourse involves diverse political actors, both state and nonstate, reflecting its widespread presence and persuasiveness as a language of justification.

In addition, chapter 3 reviews the dimensions that characterize the humanity law regime; its changed subjectivity in the international system, as it moves beyond states to persons and peoples; its applicability beyond instances of conflict; and its guarantee of minimum order. The humanity law regime, as it extends across the law of war and human rights law, reaches beyond states and their interests and obligations, to the rights and responsibilities of persons and peoples. Despite the emergence of the humanity law regime, many institutional structures are not yet formally changing, and therefore, given institutional rigidity, there are concomitant tensions. Such tensions make it all the more important to adopt appropriate principles of interpretation, so that the transition may be managed (a subject taken up in chapter 7).

New forms of humanity-based law are aimed at bridging the gap between prevailing forms of legality and changing sources of legitimacy. In this context, the proliferation of decentered adjudicatory processes and fora is aimed at fairly representing and reconciling diverse and potentially conflicting aims, such as the aims of justice, security, and peace, reflecting their complex role in present-day politics.

Chapter 4 explains how humanity law frames the use of force, and explains its legitimacy through the lens of crime and punishment. This chapter discusses the uses of tribunals that are convened in the midst of ethnic and political conflict. In such conflicts, the transformation in the perception of the legitimacy of the use of force is seen in the imperative of adjudicating *jus ad bellum,* as well as in the prosecution of *jus in bello,* by addressing the humanitarian violations occurring in conflict. Perhaps the greatest departure humanity law makes from the long-standing understanding of international humanitarian law lies in its inclusion, among its "most serious crimes" category, of the offense of "aggression." That offense, although thus far undefined, would give the now-permanent ICC a routine, ongoing authority that would extend beyond the cessation of the conflict, as classically understood.[17] This development goes together with the "normalization" of humanity law as a regime that is applicable generally, whether in war or peacetime.

Chapter 4 ends by evaluating the complex relationship between the uses of punishment and the use of military force, as alternative means of protecting humanity rights. It begins by looking to the apparent rise of international criminal justice as means of enforcement of humanity rights. Recent foreign policy discourse reflects an evident return to the concept of the "just war" and its uses as an international sanction. At the same time, however, this return to the "just war" concept occurs against the present context of legalism and judicialization, which imposes added constraints on the waging even of an ostensible just war. This dilemma is evident in the contemporary use of military interventions, where traditional national security is being reconceived in terms of human security: the preservation of persons and peoples. This chapter explores the relationship of the classic approach to the waging of war, to the newer just war logic—showing how these approaches and logics exist in palpable tension with one another. Recognition of this tension, it is suggested, might well clarify the difficulties of some of today's military engagements, such as Afghanistan, Iraq, and most recently Libya.

Chapter 5 considers the implications of the shift toward a humanity-centered perspective for a number of areas of policymaking, where security is being reconceived in terms of the protection of persons and peoples. The expanded humanity-based legal framework has a wide-ranging impact on the meaning of the rule of law in foreign affairs—redefining the rule of law in terms not just of states, but of persons and peoples as well. This chapter will look at several case studies involving recent international controversies that raise dilemmas about the ongoing legitimation of the use of force. It examines situations where the existing legal order coexists with the humanity law regime's rights-based predicates for forceful intervention, in instances of massive humanitarian rights violations. It also asks what is the legal scheme that is normatively appropriate for, and applicable to, the "war against terror." Moreover, it inquires as to how the relevant debates about this campaign also reflect the advent of the humanity-centered response, as well as laying the basis for law enforcement–based constructions regarding who is inside, and outside, the relevant international community. Under the humanity law regime, the appeal of universalizable terms of protection, deriving from a human rights scheme, is now stronger than ever; in the humanity-centered view of agency, responsibility devolves on the individual,

Changes in legal concepts of personality and agency are inextricably associated with related procedural and normative changes in the global order. The heart of the human-centered perspective is that more and more rights and responsibilities in the international system are being reframed to extend beyond the interests of states, and to recognize the interests of persons and peoples. There is a clear expansion of the procedural dimension, in the proliferation of tribunalization and in the increased demand for the ability to adjudicate issues involving individual rights and responsibilities in a variety of spaces, such as the European Court of Human Rights; UN tribunals; and international, hybrid, and local fora. The normativity is also seen in the proliferation of institutions adjudicating *jus cogens*, norms seeking to provide a modicum of security for persons and peoples around the world. Such norms involve, for instance, protection against crimes against humanity and anti-genocide laws. These developments reflect the evolution of rights to human security, as they are transformed along a procedural/substantive divide that is importantly informing the normative meaning of global justice.

Chapter 6 articulates how the humanity law framework exposes substantive principles of justice. The rise of humanity-centered law informs a changing conception of global justice that centers on a principle of human security with formal and substantive dimensions. The rise of a discourse of "global justice" across a broad range of areas is itself evidence of the humanity law transformation.

Across a broad swathe of areas—including politics, law, economics, ethics, and public health—a vital vision is emerging, which depends on a threshold consensus on the need to guarantee the humane treatment of persons and peoples, and ensure their preservation. Hence, under the humanity law regime, political and economic rights and freedoms are not artificially separated. Rather, the humanity-centered principles of security and the rule of law *span* these rights regimes—thus constituting a modality whose locus exists between human rights and the interests of states. It is from this responsibility of care for persons and peoples that other rights and entitlements follow. This human-security focus is reflected in the discourse of a range of political and legal fora and actors—including multilateral institutions such as the UN Human Security Commission and Report, where appeals to justice are being framed and justified in humanity law terms.

Chapter 7 presents the humanity law framework as an interpretive lens, examining how its teleology and normative lens informs and shapes— consciously or, often, implicitly—the way courts and tribunals (international, regional, and domestic) interpret and apply the law that governs the disputes before them. Some of the underlying issues include: To what extent do individual rights stop at state borders? To what extent are individual rights to be recognized and enforced transnationally? To what extent are interpretations through the lenses of the humanity law framework reshaping the categories of the discourse that are dominant among political actors, and the multiple agents of globalization?[18]

Chapter 8, building on the argument of the prior chapters, seeks to distill the normative contours and significance of humanity law. It explores the implications of the shift to a humanity-centered discourse, and humanity-centered values and institutions, for contemporary international politics. In particular, it focuses on the role of judgment and of interpretation in clarifying humanity law norms in an ongoing way. Beyond the role of judgment, chapter 8 examines the parameters of the basis for the rule of law—moving beyond the state to the protection of persons and peoples—and it shows how these policy decisions forge an evolving conception of international society. In the now emerging global society, the protection of peoples is being reconceptualized—as a protection that goes beyond the protection of the state itself, and bears a dynamic connection to an overarching humanity. The force of the book's thesis is that it offers a coherent account that both illuminates present-day politics and maps the contours of an emerging vision of global social order—one with tremendous potential for transforming human relations and creating greater solidarity between peoples and across state borders.

Finally, the last chapter draws from prior chapters regarding the bases of humanity law to explore the ramifications of this logic for foreign affairs, for conflict, and for the protection of human security. Humanity law puts into motion a comprehensive value system and set of mechanisms and processes. This framework provides the basis for the legitimation of foreign policy decisionmaking. Hence, understanding how a humanity law–based perspective operates practically should elucidate and contribute to a better understanding of current foreign policy controversies, particularly concerning conflict and security. Indeed, the terms of engagement are now at the heart of political strategy, and have become an independent goal of interventions that are justified along humanity law lines. Finally, the conclusion seeks to show some of the practical takeaways of the humanity law perspective that prior chapters have articulated.

CHAPTER 2

The Faces of Humanity

Origins and Jurisprudence

THE HUMANITY LAW TRADITION

Humanity law is the product of multiple traditions and diverse commitments, which converge in a distinctive subjectivity. This subjectivity derives from the recognition of individual agency and individuals' capacity and responsibility for action in the international sphere—responsibility that is potentially independent of the responsibility of the state. The recognition of individual responsibility was, in some sense, already anticipated by Grotius, who early on saw international society as not simply constituted of states and their relations, but encompassing individuals as well. The humanity law framework also implies a standard of treatment that is based on humanity as both the subject and object of action. Lastly, humanity law's orientation or telos is the preservation of humanity—understood as being composed at the same time of individuals and of diverse peoples, each organized around its own affiliations, aims, and interests. Such peoples challenge existing states in terms of defining allegiances and identities and the distribution of sovereignty—most evidently, with claims of self-determination, both internal and external.

The oldest conception of humanity that determined who is the subject and/or the object of law within the political community—that is, who is a citizen versus who is a slave, and who is a citizen versus who is a foreigner—is evidenced in what we call constitutionalism today, the increasingly universalistic civic status that is intimately linked to the rise of human rights. This contrasts with the concept of universal humanity as a legal or moral order transcending any particular political community—a concept that comes, instead, from international law. International law generally conceives of this order as an order *among* political communities.

The synthesis or interaction of these two conceptions generates a third idea: the idea of universal order as based on the status of the human being himself or herself. Hence the increasing recognition and protection of persons and peoples, based on a conception of the human.

Since the Renaissance, secular thought has focused on the human being as *subject*. From the beginnings of the nation-state,[1] humanism's evolution has occurred in tandem with the evolution of the conception, status, and relation of the individual *within* the state, as well as the evolution of the state as the crucial actor in international politics. Human rights developed out of the individual's struggle with the state, a struggle that continues to influence long-standing debates concerning the relationship between the public and private spheres, negative and positive rights, and concerning civil, political, and social and economic rights.

The humanity norm refers to both the manner and means of human conduct, and to its ends; the human is a subject and a standard of treatment. The tensions subsumed within the idea of the "law of humanity" go beyond the long-standing problems posed by international human rights law. That leads to a key question: How do we reconcile universalism in human rights with the demands of particular forms of community and culture?[2]

THE ORIGINS OF HUMANITY JURISPRUDENCE

Let us consider the confluence of various component regimes of humanity law—especially two strands of the law of conflict, namely, *jus in bello* and *jus ad bellum*, together with human rights law, and international criminal law. *Jus ad bellum*, which concerns the justification for waging war, has its origins in the just war tradition. Over the course of the evolution of *jus ad bellum*, the tendency has been to narrow considerably the possibilities of states' resorting to armed force to enforce legal or moral norms, or as a punishment for violations of international law. *Jus in bello*, in contrast, concerns the constraints on the waging of war, the manner in which hostilities are conducted, and the effects of war on combatants and civilian populations. This field, "humanitarian law," has its deepest source in the notion—as articulated by Hugo Grotius, the founder of modern international law—that there are some natural limits on what can be done even in the heat of battle, that is, limits inherent in the nature of the human, some but not all of which are reflected in the positive *jus gentium*.[3] In other words, this conception sees such limits as a product not only of natural justice but also of common practice and elements of agreement or consensus among peoples or nations. Customary norms have existed for centuries. However, modern humanitarian law derives significantly from treaty law—chiefly, the four Geneva Conventions of 1949, and most notably, Common Article 3, prohibiting certain forms of violence against the person.

Finally, human rights law, as reflected in the Universal Declaration and the International Covenants on Civil and Political Rights and on Economic, Social and Cultural Rights, primarily engages state responsibility with respect to the rights that states owe their own citizens. (However, it should be pointed out that the distant origin of the idea of international human rights law is often considered to be the law of diplomatic protection, which concerned the duties that a state owed other states with respect to the treatment of *their* citizens on its territory—now reflected in the International Law Commission Draft Articles on Diplomatic Protection.[4] It is clear that most of the rights in the Covenants, and the manner in which they have been articulated, suppose the context of a domestic society in peacetime. That being said, however, if one considers some of the Covenants' limitations on rights that relate to national security and emergency situations, the drafters of the Covenants apparently intended that the rights they guaranteed would continue to apply during conflict, even if an allowance had to be made for the particular necessities imposed by war (as has been confirmed by the International Court of Justice in recent case law).

In recent decades, the bases for applying international human rights law—including in conflict situations and across national boundaries (for example, and still controversially, to conduct by a state toward other states and their citizens)—have expanded tremendously with the increase in interpretive bodies, whether multilateral, regional, or international. The Convention on the Elimination of All Forms of Discrimination against Women now explicitly applies not only to the actions of the state but also to behavior by other actors and situations, for it makes states internationally responsible for certain acts and omissions of nonstate agents.[5]

Let us now turn to the mutual interconnection and reshaping of these areas of law, in terms of the expansion of claims, the definitions of claimants and responsibilities, and the role and responsibility of states and nonstate actors. On examining these areas of law, we shall see the emergence of a framework of humanity-based rights and duties that operates across the traditionally defined doctrinal substance of these three areas.

As the discussion that follows will bear out, history tells us that the notion that these are entirely separate bodies of law is not an apt description, particularly since World War II and the extension of the Geneva

Conventions' protections beyond the persons caught up in immediate conflict, and toward other categories of vulnerable persons.

Viewing humanity law in historical perspective enables us to understand better the contemporary rise of humanitarianism. While the humanity law framework is coalescing in our own time, the current ascendance of humanitarian legalism shares affinities with developments during earlier periods that are associated with the pursuit of empire: As will be seen, the return to the "just war" concept relates to a revival of imperial or imperialistic political discourse. Yet, at the same time, humanity law exists in dynamic tension with the inherited understandings and practices of the classic interstate order, which are grounded in concepts of Westphalian sovereignty; are still reflected in the UN Charter's foundation of the sovereign equality of states; and are admittedly unstable and are changing (precisely in dynamic relation to humanity law) the dividing line between domestic matters and matters of international peace and security.

The universalist element in the notion of humanity is seen in early natural and canon law, in the beginnings of the just war tradition, and in the politics of empire. This moralizing rhetoric distinguished "just" from "unjust wars" and "civilized" from "uncivilized" nations—and in so doing rationalized a wide range of wrongs, ranging from slavery to colonialism to imperialism.[6] Even on the ruins of the Roman Empire, there was a call by humanists for natural-law restraints in war-making on "humanity" grounds.

"Jus gentium" translates as the "law of nations" or, more accurately, the "law of peoples." Some of the norms concerning merchants and others who are often on the move (e.g., ambassadors) became "positive" law, by virtue of incorporation in Roman law, as the legal rules applicable to Roman citizens and foreigners alike throughout the empire.[7] As the empire grew, becoming more diverse, this unifying law also expanded and evolved. Navigating between natural and positive law, "jus gentium," as it was known, consisted in shared customs, and was in no way limited to what was set out in treaties, which evolved to govern human relations in the metropolis. Historically, jus gentium applied to areas of disputed sovereignty. As we shall see, its applications became controversial, for example with respect to colonization and slavery.[8]

Yet in this way, jus gentium becomes available across the world, as a set of rules of conduct that were equally valid everywhere. According to Francisco Suarez, "although the totality of men was not gathered into *one* body politic, but...divided into various communities, nevertheless, one would observe some general laws as it were by common treaty and consent among themselves—and these are what are called 'the laws of nations,'— which have been introduced more by tradition and custom than[9] by some constitution."[10] Suarez conceptualizes jus gentium in terms of the Christian natural-law tradition, whereas, as we shall see, Hugo Grotius grounded jus gentium on a more secular basis, emphasizing commonalities in human practice or custom, such as principles guiding envoys, and other customs concerning diplomacy and the formalities of agreements regarding war and peace, an understanding that later develops into a system of interstate relations.

HUMANITY LAW AND THE GROTIAN TRADITION

As was recognized by one of the architects of twentieth-century international law, Hersch Lauterpacht, Grotius saw "an intimate connexion between the rejection of the ideas of 'reason of State' and the affirmation of the legal and moral unity of mankind. He insists that if no association of men can be maintained without law, 'surely also that association which binds together the human race, or binds many nations together, has need of law.'"[11] Grotius elaborates that at the crux of interstate relations is the law itself: "[T]he common consent of mankind has shown to be the will of all, that is law."[12]

According to Grotius,

> the "law of nations" is considered a more extensive right, deriving its authority from the consent of all, or at least of *many* nations: It was proper to add MANY, because scarce any right can be found common to all nations, except the law of nature, which itself too is generally called the law of nations. Nay, frequently in one part of the world, that is held for the law of nations, which is not so in another. Now this law of nations is proved in the same manner as the unwritten civil law, and that is by the continual experience and testimony of the Sages of the Law. For this law...is the discoveries made by experience and time.[13]

Later, Alberico Gentili would refer to injuries that threaten not only the existence of particular states but also the existence of "human society."[14] Beyond this notion of society, for Grotius, the shared legal principles, as elaborated in his *Rights of War and Peace*, center on "self-preservation" and the idea that "it shall be permissible to defend [one's own] life and to shun that which threatens to prove injurious; it shall be permissible to acquire for oneself, and to retain, those things which are useful for life."[15] Nevertheless, he sees this right as strictly limited. As Benedict Kingsbury has observed, this emphasis on self-preservation is common to the entire early modern social contract tradition, including that part of the tradition that is based on the writings of Thomas Hobbes and John Locke.[16]

Hobbes wrote:

> The right of nature, which writers commonly call jus naturale, is the liberty each
> man hath to use his own power as he will himself for the preservation of his own
> nature; that is to say, of his own life; and consequently, of doing anything which,
> in his own judgement and reason, he shall conceive to be the aptest means there-
> unto.... Whensoever a man transferreth his right, or renounceth it, it is either
> in consideration of some right reciprocally transferred to himself, or for some
> other good he hopeth for thereby.... [T]he motive and end for which this
> renouncing and transferring of right is introduced is nothing else but the secu-
> rity of a man's person, in his life, and in the means of so preserving life as not to
> be weary of it.[17]

Compare Grotius's opening words in *Rights of War and Peace*: "The disputes
arising among those who are held together by no common bond of civil laws
to decide their dissensions, who formed no national community, or the
numerous unconnected communities...all bear a relation to the circumstances of war or peace...it will be proper to treat all such quarrels as commonly happen, between nations, as an article in the rights of war."[18]

The idea of humanity had emerged in late antiquity and was present in
the Christian Middle Ages. Here, we can see the pivotal role for *lex humana*
in drawing the parameters of the international community—that is, in
drawing a line between the "civilized" and the "barbarians"— which role is
then deployed to justify various aims in international relations, from war,
to punishment, to slavery in the colonializing era.[19]

At the time, the concept of *humanitas* supplied the sense that there was a
rule of law in the international sphere, largely understood as an intelligible
line between just and unjust conflict. "In a general sense, the word *humanitas* also conveyed the meaning of 'broad humanity,' or 'human duty,' extending beyond any artificial boundaries.... In defending Roscius against the
charge of a brutal crime, Marcus Tullius Cicero states that this same universal
human feeling is strong enough to have prevented the defendant from committing such an atrocious deed against any fellow man for, as he says, *magna
est enim vis humanitatis*."[20] In turn, *humanitas* is defined in Roman law as
follows: "the humane tendency as an ethical commandment, benevolent
consideration for others. The term as well as the adjective humanus (human-
ior) appears both in juristic texts and imperial constitutions. The idea of
humanity undoubtedly exercised a considerable influence on the development
of the Roman law through interpretation and decisions of the jurists. In the
Christian Empire its influence infiltrated various providences of the law
(family, marriage, succession, slavery, penal legislation)."[21]

Years of warfare inspired by religious differences ended in the Treaty of Westphalia, whereby the sovereign was recognized as the supreme authority responsible for the care of those within the sovereign's territory, with absolute authority over internal affairs. The treaty also marked a point at which the focus of international law became, exclusively, the rights and duties of states in relation to one another. Hence, at this critical juncture, the idea that war could be justified by abstract moral principles was sacrificed to the notion of the sovereign equality of states. The law of war became a tool used by states for managing the conduct of war—and these practices were later ratified in the Hague and the Geneva Conventions, in 1864 and 1907, respectively.

A humanitarian sensibility emerged eventually. The mainstream of early modern political theory grounded the status of citizenship on the notion or fiction of a contract or compact between free, equal, and isolated individuals—abstract selves. This approach to political legitimacy, which became the normative basis for revolution and for liberal-democratic state-building, attributed or assumed a prepolitical moral status or capacity in the individual, as a precondition of social and political cooperation.[22] Rousseau's privileging of compassion as a source of public, not just private, morality would powerfully influence the early political rhetoric of humanitarianism. The nineteenth-century controversy over the morality of slavery revealed a growing awareness of the evolving norm of humanity. At the Congress of Vienna, which was convened to address the slavery issue, a core group of delegates declared the international slave trade repugnant to "the principles of humanity and universal morality."[23] Efforts to combat slavery gave rise to related endeavors concerning racial and other persecution, all in the name of "humanity."

The invocation of "humanity" would also have its role in empire; the term was employed in various imperial campaigns. For instance, in denouncing Napoleon's massacres of prisoners in the Syrian campaign, Chateaubriand said, "the heavens will avenge the violations of the rights of humanity."[24] Indeed, it was one of these last bloody campaigns that spurred the creation of the Red Cross and the drafting of the first of the Geneva Conventions, the foundations of international humanitarian law. After the ravaging effects of the 1864 Battle of Solferino became known,[25] there was a call to put some limit on the devastating effects of war. This movement in favor of constraining the waging of war would give rise to the first humanitarian treaty of its kind—a treaty that took the existing law of war in a more human-centered direction, as it aimed at the amelioration of the condition of wounded soldiers across state borders and national lines, though all within Europe.

Beyond the early twentieth-century concern to protect those who are caught up in war, based on defined statuses (e.g., of "combatant," "civilian," and so on), another strand of humanity law aims at limiting the methods of warfare that may be employed, based on the notion that certain methods are inherently inhumane or contrary to the "law of humanity."[26]

The St. Petersburg Declaration incorporated a notion of proportionality, implying at the very least that violence must be limited to that deemed "necessary" to the war's waging.[27] The use of certain weapons, such as explosive bullets, was considered to run counter to the "laws of humanity."

In 1899, the Hague Convention "Martens Clause" set out the "principles of the law of nations, as they result from usages established among civilized peoples from the laws of humanity and the dictates of public conscience": The aim was to set limits to the waging of war, deriving from the "laws of humanity."[28] Even though the clause would become incorporated in the Convention, it also seemed purposefully vague, as its language alternated between references to "law" and to "principles of humanity." The resulting ambiguity would open a space for shared custom and practice to develop, relating to conflict as a source of international humanitarian law. Moreover—and even more important—this purposeful ambiguity constitutes a predicate for an always-evolving humanity law, guiding interpretation.[29] The Hague Conventions at the time stipulated "the desire to serve the interests of humanity," and, "until a more complete code of the laws of war is issued, the High Contracting Parties think it right to declare that in cases not included in the regulations adopted by them, populations and belligerents remain under the protection and empire of the principles of international law, as they result from the usages established between civilized nations, from the requirements of the public conscience."[30]

During World War I, the "law of humanity" was invoked once again in its breach. In 1915, at the time of the massacres of the Armenians, a letter addressed to the Ottoman government denounced the "new crimes of Turkey against humanity and civilization." The reference to humanity was thought to amend the original, which spoke only of "violations against Christianity and civilization," as it was feared that this language would offend Muslims in the colonies.[31] After the war, German atrocities against Belgians, analogized to the Turkish massacre of the Armenians, were deemed to have been violations of the "laws of humanity."[32] Over time, especially during conflict, the notion of the subject of "humanity" would recur, for the brutality of war would make it clear that—despite the establishment of international agreements and institutions dedicated to managing conflict, such as the League of Nations—civilians were nevertheless more exposed to wartime abuses than ever. Humanitarian law still did not adequately recognize the extent of the threat.

The Kellogg-Briand Pact (or the Pact of Paris) aimed at a permanent peace on "humanity" grounds;[33] here one can see that a point of connection emerges between the two historical strands of *jus ad bellum* and *jus in bello* (humanitarian law). Yet this attempt would fail, and the humanitarian principle would largely be honored in the breach, and vindicated only in an ad hoc way—for example, through the so-called minority treaties, agreements that states made, at their own discretion, so as to reciprocally protect their own citizens when they resided as minorities on the territory of other states.

Like *jus gentium* as it existed earlier on, the minority treaties sought to protect persons and peoples, along religious and linguistic affiliation, even where the relevant group affiliation was not expressed via statehood. Yet it bears remembering that for the most part these were modest arrangements, limited to protecting the affected peoples' religion rights, and often in circumscribed ways (i.e., relative only to that of other citizens of majority-religion status). Furthermore, the beneficiaries of these arrangements were still always dependent on the state to guarantee the protection in question, which in turn was an equality that was always relative to the implicated constitutional regime. In the landmark *Albanian Schools* case, the Permanent Court of International Justice explained,[34] "The idea underlying the treaties for the protection of minorities is to secure for certain elements incorporated in a State, the population which differs from them in race, language or religion, the possibility of living peaceably alongside that population and co-operating amicably with it, while at the same time preserving the characteristics which distinguish them from the majority."[35]

These precedents for extending humanitarian protections beyond the state take on a renewed relevance in the present context of political disequilibria. Since World War I, the ratio of civilian to military casualties has risen steadily, and now the absolute numbers of casualties typically are greater for civilians than uniformed combatants.[36] In former UN Secretary General Kofi Annan's words, in a recent address reflecting on intervention, "it is now conventional to put the proportion of civilian casualties somewhere in the region of 75 percent. But an actual figure will always be subject to question or dispute.... [T]here is no agency whose job it is keep a tally of citizens killed."[37]

As Mary Kaldor has observed, increased civilian vulnerability can, in part, be explained by the transformation of military technology and strategy.[38] For a long time, the law lagged behind. For example, even the most recent iterations of the Geneva Conventions, namely the Fourth 1949 Geneva Convention Relative to the Protection of Civilian Persons in Time of War, and Its Protocols, the 1977 Protocol I relating to the Protection of Victims of International Armed Conflicts, the 1977 Protocol II relating to the Protection of Victims of Non-International Armed Conflicts, and the 2005 Protocol III relating to the Adoption of an Additional Distinctive Emblem, left out the issue of the aerial bombing of civilians—which has by now become a central issue in recent and contemporary interventions such as in Kosovo and Afghanistan. This lag in the law would turn out to be characteristic of the ex post way the law of humanity is generated in response to conflict. Over the years, international law in this area would continue to develop in piecemeal and reactive fashion, responding to actual interstate conflicts as they unfolded over time.

Despite frequent recognitions of the threat posed to humanity from warfare, and apart from old customary norms rarely invoked and complied with, at the beginning of the twentieth century there was still no robust accepted law of humanitarian protection. Here, one might recall the divisiveness that existed over what form post–World War I punishment of Germany's violation of the "laws of humanity" would take.[39] Despite the widely shared sense that these had been egregious contraventions of basic norms, the United States, among others, saw individualized retributive justice for crimes that had hitherto been understood as collective—such as the crime of "aggression"—as amounting to the creation of new law after the fact, and thus as arguably itself posing a threat to the rule of law.[40]

It was the minority regimes that first explicitly recognized the vulnerability of certain persons and peoples. But this recognition remained within the framework of Westphalian state sovereignty (even while pushing against that framework) since the underlying basis for the obligations was each state's interest in protecting the affiliation of its own nationals to the "nation," and, accordingly, each state's willingness to extend protection to minorities within its own territory was premised on sovereign reciprocity.

Not much would change until the end of World War II, with the experience of wartime atrocities again prompting a call for accountability. At the time, the core threat to humanity was seen as deriving from the war's unjust beginnings. Whatever the concern for civilian atrocities, it was overshadowed by the concern with state aggression. Humanity rights, as such, were still not considered to be the subject of positive international law.

The turning point occurs at the postwar Nuremberg Trials, where the three strands of humanity law appear to converge for the first time. To some extent, this moment presents a return to the early classical international law vision, which emphasizes justice in the initiation of war; but the trials go beyond the justice of war: They amount to a crossroads in the three bodies of law at stake, as they imply the existence of a later modern doctrinal evolution in the actual application of punishment as to the forms of waging war.

The tribunal conceives Germany's aggression as the central offense. Beyond the offense against the community of states are the offenses against persons who were caught up in hostilities—that is, noncombatants, or those who were persecuted for their peoplehood. (I elaborate these categories of offenses in chapters 3 and 4.) At this moment in history, for the first time, there are glimmerings of the humanity law framework. Although political observers at the time were generally quite skeptical about the uses of these trials, Judith Shklar would observe, as to Nuremberg, "that as far as the Trial concerned itself with crimes against humanity it was both necessary and wise."[41] Hannah Arendt, too, seemed to understand the conceptualization of crimes against humanity as a decisive innovation.[42]

With the adoption of the postwar human rights conventions, humanity rights begin to take a universalizing turn: Protection is extended beyond a state's nationals to "all civilians." While the early law of war was directed at those with special status or special vulnerability—such as combatants, the sick, the wounded, or those who are taken prisoner at war's end—after World War II, in the Geneva Conventions, rights protection was extended from concern with the treatment of "combatants" (and particular localities or targets) to "civilians in armed conflict."[43] In particular, Geneva 4 became known as the "Civilian's Convention." Still, despite these new conventions, it would take time before these norms were seen as shared. While International law afforded protection against civilian atrocities, only insofar as they could be linked to war.[44]

Finally, in the 1970s—going beyond the classic understanding of war as involving interstate conflict, and building on the Geneva Conventions of 1949[45]—the two Additional Protocols greatly extended the humanitarian aegis of Geneva law, so as to limit operations that might impact on civilians. In laying out "basic principles for the protection of civilian populations in armed conflict," Protocol I says that "fundamental human rights" are accepted in international law. They "apply fully in situations of armed conflict."[46] Moreover, the 1949 Conventions' "Common Article 3," which is "common" to all the conventions, extended to *any* armed conflict the "elementary considerations of humanity" that are applicable under customary international law.[47] This is a norm that has become increasingly relevant in today's world of ethnic civil wars and transnational terror. Moreover, in the late 1970s, Protocol II internationalized further, beyond Common Article 3, the protection of victims of internal conflict, providing further assurances of humane treatment—though this guarantee of protection is still not enforced except against the state.[48]

Post–Cold War politics fueled the demand for a more sweeping universal rights regime. While humanitarian norms originated in settings of inter-state conflict, contemporary developments challenge accepted understand-ings as to how to draw the line between war and peace, international and internal conflict, state actors and private actors, and combatants and civilians. As with the present increase in certain kinds of violence,[49] the law of war expands with the parameters of contemporary transnational conflict. Hence, it has become clear that evolving human rights law applies even in situations of armed conflict where international humanitarian law also applies—an overlap that has produced some confusion. For some, espe-cially within the international humanitarian law advocacy world, this indeterminacy is reconcilable only if one thinks in terms of the dominance of international humanitarian law as a specialized regime that belongs to an epistemic community of humanitarian and human rights lawyers and activists.[50] The focus on this epistemic community—by David Kennedy, for instance—may overstate the extent to which the meaning(s) of humanity law are controlled by such committed professionals—changing, sometimes in ways neither necessarily anticipated nor desired, the discourse of inter-national politics.

HUMANITY LAW TODAY: WHAT DIRECTION WILL IT—AND SHOULD IT—TAKE?

For cosmopolitans, the growing universalization of the humanitarian norms, and their application beyond the state and beyond interstate con-flicts, are interpreted as signs of progress, and some constructivists, including Kathryn Sikkink, also take this view, as does Beth Simmons, who traces both the growing uses of this discourse and its effects.[51] From this perspective, the emergence of humanity law discourse is itself a sign of an ever-expanding legal system—one that has the potential of attaining universal scope, and thus carries the allure of the promise that we may someday see a "one-law" world. Rafael Domingo advocates this position from an apparently natural-law perspective;[52] he invokes humanity to denote a very particular kind of universalism—the notion of a law whose content is binding on all human beings, everywhere, for it legitimately demands universal obedience.

This notion should be contrasted with the humanity law framework I articulate in this book, which postulates the dynamic character of the status of the human. Humanity law offers a distinctive *subjectivity:* the status of the human is a basis for new and diverse *claims*, on the part of diverse voices that are new to international law and politics. It would not easily be possible to make such claims based on the older, more particular forms of status that were previously recognized. (As we have seen, even the applicability of international human rights law depended on the status of being a *national* of a *state* that had the responsibility to fulfill the obligations created by that law).

By contrast, the realist school of international relations asserts a permanent structure of interstate power relations. According to this school of thought, insofar as legal changes are acknowledged as having real-world effects, they are generally reconceived in terms of—and as expressions of—state sovereignty. (A good example of work within this school can be found in the writings of the international relations scholar Stephen Krasner).[53]

There is also a strand of *legal* realism, influenced by realist conceptions of international relations and state power, that is even more skeptical of the notion of an apparent trend toward universal law. This account lacks an appreciation of the ongoing dynamism of meaning that is created as a result of the uses of this discourse by diverse actors in the system on this basis.[54] Meanwhile, thinkers on the right, such as Krasner and Jack Goldsmith, see the increasing reliance on the uses of legalist discourse and institutions as epiphenomenal of Enlightenment narrative. In other words, they see this development as reflective of control by certain elites; they see the juridical shift to the law of conflict as merely a way to manage the balance of power; and their view of the role of new conflicts does emphasize the importance of the legalist elites, but that is a separate point.

On the other hand, Anne Peters, writing on the value of humanity, fails to give full credit to the change in subjectivity, and to the related substantive changes, that I discuss here.[55] Thus, she conceives humanity law as the new *Grundnorm* of what, in her view, still remains a system among states, where the subjectivity remains state-centered. What remains unacknowledged is the extent to which humanity law is unleashing new kinds of subjectivity in international law and politics.

I will take up some of the implications of these diverse interpretive approaches to contemporary international law and politics in the conclusion, where I argue that the prevailing views on this subject are often distorted precisely by their choice of conceptualizing the humanity law phenomenon largely from the perspective of the prevailing interstate system and, relatedly, from the perspective of somewhat anachronistic legal debates.

Scholars of international law such as Antonio Cassese and Theodor Meron have entertained aspects of this narrative. However, the account of humanity law I set forth here differs, for one, in that it is not just about the law; instead, this account looks to phenomena beyond the development of an autonomous law, with social, political, economic, cultural, implications for politics. Moreover, unlike many accounts of international law and politics, the story told here does not depict current humanity law as the culmination of the state-centric Westphalian narrative. Yet neither does this book's story describe a pure rupture from that long-prevailing account.

David Kennedy and Martti Koskenniemi challenge any account of international law that fails to adequately recognize a historical continuity with the pre-Westphalian period of religious wars and so on, advocating a colder pragmatic view of the connection between law and violence.[56] This book's account takes a different view, while it also recognizes the continuities. I concede that we lack a continuous narrative of progressive law. Rather, we must recognize the affinities and tensions between the three regimes that inform a single framework.

One might say that there have been two master narratives about the generation of international law: imperial versus Westphalian. If so, then one way to understand humanity law, instead, is through the Grotian moment. At that moment, the tradition of the philosophers of empire— the Spanish natural-law thinkers—is bridged with the conception of sovereignty in the emerging interstate system. A possibility is glimpsed of understanding international society as a universal community of peoples that underpins and shapes interstate relations—but that very possibility is submerged when state sovereignty is given primacy at Westphalia, and in the theory of Vattel and his successors.

As the humanity law framework is extended to ever broader populations— populations that are often caught up in conflict, or otherwise displaced— contemporary manifestations of international rights regulation are predominantly humanitarian in character. The change is demonstrable in foreign affairs discourse. Yet it is also demonstrable in the international legal framework and its applications. Indeed, more and more, the contemporary rule of law is being equated with the assurance of humanitarian norms regulating violence within a coercive scheme. This is illustrated by the tribunals addressing the conflicts in the former Yugoslavia and Rwanda, and the Rome Treaty establishing the permanent ICC.[57] It is also evident in a related explosion of transnational developments in the enforcement of "crimes against humanity." I explore these instances, and the overall turn to punishment, at greater length in chapter 4.

Why is the resurgence of a humanity-based jurisprudence occurring at this time in history, in particular? Over the course of human history, the effects of post-Enlightenment thinking made abundantly clear the limits of natural law, as well as the limits in human knowledge—as discussed in the work of Jacques Derrida, Richard Rorty, and others.[58] Yet once again, as historically, the law of humanity rises to this moment of legal and political transformation, as it presents a value system that mediates natural and positive law, the public and the private, the state and what lies beyond the state.

The law of humanity affirms the role of the individual within a layered conception that also takes account of the collective character of contemporary violence. These two faces of humanity are in some conflict, as is apparent in the ways the protection of individual human rights depends on group sovereignty in some fashion—particularly wherever its protection is related to the definition of peoples. As is also becoming apparent, humanity law additionally serves the complementary—and sometimes conflicting—aims of inclusion and exclusion in times of political flux, as in the ongoing protection of persons and peoples, whereby it defines and redefines groups, particularly those groups that are politically vulnerable, as well as the larger international society. This reconstitution is now commonly occurring through judicial processes and mechanisms, to which I turn in the next chapter.

CHAPTER 3

⌒◇⌒

The Ambit of Humanity Law

An Emerging Transnational
Legal Order

The simultaneous surge in law and violence is a beginning point for understanding the current world situation, for it casts into doubt the prevailing assumptions regarding the purported relationship of the rule of law to peace and stability.[1] Indeed, as has been observed in recent political science scholarship, such as that of Edward Mansfield and Jack Snyder, the processes of democratization and liberalization have not been as linear or as obviously harmonious as some had predicted at the end of the Cold War.[2] Furthermore, political, economic, and technological changes with globalizing ramifications are now penetrating the boundaries of the state[3] and producing a shift away from the prevailing state-centric system, in ways that transform rule-of-law values in the international legal order. Present political conditions, characterized by the increased manifestation of violence, lay the predicate for an enlarged humanity law framework.

CONFLICT JUDICIALIZED: POLITICS HUMANIZED

The leading element in the transformation is a humanitarian legal regime with a greater reach. This expanded legal ordering goes hand in hand with changing conceptions of legitimacy in contemporary international politics, and bridges divergent conceptions of the rule of law—moving between them, but also creating a new set of dynamic tensions among them. Historically, international judicial processes applying humanitarian law, if they were used at all, were only deployed postconflict. The preeminent aims were to settle claims arising from the conflict, to legitimize or normalize the ongoing occupation by the victors, and to finalize the status of the new political arrangements—for example, these were among the goals of the Nuremberg Trials after World War II. Today, however, adjudicatory processes are playing a significant role in foreign policy and strategy, often in the very midst of the conflict itself.

We can see legalization as a tool for shaping *state* behavior,[4] but the phenomena in question also have broader implications and dimensions, which engage the subjectivity, norms, and capacities of actors beyond the state. Consider, for example, the injection of a humanity-based discourse into the deliberations regarding the nature of the international response to the last decades' human rights crises in the Balkans and Africa, as well as into deliberations regarding the broader democratization project in the Middle East and the "war on terror."

Humanity-based normativity has a relationship of interdependence to classic, state-sovereignty-based international law and morality. The shift to the language of humanity law aims to construct a bridge between the discourse of state power and that of transpolitical moralism. The emergence of an ethical-legal discourse reflects, in part, the apparent lack of agreed-on common political principles that are adequate for managing current crises; the political changes and fault lines discussed in chapter 1 have brought about—or at least exacerbated—this state of affairs. Humanitarian legalist discourse offers an alternative set of principles and values for global governance.[5]

The humanity-based discourse is deployable by a diverse range of actors; as will be seen, it is also amenable to a broad range of purposes. For better and for worse, this discourse can operate beyond the state's control and its forms of political accountability. Indeed, part of what is alluring about this discourse is its promise of a normative language that seems to be beyond the fray of conventional political struggle (or at least beyond the claims and counterclaims of the antagonists). This promise appears to offer a sense of order and (normative) stability in a time of substantial political disequilibrium and dissensus. Its greater reach and justificatory scope create greater bases for legitimation.

Across the political spectrum, policy actors often now call for international intervention.[6] Since the late 1990s, speeches by political leaders have illustrated a shift in the justificatory rationale guiding policies and interests—from statist to human-centric justifications. For instance,

Bill Clinton made the following remarks in a speech he give after the war in Kosovo: "Because of our resolve, the 20th century is ending, not with help-less indignation, but with a hopeful affirmation of human dignity and human rights for the 21st century. In a world too divided by fear among people of different racial, ethnic and religious groups, we have given confidence to the friends of freedom and pause to those who would exploit human difference for inhuman purposes."[7]

A striking shift is evident in the frequency of political actors' and in particular leaders' references to persons and peoples and to global security, as well as in the non-state-centered nature of the asserted aims and pur-poses justifying engagement. What is also revealing is the significant increase in the numbers of appeals to humanitarian assistance. Beginning in the 1990s, the demand for forcible "humanitarian" intervention increased dramatically, for example with the call for the first Iraqi intervention, the call for intervention in Kosovo, and Darfur.[8] In Tony Blair's words, "war is an imperfect instrument for righting humanitarian distress; but armed force is sometimes the only means." Moreover, contemporary political discourse contains frequent references to the concept of "humanitarian" intervention, in what one might call a revived "just war" discourse. For example, such a discourse was evident with respect to the Russia/Georgia conflict, and was even invoked by traditional international security institu-tions and actors, such as the Security Council and its members, all against the shifting context of appeals to a broader duty to protect (discussed in chapter 5).[9] One might also consider as well the Security Council authoriza-tion of the intervention in Libya.[10]

The role of law in setting the parameters of engagement reflects the changes that are under way regarding the prevailing regime of interna-tional law, and reveals its relevance to the transformation of legitimacy. Humanity law's ascendancy poses a number of risks, stemming from the complexity of its norms and the generalized effect of a legalized political discourse. The traditional *jus in bello*—where international humani-tarian law was premised on neutrality as between the parties in the conflict, or at least their political claims—is of restricted scope, limited to regulating or constraining the manner in which the parties conducted the conflict.

To apply this bounded and minimalist morality as a normative blueprint for policymaking in general may impoverish the discourse of international politics. A "thin" negative consensus may well pass for an attitude of neu-trality toward competing political claims. Yet it is evident that while under the humanity law regime the "other" is generally depicted in absolute terms—as a criminal or a lawbreaker—there is still always an "other," and therefore political judgment continues to be salient, even if such judgment is somewhat hidden or obscured. Moreover, this is true whether the "other" is "the terrorist," "the rogue state," or "the outlaw regime." (Of course, the characterization does not fully address the self-understanding of the "other," who may well resist or reject the notion of neutrality within the political.) Thus, in a development that is reminiscent of the process that gave rise to the origins of international law, the emerging framework serves to lay the basis for a constitutive international society.

This discourse has had more and more currency, given globalizing changes that reach beyond the limits of the traditional state. It also shapes the representation of other asymmetric conflicts, as in the Middle East (e.g., in the 2006 Israeli operation in Lebanon) where humanity law discourse is somehow displacing other political evaluation[11] by framing the relevant issues primarily in terms of humanitarian rights and numbers of casualties, abstracting from the challenge of a just and viable political settlement in the region. In the Middle East, the Goldstone Report and the controversy it generated upstaged, and perhaps undermined, the tentative efforts to move forward the peace process. This type of framing is evidenced in recent studies and other reports analyzing a number of regions where the relevant legal order or regime is guided by humanity law.[12]

HUMANITY LAW'S DIFFUSION: OF PERSONS AND PEOPLES

One never governs a state, a territory or a political structure. Those whom one governs are people, individuals or groups.
    Michel Foucault, *Lecture at the Collège de France (1978)*

Historically, the scope of the humanitarian regime was carefully circumscribed.[13] It conferred a protected status only on a narrow range of persons, and only in certain very limited situations, associated with conflict. This was a small subset of all the persons who were at risk from the conflict in question, that is, combatants who had put their weapons down and were in detention. This understanding of the relevant protected status began to change with increasing civilian exposure to conflicts. But even where the Geneva Conventions were extended to civilians, the protections were still seen in terms of certain specific periods or phases of the conflict—that is, phases where persons found themselves in enemy hands, with the enemy understood, again, only in state-centric terms. Thus, a person could find himself or herself in a situation where the relevant protections run along nationality/citizenship lines; for example, consider the recent Balkans conflict. A good example of this type of protection can be found in the Fourth Geneva Convention: "Persons protected by the Convention are those who, at a given moment and in any manner whatsoever, find themselves, in case of conflict or occupation, in the hands of a Party to the conflict or Occupying Power of which they are not nationals."[14]

Yet today there is a demand for broader legal protection: as Judge Bruno Simma explained in his opinion in *Armed Activities on the Territory of the Congo (Democratic Republic of the Congo v. Uganda)*, "attention must also be drawn to Article 3 common to all four Geneva Conventions, which defines certain rules to be applied in armed conflicts of a non-international character. As the Court previously stated in the *Nicaragua* case: 'There is no doubt that, in the event of international armed conflicts, these rules also constitute a minimum yardstick, in addition to the more elaborate rules which are also to apply to international conflicts; and they are rules which, in the Court's opinion, reflect what the Court in 1949 called 'elementary considerations of humanity.' ' "[15]

Beyond the destabilization of the fundamental war/peace dichotomy just described, is the challenge to any fixed, circumscribed meaning of "protected person" and the expanding influence of the humanity law framework over the definition of the subject of the international regime. In referring to persons whose rights have been violated but are not fully represented via traditional—that is, diplomatic—protection, in the Uganda conflict, Judge Simma opined, "international humanitarian law provides for protection under Article 75 and common Article 3 so that such persons do not remain without certain minimum rights...there is 'in respect of these matters...no legal void in international law.' "[16]

At the same time, there is an extension of individual responsibility, challenging traditional limits on legal accountability, such as, for example, sovereign immunity. Consider the cases of Slobodan Milosevic, Saddam Hussein, and Muammar Qaddafi or before that Chile's Augusto Pinochet, the Congo's Abdoulaye Yerodia Ndombasi, and Sudan's Omar Bashir.[17] (I discuss these controversies at greater length in chapter 4.) In *Congo v. Belgium*, the ICJ, in the opinion of the court, held: "Immunity from jurisdiction enjoyed by incumbent Ministers for Foreign Affairs does not mean that they enjoy impunity in respect of any crimes that they might have committed, irrespective of their gravity." In other words, there would be no basis in international law for such individuals asserting immunity against civil or criminal prosecution once no longer in office. In 2003, a Parisian magistrate issued an arrest warrant against Zimbabwe's president, Robert Mugabe, on charges of torture, the French court ultimately ruled that

Mugabe was entitled to immunity from prosecution as a sitting head of state.[18] "Immunity from criminal jurisdiction and individual criminal responsibility are quite separate concepts," the court stated. "While jurisdictional immunity is procedural in nature, criminal responsibility is a question of substantive law. Jurisdictional immunity may well bar prosecution for a certain period or for certain offences; it cannot exonerate a person to whom it applies from all criminal responsibility."[19] As is illustrated by the cases of Bashir and Qaddafi, the ICC jurisdiction extends to incumbent political leaders, a further fundamental erosion of immunity unthinkable in earlier times.

However, in the 2000 case in England of *R v. Bow St. Metro. Stipendiary Magistrate and Others, Ex Parte Pinochet Ugarte (No. 3)*, the Queen's Bench Division ruled on the scope of Pinochet's sovereign immunity as a former head of state.[20] The question in the case became whether "international crimes in the highest sense," such as torture, can ever be regarded as the official acts of a head of state. Lord Hutton opined as follows: "The alleged acts of torture by Senator Pinochet were carried out under colour of his position as head of state, but they cannot be regarded as functions of a head of state under international law when international law expressly prohibits torture as a measure which a state can employ in any circumstances whatsoever and has made it an international crime."[21] Lord Phillips, taking a still broader view, explained that no immunity can be claimed by a government official for an act that violated customary international law: "An international crime is as offensive, if not more offensive, to the international community when committed under colour of office. Once extraterritorial jurisdiction is established, it makes no sense to exclude from it acts done in an official capacity."[22]

Later cases in special courts, such as that of Sierra Leone, would bear out the principle of individual responsibility. "Where jurisdiction is universal, a State cannot deprive another State of its jurisdiction to prosecute the offender by the grant of amnesty."[23] Contestation over the parameters of immunity is on the rise in the context of the demand for greater enforcement of humanity law.

This trend began in the mid-twentieth century, arguably with the postwar Geneva Conventions, which as to "grave breaches," the most serious war crimes already contemplated remedies incorporating notions of universality. Now the trend has become more and more evident, not only with the lifting of state immunities in a number of areas but also with the extension of the principle of liability for actions taken by state or nonstate actors wherever they are wielding public power. This development was foreshadowed by the work of leading international law scholars—such as Hersch Lauterpacht.[24] Thus, one can trace universal jurisdiction to World War II: At Nuremberg, the protections of the law were extended beyond nationals under occupation, to "*any* civilian population."—already reflecting a universalizing of the offense beyond a particular state. However, because of the novelty of the jurisdictional expansion at the time, and its vulnerability to challenge, jurisdiction was only actually exercised where the acts in question took place in the context of hostilities. Indeed, at the time, the preeminent offense was "aggression"—defined as a threat to the peace and stability of the interstate system, following a classic conception of the primacy of international security.

The postwar 1949 Geneva Conventions, for the first time, recognized a form of universal jurisdiction.[25] Though the concept yielded to postwar politics at the time, the concept of universal jurisdiction was, in 1973, in the International Convention on the Suppression and Punishment of the Crime of Apartheid, the convention recognizing South Africa's apartheid as a crime against humanity. Later, the Convention Against Torture and Other Cruel, Inhumane or Degrading Treatment established the duty of the state to prosecute torture, where to do so was within its jurisdiction, foreshadowing a relation of complementarity between the domestic and international society.

FROM WAR TO PEACETIME, FROM INTERNATIONAL TO INTERNAL CONFLICT

The wars of the last half century have ushered in a sense of a transformation of interstate security and, relatedly, a reconceptualization of the law of conflict—for an increasing number of *internal* conflicts now have *global* import.

Consider a relatively early example: the struggle against apartheid in South Africa. This struggle—originally conceived of as an "internal matter"—came to be reconceived as a matter of international peace and security, that is, as being fully within the UN Security Council's mandate. This change reflects the somewhat paradoxical political situation that characterizes the moment of post–Cold War democratization: One can see new exercises of self-determination, political fragmentation, and a discernable increase in transnational tensions and often in violence. Wherever internal armed conflicts are based on transnational affiliations, such conflicts have transborder, and even global, consequences. Indeed, the humanitarian-law

regime now applies to a diverse range of internal and transboundary conflicts, where the distinctions between the state of war and ordinary times
are neither dispositive, nor even determinate. Here, once again, the 1990s
Balkans and contemporary Iraq are illustrative. The tension is increasingly
apparent, as more and more of the controversies the ICJ is called on to
decide have posed challenges to adherence to that simple view, whether on
nuclear weapons, the security fence between Israel and the Territories, or
violent conflict implicating nonstate actors.

In the Statute of the International Criminal Tribunal for the former
Yugoslavia (at Article 5), jurisdiction is accorded to the Court to prosecute
persons who are responsible for certain crimes "when committed in armed
conflict, whether *international* or *internal* in character, and directed against
any civilian population."[26] In the tribunal's groundbreaking case law regarding
the Balkans, the meaning of Article 5 has been developed even further, as its
leading jurist has observed.[27] In adjudicating the "crime against humanity"
norm, the new tribunals proscribe "persecution against any identifiable
group or collectivity on political, racial, national, ethnic, cultural religious,
[or] gender... grounds," whether or not the state is involved in that policy.

When the ICJ was asked for its advice on the legality of the threat or use
of nuclear weapons, it rejected arguments that sought to circumscribe unduly humanity rights—that is, it rejected the notion that "the
Covenant was directed to the protection of human rights in peacetime, but
that questions relating to unlawful loss of life in hostilities were governed
by the law applicable in armed conflict."[28]

In its advisory opinion of July 8, 1996, on the legality of the threat or
use, the ICJ found that the human rights claims were valid—wherever they
were reconcilable with international humanitarian law—even, and most
important, when it came to the "right to life." In the court's words:

[T]he protection of the International Covenant of Civil and Political Rights does not
cease in times of war, except... whereby certain provisions may be derogated from
in a time of national emergency. Respect for the right to life is not, however, such a
provision. In principle, the right not [to] arbitrarily to be deprived of one's life
applies also in hostilities. The test of what is an arbitrary deprivation of life, however, then falls to be determined by the applicable *lex specialis*, namely, the law applicable in armed conflict which is designed to regulate the conduct of hostilities.[29]

Similar conclusions have been reached in regional tribunals, such as the
European Court of Human Rights, in *Isayeva v. Russia*; and the Inter-
American Court and Inter-American Commission on Human Rights, in
Abella and *Barrios Altos*. In its report on terrorism and human rights, the

Inter-American Commission asserted that "the international human rights commitments of states apply at all times, whether in situations of peace or situations of war."[30] As will be further elaborated, this is no longer an isolated claim, but a claim that has been asserted by more than one tribunal—and is emerging across conflicts and regions.

A CHANGING TELEOLOGY OF HUMAN SECURITY: CONTEMPORARY ILLUSTRATIONS

Further quandaries regarding human protection arise from the blurring of the lines between war and peace, and between international and internal borders. In *Case Concerning Armed Activities on the Territory of the Congo (Congo v. Uganda)*,[31] the Democratic Republic of the Congo instituted proceedings in the ICJ against Uganda, after Uganda had both occupied and perpetrated acts of armed aggression in the territory of the Congo in violation of the Charter of the United Nations and the Charter of the Organization of African Unity. The court invoked an earlier ruling, *Legality of Nuclear Weapons*, which stated, "to conclude that humanitarian law does not apply to nuclear weapons would be incompatible with the intrinsically humanitarian character of the legal principles in question which permeates the entire law of armed conflict."[32] These words—written more than two decades ago—foreshadow the humanity law framework, and the related interpretive practices concerning the evolving understandings of state responsibility aimed at a threshold level of human protection.

In other instances, as a result in part from post–World War II decolonization and the attendant rise of self-determination as an international right, there is a related expansion in the notion of "occupation"—beyond the context of territory that is held immediately subsequent to armed conflict, and extending to situations in which territory is contested, for example Israel/Palestine; Congo/Uganda. These developments are reflected in postwar treaty law in Geneva Convention IV, which is largely aimed at the protection of civilians, and goes beyond declared wars or other hostilities pertaining to states.[33]

Another factor, the post-9/11 "war on terror," has challenged the already unstable categories of combatant and civilian—that is, the long-held "principle of distinction" under the law of war. The result has been to leave civilians increasingly vulnerable to being affected both by the acts of terrorists and by counterterror operations. (I discuss this subject, raised in chapter 2, at greater length in chapter 5.) Concern for the protection of civilians animates the First Protocol, barring harmful effects on civilians of attacks that are deemed "excessive" in terms of military interests. This balancing test spurs teleological interpretations, in which human security constitutes the independent ultimate interest.

The tensions between state security and human security were brought squarely into relief in the ICJ opinion concerning Israel's construction of a miles-long barrier in occupied territory extending into the West Bank, "The Legal Consequences of the Construction of a Wall in the Occupied Palestinian Territory."[34] Confronted with a dispute over whether the international human rights conventions to which Israel is party apply within the Occupied Palestinian Territory, the Court opined, "to determine whether these texts are applicable in the Occupied Palestinian Territory, the Court will first address the issue of the relationship between international humanitarian law and human rights law and then that of the applicability of human rights instruments outside national territory."[35]

Here, the fundamental question was that of so-called dual application, given the varying origins, subjects, and values of the two legal orders at issue. Humanitarian law is the protection granted in a conflict situation, such as the one in the West Bank and Gaza Strip, while human rights treaties are intended for the protection of citizens vis-à-vis their own governments primarily in times of peace. In the words of the ICJ,

> the protection offered by human rights conventions does not cease in case of armed conflict, save through the effect of provisions for derogation....As regards the relationship between international humanitarian law and human rights law, there are thus three possible situations: some rights may be exclusively matters of international humanitarian law; others may be exclusively matters of human rights law; yet others may be matters of both these branches of international law. In order to answer the question put to it, the Court will have to take into consideration both these branches of international law, namely human rights law and, as lex specialis, international humanitarian law.[36]

The question of what this will amount to normatively remains controversial. The controversy has persisted at the United Nations, with the Goldstone Report and the question of what norms ought to apply concerning the use of force in Gaza. Though controversy remains, the report asserted that it was evaluating the situation in the territories from a humanity law framework: "Israel has failed to fulfill its obligations to protect the Palestinians from violence by private individuals under both international human rights law and international humanitarian law."[37] Again, here, a conflict situation has become transmuted from the political sphere, into a question of law and related rights protections—arguably informing the predicates for political process.

ACCOUNTING FOR HUMANITY: FILLING THE LEGAL
GAPS IN HUMAN PROTECTION

Consider *Bosnia v. Serbia*, a contentious case arising out of the Balkans conflict, where the ICJ held that genocide had occurred in Srebrenica but rejected the claim for collective reparations, while finding that Serbia had failed to perform its obligation to prevent and to punish. One might say that in a fashion, the court deferred to the primacy of individual criminal responsibility as a means of accountability, and thus to the UN Security Council's vision of the central role of the ICTY—the tribunal presiding over the conflict. At the same time, however, the court did not accept the ICTY's broader view of "overall control," as applied in individual cases to the question of what individual behavior and responsibility was enough to establish attribution to the state. Instead, the court reverted to the stricter standard of "effective control" as had been annunciated in *Nicaragua v. US*.[38]

Yet other courts—domestic and regional—have used humanity law to interpret what "effective control" means, such that there is a guarantee of meaningful protection: For instance, the House of Lords in *Al-Skeini v. Secretary of State for Defence* held: "Effective control here is equated with *immediate presence and power*....If effective control jurisprudence of the ECtHR marches with international humanitarian law and the law of armed conflict, as it clearly seeks to do, *it involves two key things: the de facto assumption of civil power by an occupying state and a concomitant obligation to do all that is possible to keep order and protect essential civil rights*. It does not make the occupying power the guarantor of rights; nor therefore does it demand sufficient control for all such purposes. *What it does is place an obligation on the occupier to do all it can*."[39]

Although, for the most part, the ICJ confirmed the effective-control standard in the *Armed Activities on the Territory of the Congo (Democratic Republic of the Congo v. Uganda)* and *Application of the Convention on the Prevention and Punishment of the Crime of Genocide (Bosnia and Herzegovina v. Serbia and Montenegro)* decisions, the Court appears to be divided as to whether this threshold is still in conformity with contemporary international law or whether there is a change underway as to the standard for state responsibility.[40] In a separate opinion in *Congo*, Judge Peter Kooijmans questioned the effective-control standard and argued that the ICJ had ignored the operational code that was evident in the international community's reactions to the 2001 attacks by the NATO Coalition against the Taliban, Operation Enduring Freedom.[41] In Kooijmans's opinion, Taliban support for Al Qaeda fell far below the bar that had been set in either the *Nicaragua* or *Tadic* judgments: "If the activities of armed bands present on a State's territory cannot be attributed to that State, the victim State is not the object of an armed attack by it. But if the attacks by the irregulars would, because of their scale and effects, have had to be classified as an armed attack had they been carried out by regular armed forces, there is nothing in the language of Article 51 of the Charter [of the United Nations] that prevents the victim State from exercising its inherent right of self-defense."[42] Similarly, Judge Simma stated: "[T]he lawfulness of the conduct of the attacked State in the face of such an armed attack by a nonstate group must be put to the same test as that applied in the case of a claim of self-defence against a State, namely, does the scale of the armed action by the irregulars amount to an armed attack and, if so, is the defensive action by the attacked State in conformity with the requirements of necessity and proportionality?"[43]

Simma further opined: "I will be very clear: I consider that legal arguments clarifying that in situations like the one before us *no gaps exist in the law* that would deprive the affected persons of any legal protection, have, unfortunately, never been as important as at present, in the face of certain recent deplorable developments."[44] Deploying a teleological interpretation grounded in the need for the sustained protection of humanity, Simma suggested: "If the international community allowed such interest to erode in the face not only of violations of obligations *erga omnes* but of outright attempts to do away with these fundamental duties, and in their place to open black holes in the law in which human beings may be disappeared and deprived of any legal protection whatsoever for indefinite periods of time, then international law, for me, would become much less worthwhile."[45]

Expanding on the concept of "erga omnes," that is, those obligations owed to the entire global community, Simma further explained:

> As against such undue restraint it is to be remembered that at least the core of the obligations deriving from the rules of international humanitarian and human rights law are valid erga omnes. . . . In its Advisory Opinion on the Legality of the Threat or Use of Nuclear Weapons the Court stated that "a great many rules of humanitarian law applicable in armed conflict are so fundamental to the respect of the human person and 'elementary considerations of humanity' . . . that they are "to be observed by all States whether or not they have ratified the conventions that contain them, because they constitute intransgressible principles of international customary law."[46]

These obligations were seen to extend beyond states to actions of others actors operating in the context of the law of war which may have implications as to their own responsibilities under the law of war and international criminal responsibilities.

Building on the Geneva Conventions of 1949, Common Article 3 extends, under customary international law, elementary considerations of humanity to any armed conflict—regardless of whether or not that conflict is international. Furthermore, the Geneva Conventions' "grave breaches" approach contemplated mandatory humanitarian-law enforcement in dealing with offenses of the greatest gravity, wherever there is "a duty and a right of all Contracting States to search for and try or extradite persons allegedly responsible for grave breaches." At the time, a form of universal jurisdiction was contemplated for offenses with an international component, i.e., states had jurisdiction over "grave breaches without regard for where the act occurred or the perpetrator's nationality.[47] A similar consensus had not yet been reached over protection against comparably serious violations in internal conflicts. That lack of consensus no doubt reflected the state-centric limits of the time, which—with the rise of civil wars and similar ethnic conflicts—are now being challenged.

The ICTY and the ICTR reflect a broad new scope of war crimes and crimes against humanity, which operates more and more without regard to the specific (i.e., international versus domestic) nature of the conflict at issue. In the statutes of these courts, as well as the ICC, there is an expansion of the jurisdictional reach over protected persons, as well as in the scope of individual responsibility (a topic on which chapter 4 elaborates further). Humanitarian law reaches well beyond the parameters of international armed conflict to regulate persecution and other situations *within* the state that do not necessarily involve civil war.[48]

The ICTY found the normative protections against "war crimes" and "crimes against humanity" applicable in both international and internal conflicts—relying on the postwar Geneva Conventions extending rights beyond interstate conflict. In its first challenge regarding jurisdiction the ICTY Appeals Chamber declared that the violations at issue entailed "individual criminal responsibility regardless of whether they are committed in internal or international armed conflicts.... Principles and rules of humanitarian law reflect elementary considerations of humanity, widely regarded as the mandatory minimum for conduct in armed conflicts of *any* kind."[49] The Appeals Chamber also added: "What is inhumane, and consequently proscribed in international wars, cannot but be inhumane and inadmissible in civil strife."[50] And it commented: "In the area of armed conflict the distinction between interstate wars and civil wars is losing its value as far as human beings are concerned."[51]

At its inception, the ICTY had promised that it would take a narrow view of its jurisdiction "As the first international tribunal to consider charges of crimes against humanity alleged to have occurred after the World War II, the International Tribunal...must apply customary international law as it stood at the time of the offenses."[52] Yet once cases were underway, these original parameters were quickly exceeded, and cases were decided where opinions referred often to the role of custom in the tribunal's application of the relevant law Indeed, the acceleration in the uses of customary law is bolstered by the work of jurists such as Theodor Meron.[53]

Here, we can see that challenges to the ICTY's creation and ongoing jurisdiction during conflict of an uncertain international nature spurred "teleologically based interpretation" of its statute.[54] The tribunal has invoked the Security Council's aims in establishing the ICTY in 1993 under UN Charter Chapter VII powers, which were aimed at advancing the goals of justice, and of making and preserving the aims of peace and security, and asserted that these multiple aims clearly reflected "an awareness of the mixed character of the conflicts."[55] Therefore, the Security Council is understood to have been granted jurisdiction appropriate to deal with this multi-faceted reality.[56] In appealing to the UN Charter's broader purposes, the ICTY has gone beyond the four corners of the statute. In *Celebici*, the ICTY interpreted the aims of the Geneva Conventions in terms of the protection of the human person, thus rendering essentially irrelevant the distinction between international and internal conflict in the selection of applicable legal norms.

Both human rights and humanitarian law focus on respect for human values and the dignity of the human person. Both bodies of law take as their starting point the concern for human dignity, which forms the basis of a list of fundamental minimum standards of humanity. Invoking their shared values, the International Committee of the Red Cross Commentary on the Additional Protocols refers to their common ground in the following terms: This irreducible core of human rights, also known as 'non-derogable rights' corresponds to the lowest level of protection which can be claimed by anyone at anytime.... *The universal and regional human rights instruments and the Geneva Conventions share a common 'core' of fundamental standards which are applicable at all times, in all circumstances and to all parties, and from which no derogation is permitted.* The object of the fundamental standards appearing in both bodies of law is the protection of the human person from certain heinous acts considered as unacceptable by all civilised nations in all circumstances."[57]

The jurisdictional revolution became explicit in the next international criminal tribunal established by the United Nations, the International Criminal Tribunal for Rwanda (ICTR). Despite that the offenses at issue were being committed within that country's ethnic conflict, the ICTR's statute explicitly contemplates *international* enforcement of prohibitions on genocide and crimes against humanity.[58] Here, we see that the institutionalization of the most serious offenses is being directed at protecting core individual and group humanity rights affinities beyond their nexus to the state.

In the more contemporary prosecutions based on this norm of protection, punishment policies have begun to lose their nexus to the state. This development recognizes the power of nonstate actors, particularly in weak and failed states. The extension of legal regulation to nonstate actors occurs both through broader principle of attribution in state responsibility as well as the emergence of criminal responsibility where armed conflict is pursued or directed by nonstate actors. From the very first case before the Balkans tribunal, the ICTY declared that "the law in relation to crimes against humanity has developed to take into account of forces which, although not those of the legitimate government, have *de facto* control."[59] Importantly, seen from the perspective of the threatened person or population, the public/private divide lacks relevance.

This change in focus constitutes a departure from the earlier international law of the interstate system; for instance, the ruling of the ICJ in the *Nicaragua* case, where the criterion was "effective control"—a narrow understanding of attribution of state responsibility.[60] Yet the ensuing transformed, more pragmatic precedent has been followed in subsequent cases in the international tribunals addressing conflicts such as those in the Balkans and Rwanda; where, too, jurists have looked to evidence of the policy on the ground.[61] The transformation of responsibility that is under way is also reflected in codifications, such as the International Law Commission's Draft Code of Crimes Against the Peace and Security of Mankind, which recognizes "the possibility that private individuals with de facto power . . . might also commit the kind of systematic or mass violations of human rights covered by the article."[62] This is also discussed further on in chapter 5 in reflections on the judicialization of instances of extraterritoriality in the campaign on the war on terror.

Other tribunals are similarly deploying a "teleological interpretation" guided by human-centered normativity. Wherever the humanity law framework is being extended to internal as well as international conflict, a challenge is how to reconcile this with applicable domestic law, whether that law is constitutional law or law incorporating protections for international human rights.

In *Abella v. Argentina,* which involved a standoff between the Argentine military and its police, the Inter-American Commission looked to international humanitarian law to interpret the American Convention on Human Rights Article 4 claim, asserting that *both* bodies of law—that is, human rights law and humanitarian law—apply in situations that come before internal conflict, where the regimes generally "converge and reinforce each other," as they share "a common nucleus of non-derogable rights and a common purpose of protecting human life and dignity." In so reasoning, the commission relied on the so-called most-favorable-to-the-individual clause, a principle of interpretation contemplated by the American Convention on Human Rights (at Article 29[b]). According to the Inter-American Commission, wherever both international humanitarian law and human rights law apply, any tensions between the relationship in international humanitarian law and human rights norms should be guided by this human-centered interpretation. In such situations, the Commission must give effect to the provision most favorable to the individual right or freedom in question. "Where there are differences between legal standards governing the same or comparable rights in the American Convention [on Human Rights] and a law instrument the Commission is duty bound to give legal effect to the provisions of that treaty with the higher standards applicable to the right(s) or freedom(s) in question."[63]

Guiding the interpretation of these two bodies of law is the principle of choosing what "provides the higher standard of protection." The Commission has concluded that "certain fundamental rights may never be suspended, as in the case, among others, of the right to life, the right to personal safety, or the right to due process.... under no circumstances may governments employ ... the denial of certain minimum conditions of justices as the means to restore public order. While international human rights and humanitarian law allow for some balancing between public security and individual liberty interests, this equilibrium does not permit that control over a detention rests exclusively with the agents charged with carrying it out."[64]

Indeed, a similar normative direction emerged from litigation arising out of the United States' detentions in its 1980s intervention in Grenada, *Coard v. United States*—which led to the convergence on essential standards of protections holding that both human rights and humanitarian law are applicable in "the protection of the individual," discussed further in chapter 5.[65]

THE GLOBAL UNIVERSAL: THE OFFENSE AGAINST HUMANITY

At the trial of Louis XVI, Louis Saint-Just argued: "The single aim of the committee was to persuade you that the king should be judged as an ordinary citizen. And I say that the king should be judged as an enemy; that we must not so much judge him as combat him; that as he had no part in the contract which united the French people, the forms of judicial procedure here are not to be sought in positive law, but in the 'law of nations.'" What exactly might this mean?

In the long-prevailing statist model, the international rule of law was grounded primarily on the inviolability of existing state borders. Even in the immediate post–World War II period, the guarantee of human rights protection continued to derive from the connection to the state, where it was undergirded by the principles of nationality and citizenship. Therefore, statelessness was a preoccupation of scholars of the period, such as Hannah Arendt.[66] Traditional international law had based an individual's right of protection on nationality, on the notion of their being a sovereign that can assert a right against another state to have its own national protected. Thus anyone stateless would lose any claim to protection. Nottebohm, an ICJ decision of the early postwar period, increased the risk of statelessness, by creating hurdles to the ability of a state to assert the claim of someone who has acquired the nationality of that state having abandoned their original, different nationality.[67]

Historically, as noted, the law of peoples prefigured that of states, deriving alternately from the "law of nations," as well as from the broader practices of humankind. According to Hugo Grotius, the society of states had jurisdiction over "gross violations of the law of nature and of nations, done to other states and subjects." Today, one can see that this premodern idea appears, remarkably, to be taking on new traction: Wherever there are gaps in the global subject, humanity law contributes a minimal normative threshold, as well as drawing from the law of war's coercive enforcement scheme, which lays a basis for a revived sense of political legitimacy in the present global order. To what extent is this legitimacy political in its sources, rather than (as is often claimed) transpolitical or depoliticized?

During the Cold War, the ICJ invoked this principle in its landmark review of the Convention on the Prevention and Punishment of the Crime of Genocide, the new Convention discussing "genocide," where it emphasized the norm's universality:

> The origins of the Convention [on the Prevention and Punishment of the Crime of Genocide] show that it was the intention of the United Nations to condemn and punish genocide as "a crime under international law" involving a denial of the right of existence of entire human groups, a denial which shocks the conscience of mankind and results in great losses to humanity, and which is contrary to moral law and to the spirit and aims of the United Nations (Resolution 96 (1) of the General Assembly, December 11th 1946).... [T]he *universal* character both of the condemnation of genocide and of the cooperation [was] required "in order to liberate mankind from such an odious scourge" (Preamble to the Convention). The Genocide Convention was therefore intended by the General Assembly and by the contracting parties to be definitely *universal* in scope.[68]

Further, as the Supreme Court of Israel stated in *Attorney General v. Eichmann*, "it is the universal character of the crimes in question [i.e. international crimes] which vests in every State the authority to try and punish those who participated in their commission."[69]Justice Landau, drawing upon Grotius' "On the Rights of War and Peace," articulated the bases for universal jurisdiction in the case:

> It is therefore the moral duty of every sovereign state...to enforce the natural right to punish, possessed by the victims of the crime whoever they may be, against criminals whose acts have "violated in extreme form the law of nature or the law of nations." By these pronouncements the father of international law laid the foundations for the future definition of the "crime against humanity" as a "crime under the law of nations" and to universal jurisdiction over such crimes.[70]

In a more contemporary case, in *Prosecutor v. Furundzija*, the ICTY similarly referenced this principle: "It has been held that international crimes being universally condemned wherever they occur, every State has the right to prosecute and punish the authors of such crimes."[71] The Genocide Convention requires signatories "to prevent and to punish." Reiterated by the ICJ in *Bosnia v. Serbia*, this obligation extends "so far as within their [states] powers regarding all persons over when they had a certain influence."[72]

One might think of the idea of the "crime against humanity" as expressing a cardinal, ordering value—one that, like other such core political distinctions over the years (e.g., such as that of friend/enemy in Carl Schmitt's thought) has two functions: First, it draws a line defining the very parameters of permissible politics, and second, it decides on the core—delimiting the "other" as criminal or lawbreaker, outside our own "humanity" and opposed to it.[73]

This reflects the fundamental transformation in contemporary globalizing politics: The relevant norms, by their definition, extend beyond the protection of the state to the protection and the preservation of humankind, with evident impacts on the individual, the collective, and global stability. There is a growing demand for involvement by a third party; later we will show this trend developing along a complementary basis. For some scholars, such as David Luban, this added involvement is seen as "vigilante justice" in which the criminal becomes anyone's and everyone's legitimate enemy."[74] Yet this characterization may not get at the distinctive ordering role of the law in structuring societal judgment. While classical international law has always recognized that the interests in justice transcend the state, devolving on other nexuses, whether the nationality of persons or other stakeholders in the matter, for example *Lotus*,[75] at present this third-party involvement occurs either via judiciary, through the ICC, or through other states' unilateral action. This is an observable change since the Grotian moment.

Foundational as it is to modern humanitarian law, notion of humanity is equally central to the law of human rights. The preamble of the Universal Declaration of Human Rights frames individual rights in terms of a shared human condition: "Whereas recognition of the inherent dignity and of the equal and inalienable rights of all members of the human family is the foundation of freedom, justice, and peace in the world, . . . the advent of a world in which humans shall enjoy freedom of . . . belief and freedom from fear and want has been proclaimed as the highest aspiration of the common people."[76]

This protective norm encapsulates simultaneously the protection of (1) core *human* rights of bodily integrity, life, and freedom from persecution, and equal protection on an individual basis, and (2) rights of peoplehood—with the latter dimension being framed as categorically going to status and hence, as characteristic of humanitarian law associated with conflict.

Competing affiliations—such as with ethnic groups, or ethnically based religious groupings—operate in the struggle for control and influence in weak or failed states, which often lack a fully working legal system and a functioning constitutional order or social bargain. Therefore, one might say that th velopment of the norm of the "crime against humanity" goes to the heart of circumscribing where legitimacy lies in dealing with these competitive affiliations. First, it demarcates where the regimes themselves are illegitimate, and it stipulates where, failing to control and to protect, the regimes lack the requisite conditions for legitimate rule, measured against the minimalist political morality of humanity law. Moreover, in this regard, as we will see, the state itself is not immune from critique and judgment: Are we judging the state for its inability to protect, or judging the movements in the internal struggle for putting human security at risk, or both?

For the political philosopher Judith Shklar, the postwar trials' legitimacy largely depended on the concept of offenses against humanity: "As far as the trial concerned itself with crimes against humanity it was both necessary and wise."[77] For Hannah Arendt, too, the "offense against humanity" was the norm that was fundamentally at stake.[78] Despite the political realities at the time of the war, and the asserted concern for aggression and war crimes, it was the offense against humanity that came to epitomize the case for universal judgment. The subject of this offense would remain circumscribed, limited as tied to its defining time—that is, the interim reign between the end of World War II and the Cold War's beginning.

Starting with the international community's ambivalent response—through the UN Security Council—to Adolf Eichmann's abduction from Argentina to stand trial in Israel, one can begin to discern an emerging trend toward individual responsibility, even, apparently, if accountability occurs at the expense of state sovereignty. Thus, the abduction ultimately was not condemned, despite the violation of Argentina's territorial sovereignty. This forbearance was premised on the call by Israel's prime minister for "proportionality," which itself (whether knowingly or unwittingly) drew on humanitarian law's cardinal norm—and limited itself to the declaration that such acts, if repeated, could "endanger international peace and security."[79] This example illustrates that the diplomatic arguments at the time were already being made within the humanity law logic.

In *Nikolic*, decades later, the ICTY Appeals Chamber relied on this precedent, in a case where NATO forces had apprehended the defendant across national boundaries, restating the balance between humanity and sovereignty values as follows: "The damage caused to international justice by not apprehending fugitives accused of serious violations of international humanitarian law is comparatively higher than the injury, if any, caused to the sovereignty of a State by a limited intrusion in its territory."[80]

As discussed above, Israel's prosecution of Eichmann during the early 1960s the principle of "universal jurisdiction" was deployed to allow prosecutions to reach beyond the traditional nexuses of territoriality or nationality, and to be launched on behalf of a people and their connection to common humanity, yet the norm was invoked together with other traditional bases of jurisdiction. Hence, the State of Israel's "right to punish" the accused derived, it was held, "from two *cumulative* sources: a *universal* source (pertaining to the whole of mankind) which vests the right to prosecute and punish crimes of this order in every state within the family of nations; and a *specific or national* source which gives the victim nation the right to try any who assault its existence."[81]

. Ultimately, the Eichmann case would prove to be a major precedent, which clearly shows the demonstrable nexus between the attack on the particular group and that on the humanity-based universal. What was the right body of judgment? And what are the broader consequences of such judgment?

Later, in 1980s France, embarking on the long-delayed trials of the Nazi-era war criminals Klaus Barbie and Maurice Papon required displacing domestic law principles; some such principles go to procedure, others go to more fundamental issues regarding the nature of the charges. Yet even so, the tension was that, ultimately, rights could only be seen to be protected within the parameters of a distinct political context, jurisdiction, and related principles. Whereas historically the adjudication of "crimes against humanity" has drawn from normative universalism, over the years it has become evident that the politics of transitional justice draw also from its particular social and political context. The *Barbie* trial in Lyon, while a revival of the concept of "crimes against humanity," nonetheless served as a rallying point for the affirmation of political identity, and the representation of the heroic role of the country's resistance—allowing a strategy of national vindication and identity.[82] Still, the postwar trials ignited an important debate regarding the legitimate subject of "humanity," and whether the notion extended beyond those civilians caught up in conflict to others caught between the two regimes of war and peace. In light of the Resistance, the bases for protection extended beyond civilians to combatants and, in so doing, clearly showed the partial openness of the "humanity" norm.

Relying on the postwar precedents, the ICTY, in *Prosecutor v. Kupreskic*, interpreted the reach of the crime against humanity more broadly—to include a systemic attack that is not necessarily limited to the civilian populations, or even to wartime per se. The ICTY held that the normative offenses relating to persecution "possess a broader humanitarian scope and purpose than those prohibiting war crimes," whereby "inhumane acts and persecution committed in a systematic manner, in the name of a State practicing a policy of ideological supremacy, not only against persons by reasons of their membership of a racial or religious community but also against the opponents of that policy, whatever the form of their 'opposition' could be considered a crime against humanity."[83] In so holding, the court also relied on the surrounding Security Council Resolution 780, on the interpretation of Article 5 "crimes against humanity," which suggested that the contemplated protection of civilians (by the specially appointed court) ought not be interpreted in a zero-sum way vis-à-vis other persons.[84] In the ICTY's words, "information of the overall circumstances is relevant for the interpretation of the provision in a spirit consistent with its purpose."[85]

Again, we see the "teleological" approach, which—since the ICTY's first decision establishing the scope of jurisdiction—has animated the court's jurisprudence, rationalizing that its adjudication is always aimed at the protection and preservation of the human being, in its articulation of rights and responsibilities in present-day political situations.[86] Under this approach, persons are subject to jurisdiction on humanity law grounds, and across state boundaries, for rights violations affecting persons and peoples. Indeed, one can see the trend toward a humanization of what was hitherto conceived largely as a matter of state-centric transitional justice.

In the case of General Pinochet, *Regina v. Bartle*, the British High Court accepted the possibility of universality jurisdiction with respect to a small number of grave offenses. In Lord David Hope's words, "it is just that the obligations which were recognized by customary international law in the case of such serious international crimes by the date when Chile ratified the (Torture) Convention [UN Convention Against Torture and Other Cruel, Inhuman or Degrading Treatment or Punishment] are so strong as to override any objection by it on the ground of immunity . . . to the exercise of the jurisdiction over crimes committed."[87] The case reflects the heightened demand today for the enforcement of the law with respect to humanity law violations, even where that enforcement is far removed from the site of the original wrongdoing.

The heart of the shift is that in the present humanity-based scheme, jurisdiction follows the norm—and the person. Yet this shift also implies expanding responsibilities and duties for the state. This in turn raises questions about what relationship the principle of universality bears to the context of the prevailing interstate system. In other words, exactly where do persons and peoples fit into the prior and now-changing system? How do these concerns engage with one another?

Cases like Pinochet's reflect the evident potential for tensions vis-à-vis the state, as international law scholars have observed. For example, Paul Kahn argues that "community self-determination" remains a "compelling value" of equal weight.[88] The ramification of "universality" still, in some sense, ultimately depends on the state, on treaties of extradition, and on the relevant political actors that are involved in implementation of the law at the time.[89] Issues continue to arise regarding the assertion of traditional state sovereignty, if that sovereignty is understood to involve discretion over enforcement and the application of the law. In the *Pinochet* case, "universal" jurisdiction ultimately brought humanity law back home. There, despite the state's inaction, responsibility was held to be directly attributable to Pinochet. Yet the role of private actors, and the transnational assertion of jurisdiction against the former political leader, highlight the shift from the previously prevailing state-centricity to the newer, humanity-centered order.

One might think of this as a relativization of sovereignty. Hence, the Spanish Supreme Court, in reviewing Spain's "universality jurisdiction" law, held that "the limits of said principle are set by the application of other principles equally recognized under public international law."[90] This illustrates the attempt to reconcile long-standing state-centric interstate law with the growing human-centric law (and practically, it helps to explain instances where universality was ultimately reversed—e.g., in Belgium, where it has been evaluated in the broader context of other international law principles).

Indeed, the contextual approach has been followed more broadly. In a 2001 study of universality jurisdiction, more than 125 countries had adopted statutes conferring such jurisdiction over one or more crimes.[91] Yet few of these were instances of "pure" universal jurisdiction, that is, where jurisdiction is theoretically exercised without any nexus between the alleged offense and the exercising states.[92] Rather, they varied tremendously in terms of their nexus to the state. As of 2001, Belgium and Spain[93] were the only states to have adopted "pure" universal jurisdiction;[94] and still, even here, there is often in practice an added nexus. Here we might consider the Spanish judiciary's apparent ongoing involvement in judgment regarding some of the Central American successor regimes, such as those in Chile, Peru, Guatemala, and El Salvador, inter alia.

The ramifications of *Pinochet* continue to be played out in Spain, Europe, the Americas, and beyond. For example, in a case initiated by the Nobel laureate Rigoberta Menchú concerning the atrocities against Mayan Indian communities in 1980s Guatemala, Spain's highest court interpreted universality jurisdiction to reach genocide but—once again—in tandem with other international law principles such as that of "passive personality," that is, the principle of protecting victims who happened to be nationals. That principle has also been invoked in a later such case, where an indictment was sought for the notorious killings of various Salvadorean priests and nuns, several of whom were of Spanish descent.[95] In *Scilingo,* the Spanish High Court convicted a former Argentine navy captain of crimes against humanity in that country's "dirty war," led by the military junta against suspected left-wing dissidents. *Cavallo* involved an extradition in 2003 to Spain for genocide charges on "universality" grounds.[96] Seen in the light of the colonial past and its humanity law, one can better understand the modern deployment of judicial power in a way that complements other local responses regarding violations of the law of nations and hence aims at bolstering protection in instances of weak states and vulnerable populations.

Tensions in the framework and in its reconciliation with state sovereignty can be seen in the "presence" limitation to universal jurisdiction, that is, in the recent amendments to laws in both Belgium and Spain limiting the applicability of universal jurisdiction. Thus, in 2003, a legislative amendment limited Belgium to the exercise of universal jurisdiction only where the country was otherwise obligated to prosecute under a treaty obligation, for example the UN Convention against Torture and Other Cruel, Inhuman or Degrading Treatment or Punishment;[97] and added a requisite nexus based on the principle of active and passive personality: This principle holds that where the accused is not present, there is prosecutorial discretion to dismiss a case.[98] In France, this concept effectively prevents prosecutors from investigating crimes abroad unless the suspect is present on French soil. However, at the same time, French law allows trials in absentia; hence, a criminal action may proceed with or without the defendant's presence—as illustrated in the case of Ould Dah, involving an indictment initiated by victims, for torture during the 1990–91 clashes between various ethnic groups in Mauritania.[99] After a trial in absentia, in 2005, he was convicted for torture at the Jreida death camp (as at the relevant time, the UN Convention against Torture and Other Cruel, Inhuman or Degrading Treatment or Punishment of 1984 had already come into force in 2008, and it had been incorporated into French law). The rejection of Ould Dah's appeal reaffirms the universal jurisdiction of the French courts to judge the crime of torture through the application of the 1984 Convention Against Torture, without consideration to the place where the crimes were committed or the nationality of the presumed perpetrator. In March 2009, the European Court of Human Rights declared that France had exercised its jurisdiction according to the European Convention on Human Rights on jus cogens grounds.[100]

In other instances, we can see the application of universality jurisdiction where the state could otherwise rely on traditional bases for jurisdiction, such as the presence in the arresting or prosecuting jurisdiction of the defendant or the victim.[101] When Senegal's courts failed to convict the Chadian dictator Hissene Habré—who was accused of killing forty thousand people and torturing his political opponents, and who fled from Chad to Senegal in 1990—his victims filed a complaint in Belgium, under its universal jurisdiction law,[102] where it would be four years before an international arrest warrant could be issued.[103] The Belgian prosecutorial activities provoked the African Union to call on Senegal to prosecute Habré "in the name of Africa" rather than Europe.[104] Belgium filed a request in February 2009 with the ICTR "regarding Senegal's compliance with its obligation to prosecute" Habré "or to extradite him to Belgium for the purpose of criminal proceedings,"[105] basing its claims on the United Nations Convention on Torture and Other Cruel, Inhuman or Degrading Treatment or Punishment, and on customary international law.[106] Claims of universality jurisdiction have been taken up by the African Union, which is calling for a hybrid tribunal with the input of Senegal and the AU, reflecting the shift to diverse actors and multilevel politics.[107]

Most common is a notion one might term "universal jurisdiction plus," where there is another added linking connection to more familiar bases of jurisdiction, such as those requiring some nexus to the defendant—that is, to a state's territory or to its interests. Hence, for instance, Section 7(3.71) of the Canadian Criminal Code "allows for retrospective jurisdiction over the crimes of genocide, crimes against humanity, and war crimes, provided that, at the time of the crime, the conduct constituted a crime under international law as well as under Canadian law, the defendant was within the territorial jurisdiction of Canada, Canada was at war with the country when the crime occurred, and the crime occurred in the territory of that country or was committed by one of its citizens."[108] Some scholars, such as Cherif Bassiouni, argue that these developments amount to a limited support for the notion of universality evolving into customary international law.[109]

Every instantiation of humanity law's universality has its particularist dimension—as its application inevitably arises in a particular context and reflects distinct interests of state and community, even as it still continues largely to depend on state legislation and other related implementing mechanisms for its positive operation. At the same time, we can also see that the relevant normativity clearly transcends the state and relativizes sovereignty. Against the context of the appeal to universality in the abstract such assumptions of humanity-based jurisdiction always reflect their relevant context— shaped by the needs of persons and peoples in the relevant jurisdictions— which in turn contributes to the built-in indeterminacy in humanity law.

GESTURING TOWARD A GLOBAL RULE OF LAW

The increasing recognition of crimes against humanity goes to the heart of the emerging global rule of law. It expresses the change in the rule of law by sending a message that "humanity rights" are inviolable, and by expressing the value of protection—that is, of freedom from persecution by the state or other state-like entities—on a global basis. Indeed, this offense encapsulates the paradigm shift in normativity, as it expresses the status of the new subject and defines the place of the individual—in terms of and connected up on the basis of the collective, as well as other transnational affiliations. As to the nexus between the individual and the collective, as its universality dimension reflects, the humanity norm's substance retains the capacity for change as a result of human engagement and conflict.

As a result, in present political conditions, the pursuit of humanity-based justice often appears far more promising than—and indeed, superior to—other projects within human rights, which generally may depend on the state to a greater degree than humanity-based justice does. Thus, where justice processes aim beyond the state and aspire to some level of universality, they have often taken the form of criminal justice. For some, such as Larry May, the conception of the crime against humanity insofar as it represents "harm" to the international community is at once too narrow and too broad.[110] Rather than essentializing the offense, a look at instances of its expanded enforcement under the law reveals instead a universalizable normativity.

Thus, as a practical matter one can see that, for example, the ICC relies in great part on the basis of state consent to assert jurisdiction over the prosecution of nationals, even state leaders. But state consent also apparently can be dispensed with where there is an *ex proprio motu* prosecution or Security Council referral—such as occurred in the case of Darfur or more recently the conflict in Libya. Indeed, in some instances, even the political leaders of nonstate signatories may end up in the dock.[111]

As to the "crime against humanity" in the Rome Statute of the ICC, at Article 7(1), it establishes jurisdiction regardless of the nature of the conflict and defines a "crime against humanity" as a set of inhumane acts "committed as part of a widespread or systematic attack directed against any civilian population, with knowledge of the attack." Moreover, any state can prosecute a crime against humanity, as a matter of universality.[112] And doing so, as the statute sets out, is seen as an obligation.

For these reasons, one might say that the contemporary recognition of the "crime against humanity" expresses the core global rule-of-law value that is predicated on a generally applicable human rights law: namely, its complementarity. The aim of recognizing crimes against humanity is to ensure that there is no site where humanity law's protective force is eluded. In this sense, recognizing such crimes has gap-filling, glue-like, "seal-tight" dimensions. This is also a determination that—as it is informed in part by practice[113]—it is made anew with every generation and, likewise, is contingent on the ethnic and other affiliative divisions within the state.

The "crime against humanity" defines the outer limits of political legitimacy, as scholar David Luban has observed. Now we can see that international and regional judiciaries, with their statutes and arrays of coercive sanctions, are aiming to make this normative regime real in so doing illustrating the norm itself. In principle, no one is exempt from judgment, from those in the top echelons of political power on down (although we must bear in mind the persistence of some limited recognition of various types of official immunity). Humanity law offers no implied basis for immunity of political actions. The new international court's existence enables the jumpstarting of a profound transition, whereby the Westphalian model respecting the borders of the state is displaced by the "Rome" view, which penetrates the state itself.

By its very definition, in "humanity" terms, universal jurisdiction retains a built-in indeterminacy: It is capable of evolving, and it has already been extended to a handful of other humanity law offenses. One can see this extension in contemporary conflict situations. Thus, in *Prosecutor v. Furundzija*, the ICTY extended the principle of universal jurisdiction to torture—an offense that lies at the convergence of the laws of war and peace, but had generally been seen as a norm protected as a matter of state responsibility: The tribunal reasoned that "one of the consequences [of universal jurisdiction] . . . is that every State is entitled to investigate, prosecute and punish or extradite individuals accused of torture, who are present in a territory under its jurisdiction."[114] The tribunal went on to say that it "would be inconsistent on the one hand to prohibit torture to such an extent as to restrict the normally unfettered treaty-making power of sovereign States, and on the other hand to bar States from prosecuting and punishing those torturers who have engaged in this odious practice abroad."[115]

In recognizing the breadth of protection, the tribunal has ruled that protection against torture transcends the rule of the state, binding even nonstate actors, and therefore it has concluded that private parties could be found liable for torture.[116] This conclusion reflects the convergence of legal orders: as the tribunal declared in *Kunarac*: "In the field of international humanitarian law, and, in particular, in the context of international prosecutions, the role of the state is, when it comes to accountability, peripheral. Individual criminal responsibility for violation of international humanitarian law does not depend on the participation of the state and, conversely, its participation in the commission of the offense is no defence to the perpetrator."[117]

While humanity law is enforceable on the basis of universal jurisdiction, without the state; of course, its actual exercise reflects an accommodation with political realities—a look at which may illuminate law's role in current global politics.

Perhaps the greatest tensions in the application of humanity law are most evident when the challenge at issue is to state control over justice—and, in particular, when there are claims of state terror—and hence ostensibly competing claims to human security. So, for example, drawing from the "global war on terror" in Germany, complaints were filed—but quickly dismissed—against former U.S. secretary of defense Donald Rumsfeld and others, alleging the torture of prisoners at Abu Ghraib.

In another high-profile case, in 2009, the same magistrate who was notorious for presiding over the Pinochet case opened an investigation into the alleged torture of terror suspects by the Bush administration at Guantánamo Bay. Acting under Spain's principle of universal justice,[118] Judge Baltazar Garzón declared that documents that were declassified by the Obama administration reflected the systematic nature of the practice, inviting action from the political arm of the government in Spain. However, the legal action was dismissed by Spain's attorney general for lack of merit, and moreover in 2010, Garzón was temporarily suspended.[119] Following his suspension by the Supreme Court of Spain, he was charged with

ignoring a 1977 amnesty law during his investigation of the disappear-
ances of more than one hundred thousand people during Spain's 1930s
Civil War.[120] Despite this resistance on the part of other entities of the
Spanish state, Garzón has stated: "The principle of universal jurisdiction
has in fact germinated and is a conquest that cannot be lost and will not
be lost." He added, "as always happens with international justice, it's about
two steps forward, then one step back,—so we advance with a lot of
difficulties."[121]

Between 2006 and 2009, globally at least thirty-four investigations
were initiated that were grounded on the principle of "universal jurisdiction." Of these, the majority were initiated by victims and/or NGOs clearly
reflecting the principle of complementarity. Twice as many complaints
were filed by third parties as by state authorities, including cases that were
initiated by way of extradition requests (although the actual number of
cases initiated by national authorities is likely to be higher). Private parties
proceeded as "parties civiles," wherever permitted under national law, for
example France or Spain, or by filing complaints with the relevant national
authority.[122]

Those invoking this principle have thus far faced a mixed record of success: A Belgian court convicted Bernard Ntuyahaga, a former Rwandan
army general, of grave violations of humanitarian law; the Netherlands and
France both convicted perpetrators of torture; in 2008, Norway convicted
a Bosnian of war crimes for 1992 crimes against Serbian civilians; and
Canada convicted Desire Munyaneza of genocide, crimes against humanity,
and war crimes.[123] In a sense, "universality" also laid the basis for the first
prosecution of atrocities committed in the Balkans, whereby Germany's
arrest and indictment of the paramilitary Dusko Tadic under its own laws
led to his being turned over to the Hague ICTY, where despite his being a
private actor operating in a largely internal conflict, he was ultimately tried
and convicted of "crimes against humanity."[124]

In all these cases, the extension of universal jurisdiction reflects a
humanity law view of justice. Humanity law abhors any gap in the protection of humanity; so in the presence of persistent violence, often without
state action, this legal framework engages and expands international
responsibility, and the capacity to enforce that responsibility.

BEYOND COMPLIANCE

How do we judge success in the arena of crimes-against-humanity prosecutions? Where transitional justice's aims are reconciliation and state-building,

such trials are often eschewed. But where the offense is conceived in terms of "humanity," what exactly is the relevant community and whom does it include? Insofar as the recognition of the crime against humanity expresses a core equality norm and a right to freedom from persecution, this offense expresses a critical element of the rule of law on a global basis.

As I elaborate in chapter 4, recognizing the crime against humanity can also contribute to a sense that there is a shared minimum of global justice. Meanwhile, trials can serve to isolate individuals, and thus redefine international society—as occurred with Charles Taylor vis-à-vis Liberia, Lubanga, and others now in dock regarding Africa more broadly, and with Milosevic in the Balkans. This enables a new process of reengagement at the individual level and beyond the state. The prosecution of prominent political leaders for persecuting their own citizens reflects the way a normativity has penetrated traditional understandings of state sovereignty and territoriality. Currently, we are framing new answers to the questions of what matters are relevant to the international community and, further, what behaviour is at stake in supporting a globalizing order of heightened engagement and intervention.

Yet the full weight of norm transformation rarely can rest solely on the law. Indeed, this point has been driven home in instances where tensions among the various aims of humanity law enforcement policies have been evident—for example, in the adjudications coming out of Iraq. The Special Iraqi Tribunal attempted to focus on the substantive bases of jurisdiction in order to circumscribe potential countervailing challenges to the occupation. Its jurisdiction was circumscribed to "genocide, crimes against humanity," war crimes, and certain crimes under Iraqi law. In this way, it was limited to what Saddam Hussein did to his *own* people, in order to establish the illegitimacy of his prior regime and therefore, at least by implication, the legitimacy of forceful intervention.[125] One can see that the process here represents the shift away from the state-based approach and toward a disaggregated, law-based approach to rights protection.

The surge in judicial enforcement mechanisms is taking place against the context of the inadequacy failure of multilateral institutions (most notably the Security Council) to coordinate state action to protect international peace and security, reflecting the presence of a conflict of norms and interests that is not evidently soluble through classic interstate diplomacy and politics. It is in this politico-diplomatic context that humanity rights come into conflict with the traditional sovereignty rights that are protected by the international legal system, sparking strong tensions. And when the Security Council does act today, the Council itself invokes the aims and methods of humanity law, as exemplified in Resolution 1973, authorizing air strikes where necessary to protect civilians in Libya.[126]

What we are seeing is that, in a time of instabilities and dislocations, there is surfacing an evident and growing pragmatic approach to the issue of responsibility to ensure some degree of protection and minimal rule of law, where the normativity is transnational. When and where domestic options are unavailing, transnational, regional, and international institutions step into the breach. What distinguishes these institutions and processes is their capacity to assert authority across traditional jurisdictional lines and substantive doctrinal boundaries or divides—such as public/private, state/nonstate, and so on—in essence, rendering humanity itself their compass.

Further, there is an enhanced role, beyond states, for persons and peoples in the assertion, or normalizing, of the now-transforming body of humanity law.[127] As humanity law operates largely on persons, and it is individuals who are made subject to its sanctions, this means reconceiving complex conflict situations from a perspective that looks beyond the state—and sees such situations in terms of a variety of diverse actors: for example individuals, states, and nonstate collectivities.

Developments in judicial mechanisms, reaching beyond the borders of the state, create the perception of an increasingly law-based order, as the additional enforcement power gives the humanity law norms an added sense of legal authority, and the heightened degree of regular applicability that is associated with established rule-of-law systems in ordinary times.[128]

The fundamental development that is identified here reflects a move away from the single-minded conceptualization of interstate relations premised on state interests and toward, instead, the legalist discourse of humanity rights pertaining to persons and peoples, as instantiated in alternative sites such as courts of law. Through juridical processes, matters of policy are convertible into matters for the law.[129]

Although universal jurisdiction has generally been exercised as a matter of criminal law, international law is permissive of the application of civil jurisdiction based on similar principles. Indeed, one might say that generally such instances run less afoul of state-centricity. Hence, one can see that domestic courts have been providing civil remedies for victims of piracy.[130] As I will discuss at greater length in chapter 7, the U.S. Alien Tort Claims Act (ATCA) provides a means by which an alien may pursue, in U.S. courts, a cause of action in tort for a violation of the law of nations. In a landmark ATCA case, *Filártiga*, the U.S. Court of Appeals for the Second Circuit held that "deliberate torture perpetrated under colour of official authority violates universally accepted norms of the international law of human rights, regardless of the nationality of the parties." In finding the arch-offense of torture to be a clear violation of the law of nations, the court asserts: "The prohibition is clear and unambiguous, and admits of no distinction between treatment of aliens and citizens."[131] In other words, in the court's view, the prohibition on torture applies irrespective of the victim's citizenship or nationality.

In *Kadic v. Karadzic*, the same court made it clear that the body of law that was applied in *Filártiga* derived from the customary international law of human rights. It also made clear that whereas in the human rights context torture is proscribed by international law only when committed by state officials or under the color of the law,[132] atrocities including torture are actionable under the ATCA—*with or without state participation*—to the extent that the criminal acts were committed in pursuit of genocide or war crimes.

This basis for liability has been invoked more recently in a number of cases growing out of conflicts within the so-called global war on terror, where we see a growing number of instances of the individuation of remedies.[133] Here, the turn toward judicialization for enforcement of the law of nations is often taken completely out of the traditional realm of interstate diplomacy (indeed, it can be at odds with state interests). Here, the courts have not been particularly deferential to the political branches in instances where they have opposed recognizing individual claims.[134] Once again, this reflects the deep penetration of humanity law into the legal system.

JUDICIALIZATION, REGIONALISM, AND HUMANITY LAW'S ASCENDANT ROLE IN THE MANAGEMENT OF CONFLICT

For some time now, international legalism's regular justificatory processes have aimed to rationalize the interstate system and to create the perception of global order.[135] The transformation in the international-humanitarian-law regime represents a shift not merely to an expanded legalism but also to a new and distinctive discourse of justice. The turn to humanity rights strategies reflects the liberal form of the rule of law—its remedies, processes, and institutions.

More and more, with the proliferation and globalization of processes of justice, the meaning of international rule of law takes the outside veneer of domestic law enforcement. With humanity law no longer relegated to international conflicts, its normative potential transcends the exceptional regulation of extraordinary circumstances in wartime, so as to contribute more regularly to law enforcement operations. This occurs against a backdrop of heightened political instability. The apparent consensus on the normative foundations for a permanent ICC, despite disagreements about the specifics of the institution and its place in international politics, reflects the way these norms—via a system of judgment and sanctions—have now become an integral part of global rule of law.[136]

Beyond the ICC and the exceptional ad hoc tribunals are the growing number of so-called hybrids that can be found in Sierra Leone, Kosovo, Lebanon, East Timor, and Cambodia.[137] Though framed in terms of affording protection for violations of humanity rights, these courts are characterized by their mix of universal and domestic jurisdiction and international and domestic legal systems, by the gravity of the offenses they address, by their institutionalization, and by their normative character. For these reasons, they well reflect the nature of contemporary crises—which involve diverse but overlapping rule-of-law values, are characterized by fluidity in their legalities, and require pragmatic innovation and accommodation in the mix of the procedural and substantive dimensions of internationalism. Perhaps more than any other courts, they epitomize the situation-based nature of contemporary applications of the humanity law norm.

These innovative hybrid judicial institutions involve sui generis blends of the international and the national, and apply a continuum of humanity law as a complement to the state's prosecutorial processes, contributing to the diffusion of these norms on a transborder basis. So, for example, in the UN Interim Administration in Kosovo, special judicial panels have brought together international and domestic judges,[138] with substantive jurisdiction over a variety of domestic and international crimes, including war crimes and genocide.[139] In East Timor, "special panels" were established for the prosecution of "serious crimes," including war crimes, genocide, and crimes against humanity.[140]

Another hybrid judiciary, the Special Court for Sierra Leone, comprised of both domestic and UN-appointed judges, was established to oversee the prosecution of those responsible for the atrocities that occurred in the country's ten-year civil war, for crimes against humanity,[141] having been given "the power to prosecute persons who bear the greatest responsibility for serious violations of international humanitarian law and Sierra Leonean law."[142] As a hybrid, the court enjoys a certain nexus to the region and related accountability and legitimacy.[143] Yet from the get-go it has been subject to challenge on political and other grounds, hence the prosecution of former Liberian president Charles Taylor for war crimes and crimes against humanity arising from his alleged role in the bloody civil war in Sierra Leone, has been ongoing since 2003.[144] The case demonstrates the relationship between state and non state actors by following the weapons sales and blood diamond resources used to fund the war.

After lengthy negotiations, UN-backed "Extraordinary Chambers"—another hybrid institution—was created in Cambodia's own domestic courts[145] and yet with jurisdiction over international offenses such as genocide,[146] crimes against humanity, and grave breaches of the Geneva Conventions.[147] While the Extraordinary Chambers has had difficulty remaining impartial in the face of continued influence by the Cambodian government, yet trials have recently been commenced for abuses of the Khmer Rouge three decades past. Since the conviction of Kaing Guek Eav (Duch) for war crimes and crimes against humanity,[148] it remains to be seen whether the Chambers, through the high-level trials of Khmer leadership, will serve their stated goals of deterrence and advancing reconciliation in the region, while making a clear normative contribution.[149] The role of the state in these cases highlights the importance of independent judgment.

In 2002, Secretary-General Annan reiterated a challenge first made to UN members in 1999, urging the Security Council to discuss "the best way to respond to threats of genocide or other comparable massive violations of human rights." Recall that in an earlier advisory opinion, the ICJ had considered whether a reservation to the Convention on the Prevention and Punishment of the Crime of Genocide, with respect to monitoring and enforcement, was consistent with the purposes of the court. The ICJ observed that there was a link between the normativity of the Convention on the Prevention and Punishment of the Crime of Genocide and the demand for its enforcement in the court, noting the need to revisit earlier understandings that had seen such treaties' force as purely a matter for state consent, and instead pointing to the developments in other tribunals, and the growing sense, associated with such human rights treaties, that assumes some agent of accountability for enforcement. Later, five judges of the ICJ in *Armed Activities on the Territory of the Congo v. Rwanda* remarked, at the time of return of violence to the Great Lakes, that "it is a matter for serious concern that at the beginning of the twenty-first century it is still for states to choose whether they consent to the court adjudicating claims that they have committed genocide. It must be regarded as a very grave matter that a state should be in a position to shield from international judicial scrutiny any claim that might be made against it concerning genocide. A state so doing shows the World scant confidence that it would never ever commit genocide, one of the greatest crimes known."[150]

Here, the dilemmas of judicial enforcement are seen as inextricably linking the state and nonstate actors, as well as affecting the ongoing vitality of the norm—going to the questions of interpretation of humanity law as an international framework (taken up in chapter 7).

Hence, not surprisingly, from the Americas to the heart of Europe, there are a growing number of cases in which conflict is being taken to the courts on the basis of humanity law principles. Regional courts are also confronting new claims that are framed in humanity law terms. From post–Cold War transitions from repression in the Americas to the Balkans the Inter-American Court for Human Rights and the European Court of Human Rights have had to address the growing corpus of the law of humanity.

Behrami and *Saramati v. France*, two companion European Court of Human Rights cases, arose out of human rights violations committed in the Kosovo conflict, where the subsequent NATO intervention raised the issue of the extent of UN responsibility given its peace operations for human rights violations in that conflict. At issue was how to interpret the interconnection between two systems, and how to reconcile the aims of the prevailing interstate security system with those of the European Court of Human Rights (i.e. regional court) human rights system. In particular, at issue was the "right to life," and whether and to what extent this peacetime right might also be applicable in conflict. What actor, or actors, might be responsible to guarantee this right? In a world of greater apparent and unstable proximity, the law becomes ever more important to delineate where responsibility lies.

These important questions of agency and responsibility arose where rights violations have occurred in the context of the operation: For example, exactly who was in control during the NATO bombing, and what are the applicable norms of behavior? The European Court of Human Rights opined in its decision in *Behrami* and *Saramati*: "It is evident from the Preamble, Articles 1, 2 and 24 as well as Chapter VII of the [UN] Charter that the primary objective of the UN is the maintenance of international peace and security. While it is equally clear that ensuring respect for human rights represents an important contribution to achieving international peace (see the Preamble to the Convention [European Convention on Human Rights])."[151] Here, the European Court of Human Rights is wrestling with the fulfilment of humanity rights—but not human rights per se—for, above all, in the court's attempts to reconcile the norms of both systems, it appears to have been guided by the telos of human security and, therefore, to have ultimately elected to interpret matters using these terms of security, first and foremost. The court thus wrote, "since operations established by UNSC Resolutions under Chapter VII of the UN Charter are fundamental to the mission of the UN to secure international peace and security ... the Convention [European Convention on Human Rights] cannot be interpreted in a manner which would subject the acts and omissions of

Contracting Parties which are covered by UNSC Resolutions and occur prior to or in the course of such missions, to the scrutiny of the Court."[152]

In later cases also seeking to reconcile harms in domestic or regional contexts the UN Security Council resolutions arising as a result of the war on terror, the recognition within the judiciary is that—particularly where human rights are concerned—there is a need to apply and interpret plural and overlapping legal orders. Thus, for example, in *Kadi and Barakaat v. Council and Commission*, which involved targeted sanctions such as freezing of assets of individuals under a UN Security Council resolution, the European Court of Justice (Grand Chamber) asserted that it had the authority and obligation to review these contested sanctions and related processes within the ambit of the European Union order so as to see whether they violate European Community basic norms, given the individual rights to access to judicial review at stake.[153]

From the perspective of humanity law, one can see the introduction of the issue of civilian or human security posing tensions for international peace and security and their protection. Ever since 1990s Iraq, there has been an evident reconceptualization of the means of human rights enforcement in light of the human effects of collective sanctions. In former Secretary-General Annan's words, "sanctions...are a blunt instrument, they raise the ethical questions of whether suffering inflicted on vulnerable groups in the target country is a legitimate means of exerting pressure on political leaders whose behavior is unlikely to be affected by the plight of their subjects."[154]

Thus, human-centered logic led inevitably not just to the move to the individuation of sanctions but also—as *Kadi* reflects—to a related rule of law regarding the means of such restrictive measures including access to judicial review. In *Kadi*, the European Court of Justice held that "respect for human rights is a condition of the lawfulness of Community acts...and that measures incompatible with respect for human rights are not acceptable in the Community....It follows from all those considerations that the obligations imposed by an international agreement cannot have the effect of prejudicing the constitutional principles of the EC treaty, which include the principle that all Community acts must respect fundamental rights."[155] Some of the further consequences of this precedent for the fragmentation of international law are taken up in chapter 7, discussing interpretive approaches in humanity law.

In *Isayeva v. Russia*, claims were brought against the Russian Federation for the indiscriminate bombing of civilians in Chechnya, raising the question: What standard of protection ought to apply? Although the situation in Chechnya had been characterized as an "internal" armed conflict, the European Court of Human Rights declined to articulate the applicable rules of international humanitarian law, instead blurring the distinction between humanitarian law and human rights law. Hence, the court applied what it called the "law on the right to life," developed in a law enforcement context, to a large-scale battle between Chechen fighters and the Russian army in 2000. While ostensibly applying the principles of the European Convention on Human Rights that are aimed at protecting peace-time human rights, the court's interpretation was also informed by the law of conflict, for it accepted that Russia was justified in using armed force on the occasion in question, which suggested an armed conflict situation under the law. Yet the court found, nonetheless, that the state was in violation of Article 2 because force was not employed "with the requisite care for the lives of the civilian population."[156]

The ECHR explained its ruling: "In the light of the importance of the protection afforded by Article 2, the Court must subject deprivations of life to the most careful scrutiny, taking into consideration all the surrounding circumstances. In particular, it is necessary to examine whether the operation was planned and controlled by the authorities so as to minimize, to the greatest extent possible, recourse to lethal force. The authorities must take appropriate care to ensure that any risk to life is minimised."[157] Moreover, the court held that this responsibility extends, beyond the state, to the failure to protect persons from private action,[158] and finally, that this obligation to protect life—together with the Convention's duty, under Article 1, to secure rights—"requires by implication that there should be some form of effective official investigation when individuals have been killed as a result of the use of force."[159]

The earlier, state-centric view saw the struggle for recognition by groups and in the name of their own survival in terms of self-determination, sovereignty, and statehood. At present, the rights at stake are just as likely to be framed in terms of the claims of groups that—while they operate subnationally—often *compete* with the state for particular attributes of sovereignty, such as identity, recognition, and control on the ground.[160]

JUDICIALIZATION, POLITICS, AND THE ALLOCATION OF INSTITUTIONAL AUTHORITY

Historically, in some empires or imperial constellations, courts performed the function of managing societal conflict or even governing faraway territories. By analogy, there is a remarkable resurgence, at present, of extraterritorial law and courts, renewing the demand for the judicial regime's managerial potential.[161] Jurisdiction, as we have seen, is being brought to bear beyond state borders, echoing and expanding on earlier understandings of the role of the "law of nations," going back to the Grotian moment discussed earlier.[162]

The tensions that are emerging in the new humanity law processes and institutions concern the normalization of the workings of the older judicial institutions (the ICJ is the leading example)—institutions that were aimed at reinforcing the existing international scheme on the use of force—with the newer processes and institutions. Insofar as these newer processes and institutions are aimed at the protection of the ongoing human rights of individuals and peoples, this normalization may present dilemmas involving the conflicts between various schemes regarding the law on the use of force. (This interaction—which can be seen to involve the law of war, both *jus ad bellum* and *jus in bello*—is the subject of chapter 4.)

"Jurisdiction is one of the means of expressing the sovereignty of a State."[163] Therefore, wherever courts operate on their own—lacking an effective relationship or dialogue with functioning political institutions— they bear a heavy burden to deliver a sense of security and of the rule of law. Simultaneously advancing the purposes of justice and peace often presents tensions, and its feasibility depends on the context. Can a distant court be relied on to quell conflict, respond to humanitarian crisis, and do justice, as was sometimes promised in the midst of the Balkan wars?

Or, to invoke a more recent illustration, the Security Council's "referral" of the situation in Darfur to the ICC—in the midst of the violence that occurred then, continued, and is still ongoing—raised real questions about which international institution (and what processes) are best for dealing with a given conflict.[164] In Darfur, despite the fact that the majority—a full two-thirds, by recent accounts—of a population is threatened, and despite humanitarian needs, geopolitical strategies have reached an impasse, in part because of the veto of states that are involved in political and economic relations with Sudan.

One can see that the Security Council's referral of Darfur to a court in this light, it is an attempted depoliticization that permits responsibility to be reconceived on an individual basis and in a nonpolitical light, while enabling continuing interstate engagement and political development. It is also a move that reflects a role for judicialization—beyond state compliance. This is further exemplified in the recent UN Security Council referral to the ICC on the situation in Libya, although unlike in Sudan, this would also spark the building of political consensus and the forging of a coalition on military intervention.[165]

The same is true of the Uganda referrals to the ICC, as the subsequent peace accords were bargained in the "shadow" of the law, including tribunal indictments.[166] Indeed, the ICC itself refers to the "shadow of the court" as its impact beyond the achievement of individual convictions.[167] Justice and judicialization have the effect of changing the political context and the conditions for conflict resolution. Thus, the Ugandan agreements appeared to allow deals on lower level indictments, with less negotiability regarding the more politically significant prosecutions at the top.[168]

Thus, one might say that the surge in legalization and judicialization, especially where they occur along a complementarity basis, reflects a trend that aims at filling globalization's accountability deficit. That deficit has been increasingly apparent, given the growing number of nexuses and the greater dependence among nations—a development related to globalization that is spurring demand for a coherence derivable from law.

The indictments express international society's condemnation and judgment; at the same time, they guarantee neither the pursuit nor the arrest of the accused, revealing a continued dependence on state cooperation for the law's effectiveness. Similar concerns are pertinent to other situations that have arisen in the world: Just how is it that enmeshing the law in a conflict, during hostilities, will help end the conflict? Indeed, in some instances, there is reason to think that throwing the force of law behind one position or another might well actually exacerbate the conflict, rather than being a force toward its resolution.[169]

The judicialization trend also poses serious questions concerning the purposes of law's growing role in world politics. Extraordinarily weighty expectations for delivering the rule of law are being generated and borne by the courts. For some, there are reasons for second thoughts about judicial engagement, which are analogous to those that are often raised in the domestic context. Such concerns are, perhaps, made even stronger in the international setting, where the relevant judicial institutions are often seen as perhaps even more lacking in political nexuses to the relevant region and, therefore, as lacking in democratic accountability.[170] Other scholars have written of the law and economics of justice-seeking in situations of civil war, arguing that there are fewer incentives in such periods for state accountability.[171]

Nevertheless, there are also more forceful counterarguments that may well favor such judicial roles, and may clarify the trend in the direction of the greater individualization of responsibility, irrespective of conflict. For it is precisely in a changing international system associated with the end of bipolarism, globalization, and a related democracy deficit—a system where other institutions with greater legitimacy and political accountability are lacking—that the courts may well serve a needed representation-reinforce-ment role in political conflict and, relatedly, may be capable in some con-texts of bolstering legitimacy.

In conclusion, the developments I have discussed in this chapter promise a demonstrable form of accountability, which visibly operates at the level of the individual in a globalizing regime. One consequence of the humanity law framework's new law enforcement approach—and, particularly, of its coercive sanctions—is its injection into the global legal system of a visible measure of what justice is. That measure consists in certain processes and sanctions that constitute a basic threshold legality; and a set of responses and sanctions that symbolize legality and its effectiveness, even if, as an empirical matter, it may well not be directly responsible for "compliance."

Law enforcement processes that operate on the person uniquely render the individual the subject of both rights and responsibilities, in the global-izing regime. Beyond the state, the norms in question are being applied by courts and to individuals, and are distinguished by their coercive nature in conditions of diminished political accountability. Insofar as they highlight individual rights and responsibilities, these processes can be understood to lend a necessary corrective to a political system that too often leaves indi-viduals out—both allowing the perpetrators to act with impunity and allowing the victims to be subjects of ongoing harm in a time and in places of persistent political violence in need of regulation.

CHAPTER 4

✧

Peacemaking, Punishment, and the Justice of War

The Humanity Law Framework and the Turn to International Criminal Justice

> Those regimes that break the rules must be held accountable. Sanctions must exact a real price. Intransigence must be met with increased pressure—and such pressure exists only when the world stands together as one....
>
> But as a head of state sworn to protect and defend....I face the world as it is, and cannot stand idle in the face of threats to the American people. For make no mistake: Evil does exist in the world. A non-violent movement could not have halted Hitler's armies. Negotiations cannot convince al Qaeda's leaders to lay down their arms....The world must remember that it was not simply international institutions—not just treaties and declarations—that brought stability to a post–World War II world.
>
> Barack Obama, *Nobel Peace Prize Acceptance Speech (2009)*

President Obama's speech harks back to a resilient tradition in Western thought.[1] The concept of the just war is enjoying a revival, although the foundation now is different—that is, secular and humanist, not religious.

The medieval just war tradition endorses the sovereign's use of force against other sovereigns and peoples as punishment for wrongs against the sovereign and against God. In early classical modern international law, the attempt to ground and limit punitive force on a humanity basis was also an effort to limit or contain holy war.[2] For Grotius, the power to punish proceeds from the law of nature: "Where the methods of justice cease, war begins."[3] The notion of force as legitimate punishment was understood by Grotius as limiting and self-limiting—as both a justification and a constraint. Indeed, it is just this balance that is vital for our own time. While arguably the most moralistic form of the law, punitive justice constitutes an ideal against which opportunistic, politicized uses of force may be critiqued.

Emer de Vattel in his *Law of Nations* argued in favor of much more strictly limiting the grounds for the punitive use of force.[4] He contended that force should be used only where another state has acted first to infringe sovereignty; morality is sacrificed to the goal of maintaining a stable state system. According to Vattel:

> Only the Nation has the right to make war, only it can attack its enemy, taking his life, and his goods and possessions, to whom justice and necessity have granted weapons. This is the decision of the just war from necessity, or the natural law the observation of which each of the Nations is strictly bound (Prelim, s. 7). It is the inviolable rule that each must follow in his conscience. But how to ensure that rule is honored, in the anarchic situation of peoples and sovereigns in the state of nature? They do not at all recognize a superior authority: Who will judge between them, in order to demarcate for each its rights and obligations? It belongs to each free and sovereign state to judge in its own conscience what its duties require of it, to what it can or cannot justly do. (Prelim, s. 16) If the others undertake to judge, they will infringe its liberty and injure it with respect to its most valuable rights. (Prelim, s. 15). And since each is judge in its own cause, conferring on itself all the rights of war and pretending that its enemy has none, that the enemy's acts of war are nothing but brigandry, violations of the jus gentium, worthy of being punished by all Nations. The determination of right, of the dispute will be no more advanced and the quarrel will become more cruel, more pernicious in its effects, more difficult to end.[5]

As Vattel pre-saged, the rise of statism would inevitably result in the waning of the just war tradition. Subsequently, centuries of religious wars made abundantly clear the extent to which notions of justice were inevitably tied to diverging traditions, and thus the appeal to a higher truth brought with it divisiveness and even holy war.

With the rise of the state (as discussed in chapter 2), a sharp line is drawn between the justice of war and the concern for the justice in the waging of war. Thus, in the Geneva First Protocol, which reaffirms that the protections of humanitarian law apply without regard to the causes of the conflict.[6] Though there were strong pragmatic reasons for adhering to the so-called principle of distinction, its normative foundations would prove to be shakier. In the period following World War II, a change with significant political implications is the combination of the law of war and the law of human rights, which extends beyond the state and becomes at least nominally universalizing in its reach. This expanded enforcement reflects a concomitant expanded legal personality and normativity in the globalizing system.[7] Here, the idea of the "new" personality, or subject, in the international legal realm can be better understood as continuing an earlier, pre-modern-state understanding of who is the relevant subject of international law. Indeed, going back to Grotius, notions of "international law" could be seen to subsume individual- and human-centered law.[8] At that time, there was a comprehensive view of the scope of the "law of nations," in which peoples and individuals played a role. Now, once again, both state and nonstate actors have become subjects of the regulatory regime; with implications for the significant evolution of individual responsibility under international law.[9]

International criminal law sets one party, the prosecutor, on behalf of international society against another, the defendant. In so doing, it gets beyond the approaches that are traditionally associated with the field of international human rights, where the respondent is the state. Human rights law sets down protected rights—whereas international criminal law sets down offenses. Obviously, such processes have political ramifications beyond those that are ordinarily associated with the punitive sanction; international punishment processes are said to enable reconciliation in areas of potential conflict wherever state interests may conflict with those of their populations.

International criminal justice is now playing a conspicuous role in foreign affairs—and, in particular, in the framing and regulation of ongoing conflicts, where, as we will see, the tendency is for criminal justice to eclipse conceptions of political justice in conflict situations. This tendency poses the risk that the underlying political claims and controversies may not be addressed, or may be addressed only in a manner that is distorted by the single-minded focus on the criminal responsibility of individuals.

THE TURN TOWARD INTERNATIONAL CRIMINAL JUSTICE

The trials at Nuremberg represented a unique historical crossroads for the three legal orders that form the humanity law framework. At some point, the indictment of Germany's aggression and expansionism—of its offenses against other states and the interstate order—begins to pale in comparison to the trials' vindication of the rights of persecuted persons and peoples.

The vision at Nuremberg led to new views of international criminal jurisdiction and responsibility. The radical innovation, in terms of contemporary ideas of global justice, was reaching beyond the state and its responsibility to that of the individual. Article 7 of the Nuremberg Charter provided that "the official position of defendants, whether as Heads of State or responsible officials in Government Departments, shall not be considered as freeing them from responsibility or mitigating punishment." Holding *leaders* accountable—as *individuals*—for what were traditionally *state* crimes of aggression was itself a dramatic innovation. The central charge at Nuremberg of "crimes against the peace" was thought to comprehend all other war crimes. Indeed, Justice Robert Jackson's statement for the prosecution brings the challenge to the war as unjust together with the other war crimes:

> Of course, it was, under the law of all civilized peoples, a crime for one man with his bare knuckles to assault another. How did it come about that multiplying this crime by a million, and adding fire arms to bare knuckles, made it a legally innocent act? The doctrine was that one could not be regarded as criminal for committing the usual violent acts in the conduct of legitimate warfare. The age of imperialistic expansion during the eighteenth and nineteenth centuries added the foul doctrine, contrary to the teachings of early Christian and international law scholars such as Grotius, that all wars are to be regarded as legitimate wars.[10]

In harkening back to Grotius, Jackson was well aware that he was advocating for a departure from the law prevailing at the time. As he put it,

> doubtless what appeals to men of good will and common sense as the crime which comprehends all lesser crimes, is the crime of making unjustifiable war. War necessarily is a calculated series of killings, of destructions of property, of oppressions. Such acts unquestionably would be criminal except that International Law throws a mantle of protection around acts which otherwise would be crimes, when committed in pursuit of legitimate warfare.... But International Law as taught in the Nineteenth and the early part of the Twentieth Century generally declared that war-making was not illegal and is no crime at law.[11]

Hence the pivotal significance, as Jackson recognized, of the doctrine long ago taught by Grotius—the distinction between "just war" and "unjust war"—which would thereafter become a central aim of the trial. The culpability of individuals in the political leadership for the crime of "aggression"[12] reflects a reconceptualization of an international offense of the law of war in individual terms—a development that would be carried forward into contemporary legalism when it was ratified into General Assembly principles.[13]

The turn toward individual responsibility, in the form of punishment, has wide-ranging implications. Beyond the role of judgment in the individuation of aggression, rendering these trials foundational for the evolution of human rights, what vindicated the trial was its application of more far-reaching law protecting human rights against persecution, in and through the "crime against humanity."[14]

Although the Nuremberg Trials represented the first time that international tribunals had adjudicated the crime against humanity as an international offense, this hardly meant that a new offense had been created. To the contrary, "Nuremberg has only demonstrated how humanity can be defended in court, and it is inconceivable that with this precedent extant, the law of humanity should ever lack for a tribunal. Where law exists a court will rise. Thus, the court of humanity, if it may be so termed, will never adjourn."[15]

With the Nuremberg Charter law, the "crime against humanity," entered into positive law. The corresponding recognition of this right to protection on humanity grounds links persons and peoples—thus highlighting the war's impact, first and foremost, on civilians and on their affiliative peoples. Meanwhile, the "crime against humanity" attenuates the connection to the state—by omitting an express nexus to the war, to the state, or to nationality. Notably, the Nuremberg Charter boldly authorizes the vindication of violations against, and the protection of, "any civilian populations."[16] The consequence of this shift is clear. In the words of the tribunal, "now it has been seen that humanity need not supplicate for a Tribunal in which to proclaim its rights. Humanity need not plead for justice with sobs, tears, and piteous weeping. It has been demonstrated here that the inalienable and fundamental rights of common man need not lack for a court to proclaim them and for a marshal to execute the court's judgments. *Humanity can assert itself by law. It has taken on the robe of authority.*"[17]

Despite the aspirations to universality in the Nuremberg Charter, which extended its reach over all civilians and ostensibly applied whether or not acts had occurred during the war,[18] the prosecutions would ultimately be limited by adherence to the conventional state-centric jurisdictional principles that historically had circumscribed judicial power. Perhaps haunted by worries about "victor's justice" and retroactivity, the tribunal limited its prosecution of crimes against humanity—that is, crimes with respect to the inhuman treatment of civilians—to instances where the allegations at issue could be connected to the conduct of war by the now-defeated enemy.

Mechanisms of enforcement continued to lag behind. However, by the beginning of the Cold War and the polarization of U.S.-Soviet relations, the Geneva Conventions themselves seemed highly ambiguous as to the form of their protection. Consider the Convention on the Prevention and Punishment of the Crime of Genocide, the leading postwar instrument aimed at ratifying the norms relating to the worst of crimes. Theoretically, the Convention on the Prevention and Punishment of the Crime of Genocide might have left open the question of enforcement to a prospective international tribunal. Instead, the Genocide Convention still left the protections to states to enforce.[19] In many ways, states remained firmly in control of their citizens, and the international legal system served ultimately to preserve the status quo.[20] For about half a century, the expanded humanitarian norms discussed herein had a largely exhortatory force; their values took on added meaning only later, with the transformation of international politics, which redirected the international community's sense of the potential of international law.

POST–COLD WAR VIOLENCE: A PUNISHING PEACE AND THE RISE OF THE INTRACONFLICT COURT

Close to two decades later in a Cold War–era trial, such as *Eichmann*, there were clearly tensions between achieving the goals of state-centric nation building and achieving other broader, humanity law goals. Therefore, despite so-called cumulative jurisdiction affording a basis to pursue both goals, generally a choice between the two got made. Nuremberg chose the message of unjust war over that of avenging humanity. *Eichmann* represents much later the vindication of "crimes against the people." In *Tadic*, the ICTY, asserted: "It would be a travesty of law and a betrayal of the universal need for justice, should the concept of State sovereignty be allowed to be raised successfully against human rights."[21] With the end of the Cold War, the potential of international criminal justice would continue to grow.[22]

A revisiting of the meaning of international criminal justice would occur a half century later, with the 1990s Balkans wars and the new wartime atrocities to the heart of Europe. The question asked: What is the role of international criminal justice *during* conflict? Convened in The Hague in the very midst of a bloody conflict, the ICTY had a strong mandate—and its mandate was hardly to ratify the gains of a hard-won peace. The ICTY was convened to hold war criminals to account, with the aim that this would help produce the peace. Indeed, the UN Resolution establishing the tribunal stated that "the prosecution of persons responsible for serious violations of international humanitarian law...would contribute to the restoration and maintenance of peace."[23] The tribunal had its flaws: It was not properly situated to prosecute aggression, given the ongoing nature of the conflict; and it suffered from the lack of clarity as to the justice of the initiation of conflict.

When the UN Security Council received reports of terrible abuses—including mass expulsion, civilian deportations, mass killings, torture, imprisonment, and atrocities in detention camps—it convened the first commission of experts since World War II to investigate the atrocities in Europe.[24] The commission concluded that there had been willful killing, organized massacres, torture, rape, pillage, and destruction of civilian property,[25] amounting to a campaign of "ethnic cleansing,"[26] and moreover that in some parts of the country, such ethnic cleansing had constituted part of a larger attempt to commit genocide against Bosnian Muslims and other non-Serbs.[27] However, ethnic cleansing broadly understood—the forcible deportation of a population—is defined as a crime against humanity under the statutes of both the International Criminal Tribunal for the Former Yugoslavia (ICTY) and the International Criminal Court (ICC). The gross human-rights violations integral to stricter definitions of ethnic cleansing are treated as separate crimes falling under the definitions for genocide or crimes against humanity of the statutes. This finding put into motion a track of independent judgment that was aimed at getting beyond the political stalemate. Established by the Security Council in the very midst of the Balkan wars, through its Chapter 7 powers, the ICTY explicitly linked punitive justice with peacemaking.

The tribunal would play a significant, ongoing role in constructing how the conflict was understood and the responses it would provoke. Though not simply the product of war between states, the humanitarian-law violations in the Balkans were seen as threatening "international peace and security." The establishment of the ICTY was followed less than two years later by the Rwanda tribunal.

Still, until Kosovo in 1999, forceful humanitarian intervention was not marshaled to stop the atrocities. Instead, under its Chapter 7 "peacemaking" powers, the Security Council convened an international tribunal as "a measure to maintain or restore international peace and security." According to the postwar Geneva Conventions and Convention on the Prevention and Punishment of the Crime of Genocide, the atrocities in the Balkans could be punished as war crimes, such that the bringing of individuals to justice was aimed at the "restoration and maintenance of the peace."

The ICTY's location, far from the war zone, meant that its brand of punishment took place in what might be seen as a political no-man's-land—in sharp contrast to the victors' justice that was meted out at Nuremberg to a vanquished enemy. This lack of power—whether regarding the ICTY's control over evidence or its custody over suspects—was reflected in the tribunal's decades-long struggle to bring to justice those belonging to the top political and military echelon in the region.

War crimes trials that occur during conflict, such as the World War I French trials of German soldiers,[28] have commonly been aimed at deterring the commission of further atrocities.[29] Yet, the ICTY's prosecutions hardly held much promise of creating deterrence, at least in the short run. After all, genocidal massacres, such as those that happened at Srebrenica, occurred despite these ongoing processes, thus challenging the notion of international punishment advancing the aim of deterrence, at least in the short run. That raises an important question: When are such expectations reasonable to possess, with respect to new processes and institutions?[30]

The other expectation was that this would be a court of reconciliation. According to the opening statement of the ICTY chief prosecutor, Richard Goldstone, in 1995, the "public record will assist in attributing guilt to individuals and be an important tool in avoiding the attribution of collective guilt to any nation or ethnic group."[31] The ICTY developed an exemplary cases policy—whereby the abuses represented are to cover the entire time period, from 1991 through the fall of the safe havens in 1995, and to include the full spectrum of war crimes and crimes against humanity committed in the region. These would encompass the setting up and implementation of detention camps; the Serb military takeover of towns; campaigns of terror; the firing of rockets into cities; the deportation of civilians; shelling of civilian gatherings; plunder of property; destruction of sacred sites; sniping campaigns against civilians in Sarajevo; and the targeting of peacekeepers and their use as human shields.[32]

Moreover, though the overwhelming number of the indicted are Serb nationals, the ICTY recognizes perpetrators and victims by their ethnicity and gender by taking note of these factors in the adjudication telling a complex story, that goes beyond the violation of individual human rights to reach ethnic conflict and the attack on peoples.[33] At the ICTY, mass rape and forced pregnancies are prosecutable as "crimes against humanity."[34] They are conceived as tools of destruction of the group, at the interface of gender and ethnic persecution, rendering what might have been construed as private violations as, instead, also threats that resonate in public and international terms.[35]

In supporting the establishment of the ICTY at the Security Council, the U.S. Secretary of State, Madeline Albright, declared, "the only victor that will prevail in this endeavor will be the truth," recognizing that the ICTY's brand of justice would be defined by its unique context of conducting autonomous judicial processes of inquiry and indictment—independent of any military victory and settlement. Nevertheless, as the processes unfolded, there were clearly tensions between the ICTY's efforts to construct truthful narratives, achieve the aim of reconciliation, and dispense criminal justice. Indeed, it is this last, overarching purpose, the purpose of dispensing criminal justice, that best explains both Milosevic's extended trial and the sense that it was ultimately a failure, or that the pursuit of historical justice necessitated a broader lens than the one individual trials afforded. Instead, in the Balkans, a full account would require working through the region's complex and conflictive political history, a still incomplete process.

Given their multiple purposes, the proceedings at The Hague couldn't help but fall short. In other words, they could not both punish culpable individuals and provide the thick form of reconciliation necessary for reconstructing a community of citizens. Yet the tribunal's international authority did have one singular advantage: By intervening unambiguously from outside, it operated beyond the strained political circumstances that continue to trap participants within the Balkans.[36] Still, this perceived advantage also underscored the ambivalence of the law of humanity: for insofar as such adjudication attempted to depoliticize the problem of dealing with conflict, it risked failing to deliver long-lasting solutions that were grounded in local accountability and the rule of law.

Since the ICTY's lack of perceived legitimacy in the region dogged its efforts to achieve peace, whether through deterrence or reconciliation, punishment became central. In the words of the jurist Theodor Meron, the ICTY was "the first truly international criminal tribunal."[37] Here, the workings of liberal legalism in the contemporary period hark back to historical (prestatist) conceptions of international justice, conceptions in which the predicate of punishment is prefigured in offending the law of nations.[38] International criminal justice was to lay a basis for a form of accountability that could break "cycles of ethnic retribution" and advance ethnic "reconciliation." Thus, the *Tadic* prosecutor contended, "absolving nations of collective guilt through the attribution of individual responsibility is an essential means of countering the misinformation and indoctrination which breeds ethnic and religious hatred."[39]

In a landmark decision affirming the basis of its mandate in the powers of the Security Council under the UN Charter, the ICTY declared that the crimes at issue "could not be considered political offenses, as they do not harm a political interest of a particular state" and the "norms prohibiting them have a universal character." Identifying violations of the "law of nations" is one of the ways the humanity law framework is defining the subject and impact of globalization in terms of its affected personality, and its ability to transcend borders to protect diverse peoples, and persons. So, for example, if one considers the offenses prosecuted, such as "genocide" and "crimes against humanity," these can be characterized by their close nexus between individual and group identity. "Ethnic cleansing"—one ethnic group's purposeful policy to purge by terror the civilian population of another ethnic group from a defined geographic area—is being prosecuted as a series of "crimes against humanity," as "inhumane acts" that are "widespread and systematic" and are "perpetrated on any civilian population, on an ethnic basis."[40]

Reaffirming Nuremberg's central principle of the subjectivization of responsibility for war crimes, the ICTY underscores the message of holding individuals responsible for ethnic persecution. The element of intention, of persecutory motive,[41] uniquely mediates individual and group identities where there are systematic mechanisms of state or state-like policy.[42] To adjudicate responsibility for humanity means reaching both the public and the private. It means going beyond state sponsorship and embodying concern for the protected person. It also entails protecting and accounting for individuals within collectivities, by drawing clear limits on what is, and is not, legitimate state and nonstate collective exercise of power in the early part of the twenty-first century, and thus informing the threshold standard of global accountability and governance. In then Secretary-General Annan's words, "the international tribunal should apply rules of international humanitarian law which are beyond any doubt part of customary law."[43] The content of such rules is subject to contestation, however, as there is no codification of international criminal law beyond the various statutes.[44] In this way, the instantiation of international humanitarian law can be seen to delineate the central norm of the rule of law within contemporary global politics.

The Nuremberg tribunal's jurisdiction over atrocities was always tied to the conduct of a war that was conceived as unjust within the understanding of the prevailing, classical interstate system.[45] In this regard, one can see that the ICTY has greater reach, in at least two ways, than the Nuremberg tribunal did: Unlike the Nuremberg tribunal, the ICTY's reach includes acts of persecution committed in the *course* of an armed conflict (i.e., irrespective of the victory); its exercise of jurisdiction began before the conflict's end, and most of the conduct it seeks to punish would count as an offense *whether or not* the conflict at issue is international.[46] In the ICTR statute, there is a further expansion in jurisdictional reach. The genocide of approximately one million Tutsis and Hutu moderates in Rwanda was committed within the country's borders. Nevertheless, for the first time, this was seen as a matter that was deemed to appropriately be put before an international tribunal. One might say that this marked a material change in the understanding of the meaning of having an enforceable law against genocide—at least, this viewpoint was sharply distinguishable from the limitation to transnational persecution that characterized the earlier midcentury postwar understanding of genocide.

There has been a significant controversy in the ICTR about how to define the relevant peoples for purposes of identifying "genocide" under the court's statute. In some regard, this doctrinal struggle transcends the legal realm, to speak to law's role in the current politics—thus raising anew the persistent question of whether humanity law has a clear definition or, as the recent ad hoc tribunals' jurisprudence suggest instead, there are only variable definitions enmeshed in the particulars of politics in a given region. While the ICTY emphasized the intent in its condemnation of state persecution,[47] the adjudication of the ICTR pressed in another direction, seeking more fixed definitions of race that could somehow be conceived of as "neutral" and outside politics.[48] At first blush, this seemed to present a conflict in humanity law. Yet these approaches, both historically and at present, simply underscored the entanglement of humanity law with politics. The ICTR statute's range of jurisdiction over crimes against humanity perpetrated in internal conflict reflects, and indeed helps support, the globalization of the law of humanity in world affairs, as the basic rule-of-law norm.

Once there is a process and machinery with the tribunals for adjudicating humanity rights, it becomes clear that the humanitarian logic is double-barreled: It operates not only to justify intervention on a humanity basis but also to limit (or otherwise shape) intervention through the same humanitarian logic. Here, one might conclude that proofs of the kind marshaled by the tribunal perform yet another role—to offer limits on a potentially open-ended return of humanitarian war. Hence, the force of the challenges to the NATO intervention in the region in the ICJ, where these charges, too, were leveled on a humanitarian basis, going to the evidence of the numbers of civilian casualties.[49] (I will discuss this important tension and constraint from *within* humanity law at greater length at the end of this chapter, as it pertains to evaluating the logic and structure of the present project of wars of humanitarian intervention and liberation.)

The ICTY was created by international peace accords and, in the context of ongoing conflict and atrocities, was assigned the mission of transforming the course of the region—an extraordinarily ambitious mandate. In this context, the image of the rule of law symbolizes the possibility of change—away from persecutory violence, and toward the rule of law, in the region. Yet the ICTY could not, in and of itself, fully embody the rule of law. Rather, the best it could do was to represent the rule of law in a transitional form, serving an image of the possibility of liberal justice—a type of justice that circumscribes a line delimiting legitimate politics in the circumstances. International criminal justice extends the possibility of judging and punishing individuals for persecutory violence in violation of the law of nations—thus offering judgment and punishment grounded in customary law. And in so doing, it appears to offer a liberal response that does not necessarily depend on the use of force.[50]

Prosecuting "persecutions on political, racial and religious grounds"[51] as a "crime against humanity" serves to represent ethnic cleaning in local conflict in transnational, even global terms. The ICTY was distinguished by the fact that it was established, and its mission was to be carried out, during the conflict. But the very efforts to accomplish these ambitious aims would ultimately underscore the project's dependence on the rule of law.[52] So, for example, the ICTY has long been dependent on Serbian authorities for the arrest and transfer of suspected war criminals. Many had blamed the longtime failure to capture two of the most notorious suspects—Radovan Karadžić, the architect of ethnic cleansing in the war, and Ratko Mladić—on Serbia's lack of cooperation. Interestingly, after more than ten years on the run, Karadžić was finally arrested in July 2008, just weeks after the formation of a new pro-Western government that was eager to gain admission to the European Union. After years of protection, with increasing European pressure in the spring 2011, General Mladic was finally caught, the last of the ethnic war's architects.

Without a matrix of political authority, the ICTY's transformative potential was but an image of liberal legalism. The tribunal has lacked the supportive national structures that are necessary to truly advance reconciliation, or to reestablish the rule of law in the region.[53] While international justice is commonly understood to model the rule of law in the region, the concern that the ICTY raised—especially in its later stages—was how exactly to reconnect international projects to the regular, local justice institutions and processes. The answer appears clearer now, as the tribunal's exit strategy involves referral to national judiciaries in the region. Early signs are promising, such as in the work of the special court of Bosnia Herzogovina.[54] Through the ICTY's indictments, the atrocities committed in the Balkans public knowledge—and this fact may well have contributed toward shaping the peace and the course of political representation in the region, even causing disqualifications from political office.[55]

A gap remains with the aspiration to reconciliation. Yet in this regard, the relevant political project has also changed—evolving toward the broader regional context, where cooperation with the tribunal is said to signal the likelihood of broader regional cooperation in Europe—which is a condition for EU membership.[56]

The European Union welcomes the adoption by the Serbian Parliament of the declaration on Srebrenica. This is an important step for the country in facing its recent past, a process which is difficult but essential for Serbian society to go through. This is not only important for Serbia, it is the key for the reconciliation for the whole region. We appreciate the role of everyone who made such a step possible.

 While recalling the European Parliament's resolution on Srebrenica of January 2009, the European Union notes the reaffirmation to fully co-operate with the International Criminal Tribunal for the Former Yugoslavia (ICTY), in particular the arrest and handing over of the remaining fugitives, and to continue the domestic processing of war crimes. These are crucial elements for stability and reconciliation in the region and for Serbia's EU accession perspective.[57]

This evolution, and the prospect of EU membership, have been acknowledged by then European Commission president José Manuel Barroso, commenting on Karadzic's arrest[58] by a joint EU statement;[59] and by then EU foreign policy chief Javier Solana. Similar statements were associated with Mladic's arrest, connecting it up to Serbia's future in Europe.[60]

 At best, the ICTY—as an institution that is both transitional and international—appears to function as an expression of the rule of law that gestures toward an alternative future, operating to reconstitute the relevant community of judgment.[61]

 Here, one can see the role of politics in rationalizing the broader humanity (and human security) bases of these trials.

FROM EUROPE TO AFRICA: THE RULE OF LAW AS "COMPLEMENTARY"

With the establishment of the ICC, international criminal justice is further enmeshed in managing conflict itself, whether or not that conflict is international in the classic interstate sense. The ICC can now be seen to represent a normative system organized around the Rome Statute.[62] This dynamic now characterizes contemporary criminal justice on a global basis. In jurisprudence relating to recent conflict, the long-prevailing distinction between international and internal conflict is "more and more blurred, and international legal rules increasingly have been agreed on to regulate internal armed conflicts."[63] As described earlier, the classical international legal regime, premised on state sovereignty and self-determination, was inextricably associated with the growth of modern nationalism and state-building.[64] Conversely, one might see the present developments in the emergent humanitarian-law regime as being bound up with the contemporary loss of political equilibrium, political fragmentation, the presence of weak and failed states, and the phenomenon of globalization.

These political realities have also sparked efforts at UN reform, with endeavors to reconcile sovereignty with the mounting justifications for greater international humanitarian intervention based on the evolving duties of protection to vulnerable persons and peoples.[65] Although such intervention is highly controversial, and may not even be legal under the current rules on the use of force in the UN Charter,[66] at least without Security Council approval, which occurred in the case of Libya. Increasingly, humanitarian intervention is being justified, whether in Iraq by the United States in terms of the need for protection of the population or under UN Charter Article 52(1)'s authorization of regional "enforcement action,"[67] and within the emergent norm of the Responsibility to Protect ("RtoP") (as elaborated beyond the state in humanity terms in chapter 5).

In this rapidly changing political context, the expanded humanitarian legal regime reflects the reframing of the meaning of security and of the rule of law in global politics. The turn to international criminal law enforcement through punishment is connected to a number of political projects associated with the present moment, involving aims from punishment to peacemaking. The statutes of the post-Nuremberg international criminal tribunals transcend any one aim or value, as these instruments—and their related processes and enforcement institutions—give expression to dynamic norms that reflect the reconstruction of the relevant understandings of international security in terms of emerging, humanity-based subjects. And, as jurist Burke–White argues, unlike the principle of primacy, the principle of complementarity may well be a way to reconcile such enforcement with state sovereignty.[68] In a sense, this is a development with certain affinities to the political principle of subsidiarity, which is guiding the globalization of law in other settings.[69]

The ICC's jurisdiction extends to a wide array of actors who are engaged in policymaking, promoting, or in some other fashion supporting violence.[70] Indeed, notably, in its provisions addressing individual responsibility, the ICC Rome Statute Article 25, sets out a wide spectrum of potential responsibility: aiding, assisting, ordering, soliciting, or inducing the offense or attempting it.[71]

As to its substantive jurisdiction, in what appears to be an implied concession of the innovation, on June 11, 2010, the Review Conference held in Kampala, Uganda, adopted amendments to the Rome Statute, including a definition of the crime of aggression.[72] While the Nuremberg Charter merely referred to a "war of aggression," this definition appeared to incorporate already-agreed-on understandings of aggression. At the ICC, the proposal was—rather than trying to renegotiate a new definition of aggression—to adopt the definition in General Assembly Resolution 3314, which had taken many years to negotiate and had received consensus in the UN General Assembly. Article 1 of Resolution 3314 defines aggression as "the use of armed force by a state against the sovereignty, territorial integrity, or political independence of another state, or in any other manner inconsistent with the Charter of the United Nations, as set out in this Definition."[73] It defines the crime as "the planning, preparation, initiation or execution, by a person in a position effectively to exercise control over or to direct the political or military action of a State, of an act of aggression which, by its character, gravity and scale, constitutes a manifest violation of the Charter of the United Nations," but it also adds: "In respect of a State that is not a party to this Statute, the Court shall not exercise its jurisdiction over the crime of aggression when committed by that State's nationals or on its territory."[74] This new definition of aggression shields nonmembers, such as the United States, China, and Russia, from being investigated.[75] A majority adopted this definition on June 11, 2010.[76]

Since the ICC's creation, there have been debates regarding gravity and scale as well as aggression's particular object.[77] Debates going to the following questions: What actors are legitimately subject to the norm in question? Just who can be held to account for the crime of aggression? What standard will apply to individual responsibility?[78] To what extent is there a necessary connection to state action? Or, might there be a reconceptualization underway of the crime of aggression? In a globalizing politics, to what extent can this archpolitical crime also be privatized? Unlike the post–World War II Nuremberg definition, where aggression applied only vis-à-vis the leading war criminals of the European Axis countries, the ICC provision on aggression is not limited to particular states or individuals (although it does protect nationals of nonmembers from investigation).[79] (Indeed, I discuss the evolution of this threshold for responsibility further in chapter 5.)

In the ICC the recently ratified amendment defines an act of aggression in terms of an attack "against the sovereignty, territorial integrity or political independence of another State."[80] However, its operation is limited to States Parties. Fundamental issues regarding group autonomy and self determination remain that may well go to the question of the legality of intervention. One can see that the Rome system's layered aims including protection of both persons and peoples, and now with aggression, the security of the state, raise new questions about the relationship the Court will have with the Security Council.[81]

As Judith Shklar observed, "it is practically of great importance to see legalism as a matter of degree.... To do this one must step outside the haven of fundamental legal theory and ideology to see what legalism as a policy can do where there is no legal system to be dissected."[82] What is extraordinary is that this view of legalism and its virtues somehow assumes, significantly, that a legal standard exists for such condemnation or judgment that doesn't otherwise depend on the specific claims that are at stake in a particular conflict, and the perceptions of justice of the actors that are present in a particular conflict.

This, of course, has presented issues before—such as the ICTY-in-the-Hague's relationship to the particular events in the Balkans. There, the tribunal was challenged on the basis of its position as a judicial authority that seeks to operate outside traditional understandings of political sovereignty. Similar concerns arise regarding the pursuit of universality jurisdiction (as discussed in chapter 3).

The ICC has jurisdiction to prosecute only where there is "inability" and "unwillingness" on the part of domestic authorities.[83] Yet, this very determination is for the ICC to make. The system gives the ICC ultimate authority—it is the court that decides. In other words, the ICC possesses *Kompetenz-Kompetenz* in determining whether the local response is adequate within the relevant definition. Already, there have been instances in which the Security Council has made referrals and the chief prosecutor's claim's have not always been automatically accepted by the trial chamber. One example is the July 2008 Security Council petition to indict Sudan's sitting president, Omar Al Bashir (the first sitting leader to be so indicted by the ICC).[84] On July 12, 2010, the ICC issued a second warrant of arrest, charging Bashir with three counts of genocide. The campaign of apparent genocide that has afflicted Sudan's western Darfur region for the last four years has resulted in the killings of thirty-five thousand people outright and at least one hundred thousand through "slow death," and has forced 2.5 million to flee their homes. The violence there appears to be largely the result of a mix of motivations. The Sudanese government mounted a campaign that has killed hundreds of thousands of Darfurians via attacks by the Janjaweed (the government-allied Arab militia) and aerial bombardment, in which Bashir is believed to have been complicit.[85] Despite arrest warrants against Ahmad Harun, Sudan's state minister for humanitarian affairs, on forty-two counts, and against former Janjaweed leader Ali Kushayb on fifty individual counts, the Sudanese government has repeatedly refused to cooperate with the court and arrest these two suspects. In July 2010, Luis Moreno-Ocampo, prosecutor of the ICC invoked the responsibility to protect: "Bashir is attacking Sudanese citizens, the same people he has the duty to protect. Now the international community has a new opportunity to provide protection."[86]

Darfur represented a turning point in American relations with the ICC: despite the Bush administration's opposition to the court, the

United States failed to veto the Security Council's referral for investigation. Moreover, the Security Council's referral, made through Security Council Resolution 1593, obliges Sudan to cooperate with the ICC, although it is not a state party to the ICC's Rome Statute. Still, there remains opposition both on the ground, and by humanitarian organizations; for some, the indictment poses "major risks for the fragile peace and security environment in Sudan, with a real chance of greatly increasing the suffering of very large numbers of its people."[87] This view reflects the breadth of humanity law logic, since whatever aims the referral may serve, if such accountability would pose greater risk to the population, then the referral would backfire from a humanity law perspective.

Certainly it would be a mistake to understate the court's broader normative role. The idea of complementarity can also be seen as reflecting a broader understanding of generalized normativity. Advocates often stress their view of the tribunal as jurisdiction—as its first chief prosecutor, Luis Moreno-Ocampo, put it—"of last resort,"[88] a seemingly modest ambition. Yet this understanding also implies, as it operates, that its ordinary understanding of the conditions to jurisdiction is predicated on some expectation of the reliance on (though not the exhaustion of) domestic remedies in some fashion, a notion that already appears to assume its integration as a matter of practice in the law of nations.

Consider the everyday implications of the existence of a court that, according to its constitutive instrument and statements of ongoing purpose, is aimed at managing conflict worldwide. Thus far, the Office of the Prosecutor has already sought to enmesh itself in a number of conflict situations, almost exclusively involving Africa, whose states have often been in crisis (e.g., situations in Uganda, Congo, Darfur, the Central African Republic, and Kenya). Of these, for some time the furthest along was a "situation" (as described by Articles 13 and 14 of the Rome Statute) that was "referred" to the ICC for the prosecution of key members of the brutal Ugandan rebel group known as the Lord's Resistance Army. There have been indictments—in particular of the group's leader, Joseph Kony, who is widely believed to maintain a base in Sudan.[89] Interestingly, in this situation and others, one can observe that—despite the initial fears of states—in most cases, it is states that are referring private actors for their roles in conflict. This state of affairs prevailing until recently (Bashir and Qaddafi), has minimized the court's potential for rocking the prevailing international system. Moreover, on the flip side are the questions concerning the private actors who are implicated in violations of the law of nations but who lack statehood—that is, nonsignatories such as the Palestinian

Authority, which has recently sought a referral to the court regarding the situation in the Territories.[90]

The Ugandan indictments presented a profound dilemma for the court, illustrating the potential tensions regarding the assumption of jurisdiction over a situation that on the one hand demanded a political resolution and on the other—according to some observers—might well be jeopardized by judicial intervention.[91] Yet it appears that a negotiated resolution has been reached—bargaining in the shadow of the law. Moreover, the ceasefire built in the justice dimension, that serious crimes would be dealt with locally—a resolution which might well have not been achievable in a different context.[92]

In the wake of the Security Council's failure to come up with a resolution regarding Darfur, the matter was put in the hands of the ICC—a referral that may give an inkling as to how the court will operate, as the pattern appears to emulate the ad hoc tribunals in a number of ways. The exercise of such Security Council referral points to the contemporary connection between punishment and international security and illustrates how the new institutions of judgment connect to the prevailing interstate security regime. First, as the referral came from the Security Council—where, in the face of more general opposition, it garnered the support of the United States—it showed, once again, that at issue was the predicament of a completely stalled international political process, as well as a lack of political or judicial response locally. While the government of Sudan has initiated a local trials policy, apparently in order to preempt international processes, nevertheless the emphasis of this policy has been on low-level crimes such as looting, which are hardly comparable to the crimes over which the ICC has jurisdiction.[93] Hence, they may not be considered to meet complementarity standards. Nevertheless, these domestic trials do raise the interesting question of what sorts of prosecutions might be more important to ongoing human security on the ground—that is, prosecutions of looting versus prosecutions of genocide? And in any event, in an international justice system, predicated on complementarity, what counts as adequate process? In any event, the most recent developments include the issuance of a warrant for Bashir's arrest for crimes against humanity.[94]

The office of the ICC prosecutor has asserted that security in Darfur depends, instead, on the government of Sudan and, where appropriate, the Security Council.[95] Might such judicial intervention be, at best, either beside the point or even, as in Uganda, apparently damaging to the political process? The Security Council under its Chapter VII powers authorized a joint African Union–UN force for peacekeeping. The course of this operation could be problematic. Many human rights groups insist on prosecutions, and indeed, indictments have followed. Nevertheless, there is an explicit debate being waged between those groups, such as Human Rights Watch, on one side and on the other side the humanitarian organizations and their advocates, such as the International Crisis Group, who argue that the indictment could backfire unless it is woven into the political negotiations on the ground.[96]

Turning the popular image of the ICC on its head, one might reconceive this latest court as instead (recalling Grotius) underscoring the close connection between the role of coercive criminal justice and that of other, even more forceful forms of intervention (that is, ones that would have been more forceful if there had been more consensus). Indeed, this becomes clear with the more recent Security Council referral of Libya to the ICC and the almost concurrent resolution for military intervention (Security Council Resolution 1973).[97] Unlike the Nuremberg Tribunal or the ICTY, where jurisdiction were inextricably tied to the particular conflict at issue, the ICC's scope is defined by its focus on those most responsible for the "most serious crimes" in the eyes of the international community: violations of the law of humanity. Moreover, the ICC statute enumerates the offenses as agreed to by a substantive consensus of international society, integrating international-humanitarian-law responses to conflicts over human history. While nominally "international," this site ties jurisdiction to a normativity that is not centrally focused on justice *between* states.

So the statute for the ICC (the Rome Statute) extends to offenses—many of which had already been recognized as the most heinous human rights violations in customary law—known as *jus cogens*. In "crimes against humanity," we can observe the expansion of international humanitarian law to protect a pluralistic human rights, i.e., protecting persons and as peoples. This is evident, for example, in the ongoing evolution of the legal definition of "persecution."

According to the ICC statute, a crime against humanity comprehends "persecution on political, racial, national, ethnic, cultural, religious, or gender grounds."[98] Indeed, there is a move now under way to entrench this norm in a convention.[99] In November 2009, at the Fifth Colloquium of Prosecutors of International Criminal Tribunals, prosecutors from the ICTR, the ICTY, and the ICC, among other bodies, unanimously called on states to "seriously consider the adoption of a convention on the Suppression and Punishment of Crimes against Humanity."[100] What might the adoption of such a convention achieve? As Judith Shklar observed of the postwar trials, "the entire trial can only be justified by what it revealed and said about the crimes against humanity."[101] For these crimes "do not enjoy the traditional approbation which war evokes." For Shklar, legalism was most at odds with the crime against humanity.[102] Might fixing its meaning for all time risk the loss of its ongoing normative force?

HUMANITY LAW'S NORMATIVITY: BEYOND COMPLIANCE

An evident aim of the newly established enforcement machinery, in the form of independent international institutions dedicated to enforcing humanitarian law, is to impose sanctions. A regular role for law enforcement, criminal sanctions, and independent institutions supports the perception of a heightened international rule of law, but the question is why. Here, it is clear that criminal sanctions are a distinctive dimension of legal norms.[103] Criminal sanctions have a particular constructive potential that plays a distinct role in today's political context.

Historically, not all violations of the law of nations would afford a basis for interstate engagement, precisely because—as Grotius observed— expanding the set of violations in the absence of a neutral tribunal might run the risk of increasing conflict, as these engagements might take the form of forceful intervention across state lines. Instead, punishment has long played a significant regulatory role in these extreme conditions—that is, conditions involving the commission of the most serious offenses against international society.

This point was most visible in times of imperial rule, but also has been seen more recently, on an exceptional basis, associated with conflict or postconflict rule. In all of these instances, historically, states were judges— either in their own cause or analogously, through various forms of "victor's justice." What we now see, however, is that the basis for the new judicialization and system of justice regarding war has become in significant measure independent from the inherited understanding of state sovereignty and consent. This development reflects contemporary conflicts that do not fit within traditional understandings of war.

Under the aegis of humanity law, heightened legal protection extends to *any* civilian population, applies without regard to nationality or citizenship, and applies whether or not those who belong to that population find themselves in armed conflict. The salient question is, instead, whether the offenses in question had a persecutory and systematic state-like quality— that is, a deliberate collective dimension—and whether the conduct itself is characterized as widespread or systematic. As the ICTY declared in its ruling in *Kupreskic*, "the crimes must, to a certain extent, be organized and systematic. Although they need not be related to a policy established at State level, in the conventional sense of the term, they cannot be the work of isolated individuals alone. Lastly, the crimes, considered as a whole, must be of a certain scale and gravity," generally relating to derogations in the protection of persons and peoples, and dimensions of humanity.[104]

These developments reflect how human rights overlap with elements of the offense in international criminal law.

We can also see the ways that processes of condemnation and punishment can create a source of community. This was so in the Grotian tradition.[105] Indeed, this link was said to be at the heart of the function of punishment that was given great emphasis by Immanuel Kant, who argued that even if a desert island community were to disband, its members should first execute the last murderer left in its jails, "for otherwise they might all be regarded as participators in the [unpunished] murder."[106] This Kantian idea—that the failure to punish wicked acts may constitute a message that society endorses them—has been reflected in the responses to the way the ad hoc tribunals create a society of judgment. And the role of the, expressive view of punishment connects the two.[107]

What may be more interesting, for our purposes, is the particular function of adjudication in global politics. Thus, the philosopher Joel Feinberg suggests that in the preoccupation with traditional punishment aims such as deterrence and reform, we may well lose sight of other purposes of punishment that are of an expressive nature, such as the purpose of "authoritative disavowal." Indeed, we might imagine this social function of punishment—express disavowal—playing an important role nowadays, given the greater number of points of contact of state and nonstate actors in globalizing conditions. Not surprisingly, therefore, we see that the new humanity law has had the effect of placing more and more pressure on states, by insisting that a state whose agent has unlawfully violated the complaining nation's rights should punish the offending agent. For Feinberg, disavowal is critical to the state's distancing itself from what could otherwise form the basis for just war. Indeed, while Feinberg does not single out international law violations, one might imagine that—given the rationale for disavowal—these would be the most serious. In Feinberg's words, "failure to punish the pilot tells the world that government A does not consider him to have been personally at fault. That in turn is to claim responsibility for the act, which in effect labels that act as an 'instrument of deliberate national policy' and hence an act of war. In that case either formal hostilities or humiliating loss of face by one side or the other almost certainly will follow. None of this scenario makes any sense without the clearly understood symbolism of punishment as reprobation."[108]

Whatever its significance for ordinary crime, one might imagine that this kind of disavowal is most important where international law violations are at stake. Moreover, one might add that the scenario has become even more serious with the new tribunalization. Here, one might observe a fortiori that perhaps the recognition of a number of different rungs of disavowal may well be in order, on a complementary basis—that is, based on whether the disavowal is that of the state of nationality, the territorial state, or international society. Such a view of disavowal might perhaps go some way toward illuminating the varying degrees of interests in such criminal justice processes.

The humanity law framework here involves both the declaration of changing norms (i.e., their discursivity) and their implementation and enforcement, giving them a sense of added positivity and reality. The shift enables a move away from a purely political discourse of state interests that is realizable and rationalizable in collective exercises of self-determination and toward a legalist rhetoric of rights-claims that are enforceable in courts of law. Juridical processes tend to convert matters of policy into matters of transpolitical law. Furthermore, the language of law, in particular, mediates between the rhetoric of pure politics and that of pure moralism; this is particularly true of the discourse of criminal law, law's most moralizing modality. The new humanitarian legalism's justificatory processes offer the potential for rationalizing international policymaking. Public processes, offering structured justification, may afford an alternative sense of global order.

Humanitarian norms are constitutive of the emerging global order, in part, by serving a central discursive function. More and more, a depoliticized, secular, legalist language of rights and wrongs, claims and duties, is complementing discourse of state interests—while this language also becomes, at the same time, a new language of politics. An expanded humanitarian discourse ultimately contributes an alternative basis for global governance, where the concept of the rule of law takes the form of a law-enforcement-based approach to conflict resolution.[109] Further, the humanitarian-law regime enables us to reconceptualize the interests that are at stake in contemporary international conflict. Whereas international legality and stability have classically been defined largely in terms of state interests and state security, the new humanitarian rights redefine security in other ways, for the benefit of persons and peoples.

What is the relationship between the pursuit of individual (as opposed to collective/state) responsibility and human security? A turning point as was discussed earlier here is the *Tadic* judgment involving the trial of Dusko Tadic, a Bosnian-Serb café owner, became the first defendant indicted before the ICTY. The charges were based on his participating in and aiding and abetting rape, gang rape, sexual mutilation, and other violence at the detention camps. The ICTY found that "[Tadic] in some instances was himself the perpetrator and in others intentionally assisted directly and substantially in the common purpose of inflicting physical suffering...and thereby aided and abetted in the commission of the crimes and is therefore individually responsible for each of them."[110] Similarly, in *Prosecutor v. Rutaganda*, Georges Rutaganda, an agricultural engineer and businessman, ordered killings and the causing of serious bodily harm to Tutsis.[111] Ever since the establishment of the ICC, its docket has been dominated by indictments of nonstate actors—starting with the referrals by Uganda of the Lord's Resistance Army.[112]

The statutes of both the ICTR and the ICTY contemplate that a person who "planned, instigated, ordered, committed or otherwise aided and abetted in the planning, preparation or execution of a crime … shall be individually responsible for the crime."[113] Similarly, the Rome Statute of the ICC states: "a person shall be criminally responsible and liable for punishment for a crime within the jurisdiction of the Court if that person … [f]or the purpose of facilitating the commission of such a crime, aids, abets or otherwise assists in its commission or its attempted commission, including providing the means for its commission." Where criminal responsibility is engaged by ordering.[114]

Courts have already held individual actors responsible for violations of the law of nations, by drawing on international criminal justice precedents—albeit, in a civil setting, within ATCA suits in U.S. courts.[115] As Judge Robert Katzmann reasoned in his concurrence in an ATCA case that came before the U.S. Court of Appeals for the Second Circuit, "viewing aiding and abetting in this way, as a theory of identifying who was involved in an offense committed by another rather than as an offense in itself, also helps to explain why a private actor may be held responsible for aiding and abetting the violation of a norm that requires state action or action under color of law. … Recognizing the responsibility of private aiders and abettors merely permits private actors who substantially assist state actors to violate international law and do so for the purpose of facilitating the unlawful activity to be held accountable for their actions."[116]

Imperial and colonial courts operated extraterritorially, where judicial power was explicitly engaged as an agent in norm transformation. Since coercive norm change is unpopular, it is perhaps not unsurprising that the task falls more often to distant courts. Historical practices may well help to explain the pull of exceptionalism, as well as the apparent fluidity between resort to the juridical and resort to the political as alternative sources of rationalizing regulation. Still, the foregoing analysis also leads us to reflect on these expectations, and to ask: Are they realistic?

Nuremberg's success, and arguably, its most lasting legacy, might well have derived from its bounded internationalism: That is, Nuremberg ought be best understood not for its international dimensions but for its decidedly mixed legal status. It was a court convened not in a removed locale but *on site*, in Germany, and a court initiated by a rather limited internationalism, via an agreement of occupying powers. Nuremberg also invoked other related normative imperatives, rendering it closely tied to the country's domestic-criminal-law values.

Mixed tribunals may well best do the work of domestic norm change. Consider the more contemporary experiments involving site-specific fora such as those of Sierra Leone or East Timor, or the special chambers that are under way in Bosnia-Herzegovina.[117] The Special Tribunal for Lebanon offers a recent example: It was established, according to Security Council Resolution 1664, to "try all those who are alleged responsible for the attack of February 14, 2005 in Beirut that killed the former Lebanese Prime Minister Rafiq Hariri and 22 others."[118] While the tribunal recently announced that it was "getting closer to identifying the suicide bomber who carried out the attack" and filed its first draft indictment over the 2005 killing of Prime Minister Rafik al-Hariri,[119] it has been limited by claims of politicization.[120]

In these fora, international criminal justice has a distinctive constructive potential, because of the criminal law's expressive and functional dimensions, as well as its flexibility in the characterization and judgment of conflict situations. As has been seen in one of the ICC's first trials, of Thomas Lubanga, where pre-trial chambers characterizing the Congo's inter-ethnic conflict as "international," so signaled the seriousness of conscription of children and other offenses "sending a message," as Deputy Prosecutor Bensouda put it, about behaviour that will no longer be tolerated by the international community. The foregoing thread of analysis highlights dimensions of the humanity norm's law-like nature: Recent developments involving centralized judicial institutions with coercive jurisdiction, imposing shared sanctions concerning the most serious crimes for international society, render these developments candidates for "basic norms" in an emerging global rule of law—norms that might themselves serve as a recognition rule.[121]

The expanded enforcement that is associated with the international law of armed conflict enables the transformation of traditional understandings of responsibility in the international sphere, from the national to the international, and from the collective to the individual. One can see newfound accountability arising from the recognition of added legal personality among agents operating in a globalizing system. In some sense, this is a revival of an historical understanding of the subjects of international law that can be seen in the writing of Grotius, where there was a more comprehensive view of the scope of the "law of nations," suggesting that this law aimed beyond states, to govern an international society.[122]

In the older justice tradition, forcible intervention was seen as a form of punishment and as a means of prevention and enforcement. With the ICTY, the goal of punishment is served instead by individual responsibility; and the intervention limited to goals of prevention and protection.

WAR'S JUSTICE?

I believe that force can be justified on humanitarian grounds, as it was in the Balkans, or in other places that have been scarred by war.... When there is genocide in Darfur, systematic rape in Congo, repression in Burma—there must be consequences. Yes, there will be engagement; yes, there will be diplomacy—but there must be consequences when those things fail....

Where force is necessary, we have a moral and strategic interest in binding ourselves to certain rules of conduct. And even as we confront a vicious adversary that abides by no rules, I believe the United States of America must remain a standard bearer in the conduct of war. That is what makes us different from those whom we fight. That is a source of our strength. That is why I prohibited torture. That is why I ordered the prison at Guantánamo Bay closed. And that is why I have reaffirmed America's commitment to abide by the Geneva Conventions. We lose ourselves when we compromise the very ideals that we fight to defend.

Barack Obama, *Nobel Peace Prize Acceptance Speech (2008)*

The Grotian tradition, in referring to the "just war," understood the phrase to encompass the justice of the war's causes, while also setting out, in Lauterpacht's words, to humanize the rules of war. However, it is important to remember that for Grotius, the justice of a war depended on both the justification—that is, the causes for the intervention—*and* the way it was waged. Indeed, it is precisely because of this Grotian, law-based view of justice that war can be a remedy only where legal institutions and remedies are otherwise unavailable.[123] "For," Grotius writes, "where the methods of Justice cease, War begins."[124] The trend in tribunalization just discussed reflects both an expansion in law enforcement and an expansion of the regulatory purview over conflict. The questions now are whether, and just how, to reconcile the two dimensions of justice in war. In the contemporary moment, the return of the earlier just war tradition is taking place against the backdrop of a fully elaborated humanitarian-law framework, resulting in a complex normative scheme by which to evaluate the justice of war. To what extent do these developments muddy the waters?

Here, I want to reconnect the two dimensions of the tradition regarding the justice of war, which I discussed in my earlier treatment of the ICC regime. At present, one can see that there is a much closer nexus between the just war dimension and the international-humanitarian-law dimension of adherence to the laws of war—one that includes, but also goes beyond, the prevailing humanity law regime. Contemporary rethinking of the relationship between the two dimensions refers to multiple bases—post–Cold War internationalization, globalization, and the privatization of war-making—all of which go to the redefinition of the subject of the just war regime. At a time when the conception of war is changing, one must concede that there is no stable concept of war that prefigures these considerations and rules; instead, one might say that the practices and customs of war, including the privileges themselves, shape how war is conceived. It follows therefore that developments in *jus in bello* shape *jus ad bellum,* and reflect a degree of continuum between these two dimensions. In a number of areas, we can see that there is a revisiting of the inherited dualism and the prevailing "principle of distinction," as it has been known in the traditional law of war.[125] We know a "just" war not merely by its aims or purposes, as expressed in the "best interests" of actors, but also—and perhaps even more important— by its forms and the ways such intervention is actually conducted. Relatedly, the very question of what regime applies is increasingly raised in instances of the growing convergence of the two dimensions of the regime regulating conflict.

Developments in the humanitarian-law regime, as well as in the Geneva Convention (such as Article 1, Protocol I, supporting wars of "self-determination") go to the question of the ongoing viability of adherence to the long-standing notion of "principles of distinction," which is now vulnerable to academic and other challenges.[126] Thus, there have been important institutional changes where the two strands of just war theory are increasingly brought together—with the potential for either collision or harmonization. Thus, for example, there is the extent to which the ICC's statute contemplates the same enforcement scheme for prosecuting both war crimes and aggression.[127] Or, since 2005, there has been the growing recognition at the United Nations of the Responsibility to Protect, a duty that in certain contexts might well extend even to an explicit duty of intervention (exercised albeit on a complementary basis) to undertake to save civilian lives wherever threatened. Indeed, such a duty to protect is being invoked regarding the recent crisis in Libya with the Security Council's Resolution 1973, authorizing "necessary measures to protect civilians under threat of attack in the country."[128] President Obama invoked similar language, warning Qaddafi that "all attacks against civilians must stop."[129]

Other limiting conditions, therefore, will appear, with implications for a changing view of the ongoing morality and legality of the use of force, under the UN system, for reasons that go beyond mere self-defense.[130] As Judge Simma explained in his separate opinion in *Armed Activities on the Territory of the Congo (Democratic Republic of the Congo v. Uganda),* attention must also be drawn to Article 3 common to all four Geneva Conventions, which defines certain rules to be applied in armed conflicts of a non-international character. As the ICJ stated in the *Nicaragua* case: "'There is no doubt that, in the event of international armed conflicts, these rules also constitute a minimum yardstick, in addition to the more elaborate rules which are also to apply to international conflicts; and they are rules which, in the Court's opinion, reflect what the Court in 1949 called 'elementary considerations of humanity.'"[131]

The stakes are high, as is further discussed in the chapters that follow, given the apparent rise in the wars of "liberation," that is, the wars in Iraq and Afghanistan, and arguably as well as in the campaign or "war" "on terror." Some see a rise in terror, an evil conflict with effects on the immunities regime. But one might argue, conversely, that from a humanity law perspective, one would expect the laws of war to be most closely observed precisely where the claim is to a "just war" and that, moreover, the very conduct of the waging of war (jus in bello) would become a part of what goes into a just war—that is, an important sign of the justice of the war.

Indeed, one might very well expect that just wars should foster better behavior in warfare. This would be particularly important where the relevant wars are not clearly ones of self-defense[132] and, therefore, necessitate some demonstrable proof of good intentions. Indeed one can already see evidence of this understanding: The Independent International Commission on Kosovo recommended that military operations in humanitarian interventions should be conducted according to especially strict rules of engagement.[133] Moreover, one might further expect that it is precisely where both sides claim to be waging a just war that looking to each side's practices regarding the waging of war could well be a tiebreaker. As President Obama implied in his Nobel address the return of notions of just war would hardly militate in favor of diminished adherence to the laws of war; to the contrary, it would only warrant stricter adherence to such norms.

RECONCEIVING THE JUST WAR IN LIGHT OF THE HUMANITARIAN BIND: THE NEW WARS OF HUMANITARIAN INTERVENTION

The justice of war is no longer understood merely in terms of its root causes (i.e., as set out in the UN Charter and its self-defense exception) but—as proposed here—is now also justified in terms of the ways the war is, and will be, waged. In part, one might see that the forward-looking view was always part of the just war calculus—that is, the calculation of the likelihood of success, as discussed by Michael Walzer and Ariel Colonomos.[134] But this point goes to the practices themselves: The new humanity law calculus involves holding in one's sight simultaneously the two strands of what had hitherto been seen as separate areas of law, and rejecting the core dualism that has, for decades, been associated with the stability of the traditional interstate security system. This rethinking, as we will see, is now having significant implications for the future of war, and its practices.

The inherited humanitarian law regime is largely the product of state agreement or consent at an earlier historical period. Yet in today's world the regime has to be applied to states and indeed other actors who did not participate in its making, and to conflicts and to methods or warfare often different than those supposed by the regime's framers. The pace of events has far outstripped the capacity to address this issue through formal amendment of multilateral conventions. And there is the lurking question posed by H. L. A. Hart with respect to transitional states and the legitimacy of those who did not participate and explicitly consent in the creation of the norms being bound.[135]

Understanding the action taken in Kosovo requires that the conflict be placed in context—specifically, that it be seen as occurring at the end of a decade of particularly savage conflicts. Civilians, not soldiers, are increasingly recognized as the primary targets and victims of modern war; civilian suffering is often the direct objective of military action. The war in Bosnia, culminating in the massacre at Srebrenica, is emblematic of this brutal trend. The atrocities that amounted to genocide in Rwanda represented the ultimate targeted attack on civilians.[136]

Consider—or reconsider through a humanity law lens—a humanitarian military intervention such as that which was launched in 1990s Kosovo. Given its explicit "just war" justification, the NATO intervention would have been vulnerable to criticism had the attacking force incurred high civilian casualties. For the report of the Independent International Commission on Kosovo had recognized the need to protect civilians who were targets of Serbian attacks. Whereas in the NATO Operation there were high-profile instances, certain attacks—that is, attacks on hospitals and other places that were civilian rather than military—that hit too close to home, given the justification for the campaign. These kinds of attacks—had they warranted more than investigation—would have put the intervention in jeopardy.[137] Such attacks, as well as the bombing of Belgrade, reflect the uneasy mix of humanitarian objectives with the political aim of putting pressure on Milosevic's authority to rule within Serbia—that is, exerting pressure to force regime change.

By way of comparison, where similar human-centered justifications were deployed in the war in Iraq—with the claim that it was a war of "liberation," ostensibly undertaken for the benefit of the Iraqi people—then one might see that this rationale generated legitimate expectations regarding the care and the treatment of the country's peoples, the restoration of the rule of law, and state-building. The expansion of just war discourse—particularly in the context where such military intervention is justified in the name of human rights—would, one might imagine, demand the scrupulous observance of civilian immunities, particularly in the affected country.

The human costs and military failures that followed from Operation Iraqi Freedom suggested to some that the appeal of humanitarian intervention would now wane. Samantha Power, senior director of multilateral affairs on the staff of the Obama Administration Security Council, argued that Iraq wrecked the Kosovo precedent for the future.[138] But in the case of Libya the humanity law logic would prevail, albeit after hesitations and qualifications that certainly could be interpreted at least in part by deriving from the "lessons" of Iraq.

As argued in this chapter, as a steady, persistent outgrowth of the changes in the law that have been identified here—namely, the advent of humanity rights within the context of the prevailing interstate security system. With this point in mind, we can better understand the Obama administration's recent call for a just war in Afghanistan: The president affirmed that "evil does exist in the world. A nonviolent movement could not have halted Hitler's armies." And he stated that "force can be justified to protect civilians."[139] We can also better understand the first Security Council authorized humanitarian intervention of the twenty-first century in Libya, which was similarly justified on the grounds of the protection of civilians.[140]

"GOOD WARS" GONE BAD; "BAD WARS" GONE WORSE

Thus, what makes a "good" war turn "bad" is not just political or military error; rather, the evaluation is shaped now, in an ongoing way, by the effects of the war on civilians.

Consider the changing evaluation of the war in Afghanistan: After 9/11, by late 2002, the war was being conceived as a justified war of self-defense. In Resolutions 1363 and 1373, in the wake of the 9/11 attacks, the Security Council affirmed the applicability of the right of individual and collective self-defense in the United Nations Charter in responding to terrorism. In addition, Resolution 1373 requires states to take "the necessary steps" to prevent the commission of terrorist acts, not excluding the possibility that this could require the use of force.[141] Now, the Afghanistan war's justice has been put in question due to humanity-related concerns such as those arising from the subsequent aerial bombardment and an unacceptably high number of killings of civilians.

In the U.S.-controlled Afghan province, the high level of civilian casualties makes it difficult to win over local people. Indeed, at some level, the war in Afghanistan has become a war of "hearts and minds"—hence is associated with the challenge presented by Vietnam—which was, as

Michael Walzer put it, "the first war in which the practical value of jus in bello became apparent."[142] Differences of opinion exist among NATO and U.S. forces in Afghanistan as to acceptable tactics for fighting Taliban insurgents, and there are concerns among soldiers on the ground about the consequences of civilian casualties.[143]

While a precise tally of civilian casualties is difficult to pin down, there have been hundreds of such casualties in the last two years—as a result of the uses of aerial bombardments—with the vast majority caused by foreign and Afghan forces.[144] Indeed, this problem is new and growing—as the problem of aerial attacks on civilians was inadequately addressed by the 1949 Geneva Conventions. The disparity occasioned by new weaponry has led some to suggest that we need a full reconsideration of the standards of international humanitarian law.[145] Meanwhile, some in the American Special Forces have justified these attacks on "necessity" grounds—as being "essential" to NATO's efforts to clear out Taliban insurgents.[146] By now, it is clear that new policymaking, deriving from U.S. command in the region, is under way regarding the norms as to the protection that is owed civilians in aerial bombardment.

U.S. Army General Stanley A. McChrystal, speaking at the International Institute for Strategic Studies in London, noted the importance of the minds and the perceptions of the Afghan people. He commented: "A tremendous number of villagers live in fear, and we have officials who either cannot or do not serve their people effectively, and violence is up."[147] More recently, Afghan leaders have repeatedly urged Coalition troops to curb civilian deaths. According to an annual report issued by the United Nations, in Afghanistan in 2010, there was "a 15 percent increase in the number of civilians killed to 2,777."[148] That year, Hamid Karzai, addressing Parliament as it opened its winter session, held up a picture of an eight-year-old girl— the only survivor when NATO rockets hit a home on the second day of the offensive.[149] "We need to reach the point where there are no civilian casualties," McChrystal said, when commander of Western forces in Afghanistan, where he ordered troops to exercise all possible care, a stance that was characterized as a policy of "courageous restraint."[150]

There are similar concerns regarding Iraq—a war that is viewed by many as having been illegal from the beginning,[151] and where we are seeing a worsening in the situation, with millions displaced and hundreds of thousands of Iraqi casualties.[152] The war is "over" as a legal matter—that is, pursuant to the formal juridical conception based on the UN Charter and the Security Council resolutions. Yet, the challenge of assisting the local and legitimate government to suppress terrorism wears on—with the urgent need to determine what policy will result in less harm and suffering to civilians. This situation, once again, well illustrates the ways a close relationship appears to exist at present between the justice of a war and the justice of its waging. It also illustrates the point that the normativity in this area of the law of war calls for an even closer adherence to international humanitarian law when the issue of the justice of war itself still hangs in the balance.

In a growing number of cases, the European Court of Human Rights appears to be more and more enmeshed in the supervision of the war on terror—supporting low tolerance for civilian casualties. In *Isayeva v. Russia*, the court concluded that in the counterterror campaign in the village of Katyr-Yurt, authorities did not take "appropriate care to ensure that any risk to life is minimized."[153] Any resort to lethal force must be "absolutely necessary."[154] "Authorities make take appropriate care to ensure that any risk to life is minimized."[155] Importantly from our perspective here, the court asserts that states have responsibility even where nonstate actors are involved in the civilian casualties: "The State's responsibility is not confined to circumstances where there is significant evidence that misdirected fire from agents of the state has killed a civilian. It may also be engaged where they fail to take all feasible precautions in the choice of means and methods of a security operation mounted against an opposing group with a view to avoiding and, in any event, minimizing, incidental loss of civilian life."[156] The European Court of Human Rights goes on to conclude that the "use of this kind of weapon [i.e. aerial bombing] in a populated area, outside wartime and without prior evacuation of the civilians, is impossible to reconcile with the degree of caution expected from a law enforcement body in a democratic society."[157]

This underscores a crucial dilemma that must be confronted in the waging of a "just war" against terror. Insofar as the "just war" argument for the use of force against terror goes beyond justifications of self-defense, it often emphasizes the illegitimacy of the terrorist's common practice of the deliberate targeting of civilians. Indeed, it is precisely this refusal to respect civilian immunities that is commonly the practice of weaker powers fighting guerilla wars. It follows that any persuasive claim of a just war against terror would have to be reconcilable not only with the laws of war, protections particularly of civilian immunity, but with scrupulous adherence to these rules. For the very justice of the counterterror war would be on the line if these rules and protections were flouted.

In sum, increasingly, the justice of war is being measured less exclusively in terms of the defense and interests of the state and more in terms of the treatment and protection of persons, peoples, and a community of nations.[158] Indeed, beyond the initiation of war, such concerns are now also transforming the way occupation law is being reconceptualized. In particular, these concerns raise the question whether the treatment of persons and peoples may prove to offer a way of distinguishing among benevolent and other occupations. As these transformations continue, they will have sweeping implications for a new global rule of law, where the treatment of individuals, collectivities, and their rights move from the periphery to the center—the very place the state has, over history, occupied.

This chapter has explored the growing phenomenon of international criminal justice and its link to war and peace, with an eye to illuminating its role in contemporary politics. My exploration of the foregoing issues points to the connection that humanity law bears to a world of persistent conflict. Humanity law is at once universalizing and comprehensive enough to direct itself to the changed subjects of contemporary global politics. And by positing parameters on the exercise of power affecting persons and peoples, international criminal justice appears to offer a promising basis for the globalizing order.

CHAPTER 5

❮❮❯

Protecting Humanity

The Practice of Humanity Law

BEYOND THE LAW OF WAR:
GLOBALIZING THE REGULATION OF VIOLENCE

The previous chapter considered humanity law in terms of punishment and justice in war. This chapter does so with an emphasis on protection and prevention. The humanity law framework provides a normative basis for extending the regulation of violence beyond the traditional scope and categories of the law of war as it evolved in the nineteenth and twentieth centuries; many of the violent conflicts that engage the concern of the world community today are not in the first instance or even at all interstate wars, waged by state actors such as uniformed soldiers. Given the gaps in human protection left open by the law of war, and its limited applicability to many of these conflicts and many of the relevant actors, the humanity law framework draws on human rights law and conceptions of transnational or international criminal justice, truly to globalize the regulation of violence and, in principle, to protect all those who are vulnerable in situations of violent conflict.

The modern law of war addressed itself to the behavior of states during armed conflict, while human rights law has aimed to constrain the state's conduct toward its citizens in peacetime.[1] The law of war was long based on reciprocity between sovereigns. Those protected, and the nature of the protections, were identified by status (e.g., combatant/noncombatant). Historically, the normative force of the law of war was based largely on convention: States agreed reciprocally to constrain themselves by setting the bounds of permissible conflict. The law of human rights, although formally based to a large extent on treaty norms, also drew its legitimacy from general notions of right and extended protection to persons on a putatively universal basis, not limited by status.[2] Elements of both of these bodies of law have influenced the humanity law framework. Yet this framework has its own distinctive approach to rights and global order. This chapter will discuss the framework, for example, in light of the dilemmas of humanitarian intervention, the emerging responsibility to protect, and the global war on terror.

In the humanity law framework, protections deriving from the law of war are being extended beyond the state, as well as beyond the conditions of international armed conflict—to civilians in peacetime.[3] In contrast, under the traditional law of war, the parameters of normative protection were generally defined by the interstate character of the conflict—thus giving rise to the anomaly that nonnationals might well be extended greater protection than nationals.[4] Historically, the law of war protected so-called enemy aliens in conditions of international armed conflict. By contrast, human rights law gave rise to other grounds for protection, which were more universalizing, but still state-connected.[5] The emerging humanity law framework closes the gap, by requiring protection that is not dependent on nationality, *or* a nexus to a specific state.

A central dimension is the shift in scope and concern to the preservation and protection of humanity, seen in humanity law's aspiration to global coverage, and the protection it affords along the lines of human security under the law. The "inquiry turns not on the presumed victim's nationality or presence within a particular geographic area, but on whether, under the specific circumstances, the State observed the rights of a person who is subject to its authority and control."[6]

PROTECTING HUMANITY AS SUCH:
A TRANSFORMED MINORITIES REGIME

In the nineteenth and early twentieth centuries, and particularly after World War I, countries in the Balkans entered into treaties aimed at protecting ethnic minorities who were vulnerable to oppression within the states where they resided.[7] While the "minority treaties" afforded some degree of protection for national minorities, these arrangements, which were modest to begin with, faltered on the difficulty that minorities depended entirely on two-state agreements for the protection and enforcement of the rights in question. Moreover, the protection that was afforded on the basis of minority status, such as for religious exercise, were circumscribed by the classic interstate-system conceptions concerning territorial boundaries.

In light of the wartime experience, the categories of protected groups expanded beyond nationality and religion to other categories.[8] Eventually, the scope of the protection that international law afforded was extended to "humanity" itself. This connection between the individual and the collective under the law has taken on a greater importance in the modern period, where it is seen in the scholarly writing of postwar philosophers: Thus, in her account of the Eichmann trial, Hannah Arendt strives to explicate just how the offense of "the destruction of the Jewish people" implies an attack on humanity as such.[9]

The Charter of the United Nations, in its opening chapter, refers to the aim of "friendly relations among nations" based on "the self-determination of peoples." Both of the UN human rights covenants refer to the rights of "all peoples." Bases for group affinity define protected classes in the provisions on equality; these bases include "race, color, religion ... [or] national or social origin." Similarly, the ICC statute criminalizes "persecution against any identifiable group or collectivity on political, racial, national, ethnic, cultural, religious, gender ... or other grounds" as a "crime against *humanity*" (Article 7[1][h]; emphasis added). The ICTR held that any "stable and permanent group" is protected for purposes of genocide.[10] Although not consistently followed in the jurisprudence, this definition of the protected group created a historic openness with respect to the evolution of the identity of the peoples of humanity based on political realities.

Premising the scope of international jurisdiction on "peoplehood" has the effect of extending preservative rights beyond their nexus with citizenship and nationality, in at least two ways: First, core understandings of global rule of law are being applied in a partly deterritorialized manner. The second, less transparent dimension goes to the nature of the protected rights. Consider the following definition of ethnic cleansing as an offense: "a purposeful policy designed by one ethnic or religious group to remove by violent and terror-inspiring means the civilian population of another ethnic or religious group from certain geographic areas."[11] The rights that have surfaced as the most fundamental, and that are enforced extraterritorially (as prior chapters discussed) bear some relation to the movement of persons and peoples and hence to globalizing political transformation—for example, the right to humane treatment, life, and judicial access and protection.[12]

According to the statute of the ICTY, "crimes against humanity refer to inhumane acts of a very serious nature ... committed as part of a widespread or systematic attack against any civilian population on national, political, ethnic, racial or religious grounds." In the Balkans, often the inhumane acts took the form of so-called ethnic cleansing.[13] Under the ICC statue, the basis for the ICC, Article 7(1), jurisdiction exists for the ICC regardless of the nature of the conflict; and a "crime against humanity" is defined as inhumane acts "committed as part of a widespread or systematic attack directed against any civilian population, with knowledge of the attack."[14] An inhumane act includes "persecution," defined as "the intentional and severe deprivation of fundamental rights contrary to international law by reason of the identity of group or collectivity."[15] Another basis is the International Convention on the Elimination of All Forms of Racial Discrimination, as argued in the ICJ case *Application of the International Convention on the Elimination of All Forms of Racial Discrimination (Georgia v. Russian Federation).*[16]

As is reflected in contemporary developments in the understanding of the concept of a "crime against humanity,"[17] these norms have often been interpreted to go beyond conventional or consent-based foundations in international law, and arguably represent an expansion of *jus cogens*. Rights protections are being extended to persons and peoples—to a significant extent, independently of their connections to particular states.[18] Insofar as the humanity law framework extends its protective treatment to persons and "peoples" organized along affiliative bases—such as, but not limited to, political, racial, national, ethnic, cultural, religious, or gender identities,[19] that framework reflects the current relativization of state sovereignty. If, for Schmitt, the sovereign is "he who decides," then for humanity law's purposes, the sovereign is "he who protects [persons and peoples]"— although, given Schmitt's contempt for the discourse of "humanity," at times Schmitt himself seemed, through Hobbes, to recognize a connection between sovereignty and protection.

If and when state mechanisms fail, humanity law protection provides a basis for some form of international intervention, whether at the level of a family of states or at the level of humanitarian aid to persons and peoples or through access to adjudication whether national and regional judiciary. Hence, this is a rights scheme that can be characterized as "watertight and inescapable."[20] As Judge Simma pronounced in his separate opinion in *Armed Activities in the Congo*, "I consider that legal arguments clarifying that in situations like the one before us no gaps exist in the law that would deprive the affected persons of any legal protection, have, unfortunately, never been as important as at present, in the face of certain recent deplorable developments."[21] A similar concern with an "excessively formalistic" approach to protection was raised in *Georgia v. Russia* (joint dissenting opinion, ICJ).[22]

HUMAN SECURITY: POLICYMAKING IN THE SHADOW OF THE LAW

Humanity law redefines security in a manner that transcends the traditional distinction between war and peace, conceptualizing conflict along a continuum of situations that require ongoing protection of those who are affected or threatened.

According to the report of the Secretary-General's High-level Panel on Threats, Challenges and Change, a broad concept of security includes protection from economic and social threats and environmental degradation.[23] In elaborating the meaning of "collective security and the challenge of prevention," the report refers to "any event or process that leads to large-scale death or lessening of life chances and undermines States as the basic unit of the international system is a threat to international security. So defined, there are six clusters of threats with which the world must be concerned now and in the decades ahead: (1) Economic and social threats, including poverty, infectious diseases and environmental degradation; (2) Inter-State conflict; (3) Internal conflict, including civil war, genocide and other large-scale atrocities; (4) Nuclear, radiological, chemical and biological weapons; (5) Terrorism; and (6) Transnational organized crime."

Furthermore, in the UN Secretary-General's report "In Larger Freedom," there is a similarly broad conception of "security": "The threats to peace and security in the twenty-first century include not just international war and conflict but civil violence, organized crime, terrorism and weapons of mass destruction. . . . They include poverty, deadly infectious disease and environmental degradation since these can have equally catastrophic consequences. All of these threats can cause death or lessen life chances on a large scale. All of them can undermine States as the basic unit of the international system."[24]

One can see how the protection of human rights poses a direct challenge to the preeminence of state security and, indeed, how the shift to a humanity-based regime reflects a change in the very meaning of international security. As the humanity law framework in important respects, modifies (without wholly replacing) older norms based on territoriality and the protection of state borders, it produces a transformed understanding, whereby international security becomes part and parcel of human security, the security of persons and peoples. A humanity-based scheme protects individual and collective rights across state borders, as is necessary for stability in a globalizing politics.

The emergence of humanity law rights could be understood as protecting humanity "as such," in that these rights protect against persecution and other acts that potentially threaten the survival of persons and peoples that make up humankind.[25] Reconceptualizing the international legal situation according to a humanity-based order implies that we use a set of alternative constructs, as will be explored in chapter 8. Threats to a collective's preservative rights not only threaten the survival of a population but also can often have destabilizing effects on other states, persons, and peoples—which may well endanger peaceful global coexistence. Whereas under the received norm of state sovereignty self-determination might well point in the direction of ethnic secession, the expansion of international humanitarian jurisdiction aims to stabilize the global order, by protecting against the persecution and migration of peoples—which threaten not only the peoples themselves but also the territorial integrity in surrounding areas, and the balance of power in the global order. The received international rule-of-law understanding can be understood as being predicated on traditional definitions of the state, as seen in terms of the self-determination of populations within fixed territorial boundaries. Under the humanity law framework, one might understand the protection of ethnic and other group-related rights as positing a limit to the prevailing ethos of self-determination as the defining dimension of security. Consider the conflict between Russia and Georgia regarding South Ossetia.[26]

The reinvigorated humanitarianism of humanity law sparks a rethinking of the prevailing basic categories and distinctions in international legal and political order—such as the international/national, public/private, and war/peace divisions. Yet in practice, the new rule of law, to a great extent, sustains the status quo, reinforcing the present territorial balance, while facilitating globalization processes. Humanity rights against "persecution" and "ethnic cleansing" have both individuals and groups as their subjects, and can be understood as rights analogous to that of state sovereignty in the interstate system, amounting to protection of a threshold preservation of humanity. What is humanity law's meaning at present? In the current humanity-centered regime, the threshold aim of preservation is seen as connected to security and territorial security.[27] The security or self-preservation rights that are associated with the humanity law framework reflect contemporary globalizing conditions, and the abiding expectations regarding the movement of peoples. Thus, the emergence of the instant juridical regime hardly reflects ideal rights norms; rather, it constitutes a set of provisional measures that are aimed at the regulation of violence, that is, governance in the currently prevalent context.

THE DILEMMAS OF HUMANITARIAN INTERVENTION

[If a ruler] should inflict upon his subjects such treatment as no one is warranted in inflicting, the exercise of the right vested in human society is not precluded.

Hugo Grotius, *De Jure Belli ac Pacis*

I believe that force can be justified on humanitarian grounds, as it was in the Balkans, or in other places that have been scarred by war. Inaction tears at our conscience and can lead to more costly intervention later. That is why all responsible nations must embrace the role that militaries with a clear mandate can play to keep the peace.

Barack Obama, *Nobel Peace Prize Acceptance Speech (2009)*

In his opening address to the Fifty-fifth General Assembly, then Secretary-General Annan called for a new principle of humanitarian intervention, which accordingly became known as the "Annan Doctrine."[28] In his report on humanitarian crises, Annan observed that human rights abuses—such as war crimes, crimes against humanity, and threats of genocide—constitute legitimate justifications for Security Council intervention under Chapter 7 of the UN Charter. The "[s]cope," Annan asserted, "of the breaches of human rights and international humanitarian law including the number of people affected and the nature of the violations" are considerations that may justify intervention based on breaches of the new humanitarian law.[29] Disagreement over the NATO intervention in Kosovo illustrates the potential of the new normativity[30] to destabilize the conventional understanding of the use of force, driving a wedge between legality (according to the strict requirements of the UN Charter) and legitimacy.[31] Thus, states that participated in, or supported, the NATO intervention—such as the Netherlands—would come to observe that "a gradual shift is occurring in international law" whereby respect for human rights has a primacy that challenges or modifies the status of state sovereignty as a preeminent norm of the international legal order.[32]

Policy debates concerning intervention—even preemptive action—in other regions, such as the Middle East, reflect similar shifts in the relevant discourse. Consider the deliberations regarding whether or not to enter Afghanistan: The question whether to intervene was not framed, as one might have expected after the events of 9/11, primarily in terms of state interests such as self-defense; instead, the question was also frequently cast in terms of the security of "humanity"—whether that involved the "liberation" of the Afghan "people" or, in terms of world security, the "war on" the global terror threat.[33] Subsequent interventions, such as in Iraq, would be rationalized in ambiguous yet analogous terms—not primarily in terms of state interests but in humanity terms. More specifically, justifications invoked the liberation of the local peoples and the need to protect human security. Clearly, the course of the war would have consequences for the ongoing persuasive force of such arguments.[34]

The trials that are wrapping up at the ICTY have introduced a remarkable aim for criminal processes: the "deterrence" of humanitarian abuses involved in ethnic conflict so as to achieve peace and reconciliation between the peoples of humanity.[35] Standing alone, the notion of reliance on international law as a means or road to peace is hardly new; it was found in the eighteenth century, particularly in the Kantian vision.[36] Yet what is emerging in its more current form is a legalist view that is hardly the purview of utopians. Political theorist Judith Shklar observed: "It was urged not only that international law was a means to peace, but that it was the only road to that end. All other forms of political action not only could be neglected; they were regarded as undesirable."[37] There are also resonances with early international law ideas regarding the potential legality of intervention in some very limited cases.[38] Yet what may well be questionable is the expectation that somehow law can, in and of itself, advance peace and stability, internationally—and, moreover, that law can somehow displace and/or complement the politics needed to address and resolve international conflict.[39]

So far, the impact of these legal mechanisms at the international level remains an open question, as heinous massacres continued in the Balkans—in Srebrenica, for example—despite the convening of, and ongoing prosecutions at, the ICTY at the time.[40] Similar doubts have been raised about the legal responses to the Rwandan genocide and the prospects for contributing to the laying down of the rule of law there, whether in the country or in the region.[41] Indeed, so far, the nexus between international criminal justice and humanity rights protection would seem indirect. While the relevant normativity may well transcend a sense of compliance, whether in the short or long term, problematically, the key neutrality of the humanity law discourse and regime, while helping in building solidarity, may obscure the political avenues that need to be traveled in order to achieve long-standing peace.

To what extent might the growing humanity-centered justifications for intervention pose a challenge to the UN Charter–based regime on the use of force, with the risk of setting the humanity law regime in contradiction with itself? So far, humanitarian intervention is still seen as posing a challenge to the UN Charter's commitment to state sovereignty and, similarly to its near ban on the use of force against the political independence or territorial integrity of any state, except where authorized by the Security Council. The narrow exception is for the inherent right of "self-defense." This regime of *jus ad bello* does not seem to provide much of a window for humanitarian intervention. Is case-by-case Security Council authorization the answer to this difficulty, as with Libya?

What is also coming to light is the layered complexity of global rule of law and the way it comprehends multiple interests and values—as was illustrated, for example, by proceedings following the events in Kosovo, where the Independent Commission on Kosovo concluded the NATO intervention to be "illegal, yet legitimate."[42] This legality gap reflects the point that the same norms can pull in potentially opposite directions, and shows that the humanity-based rule of law, as it is currently framed, constitutes a comprehensive but indeterminate regime—and a framework that may lend itself to politicization, with consequences for the perception of the rule of law.

PROCESS'S PROMISE?

The new legalism that has been displayed in the adjudication of humanity law claims constitutes a particular route to international security. In human rights crises from the Balkans to Africa, parties are resorting to the law, as well as to diverse international judicial processes, such as those of the Security Council–appointed "Chapter 7" courts: ad hoc international tribunals that are chartered during conflict, with the ambitious mandate of peacemaking through justice. While, historically, trials came ex post, at war's end, in the regime now surfacing, humanity-law-based processes operate not just postconflict but also ex ante. There is a more regular, ongoing relationship in which law rationalizes the use of force in the name of the protection of persons and peoples—thereby creating a normative scheme of protection that would not otherwise be recognized within the existing interstate system. The processes implementing and enforcing humanity law offer a source of normative guidance that goes beyond the guidance offered by existing international law, and that is informed by, and overlaps with, the hitherto independent regime of just war. From the long-standing discourse of conflict resolution to the judicialized discourse of law enforcement, the shift in normative language has ramifications for the prevailing principles regarding the use of force. Process offers a way to balance potentially conflicting rule-of-law norms. Adherence to process can also advance important rule-of-law norms, such as nonunilateralism, deliberation, and transparency.

According to Hugo Grotius, for war to be "called just...it is not enough that it be made between Sovereigns, but it must be undertaken by public Declaration."[43] Bringing diverse state interests into decision-making processes may well afford some constraint against the uses of humanitarianism for states' self-interested ends. Multilateral processes can be useful to smoke out pretextual interventions, such as the sort of self-serving engagements that historically had characterized the invocation and exercise of humanitarianism, some of which were discussed in chapter 2. Indeed, this was at the crux of the instance of multilateralism in the Libyan intervention. In President Obama's words, "the United States is acting with a broad coalition that is committed to enforcing United Nations Security Council Resolution 1973, which calls for the protection of the Libyan people....and the writ of the international community must be enforced. That is the cause of this coalition"[44] Furthermore, the exercise of various forms of multilateral process might well encourage decisionmaking through deliberation. Here one might compare the processes surrounding the interventions in Bosnia, Iraq, and most recently in Libya. An open, deliberative process could go some way toward sorting out plausible from implausible interventions, thus focusing on an important factor in gauging an intervention's justification, multilateral process can advance the transnational dimensions of the rule of law by offering principled guidance in humanitarian crises.

THE LIMITS OF PROCESS

The operation of multilateral processes and institutions dedicated to the humanity law framework may well contribute to advancing certain rule-of-law values. Yet process, in itself, does not necessarily advance the actualization of liberal aims, nor does it guarantee intervention that is just. Indeed, one evident area of tension is the potential disconnect between the growing reality of the humanity law scheme and the previous era's processes and institutions. Thus, no matter how justice is defined today, a UN Security Council consensus is hardly synonymous with justice. Indeed, the prevailing system's decisionmaking processes are often in tension, for the most part, with non-state-centric interests and values. As the crisis in Kosovo shows, evidently a gap remains between liberal process and its purposes; process, in and of itself, doesn't always make for the rule of law. In the 1990s, the conceded failures of multilateralism in Bosnia and Rwanda spurred the drumbeat for humanitarian intervention. At the time, human rights advocates were unabashed unilateralists, arguing for humanitarian intervention with or without procedural authorization or multilateral political backing. Thus, while lacking authorization under the UN Charter, NATO intervention in Kosovo gave rise to a dawning recognition that legalism was not tantamount to legitimacy. As the Independent Commission on Kosovo would conclude, the intervention was "illegal, yet legitimate," restoring, for the first time in years, the sense that justice could be found in war.[45]

Existing international processes have not yet provided a full answer to the liberal quandaries raised by the new interventionism. While appealing to universality, these continue to reflect the limits of politics, and of the prevailing international institutions, that were legacies of the last world war. While UN reform is under way, these changes are unlikely to be enough to forge a new political consensus.[46] There have been a variety of proposals for UN entities, new compacts, and the like that might be called on to play a greater role in ensuring more effective conflict resolution in crises.[47] At least in the short run, however, consensus remains elusive particularly in light of the marked imbalance of power that goes to the issue of the very possibility of a state-centered system. Pronounced differences remain, regarding the legitimacy of the use of forceful intervention as a tool of international policy; these differences could be seen, for example, in the debates over the establishment of the ICC. A new generation of humanitarian-centered institutions and processes contribute alternative understandings and legalist approaches to international security, which are represented by both the exceptional and the permanent international criminal courts, as well as other, more mixed institutions.

Finally, a troubling ramification of the spread of humanity-based discourse is that as it becomes more entrenched in the law and its processes, there is a risk that it will inspire false confidence in its own effectiveness. This risk is especially problematic where humanity-based law may displace and/or shift attention from—rather than complementing—other potentially more effective and long-acting political processes and solutions. Indeed, the risks associated with the present confusing shift in discourse—from the prevailing orientation toward conflict resolution and its mechanisms and machinery to an emphasis on normative law enforcement, particularly where exercised within institutions such as the Security Council—has already surfaced in a number of instances, such as in the deliberations surrounding the intervention in Iraq.[48] Another more contemporary instance concerns the nearly simultaneous turn both to the Security Council and the ICC concerning international action in Libya.[49]

A "RESPONSIBILITY TO PROTECT"?

Recognition of the "RtoP," as proposed in the World Summit UN reform project,[50] is aimed at mediating the present gaps created by the often-competing obligations relating to the protection of both state and human interests. There was a subsequent adoption by the Security Council, where it has already garnered some degree of interstate consensus.[51] Soon after the terrorist attacks of 2001 made clear the limits of the interstate security system, the International Commission on Intervention and State Sovereignty filed a report whose central idea was to get beyond existing ideas regarding humanitarian intervention—which seemed defined by a running paradox that pitted humanitarianism against intervention/sovereignty issues. The 2005 World Summit adopted a resolution in this regard, which was subsequently endorsed by both the General Assembly in the form of General Assembly Resolution 63/308 and the Security Council in the form of Security Council Resolution 1674. Security Council Resolution 1674, adopted by the Security Council on April 28, 2006, "reaffirm[ed] the provisions of paragraphs 138 and 139 of the 2005 World Summit Outcome Document regarding the responsibility to protect populations from genocide, war crimes, ethnic cleansing and crimes against humanity" and committed the Security Council to action to protect civilians in armed conflict.[52] This is recently evident in Security Resolution 1973, authorizing "all necessary measures" to protect the civilians of Libya.[53]

Resolution 1674 postulated that "sovereign states have a responsibility to protect their own citizens from avoidable catastrophe"—a formulation that, through its very language, aims to make the paradox disappear. The acceptance of RtoP expresses some degree of international consensus on a duty to protect civilians. The distinctions between humanitarian intervention and RtoP lie mostly in the fact that RtoP is not delimited by the in-state/outside-state line, nor is it limited to state-based "intervention." Rather, RtoP is conceived in complementary terms of doing more ex ante to serve the aims of prevention.[54]

The full implications of the recognition of a duty to protect remain uncertain, raising questions such as: What context or situation triggers the responsibility and who bears the duty? Indeed, to whatever extent the Security Council committed in the abstract to new responsibilities, it will likely soon confront the problem of the prevailing injunction against the use of the force—even in the name of humanity. The RtoP arguably pits human rights against the prevailing norms protecting states. Yet in his report on the status of the implementation of the

Millennium Declaration (2005), Secretary-General Annan called for states to embrace the "emerging norm of the Responsibility to Protect," exhorting the Security Council's ability to play a role in humanitarian crises: Annan urged: "Whenever a particular state is unable or unwilling to protect its citizens against extreme violence, there is a collective responsibility of all states to do so—a responsibility which must be assumed by this Council."[55] This position, on Annan's part, reflects the same principle or concept that informs the basis for interstate intervention in the area of legal capacity in the ICC's Rome Statute—that is, "complementarity."

In a later statement toward the end of his term, Annan said he saw himself as moving toward "a culture of prevention." And, indeed, by recognizing an "international duty to protect," the United Nations took a significant step, going beyond its prevailing concern for the mere stability of the interstate system—a step with implications for the potential necessity for multilateral action. For the United Nations sought to both recognize and cabin the new predicates for such intervention, which was potentially forcible, by insisting that such duties to protect should only be the subject of multilateral action. This led Annan to call for such action in Sudan—and the failure to protect the people of Sudan, he has said, has made "a mockery of our claim, as an international community, to shield people from the worst abuses."[56]

Later, similar exhortations were made by Secretary-General Ban Ki-moon, who declared his intent "to strengthen our mechanisms for the prevention of human rights violations and to work for steps to make operational the concept of the responsibility to protect[57] so as to insure timely action when populations face genocide, ethnic cleansing, and crimes against humanity."[58] So far, the resolutions the Security Council has adopted serve only to express the tensions that are involved in the reformulation that is identified here: While reaffirming a commitment to the sovereignty of the government of Sudan,[59] the resolutions also reaffirm Resolution 1674, on the protection of civilians in armed conflict—thus reaffirming prior commitments to protect populations from the crimes of genocide, war crimes, ethnic cleansing, and crimes against humanity.[60] In a 2008 speech, Secretary-General Ban Ki-Moon sought to clarify the meaning of RtoP by distinguishing it from humanitarian intervention. In particular, he sought to stress the implications of the concept of RtoP for reinforcing understandings of the expectations of states in the interstate system:

> We need a common understanding of what RtoP is and, just as important, of what it is not. RtoP is not a new code for humanitarian intervention. Rather, it is built on a more positive and affirmative concept of sovereignty as responsibility.... The concept of responsibility to protect rests on three pillars.

First, Governments unanimously affirmed the primary and continuing legal obligations of States to protect their populations—whether citizens or not—from genocide, war crimes, ethnic cleansing and crimes against humanity, and from their incitement. They declared—and this is the bedrock of RtoP—that "we accept that responsibility and will act in accordance with it."

The second, more innovative pillar speaks to the United Nations institutional strengths and comparative advantages. The Summit underscored the commitment of the international community to assist States in meeting these obligations. Our goal is to help States succeed, not just to react once they have failed to meet their prevention and protection obligations.... The magnitude of these four crimes and violations demands early, preventive steps—and these steps should require neither unanimity in the Security Council nor pictures of unfolding atrocities that shock the conscience of the world.

The third pillar is much discussed, but generally understood too narrowly. It is Member States' acceptance of their responsibility to respond in a timely and decisive manner, in accordance with the United Nations Charter, to help protect populations from the four listed crimes and violations. The response could involve any of the whole range of UN tools, whether pacific measures under Chapter VI of the Charter, coercive ones under Chapter VII, and/or collaboration with regional and subregional arrangements under Chapter VIII. The key lies in an early and flexible response, tailored to the specific needs of each situation.[61]

Next, Ban Ki-moon addresses the concern about whether RtoP is tantamount to a license for intervention, asserting, in this regard:

Our conception of RtoP, then, is narrow but deep. Its scope is narrow, focused solely on the four crimes and violations agreed by the world leaders in 2005.... At the same time, our response should be deep, utilizing the whole prevention and protection tool kit available to the United Nations system, to its regional, subregional and civil society partners and, not least, to the Member States themselves.... We need to strengthen the capacities of States to resist taking the path to genocide, war crimes, ethnic cleansing and crimes against humanity.[62]

Even more recently, in July 2010, the Secretary-General released a report on the implementation of RtoP; while the primary responsibility is that of each state, when a state was "manifestly failing" to protect its population, the international community was prepared to take collective action in a "timely and decisive manner" through the Security Council and in accordance with the Charter of the United Nations.[63] As framed, the report summary would appear to contemplate that even the international community's collective action in the service of the RtoP is not inconsistent with the prevailing UN Charter state-centric obligations and system.

A recent U.N. response invoking RtoP relates to the situation in Kenya, in which "Secretary General Ban Ki-moon urged leaders on all sides, as did the Special Adviser on the Prevention of Genocide, Francis Deng, to call publicly for an end to the violence and to statements inciting violence, noting that political and community leaders could be held accountable for violations of international law committed at their instigation."[64] Similarly, with respect to the U.N. response to the Myanmar cyclone, "the Special Rapporteur [of Myanmar] reiterates the pressing need for State institutions to receive and fully investigate all complaints of human rights abuses and to prosecute, where necessary, in accordance with international standards. The State must assume the responsibility to protect and promote the well-being of its people."[65]

Overall, the debates regarding RtoP make clear that once the shift toward the protection of persons and peoples is made, there is no clear distinction on the basis of causation, and there would seem to be a significant normative aim—which is still framed in terms of states and their responsibilities, as Gareth Evans and others have exhorted should be the case.[66] Yet this potential unboundedness of RtoP may well explain in part the trend toward turning to legal processes to identify and hold to account perpetrators of the relevant offenses, via the assumption of jurisdiction by the newer international institutions, such as the ICC, which is vested with permanent and ongoing authority to superintend the humanitarian order.

On the one hand, the ICC (Rome) Statute is aimed at the protection of "millions of children, women, men, victims of unimaginable atrocities that deeply shock the conscience of humanity."[67] Yet the ICC (Rome) Statute also appears to go beyond the traditional law of war (that is, its *jus in bello* side) to also include within its jurisdiction the crime of aggression (in Article 5). Yet the Rome Statute lacks an adequate definition of that crime, and lacks implementation mechanisms.[68] Moreover, the risks of making such a change may well stymie these amendments. As with the codification of "aggression," we can also see the return of the "just war" concept as a development with potentially complex potential. The new enforcement adds to the existing international juridical regime regarding "aggression," and raises the implication of the possibility of a revived legality, and the related legitimacy of a humanity law basis for the waging of a "just war."

Here, very evidently, with this institutionalization, humanity law's scope extends beyond the regulation of the waging of war to its very justification and rationalization—and in so doing, it harks back to the premodern view, previously discussed, of the relationship of justice to the use of force.

Judicialization reflects the demand for public processes that make clear in some fair and neutral way the contours of humanity law, thus providing a basis for further international engagement, whether political or even military. Consider the enormous devotion of international resources to the problem of accountability. Humanity law challenges the notion of any immunity from accountability; the acting political leadership is held responsible for its decisions concerning the use of force. The tendency is thus toward a comprehensive justificatory framework regulating the use of force.[69]

Humanity law's presence in the realm of war offers an alternative, or counterbalance, to a security system that is increasingly ill adapted in the context of the political conditions of the post–Cold War era. The international legalism that is now surfacing constitutes a counterforce to current politics—through processes and mechanisms that are in and of the international realm and whose legitimacy is being reconceived and reconstructed. Humanity law offers another option, besides unilateral judgments regarding just war and related interventions.

A "DIFFERENT KIND OF WAR"?
COMBATING TERROR FOR THE SAKE OF HUMANITY

As White House Counsel Alberto Gonzales put it in a draft memorandum to then President George W. Bush, "the war against terrorism is a new kind of war."[70] Both terrorism and counterterrorism have fueled the expansion and elaboration of the humanity law framework. What is interesting is that all sides in this conflict invoke a humanity-centered discourse in shaping the course of their campaigns—which is surely testament to the discourse's influence. Indeed, the surge in international terrorism goes to the very essence of the humanitarian-law model regulating the use of force in the present international system: Both the original terrorist terms and acts and the responses in the counterterror campaign have lent themselves to being debated in humanitarian terms, as their definition raises issues regarding the justification and legitimacy of the use of force—which is always deployed in the name of humanity.

Thus, it is the struggle for the survival of "humanity" that is often said to be the animating value of the war against terror, with the lines being drawn as they were historically—in "we-they" terms, dividing ostensible barbarism from ostensible humanity. In one version of the counterterror narrative, Al Qaeda and other Islamic militants are depicted as promoting a strategy to establish a radical Islamic empire, ranging from Europe to Asia, a supposed enterprise that is said to constitute waging a "war against humanity."

The humanity-based account also goes to the heart of the problem of defining and circumscribing terrorism, for this framework enables us to comprehend the violence committed by nonstate actors. One might see terrorists, by opting for a violence that is characterized by pointed attacks, and is ordinarily directed not against combatants but against innocent civilians, as defining themselves as being outside humanity. Here one might look to some attempts to characterize acts of "terrorism," right after the 9/11 attacks, as "crimes against humanity" and violations of the "law of nations."[71] Such characterizations—grounded on humanity law and its violations and used to define who is *in* and who is *out* of a legitimate international society—are seen in a wide variety of areas. They are even deployed in contemporary demands for the exclusion of various leaders who have aided or assisted terrorism from possible diplomatic discourse, with a wider potential for reconstituting international society.[72]

For their part, terrorist groups also manage to use—and, some might say, subvert—the humanity-based discourse. For example, consider the extent to which Al Qaeda defines its identity by both invoking affiliations with a protected peoplehood in transnational terms, and employing a discourse that is rife with universalizing humanitarian-value-laden terms, such as the aim of promoting social justice.[73] Osama bin Laden, in a video released in 2004, said, "security is an important pillar of human life. Free people do not relinquish their security."[74]

Other movements, too, such as Hamas and Hezbollah, derive their popular support from their self-identification in similar humanitarian terms—that is, in terms of their relative capacities, vis-à-vis state actors, in the provision of human security. Ismael Haniyah, a senior leader of Hamas, has cited "UN Resolutions 2955 and 3034, which affirm the 'inalienable' right of all peoples to self-determination and the legitimacy of their struggle against foreign domination and subjugation 'by all available means.'"[75] What might the self-characterization effects be, regarding the question of what legal status and what kinds of treatment are proper under the relevant humanity law? Moreover, we will see that it is in this capacity that humanity law becomes central to the struggle over the capture of legitimacy in the region.

Since 9/11, there has been a renewed interest in the notion of preemp-tive self-defense and preventive war.[76] Charter purists have cautioned that such a broadening of the concept of self-defense may well serve to under-mine the coherence and effectiveness of the limits of the use of force in the UN Charter.[77] This debate has been looming ever since the Six Day War, and of late it centers on, inter alia, the possibility of a preemptive strike on nuclear facilities in Iran. Moreover, what we see here is that—like the debates over aggression discussed earlier—so far, the debates over the changing legality of preemptive action have departed from the prevailing international relations discourse. These debates are being waged not, as they had been traditionally, primarily in terms of what would constitute sufficient state interests but, far more commonly, on humanity-security grounds. Actions are justified in terms of the asserted aim of protecting civilians, whether locally, regionally or worldwide. Of course, the appeal of this discourse is plain: It can be deployed by any side—for example, it is invoked by both Israel and Hamas in the Gaza conflict.[78]

While the UN Charter recognizes the right of self-defense against an "armed attack" (Article 51), these rules were developed with state action in mind. Nevertheless, it is now recognized—by the Fact-Finding Mission on the Gaza Conflict, for example—that the repeated launching of rockets by Palestinian militants against Israel would count as a legitimate reason for some level of armed response.[79] Questions loom about the applicability of concepts such as necessity and proportionality to such defensive actions against nonstate actors, consider in this regard the ICJ's opinion in *Armed Activities v. Uganda*, discussed earlier at chapter 3; as well as to what extent nonstate actors themselves are bound by the rules on the use of force and of humanitarian law. Indeed, these topics would become the subject of a UN-established commission.[80] Since the conflict in Gaza pits the state of Israel against a nonstate organization, Hamas, the applicable rules are those that govern "non-international conflict"—as spelled out in Common Article 3 of the Geneva Conventions and in customary international law, which requires that any war undertaken in self-defense must be limited so that its extent is proportionate to the threat it is designed to counter. Yet since Gaza is not an independent state, ambiguity persists about how these rules would apply. And, to what extent would it be relevant if there were to be an absence of any other clear military options?

Beyond these questions, too, are the questions of *jus in bello*—that is, the long-standing norms concerning the waging of the conflict that were codified in the Geneva Conventions of 1949 and associated treaties, and in a body of customary rules. One of the central questions raised in the so-called war on terror has been to what extent these treaties and rules are applicable—that is, who is a legitimate target? Common Article 3 forbids the use of violence against anyone "taking no active part in the hostilities." Moreover, there is substantial agreement that customary law also forbids the targeting of civilians who are not directly participating in hostilities.

Although Common Article 3 does not forbid indiscriminate attacks in noninternational conflicts, some authorities, such as the International Committee of the Red Cross, believe that such attacks are forbidden by customary law. In the Gaza conflict, both sides are believed to have violated this evolving customary law. For example, Hamas's rocket attacks are believed to violate that law because they are fired at targets with little military significance. Insofar as Israel has launched attacks causing extensive civilian casualties, Israel, too, might well be in violation.

Many of these questions may end up in the ICC, where at the behest of the Palestinian Authority, they have been referred and are being reviewed for admissibility (the Palestinian Authority is not a party to the ICC statute, raising important threshold jurisdictional issues).[81] Again, this is an illustration of humanity law in operation—reflecting the judicialization or at least juridification of political struggle and military conflict. Adjudication offers a mechanism that seems to go beyond conflict management to actual problem resolution according to a fixed normative scheme above the claims of the parties, so to speak. Similarly attractive are the neutrality of the forum and its apparently nonpoliticized response, and the ostensible equality of parties, irrespective of whether they are state or nonstate actors.

On the other hand, clearly problematic is the fact that the framing here is narrow, and avoids anything other than *jus in bello* in a very narrow time period and context. Thus, the process has no interest in the justifications regarding the use of force—that is, the Goldstone Report. Even more problematically, these uses of the law are largely backward looking, selecting relevant parties on those terms and not necessarily those that might advance the political negotiation of the international controversy. This point may well be behind the recent retraction of elements of the Report that would have prevented a more even handed context for the return to peace talks.

Humanity law's influence is further reflected in ongoing debates over what legal order ought to apply to the rise of terrorism and the related counterterror campaign. To think about the controversy as simply pitting state security against human rights is to accept an artificial dichotomy. Human rights advocates insist that the problem of terrorism presents nothing new, and that the appropriate rules are merely those that pertain to judicialism and particularly, those of the ordinary domestic courts and established processes.[82] In turn, the Bush administration and its allies had argued for conceiving of the relevant conflict in terms of a "war," rather than in terms of crime control—yet they postulated conflict that is open-ended both spatially and temporally and hence, as reflected in the debates about enemy combatants, is not fully accounted for within the existing law of war: There are no fully comprehensive categories, statuses, or treatment protocols there, either.[83]

This characterization of the relevant regulatory regime thus appears incoherent, and ultimately defiant of the rule of law—apparently yielding only a "no regulatory scheme, no law" position.[84] Here the reigning position is highly contradictory: On the one hand, terrorism is "war," and therefore domestic criminal law and its related rights are relevant. On the other hand, somehow the law of armed conflict, such as the Geneva Conventions, does not apply, because terrorists, as "unlawful enemy combatants," are not legitimate subjects of this legal regime either.[85] Of Al Qaeda, the Bush administration said that it is "not a state party to the Geneva Conventions, it is a foreign terrorist group." While the Obama administration has a somewhat different take on this issue, its stance still exhibits a degree of continuity in this regard. Discussion of Al Qaeda is still cast in terms of war; now, members of Al Qaeda are referred to as "alien belligerents."[86]

Some, such as Ralph Wilde, have raised the spectre of a legal "black hole" having been created by locating the largest detention prison outside of the United States, at the prison camp at Guantánamo.[87] But the central question increasingly appears to be not whether or not there is law but what exactly is the relevant order. Insofar as there have been any relevant constraints imposed on the counterterror campaign, these have been judicialized, reflecting the limits of asymmetry in litigation in the highest courts. Where terrorism has been framed in terms of "war" and its conditions, courts have granted greater latitude than would otherwise be afforded, in terms of the peacetime rights that are associated with criminal law enforcement and due process. At the same time, the sought-for characterization eludes the minimal relevant legal constraints and associated protections associated with the international humanitarian-law regime. Where this ends up normatively is in a minimalist position necessitating a modicum of humane treatment and access to courts—a position I explore further at the end of this chapter.

The "war on terror" is hardly being waged as a conventional war. In this context, there is an evident struggle over whether there is any right to meaningful judicial review—that is, review before state tribunals in the first instance, for accountability. This question arises largely in counterterror campaigns, and involves questions regarding the vindication of other substantive rights—such as rights to due process, implying constraints on current policies. For example, consider the tension between the powers arrogated by the U.S. executive in the interstate system and countervailing judicial powers that are aiming to set rights-based limits. Since 9/11, the political branches, and particularly the executive, have assumed extraordinary powers that are challenging to the constraints of prevailing international law. Whatever the military tribunals' connection to 9/11, they illustrate the remarkable exploitation of contemporary political conditions in the expansion of executive power. Lacking a classic declaration of war, the point of departure for this exceptional conflict is largely the executive's claim to power, subject only to the constraints of relevant legislation. In the absence of the sort of judicial appeal that is ordinarily associated with the rule of law, at the very least, in the limited context of the asserted state of emergency, the relevant inquiry goes to the proportionality of the counteraction taken, such as the secret detentions and military tribunals. As will be seen, these claims will culminate in the humanity-based rule of law.

Another place this dynamic can be seen is in the regional systems, where even the counterterror campaign is deemed to be subject to the constraints of rights emanating both from human rights law and international humanitarian law. In *Barrios Altos*, a 2001 case arising from Peru's counterterror campaign, the Inter-American Court of Human Rights, in what can be seen as an instance of humanity law framework adjudication, relied on both international human rights law and international humanitarian law to conclude that the domestic amnesties violated core victims' rights that were at stake: the rights to life, to humane treatment, and to judicial protection.[88]

It is possible that the campaign against terror defies full regulation by, or aspiration to, the rule of law—whether within domestic constitutional law, or international law, or both. But, even more fundamentally, the campaign against terror reveals the anachronisms in the perpetuation of the debate in this form: This debate sidesteps the developments in the law of humanity that are raised in this book (and discussed, especially, in chapter 3), which reflect the substantial overlap between international humanitarian law and the law of human rights.

When the humanity-based law framework is applied to the "war on terror," difficult questions arise: First, who is the subject of the legal regime? The terrorist, the enemy combatant, unlawful combatants, or ordinary criminals? Second, where terrorists, such as Al Qaeda, have defined themselves by refusing to follow the ordinary rules of engagement for war, what law ought to apply? Should the relevant law be law at the level of the state or of the individual person—that is, humanity law? And if law at the level of the state should apply, should it be the law of the relevant territory where the conflict is being waged? What should the rule be when instances of interstate conflict are involved in an area that also is the site of terrorist activity, as has occurred in Afghanistan? In the context of a more interconnected and interdependent world, there is a heightened concern with the subject of the legal regime, and with the drawing of juridical categorizations and distinctions (such as the distinction between combatants and civilians) so as to, at the very least, avoid the total-war scenarios that would tend to undermine any rule of law.

The judicialization of the war on terror reflects its globalization—that is, its spread and regulation beyond the state, and beyond the political. In this regard, the course of the war on terror, and that of the counterterror campaign, are illuminated by a humanity law approach. Who is the subject and the relevant self in this regime? What is the relevant applicable regime in the "war on terror?" Not surprisingly, many of the relevant questions have become judicialized. In the first phase of the interpretation illuminating the rule-of law-limits in the "war on terror," the critical issue was the foundational one regarding the rule of law. This was the issue as to what, if any, legal norms exist for this area of conflict. Here we will see that this has been defined at the human level with a vivid struggle over access to courts, where the judicialization of certain fundamental rights in this campaign protects at least a threshold rule of law, even in a world of terror. In the words of the U.S. Supreme Court in a recent case extending habeas corpus rights to detainees (even though they may be overseas and may be aliens) "Security subsists too, in fidelity to freedom's first principles. Chief among these are freedom from arbitrary and unlawful restraint and the personal security that is secured by adherence to separation of powers. It is from these principles that the judicial authority to consider petitions for habeas relief derives."[89]

To a significant degree, rights in the war on terror are being defined not in citizenship terms but across nationality lines[90]—that is, they are being defined in terms of the human condition, deriving from the person.[91] In 2004, the House of Lords issued an opinion leveling the principle of treatment governing detention for British citizens and foreigners.[92] Also in 2004, in the United States—in one of the very first high court evaluations of the post 9/11 war on terror—the U.S. Supreme Court issued its decision in *Hamdi v. Rumsfeld*. There, one can see a similar instance of a leveling approach, reflecting the complex implications of a humanity-based, rather than citizenship-based, standard of treatment. The Court declared that "there is no bar to this Nation's holding one of its own citizens as an enemy combatant."[93] The leveling can also be seen in that these detainees are referred to as "citizen-detainees" whereas at the same time "alleged enemy combatants" are deemed to be entitled to habeas corpus rights and to special processes guaranteed to grant them a hearing for their challenges to their status.

In *Rasul v. Bush*, habeas corpus rights were accorded to "detainees," including aliens in custody, apparently without regard to nationality.[94] In *Boumediene v. Bush*, detainees who were said to be enemy soldiers being held at Guantánamo Bay were—despite their offshore location and their alien status—given habeas corpus rights (rights to judicial access) in United States federal courts.[95] Consider also that while this holding appears not to have been extended as well to other foreign nationals detained in Bagram, Afghanistan.[96] The emerging approach in the war on terror, in both judicial and political discourse, appears to be, to some extent, implicitly humanity-based, as it goes beyond the strict parameters of prevailing law based on nationality and citizenship to recognize minimal protections that must be accorded to all, on a transnational basis, at the level of the person. Of course, as an exception, there remains the troubling military tribunal order aimed at noncitizens. In *Boumediene v. Bush*, the U.S. Supreme Court rejected challenges to proceedings known as "combatant status review tribunals," which provided the sole existing processes available to detainees to establish their status.[97] In March 2011, President Obama issued a presidential order resuming military tribunals for Guantánamo Bay detainees after a two-year ban.[98] In a related case that takes up the appeals of U.S. citizens, *Munaf v. Geren*, the Court once again took a pragmatic approach about the significance of nationality to the question of access to courts.[99] The direction just described suggests that the normative principles that are applicable to the treatment of terrorists, whether within or outside the judicial system, can be best understood not from a state-centric perspective but from a humanity law perspective.[100]

This can be seen, as well, in the more profound questions that have been raised regarding the conflict—which go to the nature of the relevant rule of law, and the question of what substantive legal norm applies. It would be a full political generation after 9/11 before the U.S. Supreme Court would weigh in on the relevant norm. *Hamdan v. Rumsfeld* addressed the question of what law applied to the detainees held at the infamous Guantánamo camp.[101] In this case, the Court struck down the special commissions that had been specifically set up for noncitizens who were accused of supporting, or otherwise participating in, terrorism against the United States.

In response to the Supreme Court's decision, Congress passed the Military Commissions Act of 2006 (MCA), criminalizing the most abusive interrogation techniques that the administration was believed to have authorized and that the CIA was believed to have employed.[102] *Hamdan* also reached a deeper substantive question of what norm ought to apply. More specifically, the question is this: Where as in the so-called war on terror, the relevant conflict is asymmetric (in that it lacks state-party signatories on both sides, which were the traditional sources of authority predicate to the recognition of the applicable law in the interstate system), what rule of law should apply? In response to this question, the Obama administration has persisted in adhering to a staunchly territorially based approach to constitutional rights, as is reflected in the various attempts to elide U.S. law via offshore detentions. Yet with the globalization of law enforcement in the counterterror campaign, the question remains whether it is possible to persist in the view that the choice of this site is not fundamentally an exercise of sovereignty. Despite the arguments of the previous U.S. administration to the contrary, the evolution of the law in the "war on terror" reflects a different, more fluid, and more pragmatic approach to the assertion of sovereignty over these subjects. Under this approach, the ultimate norms at stake also reflect a broader operational and pragmatic (rather than a formal) understanding of sovereignty.

Under the classic law of war, the nature of the conflict would have laid the basis for the applicable standards. Now, however, there seems to be a substantial departure from this categorical view, particularly in light of the authority of Geneva Convention Common Article 3, barring "inhumane treatment," a right that is associated with internal—not just interstate— conflict. Indeed, the question of jurisdiction seemed of little moment to the U.S. Supreme Court, when it held that Common Article 3 of the Geneva Conventions is applicable to Al Qaeda. Exactly what the Geneva right means remains uncertain: At a minimum, it entails a guarantee to a modicum of judicial process. Relying on Common Article 3, signatory states were mandated to establish a "regularly constituted court." In the *Hamdan* case, the Court held that the sweeping executive scheme that was under challenge violated both domestic justice and the law of war.[103] The Court found the military tribunals created by presidential order to try enemies captured in the "war on terror" to be in violation of the U.S. Uniform Code of Military Justice, as well as the Geneva Conventions. In establishing courts of law, the Court held, the U.S. executive must coordinate with Congress *and* abide by international law. In Justice Sandra O'Connor's words, "a state of war is not a blank check for the President."[104] The spectacle of the exercise of political discretion may well be worked out over the subject of the detainee, but only through regular public processes. Due process rights are required, as circumscribed in Geneva Common Article 3, and as deriving from customary law and from practices protecting "civilized peoples," including the tradition of ordered liberty, procedures, and processes associated with the rule of law.[105]

Beyond access to process, what does the humanity right guarantee? Case law reflects a consensus on the impermissibility of torture, detention, or interrogation that is of an "inhumane," "humiliating," or "degrading" nature—setting a standard that, over the years, has always been understood to constitute the bare minimum of humanity.[106] Yet what does this mean?

In a number of regional judicial systems, in Europe and in the Americas, we can see a number of instances where the so-called global war on terror reflects the move away from prevailing state-centricity and toward anthropocentricism—that is, humanity law. For instance, this can been seen in the new, evident controversy over the following question: Where is the present site of accountability in situations where there is the need to reconcile regimes, because there is interconnection but not integration (that is, in the absence of judicial hierarchy)?

An interesting related case arises out of counterterror, the UN sanctions scheme targeting alleged aid for terrorism. That scheme has moved away from the state to persons and to so-called smart sanctions, such as the freezing of assets of individuals. The watershed case is *Kadi v. the European Community*, in which the Grand Chamber of the European Court of Justice declared that it would be guided by human rights as fundamental principles of the Union. The court held as follows: "In this connection it is to be borne in mind that the Community is based on the rule of law, inasmuch as neither its Member states nor its institutions can avoid review of the conformity of their acts with the basic constitutional charter, the EC Treaty which established a complete system of legal remedies and procedures.... 'It is also clear from the case-law that respect for human rights is a condition of the lawfulness of Community acts'...and that measures incompatible with respect for human rights are not acceptable in the Community."[107] In this challenge, the judicial reconciliation of the two applicable regimes, through the interpretation of the respect for human rights as a purpose of the Union, informed a "teleological interpretation."[108]

Relatedly, in *Her Majesty's Treasury v. Ahmed*, the claimants challenged so-called smart sanctions imposed by the UK government pursuant to its obligations under Security Council Resolution 1373 (2001). The high court ruled that—given the "devastating" impact on individuals and their families—the UK implementation could not be sustained without giving the sanctioned individuals meaningful rights of access to a court capable of granting an effective remedy.[109]

Al Jedda v. Sec. of State for Defence involved a British and Iraqi national arrested in Iraq and detained under British rule in Basra ostensibly "for imperative reasons of security."[110] This was an alleged violation of Article 5 of the Convention for the Protection of Human Rights and Fundamental Freedoms (also known as the European Convention for Human Rights), against arbitrary detention, as well as the fourth Geneva Convention of 1949, Article 78. In a 2005 action in the House of Lords in London, Al Jedda sought to secure his release, based primarily on Article 5 of the European Convention on Human Rights, recognizing the right of physical liberty.

Ordinarily, the case would have been compelling: Article 5 does not allow for detentions on the grounds of national security alone, and there had been no relevant derogation by the United Kingdom under Article 15 to the European Court of Human Rights. Moreover, ever since *R (Al-Skeini) v. Secretary of State for Defence*—where members of the British armed forces allegedly caused the death of six Iraqi civilians and the maltreatment of one—the Geneva Conventions' protections have extended even to British military prisons in Iraq, via a holding building on prior cases involving rights protection beyond the immediate territorial jurisdiction, on the basis of "authority and control."[111] In *Al-Skeini*, the House of Lords found that the extraterritorial meaning of the word "jurisdiction" in the UK Human Rights Act was tied to its definition under the European Court of Human Rights, and thus held that the United Kingdom is bound by international human rights law, particularly that of the European Court of Human Rights, while conducting its operations in Iraq.[112]

In these instances, "overall control" was deemed enough to trigger rights protection—for instance, in *Loizidou v. Turkey* or in *Cyprus v. Turkey*, where actions of the Turkish army were at stake. Or consider the holding in *Ilascu v. Moldova*[113] that—in a situation of conflict—both Moldova and Russia had positive obligations to guarantee due process rights, with or without effective control. In *Isayeva v. Russia*, a case arising out of the campaign against terror in Chechnya, the applicants fled the city of Grozny in October 1999 with the promise of a "humanitarian corridor" only to find themselves under "indiscriminate" attack by Russian missiles. The government claimed that the missiles were launched in response to its soldiers' being "shot by automatic weapons."[114] Even where it was hardly self-evident that the injuries at issue were attributable to state signatories under classic conceptions of state responsibility, the European Court of Human Rights took jurisdiction over the conflict.[115] The court explained that

> Article 2, which safeguards the right to life and sets out the circumstances when
> deprivation of life may be justified, ranks as one of the most fundamental provi-

sions in the Convention, from which in peacetime no derogation is permitted under Article 15. Together with Article 3, it also enshrines one of the basic values of the democratic societies making up the Council of Europe. The circumstances in which deprivation of life may be justified must therefore be strictly construed. The object and purpose of the Convention as an instrument for the protection of individual human beings also requires that Article 2 be interpreted and applied so as to make its safeguards practical and effective.[116]

Accordingly, "Article 2 covers ... the situations in which it is permitted to 'use force' which may result, as an unintended outcome, in the deprivation of life.... Any use of force must be no more than 'absolutely necessary' ... , the force used must be strictly proportionate to the achievement of the permitted aims."[117]

Similar conclusions can be drawn from disputes arising in other regional systems. For instance, consider a case arising out of the U.S. intervention in Grenada, involving a claim regarding rights violations under the American Declaration of Human Rights. There, the Inter-American Court of Human Rights adopted a pragmatic approach when faced with the question of what protection was owed detainees in the conflict; it held that a "core nucleus" of the amalgamated human rights/humanitarian-law schemes applies.[118]

The court justified its holding as follows: "While international humanitarian law pertains primarily in times of war and the international law of human rights applies most fully in times of peace, the potential application of one does not necessarily exclude or displace the other. There is an integral linkage between the law of human rights and humanitarian law because they share a 'common nucleus of non-derogable rights and a common purpose of protecting human life and dignity,' ... and there may be a substantial overlap in the application of these bodies of law." The court recognized that "certain core guarantees apply in all circumstances, including situations of conflict, ... and this is reflected, *inter alia*, in the designation of certain protections pertaining to the person as peremptory norms (*jus cogens*) and obligations *erga omnes*, in a vast body of treaty law, in principles of customary international law, and in the doctrine and practice of international human rights bodies.... Both normative systems may thus be applicable to the situation under study." Addressing the question of how to reconcile the two systems when they came into conflict, the court went on to assert the relevant interpretive principle: "An international instrument must be interpreted and applied within the overall framework of the juridical system in force at the time of the interpretation."[119]

In *Al Jedda*, the authority for his arrest was grounded in Security Council Resolution 1546 (2004).[120] Here, the law lords sought to reconcile the rights specified in the European Convention on Human Rights with the UN Security Council operation in Iraq. They were faced with the following question: To what extent might the conduct of the Multinational Force (MNF) (including the British contribution) that was not in accordance with international law be attributable not to the UK, but to the UN?

One might have concluded that the human rights claim depended on the answer to this question—for the European Convention on Human Rights would clearly not have applied to what would have been conduct of the UN. That point was made very clear by the prior European Convention on Human Rights cases *Behrami* and *Saramati*. Those cases concerned the UN Mission in Kosovo and the Kosovo Force, and involved the question of what redress was proper where there was "collateral damage" affecting individuals in the situation of the Kosovo conflict, where sanctions were directed at the state. There, the ECHR deferred to the Security Council.

As in *Behrami*, which involved rights violations arising out of the UN activity in the Kosovo conflict, the issue before the House of Lords in *Al Jedda* was, on its face, the question of attribution of responsibility where a multinational force was involved in attacks occurring in the English-run section of Iraq. In this context, where did responsibility lie?

In *Al Jedda*, the House of Lords, distinguishing *Behrami* and *Saramati*, defined the issue in terms of "effective control." For more than one justice, the prior case law was distinguishable: "The analogy with the situation in Kosovo [and hence with *Behrami* and *Saramati*] breaks down at every point."[121] "The international security and civil presences in Kosovo were established at the express behest of the UN and operated under its auspices, with UNMIK [the UN Mission in Kosovo] a subsidiary organ of the UN. The multinational force in Iraq was not established at the behest of the UN, was not mandated to operate under UN auspices and was not a subsidiary organ of the UN. There was no delegation of UN power in Iraq." For Lord Simon Brown, the essential difference between Kosovo and Iraq was that Security Council Resolution 1483 (2004) had assigned the United Nations an essentially humanitarian role in Iraq, while the security aspect (the Multinational Force) would not be under UN auspices, with Security Council Resolution 1511 and 1546 merely recognizing the occupying forces "as an existing security presence."[122] The United Kingdom, furthermore, should act in keeping with Security Council Resolution 1546 and reconcile it with any pertinent rights obligation (e.g., Article V):[123] The priority was to "ensure that the detainee's rights under Article 5 (of the European Convention on Human Rights) are not infringed to any greater extent than is inherent in such detention." Indeed, the court said that the United Kingdom ought to comply with both sources of obligations. And interpretation in similar situations involved the relevant Security Council resolution; the applicable law of armed conflict, that is, the four Geneva Conventions; and lastly human rights norms—whether of the European Convention on Human Rights, Article 5(1), or of *jus cogens*. One can see this as an illustration of the status and role of humanity.

Lastly, in *Isayeva v. Russia*, the European Court of Human Rights held that "Article 2, which safeguards the right to life and sets out the circumstances when deprivation of life may be justified, ranks as one of the most fundamental provisions in the European Convention on Human Rights, from which in peacetime no derogation is permitted under Article 15. Together with Article 3, it also enshrines one of the basic values of the democratic societies making up the Council of Europe. The circumstances in which deprivation of life may be justified must therefore be strictly construed."[124] The court asserted, "Article 2 covers not only intentional killing but also the situations in which it is permitted to 'use force' which may result, as an unintended outcome, in the deprivation of life....Any use of force must be no more than 'absolutely necessary' for the achievement of one or more...purposes."[125]

HUMAN RIGHTS RELATIVISM AND THE SEARCH FOR "LESSER EVILS": MIGHT HUMANITY BE THE STOPPING POINT?

The cases discussed here lead us to the questions of whether, and to what extent—given the rise of global insecurity—there might nonetheless be human rights that one might conceive of as absolute and nonderogable. What the waging of the "war on terror" has made abundantly clear is that humanity law need not run out—that, indeed, there is no category of persons on the globe that is not covered and protected. Indeed, by turning to the overlapping regimes, coverage can be ensured. And, by their own account, the Geneva Conventions govern all conflicts "at any time and in any place" whatsoever, and extend to all persons. Regardless of status, any human being who is detained—whether he or she is a prisoner of war, an ordinary citizen, an "unprivileged belligerent," or even a terrorist—must be afforded the Geneva Conventions' protections. One might say, then, that these protections are Geneva-based humanity rights.

Beyond the question of the applicability of the laws of war in the "war on terror," there is a broader ethical dimension of our inquiry: In a variety of rights scenarios, the principle of "humanity" appears to offer a potential a normative safeguard. Humanity's law is at once both propelled and limited by its apparently animating universalizing aim.[126] Once again, the provisional point of resolution centers on a humanity-based law, in the guarantee of minimal protection against "cruel and inhumane treatment."[127]

In light of this guiding ethos, and at a time of heightened security concerns, the question is often posed in terms of "the lesser evil." Given nightmare scenarios of insecurity, whether due to the terror or nuclear proliferation—this question has become a regular refrain.[128] Torture? Terror? Other threats? A number of legal scholars have sought to problematize—that is, destabilize—existing understandings regarding torture, some by proposing to bring its practice within the legal system, in a way that is modeled on the Israeli approach.[129] Conversely, the human rights community has sought to do just the opposite: In their view, the "lesser evils" debate threatens to corrode the legal system, as it poses grave challenges to both domestic and international civil liberties.

One might say that this is exactly what has happened in the United States already: The real significance of Abu Ghraib, one can argue, was hardly the revelation of the *fact* of torture on the ground. Instead, and more important for our purposes here, it was torture's veneer of legalization—the veneer revealed by the discovery and release of the underlying memoranda by Bush administration lawyers that reflected attempts to rationalize and legalize torture.[130] Against the seemingly unbounded security concerns (i.e., those arising from the view of enemies without borders) of the endless or "forever" war, the appeal of the law of humanity is that law's contribution of a threshold—and yet an absolute—standard at the level of the human. The parameters surrounding "humane" treatment posit a limit on the possible politicization of torture. Whatever the meaning of the indeterminate phrase "inhumane treatment" may be, one can agree that at this point in human history it refers to a limit that does not purely derive from morality, but rather is bounded within the law. Through the use of the phrase "inhumane treatment," one can regain objectivity and universality through recognizing the group's nexus to humankind. This offers a limited answer to the challenge from moral relativism.

Yet an issue here is that the banning of "cruel and inhuman" treatment doesn't offer a determinate or fixed standard. Thus, while—in the context of the counterterror campaign—the United States, and even the Bush administration, has claimed that "American values" require the "humane treatment of detainees,"[131] that phrase has seemed drained of meaning— particularly where the United States also makes parallel statements regarding "the term 'inhumane' treatment" and its "lack of "susceptibil[ity] to succinct definition."[132] Meanwhile, the struggle to guard against leakage in these norms can be seen in a variety of domestic law debates concerning counterterror, and involving so-called nightmare scenarios.

There is a newfound quest for limits—for the parameters of absolute norms that one might say constitute the operative law of humanity. Put another way, no matter the countervailing justifications, these norms must be abided by, for they derive from core humanitarian concerns. A move that is currently under way aims to derive the relevant norms outside international law, whether consisting of multilateral or bilateral agreements, and instead to locate them in the broad norms affording individuals their core humanity rights. Thus, in the United Kingdom, the House of Lords upheld a clear prohibition of torture, while remaining looser about its views of the guarantees regarding the legitimacy of the use of physical pressure— short of torture. Preventive detention was held—in and of itself—not necessarily to present a violation of the European Convention on Human Rights, so long as the relevant distinctions were rational, not arbitrary; and so long as the normative principle applicable to the treatment of detention, for example, was grounded in humanity.[133]

A similar normative direction is emerging in the United States, reflected in a steady stream of legislation, such as the Detainee Treatment Act, followed by the MCA.[134] These laws ultimately reaffirm the existing consensus in favor of the humanity-based principle—at least, at the level of legislation. Indeed, as a substantive matter, the MCA revises the prior understanding of the War Crimes Act, to clearly define torture and cruel and inhuman treatment as "grave breaches" for purposes of the Act, and specifically incorporates the humanity standard, as it strengthens the prohibition on the uses of "cruel and inhuman treatment" going forward.[135]

Nevertheless, under the MCA, the president has authority to interpret the Geneva Conventions—an authority that could potentially affect the legislative protections. In an executive order on the prohibition of cruel and inhuman treatment,[136] President Bush, interpreting the Geneva Conventions pursuant to the authority vested in him, declared that Common Article 3 applies to CIA interrogations and detentions, whereby in addition to banning "cruel and inhuman treatment," the order also prohibits, inter alia, "willful and outrageous acts of personal abuse done for the purpose of humiliating or degrading the individual" and "acts intended to denigrate the religion, religious practices, or religious objects of the individual." Nevertheless, as has often been the case in the debates concerning the war on terror, the normative reach of these declarations appears to exceed their enforcement potential. Hence, here, the executive order fails to lay out the specifics of interrogation techniques, and thus is vulnerable to challenge on the ground that, by its vagueness, it continues to allow harsh treatment. Some of these concerns are addressed by the legislative reforms under the first years of the Obama administration.[137]

Convergence in this norm is borne out in the appeal to diverse legal systems. Torture is regulated under the Convention Against Torture and Other Cruel, Inhuman or Degrading Treatment or Punishment, both as a matter of domestic law and as a matter of the ban on "cruel and inhuman treatment" under the International Covenant on Civil and Political Rights. The regulation of torture thus coalesces into a consensus, offering regulatory humanity rights as an operative regime for ordinary times. Indeed, it is this convergence of the various strands of the law of war and the law of human rights that characterizes contemporary humanity law.

THE GLOBAL HUMANITY RIGHT

The foregoing analysis may well lead us to conclude that there exist what we might conceive of as global "humanity rights." To whatever extent such rights are now emergent, they (as discussed in prior chapters) clearly imply the right of *preservation*. More specifically, as the situations just described suggest, these rights include, in the first instance, "Geneva" rights—basic norms deriving from Geneva Common Article 3. Article 3 is a norm that sets a legal and moral floor, prohibiting "at any time and in any place whatsoever with respect to persons who are out of combat as a result of detention" "violence to life and person, in particular murder of all kinds, mutilation, cruel treatment and torture" and "outrages on personal dignity, in particular humiliating and degrading treatment." One might say that Common Article 3 establishes "a minimum" code of conduct of humane treatment that parties are "bound to apply."[138]

The application of the Geneva Conventions to conflicts beyond the international—including the "war on terror" —remains a lively topic of controversy. Nevertheless, it is interesting that ever since the postwar adoption of the Geneva Conventions, it has been official U.S. policy to apply these minimum, fundamental standards to *all detainees*, whether or not their countries are parties to the Conventions.[139] As recently as 2003, the State Department's legal adviser asserted that although the United States had not signed Protocol I to the Geneva Conventions, nevertheless the United States "does regard the provisions of Article 75"—which are virtually identical to those in Common Article 3—"as an articulation of safeguards to which all persons in the hands of an enemy are entitled." Here, once again, consider that the relevant subject is "all persons."[140]

In a variety of cases regarding the conduct of the war on terror, it is this human-centered approach that appears as the basis of recent U.S. Supreme Court decisions addressing the question of what standard of treatment ought to be applied to detainees at Guantánamo. In *Hamdan,* Geneva Common Article 3 was applied as the relevant standard—yet without any clear indication of just how and why this norm had its authority.[141] Indeed, one might say that the provenance of the norm was derived from the inside out—that is, from the human condition. Here, Common Article 3 has long been regarded as being predicated on the "bare minimum of humanity." Likewise, in *Tadic,* the ICTY held that Geneva Common Article 3 "specifie[s] certain minimum mandatory rules applicable to internal armed conflicts," which "reflect 'elementary considerations of humanity' applicable under customary international law to any armed conflict, whether it is of an internal or international character."[142]

Whether as a matter of treaty obligation or policy, so long as Common Article 3 applies, it should prohibit "enhanced interrogation techniques" and disallow the admittedly degrading and humiliating techniques that have been used on detainees—for example, at Guantánamo. Such techniques also appear to be the primary modus operandi of interrogation, a set of practices that are deployed regularly in the global war on terror. The norms prohibiting such techniques are deemed to apply regionally in counterterror situations. For instance, the Inter-American Court of Human Rights found that there were applicable rights to "humane treatment" under the American Convention on Human Rights in its judgment of March 2001 in *Barrios Altos.* By now, the Obama administration has articulated its approach to the "law of 9/11," as it calls it, yet it is an approach the Administration concedes involves "more continuity than change" from prior Bush administration policies.[143]

Here, the force of the law of humanity can be seen, once again, operating at the core of foreign affairs—as it ably navigates present political changes, transcending the traditional parameters of the law, to structure the normative discourse in foreign policy making. In so doing, humanity law arguably reveals its "soft law" underbelly, as well as contributing to defining the contours of international society. The Geneva right, as legislated, was never accompanied by the sanction of criminal liability—but historically, its normative pull transcends the law in the books, to serve broader animating purposes.

In other instances, other courts have observed that the interest of human security cuts both ways. Hence, security is also precisely the justification that militates in favor of recognizing certain basic rights in detention. In *Coard v. United States,* a case involving arrests and detentions that occurred during the U.S. military operation in Grenada, the Inter-American Commission invoked human rights law—the American Declaration on Human Rights, as well as international humanitarian law as found in Geneva IV; that is, the amalgamated framework that constitutes humanity law. Based on its interpretation of these two distinct bodies of law, the commission held that it "is bound by its Charter-based mandate to give effect to the normative standard which best safeguards the rights of the individual."[144] Clearly, this is a reading that applies the human security justification throughout. (One might see this as a teleological reading—an interpretive strategy that I will discuss further in chapter 7.) Seen in this light, the commission's ruling demanded a consistency between means and ends: "The same rules which authorize this as an exceptional security measure require that that it be implemented pursuant to a regular procedure which enables the detainee to be hear and to appeal the decision 'with the least possible delay.' That regular procedure ensures that the decision to maintain a person in detention does not rest with the agents who effectuated the deprivation of liberty, and ensures a minimal level of oversight by an entity with the authority to order release if warranted."[145]

As the case law discussed here reflect, humanity law today walks a thin line. The emerging framework surfaces to rationalize current foreign policy decisionmaking, beyond sheer politicization, and in doing so it legitimizes the now-globalizing order. Yet, as this chapter shows, the humanity law enterprise also has troubling ramifications that are not yet fully transparent. The humanitarian regime essentially ensures the legitimacy of what may seem, at first glance, to be minimal preservative rights. Yet the right to the protection of the survival of persons and peoples implies a security beyond a mere constraint on the use of force: Such a right could also promote the expansion of engagement, even forceful interventionism.

Thus, proceeding beyond the long-standing purposes of protecting the state to the more complex goals of protecting "persons" and "peoples" may well come into conflict with the prevailing understanding of the international rule of law, which speaks in terms of the protection of interstate stability via state sovereignty and nonexpansionism. In these ways, a humanity-based perspective should elucidate and contribute to a better understanding of the nature of current foreign policy controversies, and offer some purchase on what might be required for their resolution.

CHAPTER 6

ᴄᴠᴏ

Humanity Law and the Discourse of Global Justice

The Turn to Human Security

Claims about the distribution of resources, opportunities, and responsibilities between and among states and peoples are increasingly cast in terms of "global justice." Humanity law makes a distinctive and significant contribution to this discourse of "global justice." It is the purpose of this chapter to articulate and explore the contribution.

The provenance of humanity law includes international humanitarian law, which contemplates a set of guarantees of protection that will be granted during conflict. These rights have a specific pedigree; at the same time, they also have a potentially wide sweep, encompassing elements of economic and social as well as civil and political rights, and both collective and individual rights. The status of being a "protected person" gave one a right to access to medicine, food, and a healthy environment. As these protections have become increasingly universalized—that is, as they have been generalized beyond interstate conflicts to also apply to internal strife and analogous crises where similar vulnerabilities arise—they have served to shape the concept of human security, and have informed related policy debates over food security, access to medicines, and minimum levels of social welfare.[1]

The evolving conception of human security now goes beyond threats derived from violent conflict to include threats deriving from other problems, as set out for the first time in the UN Development Programme's Human Development Report of 1994.[2] Yet international human rights law—the 1966 International Covenant on Economic, Social and Cultural

Rights—had already referred to the "security of the person" and to "social security" (in Article 9).

The twists and turns of the global political economy since the end of the Cold War provide the backdrop against which we may better understand these phenomena. The failure of neoliberalism as a comprehensive approach to global economic governance (and domestic governance) followed close on the heels of the failure of communism itself; there was then no obvious single economic paradigm left to explain or describe the global order. At the same time, events cried out for some set of ordering principles or solutions: The world witnessed political violence; environmental and health catastrophes of transnational scale or implications, if not global ones; and a succession of financial crises in Asia, Latin America, and elsewhere, subject to rigorous analysis by economists such as Joseph Stiglitz and Dani Rodrik.[3]

Against this backdrop, the challenge of the global political economy is being reimagined in humanity law and human security terms. This chapter argues that there have been critical transformations in the framing of the problem of global justice: These transformations go to the fundamental tasks of defining, first, the *subject(s)*, and second, the *measure* of global justice. This chapter's basic thesis is that humanity law promises to reshape these two vital tasks: It reframes the problem of global justice in terms of the human, so that the core measure of justice begins with and concerns human protection.

Half a century ago, the heady postwar moment gestured towards human rights universalism; yet as we know, with the Cold War's polarization, rights claims—concerning political, social, and economic rights—clashed with each other in the opposing rhetorics of elites in the East and West. With the Soviet collapse, the opportunity arises to revisit these ideological fractures in human rights; now, we are arguably seeing a story unfold of inclusion, even integration.[4]

By turns, this new interconnectedness spurs the greater demand for global justice, including the claims arising from greater inequality across state borders. The way of conceiving these issues transcends a purported divide between the public and the private, and is therefore conceived in terms of "global justice."

The humanity law framework helps elucidate and advance a number of debates about human rights and over global values, where they meet. For instance, there is a debate regarding the relation of both economic rights and political rights to development. Here, the law of humanity promises a distinctive human-centered global justice, a modicum of the rule of law that guarantees a measure of human security and accountability. The shift in personality has implications for the rhetoric and tone of the global-justice debate, and this shift points to a change too, in the way we think about what would constitute global justice and rule of law. This debate is often conducted in the idiom of deontological moral discourse, although of course institutional choices of social and economic policy are at issue as well. The language of human security may be seen as an attempt to bridge deontological and consequentialist discourses, neither of which is, in itself, adequate to resolve the fundamental challenges satisfactorily.

Today "global justice" is demanded by a range of political actors, NGOs, and scholars alike.[5] Yet exactly what conception of justice is conceived to extend across state borders? To what extent does the term "global justice" have a determinate, common meaning?

RETHINKING THE TERMS OF THE DEBATE: FROM INTERSTATE EQUALITY TO GLOBAL JUSTICE

In prominent debates in the Anglo-American world of ideas, the question of global justice has often been posed in terms of a choice between what might be called statism versus cosmopolitanism. Statists question whether there is any moral imperative for redistribution that extends beyond the boundaries of one's own community. In contrast, cosmopolitans challenge whether and how state borders can possibly have, coherently, such a significance for issues of distributive justice.[6] Thus, Thomas Nagel largely adheres to the statist view,[7] while Charles Beitz, Thomas Pogge, and Amartya Sen all could be considered cosmopolitans.[8] Nevertheless, there are differences in their points of reference—for instance, the "transcendental" approach associated with Pogge can be contrasted with Sen's pluralistic approach. Sen's focus on capabilities "is inescapably concerned with a plurality of different features of our lives and concerns"[9] yet both Pogge and Sen agree on global interdependence.

Once the interdependence that is characteristic of globalization is conceded to be today's practical reality, it would be surprising if it had no normative consequences.[10] Nagel has argued that the contours of distributive justice can only be legitimately defined by the state, and that any justice-based argument must be associated with a distinct political arrangement of the state. Nevertheless, even for Nagel, there is still some "moral minimum"—which is interestingly articulated in humanitarian terms, that is, in terms of a "general humanitarian claim" and a "minimum humanitarian morality," which "governs our relations with everyone in the world" and must be guaranteed on a transnational basis.[11] Therefore, one might say that the hitherto virtually obsolete question of whether or not there can be global justice is now giving way to an intense new controversy centering on the question: What is the right measure of global justice? What are the duties of protection, and where does the responsibility fall for their fulfillment?

Every regime implies a self, a subject. The problem of what perspective or view of the global order we should adopt depends on what this self or subject is. In the humanity law conception discussed here, the emergence of *persons* and *peoples* as the relevant agents and hence as subjects of the norms of justice, as associated with regimes regulating conflict (as discussed in chapters 2 and 5), presents multiple normative implications for reconceptualizing the context, conditions, and meaning of global justice.

The general problem of "global justice"—which is, arguably, the problem of "global *in*justice"—arises today as a result of the confluence of a number of phenomena that together create the *anxiety* of globalization. This is a predicament constituted by on the one hand greater interdependence in the international realm, in a host of areas—economic, technological, and environmental—and on the other a lack of integration, whether political, economic, or otherwise. Hence, we see sharp disparities and variations in the global economy and other phenomena both within and beyond the state—for instance, situations where extreme wealth is juxtaposed with extreme poverty. Here, one might contrast the focus of scholars like Thomas Pogge on global income disparities with the focus of Amartya Sen on the shared human project and human capacities. "The capability approach focuses on human life, and not just on some detached objects of convenience. . . . Indeed it proposes a serious departure from concentrating on the means of living to the actual opportunities of living."[12]

Yet this account does not fully capture the debate over the causes of these disparities. Indeed, there is no consensus on the answer to this important question, which has shaped the global-justice debates in the last few decades: Considered from a historical perspective, the problem is often posited as one of economic inequality as *between* states. From the 1960s on, the problem tended to be framed in interstate and North/South terms—in terms of the distributional inequalities between wealthy and poor states, taking into account resource differences, flows of goods, services, knowledge, and capital, and so forth.[13] After the late 1970s, however, it became more rare for the distributive claim to be made in these terms. And by the 1980s, with the debt crisis as well as the advent of neoliberalism, this kind of argument had largely disappeared from the scene: The problem of global justice was no longer understood as primarily a matter of the distribution or redistribution of economic resources and or/opportunities either within or between *states*.

Nevertheless, there are, at the same time, new and increasing expectations or demands, influenced by stronger perceptions of injustice and by the imperative for remediation, that emerge from the ascendant discourse of judicialized rights. As the last century's transitions reflect, there is a growing, acute sense of moral indignation at certain varieties of historical domination, such as postcolonial inequalities and related exploitation.

The foregoing discussion of the emergence of the human-centric approach to issues of social and economic security implies the existence of some threshold: an absolute standard (even if that standard is minimalist, in some versions of this approach) that reflects the reconceptualization of the problem in rights terms. In contrast, earlier distributive theories invoked a concept of substantive equality—an equalization of resources, concerned with relative wealth or well-being. One might say that the new emphasis on an absolute standard plays into a backward-looking view; instead of the progressive achievement of equality or the progressive elimination of inequality—inherently an aspirational and future-oriented normative vision—the concern now shifts to accountability for failing to realize a minimum, absolute standard of conduct.

Yet how exactly does the relevant question change from a humanity law perspective? To what extent does the full content of social and economic rights, as articulated in the International Covenant on Economic, Social and Cultural Rights, define the ultimate goal—which cannot be achieved unless a degree of human security is *first* attained?

Global justice emerges as *global judgment*. Here one might distinguish retrospective approaches to globalizing justice—which seem to be a variant of transitional justice in that they look to the past, sometimes even the distant past, to inform their understandings of present obligations. As an illustration of such approaches, consider for example, the 2001 Durban Conference, which conceived of global justice as largely reparatory.[14]

Relatedly, we see a number of developments—scholarly, activist, and institutional—that reflect a move toward an ideal of global justice—justice that is dedicated to judgment. From this perspective, humanity law values often appear to focus on protections stated in prohibitory terms. In other words, they adopt a negative-freedoms approach. International criminal law is, obviously, most squarely embracing of this approach, but this is changing, as is emerging law regarding international criminal responsibility, arguably setting out related positive rights to accountability. For, beyond this minimum, Pogge and others, such as Peter Singer, evaluate the current situation by looking to the current state of globalization, with its sharp inequalities, and attempting to reason a counterfactual viewpoint.[15] Thus, "Insofar as the current global institutional order does turn out to entail substantially more violence and severe poverty than would exist under a better designed alternative order, we might go on to ask *who bears responsibility* for this order having been shaped the way it was shaped and to what extent and whether these responsible parties have foreseen and could have reasonably have avoided that excess in violence, and severe poverty."[16]

This approach asks us to imagine a counterfactual alternative order that never was but should have been—and to deem a derogation from that imaginary order to constitute an injustice in the current order. Yet this judgment call, or call for judgment, is a tricky business. The problem is that one might always have an imaginary counterfactual. There has not yet been any actual agreement or collective decision about the shape of a just global order. Thus, the imaginary order is inferred from our intuitions or indignation concerning the "injustice" or "injustices" of the current order. In this sense, as a standard for judging the current order, the imaginary ends up being thoroughly tautological. Intuition and indignation cannot themselves generate a defensible normative benchmark, in any case. After all, what exactly might "more violence" and "severe poverty" mean? At what point do which agents become morally, or legally, accountable or responsible? The mere existence of disparities is clearly not sufficient to generate or trigger a coherent set of duties that can and should be imposed on defined particular actors.

Pogge proposes an "interactional morality approach," which would appear to involve *global judgment*: "We can causally trace such events back to the conduct of individual and collective agents, including the person who is suffering the harm."[17] This exercise of looking to allocate accountability for the past provides the model: Pogge writes: "We all have blood on our hands—therefore it appears to follow that we should pay *so long as there are not substantial costs*."[18] Yet how can such culpability plausibly be established, unless one could have known ex ante what policies would avoid or prevent severe poverty, and who should be responsible—and to what extent—for creating and applying those policies? In his recent work, Pogge has argued that the affluent countries violated their duty not to contribute to extreme poverty globally by choosing a set of rules and institutions that were different from some imagined alternatives, which could have eliminated the most extreme forms of poverty.

As I have explored in depth in other work,[19] when one examines the details of the imagined alternatives Pogge describes, two points become clear: First, whether these alternatives would indeed have significantly contributed to preventing or reducing severe poverty depends on many undemonstrated assumptions. Second, Pogge's approach assumes a willingness to make major changes to the international order itself (such as by placing new constraints on sovereignty)—but these changes might themselves have debatable side-effects (such as opening the door extremely wide to humanitarian intervention). Finally, the poverty-reducing and other effects of these imagined alternatives are not as clearly foreseeable as Pogge seems to argue, even though he suggests that such clear foreseeability is necessary for the imputation of backward-looking responsibility.

For some part of the human rights community, the relevant measure of global justice has become establishing who is "the most responsible" for the "most serious violations" of human rights.[20] Under this approach, unlike under Pogge's approach, there *is* a known method and intentionality, an endeavor for which there appears to be significant consensus, as seen in the ICC system, discussed at greater length in chapter 4.[21]

The demand for a measure of global justice—the backward-looking pull, reframing harm as a matter of injustice—helps us to understand why it is that in the present moment, what is commonly seen as a matter of global justice tends to be conceived less in traditional socioeconomic terms and more in humanitarian terms. In other words, this demand shows why we tend now to see global justice in terms of duties to achieve a broader human security that is tied to survival, as seen in the resources that have been devoted to recognizing the threshold duties of protection that are borne by states to their own citizens, and no longer just to their own citizens but now also to other civilians as well.

The humanity law framework draws from three corpuses of positive law—of international human rights, the law of war, and international criminal justice. Where rights are framed in human security terms, their articulation and meaning will be highly contextual, shaped by a particular crisis or emergency or by the constraints and opportunities posed by the stage of development of a particular society. Such rights may shape political discourse, and may also have an impact through existing legal and other institutions—whether, for example, through the interpretative practice of the World Trade Organization dispute settlement organs or through the guidelines of multilateral development banks on such issues as displacement of persons and aboriginal peoples' rights.

RETURNING THE HUMAN SECURITY ELEMENT TO THE DEBATE
OVER GLOBAL SECURITY

Most recently, the problem of global justice has been framed in terms of—or closely entangled with—the alternative discourse of human security How should we respond, at the global level, to the broad and varied range of threats: from natural and manmade disasters, from terrorism, from violent political conflict?

Here, one can see the crux of globalization's deep paradox: the simultaneity of the shared and the unshared, the connected and the unconnected, the dependent and the independent. There is evidently a strong sense of a shared threat, but it is set against the also evident awareness of a large continuum in recognition of diversity in points or foci of impact, which often leads to the targeting of localized harms. Indeed, it is the reality of these disparities in impact—disparities that, for instance, result from varying degrees of vulnerability and of protection—that often today appear to animate the problem of "global justice." The focus shifts accordingly from a concern with the deep structures of interstate inequality (North/South, postcolonial, etc.; as in Wallerstein)[22]—to the identification and remediation of specific crises, threats, episodes, emergencies; and to the judgments of various relevant actors in theses events against what are, ultimately, humanity-law-based standards. Above all, this shift indicates a move toward a conception of what is required or demanded for "human security"—that is, a floor of protection that can withstand sudden economic or other downturns (e.g., political or environmental catastrophes). One might term it "downturn with security."[23]

The emergence of persons and peoples as among the most relevant agents (as discussed in chapters 2 and 3) has implications for the meaning of global justice. This shift involves a significant rethinking and reconceptualization of what global justice means, as well as what agency is implicated in its coming about—that is, what its purposes are, and what or who the operative actors should be. The change in subjectivity makes for a related change in the aims and measures of global justice—which is now, due to this shift, being seen from the human perspective, and grounded in human experience. Personality, subjectivity, and normative substance are connected or interrelated, as will be seen, so that the move to a humanity-centered regime may well contribute at least three major reconceptualizations: of the relevant agents, of the implicated duties and rights, and of the content or contours of the norms in question.

First, there is a rethinking of the relevant subject of global justice— which is now viewed no longer exclusively in terms of states (and interstate equalities) but instead in terms of persons and peoples. Second, this change in focus has implications for the reframing of the problem, as well as the sources of the duty, which does not align itself necessarily with the terms and arrangements associated with the interstate system. The humanity-centric duty is now seen as global, in the rise of the perception of interdependence. Moreover, these duties, which are often transnational in nature, are naturally more often derived from law and law-like agreements, as noted, for example, in the rise of treaties, for example, in the diverse regional criminal systems—whether bilateral or multilateral. Statutes often reflect indicia of the new normativity—by going beyond the state and beyond traditional indicia of bindingness or compliance. Here it is useful to consider the nature of the commitments in the ICC institution (described in earlier chapters). However, even more pertinent here are the "Millennial Reform" projects,[24] or other proposals, for example as advocated by Paul Collier and others discussed further on.[25]

Toward the end of his life's work, John Rawls began to explore the problem of international justice: "The Law of Peoples," a project he defined as a political conception of right and justice as it, "applies to the principles and norms of international law and practice."[26] A political universe is constructed that includes "peoples" as legitimate subjects, "with common sympathies" and with potentialities for reconciling individual and collective rights, as well as for recognizing new sets of humanity rights and duties, with evident implications for global justice. Although Rawls's theory represented a move away from the purely domestic perspective on justice, this departure from a state-based view was partial and limited, falling far short of cosmopolitanism, in the sense discussed earlier. Indeed, despite the invocation of political regimes beyond the state, and beyond democracies, at the time, Rawls did not get too far in elaborating a "peoples' law" and its consequences for the state.[27] Instead, one might infer from his work the notion that over time, the right culture will take care of any potential for conflicts between peoples and the state regarding question of justice.

Nevertheless, reconceptualizing the subject, as will be seen, has consequences for global justice. Consider the ways Charles Beitz and Thomas Pogge reason from a human-being-centered perspective.[28] Sen, too, shares this with the cosmopolitans: the emphasis on the perspective of persons and peoples. In particular, Sen draws on peoples' diversity to inform his pluralistic vision.

So interstate conflict is reconceived as involving the conflict of peoples—a reconception that is already present in the expanded international-humanitarian-law regime. Nevertheless, when it comes to placing duties (as opposed to rights or claims) on duty-holders, a handful of states are said to bear the responsibility in large part. From a humanity law perspective, states remain important actors, in terms of rights or prerogatives and duties or responsibilities. Yet this continuing importance of states is now complemented by the new importance accorded to the claims of persons and peoples. Certain freedoms are conceived as a matter of right because they are, in Sen's words, "threshold conditions" of relevance, of social importance, to be included as among the human rights of the person; examples include the freedom from political violence and the freedom to receive basic medical attention.[29]

THE NEW GLOBAL JUSTICE AGENDA: A GUARANTEE OF HUMAN SECURITY?

The human security focus is reflected in the discourse of a range of political and legal fora and actors—ranging from multilateral institutions such as the United Nations, in its commitment to the Human Security Commission and report, to other contexts where appeals to justice are being framed and justified in humanity terms, including even, to some extent, the context of international economic law. Reframing global-justice claims on a humanity basis appears to be apt for institutions that are undergoing transformations in light of a globalizing politics and economics. A plethora of ramifications follow for the rethinking and reframing of the normative terms of global engagement. For instance, there is the conception of global justice deriving from an objective minimum conception of human security, which offers an alternative to relational and distributive approaches to global justice, as it reconceives global duties and responsibilities. This conception of global justice moves away from the usual domestic policy arguments, insofar as it assumes global responsibilities for a limited form of interventionism, along the lines of the human measure.

Beyond the change in subjectivity that is associated with globalization, and the increased mobility of persons, capital, and goods, global justice's redirection has profound consequences because pursuant to this vision, rights and duties as between states lose their primacy—giving way to a strong focus on "human security." Changes in personality have the effect of significantly reconceiving the meaning of security and the rule of law. More specifically, such changes have the effect of complementing the state-centered view with a view that also takes into account the rights and interests of humanity as being more and more conceived in terms of human security—rather than state security.

From the human security perspective, the preeminent concern is addressing the perceived vulnerabilities or exposures of persons and peoples. This change in perspective has real ramifications for the conceptualization of the scope of the relevant problem of global justice, as well as for its solution. Considered from a person-centered perspective, problems as diverse as political violence and climate change are reconceived as shared threats to humanity. The human security approach, by its nature, cuts across sectors. For example, Kofi Annan's words in 2000 (at the Millennium Summit), where the issues this approach reaches range from "freedom from fear" to "freedom from want":

> Human security, in its broadest sense, embraces far more than the absence of violent conflict. It encompasses human rights, good governance, access to education and health care and ensuring that each individual has opportunities and choices to fulfill his or her potential. Every step in this direction is also a step toward reducing poverty, achieving economic growth and preventing conflict. Freedom from want, freedom from fear, and the freedom of future generations to inherit a sustainable natural environment—these are the interrelated building blocks of human—and therefore national—security.[30]

One might discern three different approaches that can be seen to fall under the humanity-centric approach to global justice. First, there is the approach that puts greatest emphasis on the situation of the "poorest of the poor." Second, there is a more situational or crisis-centered approach. Third, there is an approach that seeks to offer a "human security" guarantee—conceptualized on a global basis. Where weakened or failed states cannot protect the persons and peoples within their borders, the guarantee offered by this third approach becomes a legitimate basis for intervention. Such intervention may include, for example, incursion into airspace and territory to deliver aid without the consent of the state in question, as occurred in Burma.[31]

The human security approach to global justice responds to the vulnerabilities or threats to which persons and peoples are exposed. It directly addresses situations where human security is threatened in extreme but episodic fashion.

To begin, the humanity-inspired measure appeals to *absolute* needs relating to human security. This approach indubitably draws from understandings associated with conflict, and with the idea of securing a humanitarian minimum. In a growing number of situations, one can see a steady move from the language of rights, at the level of the state and its duties, to a language regarding the person and the state's duties to provide assistance to persons. Some of these duties arise in the form of what may seem like only life- or death-related humanity rights, as they are asserted in human security crises. As previously discussed, such duties are most often asserted in the context of weak or failed states—a concept that has been ratified now at the Security Council, in its resolution on the RtoP, the context for which is human security crises, such as the crisis in Darfur.[32]

And, as we have seen, the demand for such intervention more and more turns a blind eye to the source of the human threat. This is reminiscent of the strand of the law of conflict that assured the protection of populations comprehensively. Here, a relevant claim is the claim to aid in cases of extreme poverty and hunger. Such a claim might be articulated, for example, through the notion of a right to food security, in some cases. Consider, in this regard, the Millennium Development Goals report.[33] Another claim would be access to medical aid. In this regard, the United Nations Department of Economic and Social Affairs report "Overcoming Economic Insecurity."[34] By contrast with Sen's capabilities approach, which would recognize a right to basic medical care in order that persons might achieve a state of good health and wellness, this is an ends-based—rather than a means-based—approach.[35]

At the start of the new millennium, as set forth in the Millennium Declaration of 2000, world leaders set forth a vision for humanity, asserting that they should commit "to spare no effort to free our fellow men, women and children from the abject and dehumanizing conditions of extreme poverty." This poverty is conceived in human terms. For example, Paul Collier's book *The Bottom Billion* reframes the demand in terms of the numbers of the poorest of the poor—those who survive on less than a dollar a day—so that the very standard of care is articulated in terms of a class of persons, which is redefined in economic terms.[36] Relatedly, the UN Millennium Report identifies those in "extreme poverty" with the "international poverty line," which since 2000 has been drawn at $1.08 a day.[37]

Evidently, international humanitarian law has moved from the traditional view of recognizing states' duties to protect their own citizens to a view that there is a need to protect all those in the global community. To the extent that humanity rights have been recognized under the law, the enforcement of such rights—such as the right to the protection of human security—along with human rights that were articulated and enforced, first and foremost, at the state level can and does occur *beyond the state*.

That development in turn, reflects the sense in which we are already operating in a global framework. Indeed, what may well characterize the period is the proliferation in a multiplicity of actors simultaneously of justice-related duties; therefore, there has been a diffusion of responsibility, with consequences for accountability, and arguably for legitimacy (taken up at this chapter's end).

Consider the 1994 Human Development Report, which for the first time called for a new, broadened concept of security: "Human security can be said to have two main aspects. It means, first, safety from such chronic threats as hunger, disease and repression. And, second, it means protection from sudden and hurtful disruptions in the patterns of daily life—whether in homes, in jobs or in communities."[38] Moreover, what distinguishes these threats is their increasingly transnational nature—and, therefore, the sense in which they also pose a threat or challenge to global security. As will be seen, this understanding of global threats goes to the heart of the demand for universal humanity law protection.

As the International Criminal Tribunal for the Former Yugoslavia Appeals Court put it in its first landmark case, *Prosecutor v. Tadic*:

A State-sovereignty-oriented approach has been gradually supplanted by a human-being-oriented approach. Gradually the maxim of Roman law *hominum causa omne jus constitutum est* (all law is created for the benefit of human beings) has gained a firm foothold in the international community as well. It follows that in the area of armed conflict the distinction between interstate wars and civil wars is losing its value as far as human beings are concerned. Why protect civilians from belligerent violence, or ban rape, torture or the wanton destruction of hospitals, churches, museums or private property, as well as proscribe weapons causing unnecessary suffering when two sovereign States are engaged in war, and yet refrain from enacting the same bans or providing the same protection when armed violence has erupted "only" within the territory of a sovereign State? If international law, while of course duly safeguarding the legitimate interests of States, must gradually turn to the protection of human beings, it is only natural that the aforementioned dichotomy should gradually lose its weight. What is inhumane, and consequently proscribed, in international wars, cannot but be inhumane and inadmissible in civil strife.[39]

From the perspective of the individual, these threats—whether internal or international, whether seen as natural or a product of political and social choices—are analogous and may even admit of related strategies. This point of view cuts across long-established ways of thinking, destabilizing received understandings of what is "political" or "economic" and what is the realm of the "national" and the "transnational." The global-justice debate has already evolved beyond the question of whether duties apply across state borders, and if so, which duties—into a broader reconceptualization concerning what is tolerable or a matter of misfortune versus what engages moral choices. This reconceptualization was prefigured in Sen's early work on famine, and, even earlier, in Shklar's writing on modernity and the reconceptualization of the Lisbon earthquake from tragedy to injustice.[40] Indeed, it is in this sense in which a fundamental rethinking of the meaning and measure of global justice is now under way.

This is reflected in the human rights project whose present focus on "global justice" is articulated in terms of identifying the "worst human rights violations," without regard to the relevant subject. One might recall Secretary-General Annan's call that not enough had been done regarding the most serious offenses in the fall of 2002, when he repeated a challenge he first made to UN members in 1999, urging the Security Council to discuss "the best way to respond to threats of genocide or other comparable massive violations of human rights." The human measure establishes priorities, such as the focus on the most serious human impacts of violence. This explains the three main offenses giving rise to international criminal jurisdiction at the now-permanent ICC.[41] The very demand for the creation of such an institution reflects the diminished capacity of the state (or at least the capacity of those states that are weak or failed and are currently under ICC jurisdiction) and the attendant rise in attention to other actors in contemporary politics, with consequences for global legitimacy.

The reconceptualization in the direction toward a human-centric perspective can illuminate other related developments. Traditionally, the site of interstate contacts revolved around war and trade, which have given rise to highly differentiated legal regimes. In contrast, from a humanity law perspective, one can now see complex points of contact between these areas, so that *across sectors*, the transnational point of connection, the relevant nexus, is the shared harm—a basis comprehending an array of global threats. Indeed, one might say that this perspective helps us to understand the structure of the current regime—as a largely threat-based regime and, relatedly, a security-based order.

These considerations can be seen, for example, in a move away from comprehensive collective economic sanctions—irrespective of legal regime.[42] Economic sanctions pose a distinctive set of dilemmas within the discourse of humanity law. Consider the human-centric economic impact in Iraq: In

Annan's words: "In the case of Iraq, a sanctions regime that enjoyed considerable success in its disarmament mission has also been deemed responsible for the worsening of a humanitarian crisis—as its unintended consequence."[43]

Also notable is the role of international sanctions in responding to gross human rights violations in Zimbabwe or Burma, dilemmas that reflect, as well, the prevailing limits of the various specialized international law regimes—the human rights regime, the international-economic-law regime, and the UN and customary law regarding peace and security. After a split in the Security Council regarding the direction of sanctions, both the United States and the European Union tightened up their own sanctions regimes on Zimbabwe, with the European Union focusing on "targeted sanctions" in order "to avoid anything which would harm the population."[44]

This is a classic case of what is often referred to as "fragmentation" in international law.[45] As the human consequences of sanctioning or punishing an entire people or nation become evident in light of the human rights regime, the response has been to shift the emphasis from collective sanctions to sanctions that target individuals who are directly implicated in the abuses in question, such as political and military leaders. Particularly when robust and comprehensive sanctions are directed against authoritarian regimes, it is usually—and tragically—the people who suffer, not the political elites who have the power to change policy.[46]

One can see an increasing tendency (as discussed in chapter 3) to reconceive accountability in terms of the imposition of sanctions against individual leaders and officials. A good example is the setting of prohibitions on the travel of, and the transfer of funds by, the Burmese junta.

Concerns about the economic impacts of corruption have become blended with human rights concerns. Such blended concerns are raised, for instance, by the "odious debt" financing of an illegitimate regime by means of the oppression of its own people (as occurred with Marcos in the Philippines, for example, or Mubarak in Egypt).[47] From the other side, as well, we can see the complexity of dilemmas surrounding how sanctions play out on the individual level where humanity law process concerns likewise apply and thus constrain and structure the move to targeted individual or "smart" sanctions. Among the examples here are *Kadi* in the European context and *Ahmed v. Her Majesty* (discussed in chapter 3).

GLOBAL JUSTICE AND THE HUMAN MEASURE

To what extent is the humanity norm a threshold on which to build a fuller vision of global justice, one that goes beyond a concern for security to a concern for human capacity and/or human empowerment? Amartya Sen has traced the links between economic development and democracy; his analysis transcends the narrow confines of the old debate that pits state sovereignty against globalization.[48] As discussed earlier, the critical question is one of the "capabilities" of individuals to live "freely"—wherever this may take them.

Sen's *Development as Freedom* and *The Idea of Justice*[49] reflect, in part, the post–Cold War moment; the demand for new concepts; and the move away from the prior categorizations, which dichotomized the political and the economic, and from the notion of negative and the positive freedoms—understandings that no longer appear apt. Indeed, the shift in perspective can be summed up as amounting to one of "human security."

Sen cogently elucidates the connection between political freedoms and the promotion of the satisfaction of basic human needs. This is because, as he explains in *Development as Freedom*, "focusing on human freedoms contrasts with narrow views of development, such as identifying development with the growth of the gross national product or the rise in personal incomes. But freedoms depend also on other determinants such as social and economic arrangements...as well as political and civil rights."[50] From the human-centered perspective, overlaps in the relevant threats means overlap in the responses. This, in turn, illustrates the need for the development of a cross-sectional and cross-cutting rights approach—for example, one that values the protection of both political freedoms and economic capabilities.[51]

The humanity-centered approach moves beyond this stilted formulation; indeed, from a human-centered perspective, one can see that the standard debates over political and civil rights versus economic rights lose their relevance. Rather, this now-historical central divide in human rights law is being interrogated through the notion of "capacities," which are thought to bring together notions that had otherwise been conceptualized as somehow separate—notions of economic needs and political freedoms, respectively. Clearly, this moves beyond Rawls, whose relevant work predates the recent era of globalization and reflects conditions associated with a lesser interdependence, and a more limited view of assistance—for example, assistance as seen in terms of the exceptional case of "burdened states" and as limited to the development of minimal capacities assuring "decency." Indeed, Rawlsian assumptions that in a "reasonably developed liberal society, basic needs would be taken care of" seem not to contemplate the sorts of profound global threats that can produce severe economic downturns even in well-organized societies, as has been illustrated of late.

Secretary-General Annan (in 2000) articulated the claim to basic "freedom from fear," together with "freedom from want."[52] Likewise, Sen's view of threshold conditions contemplates political freedoms as the point of departure. Moreover, and importantly, Sen shifts the view of the self at the heart of the regime, with the protection of individual capabilities cultivating freedoms, with both intrinsic and instrumental virtues.[53] While Sen begins with the development of political rights and institutions, these could be just the beginning, and ideally would lead, step by step, to the development of other capacities toward ensuring human security and well-being. In this vein, Nussbaum proposes a list of ten capabilities that would be necessary to a "life with dignity," as a part of a "minimum account of social justice."[54]

In the appeal to universality, the central claim is the priority of the "right to survival." In terms of human security, this claim generates norms that secure essential needs—that is, needs that are essential to the maintenance and preservation of life—as being widely shared. The recognition of such needs goes back to the early law of war informing and constituting international society.[55] For example, Article 23 of the 1977 Additional Protocol I declares: "Each High Contracting Party shall allow the free passage of all consignments of medical and hospital stores.... intended only for civilians of another High Contracting Party, even if the latter is its adversary. It shall likewise permit the free passage of all consignments of essential foodstuffs, clothing and tonics intended for children under fifteen, expectant mothers and maternity cases." As we can see, this right mediates the various dimensions of humanity rights that have been discussed here.

Thus, one might gather that the protection of a right to preservation involves, at the very least, freedom from warlike attack. But modern protections are unlike the previous arrangements set out in the UN Charter, which were conceived in terms of protections for above all territorial integrity of states. Issues of survival and sustenance are raised by extreme poverty; where, therefore, rights to food, work, and health would be implied in certain contexts.[56]

Indeed, among the "four traps" that Collier identifies in *The Bottom Billion* is one that relates to the effects of conflict. Here, and in *Wars, Guns, and Votes*, he argues for a basic need for good governance. Consider Susan Marks for critical discussion of Collier's argument elaborating on the role of human rights law.[57] One can see the recognition of such connections in the wider international literature that brings together democracy, good governance, development and human rights. More and more, the literature is recognizing how, particularly in weak and failed states, political and economic pathologies are entangled in many ways.

The concept of a vital core is salient here. Thus, "the rights and free-doms in the *vital core* pertain to survival, to livelihood, and to basic human dignity."[58] Put another way, a working definition of human security must "safeguard the vital core of all human lives from critical pervasive threats, in a way that is consistent with long term human fulfillment."[59] A focus on human security that is so articulated is broadly consistent with the ideas of "minimum core obligation" and "minimum essential levels" of economic, social, and economic rights, which have been articulated by the Committee on Economic, Social and Cultural Rights. The progressive fulfillment of the rights in the International Covenant on Economic, Social, and Cultural Rights clearly depends on social and political condi-tions that are fundamentally compromised in most situations of violent conflict.

A minimum of human security is in many ways a prerequisite for the social cooperation, citizen and worker participation, and good governance that are needed if the full vision of this Covenant is to be achieved in each country. Conversely, when human security is menaced—whether by economic crisis, natural disaster, or war—the received understanding of social, economic, and cultural rights can be rapidly undermined. Moreover, where human security itself is threatened by the denial of economic, social, and cultural rights, the rights in the International Covenant on Civil and Political Rights are likely to be menaced or unachievable as well. It is worth observing that as to the human security dimensions of rights such as the rights to health, to food, and to work, even nonsignatories of the Covenant have participated in various legal and policy instruments and initiatives that affirm these dimensions, including the Declaration on Fundamental Principles and Rights at Work (1998) of the International Labor Organization, or the Food and Agriculture Organization's initiatives on food security, or the World Health Organization's constitution, which affirms the right to health as fundamental.

The human security dimensions of economic and social rights are arguably already implicit in the notion of the right to life in the International Covenant on Civil and Political Rights. Indeed, the con-nection of the rights in the International Covenant on Economic, Social, and Cultural Rights to human security makes these rights something more than provisions of a specialized treaty regime. Rather, one might see these rights as a part of what the report of the Study Group of the International Law Commission refers to as the "environment" of the international legal order. This presupposes that there is a minimum substantive normativity inherent in the international legal order—a floor, grounding the aspirations and efforts of the international legal system. The notion of human security reflects this minimum substantive universal normativity.[60]

What would it mean to conceptualize a measure of human security in rights terms? One might begin with a right to self-preservation, the fundamental right or concern in the tradition of modern political theory beginning with Hobbes. In the first instance, one could consider the survival or preservation of humanity at the level of the body—that is, the level of physical existence. Here, one can see that over time, there has emerged a cluster of human security norms deriving from practices regarding bodily integrity, and functioning as the basis for a shared minimum.

Michael Ignatieff and Martha Nussbaum have postulated that the crux is tangible harm, such as pain inflicted on the body. While Ignatieff asserts that a minimum is that which humans have in common, for Nussbaum, such shared suffering offers a basis to go further, primarily through the notion of shared human vulnerabilities.[61] Yet suffering as a basis for common values may—at once—prove too much and too little: Suffering may be too general to constitute the basis for a shared humanity or humanism, as suffering is experienced by animals, as well. In this instance, a suffering- or harm-based regime may well transcend a minimum commitment to human preservation. But also one can see that such a regime may also offer too little, in terms of the potential of suffering to lay the basis for the pursuit of universalistic values underlying evolving global justice. In the conclusion I take up this question of whether such a regime can be a source for more, and in any event, whether its implementation amounts to a system of global justice.

Over history, the humanity norm has been defined in rights terms, in response to certain practices that violated the human body and its integrity. Consider, for examples, the prohibition on torture, norms with respect to humiliation, and the open-ended conception of "inhuman and degrading" treatment.[62] Yet the very notion of degradation suggests that this norm is about more than the body; it also encompasses a certain conception of humanity as related to dignity.[63] A human-threat-based approach (where the measure of threat is in human terms or along human measure) implies an alternative protective response that is relevant to our understanding today of global justice.

This understanding goes back to Hobbes and to the very beginnings of modern political philosophy; indeed, this notion of the significance of a protection against mortal threats goes to the very heart of the social contract. Accordingly, this understanding points the way to how the evolution of the global-justice debate into the human security concept reflects a reconceptualization of politics and political legitimacy, as in the work of Giorgio Agamben.[64] To some degree, this overlaps with the way Sen frames the issue today. For example, we can see the relevance of the way Sen thinks about rights—as relating to protection, or ensuring certain freedoms relating to threshold conditions.

THE PRIORITY PRINCIPLE AND THE DUTY TO ASSIST IN HUMANITARIAN CRISIS

The coherence of a theory of human security as global justice depends on its capacity to prioritize human impacts—a notion of the most vulnerable, and the most affected—that results in a case for intervention, or at least deployment of resources, when effects attain a certain gravity or intensity, gauged in terms of the human or humanitarian sensibility. This brings together the notion of an absolute minimum threshold of human need, with an appreciation of the particular vulnerability of certain peoples or classes of persons. Generally, civilians—and among them women and children—are identified as being the most vulnerable or the most harshly impacted, in the normatively relevant sense. Often, one can also see that there are compounded vulnerabilities. For instance, the vulnerabilities of historically persecuted groups—groups that have faced assaults on the basis of race, ethnicity, or religion and that find themselves exposed as threatened minorities—may be combined, in some cases, with the vulnerabilities of women, children, and/or the elderly. Indeed, where these dimensions recombine, they create *extreme* vulnerabilities, as can be recognized in the plight in particular of certain women in the Balkans, among the Roma in Europe, or children in Uganda or in Sudan.[65]

The focus on impacts just described gives rise to a situational or crisis-centered orientation of humanity-law-based global justice. Here, the measure of the right to assistance and the duty to give such assistance does not derive from history as its compass, and is not concerned with judging structures or aggregate outcomes; therefore, it operates in contrast to the critique of inequality that arises from exploitation, colonialism, and so forth. Rather than focusing on historical structures polarizing the world into perpetrator societies and victims (North v. South, exploiters v. exploited, rich v. poor, etc.), this view of humanity law introduces a measure that functions in terms of new situation-based responses to immediate, specific, and multiple threats and crises.

The measure is aimed at mobilizing diverse agents—whether in the vindication of their rights or the performance of their responsibilities. The duty to give assistance to meet the needs of human security is triggered in distinctive situations, and the duties relating to global justice on human security terms are layered, with the duty to assist triggered on a "complementary" basis. As in my earlier discussion of humanity law and the related protection of humanity rights, complementarity here operates to pose a layered set of duties: In the first instance, it is the duty of the state to deliver human security, with this duty understood in terms of state responsibility, assuming that there is a functioning state to shoulder the duty. Where the state is either unable or unwilling to discharge its responsibilities, these duties can, in turn, be shifted to others, based on their capacity or functionality on the ground, in a particular situation. Indeed, we have seen this in other contexts (discussed in chapter 5) with groups such as Hamas or Hezbollah. But the principles operate more generally with respect to the issues of aid I have raised in this chapter.

Consider the challenge posed to states by transnational humanitarian aid organizations that are organized around these principles. It is one of the implications of humanity law that there is a responsibility attaching to relevant nonstate actors—not just to states themselves. Wherever these responsibilities are not met, the duties then shift to others, on an operational basis. Hence, there may be duties undertaken by either other private actors, or the international community, to assist and aid. Even where other actors (whether public or private) are involved in fulfilling these duties, there is still a reciprocal duty, which falls on the state, to accept the aid on behalf of its people(s). And, as we have seen, the management of these duties regarding global justice has implications for ongoing legitimacy in today's global politics.

In December 2001, in a report titled "The Responsibility to Protect," the Gareth Evans–Mohamed Sahnoun Commission argued that the controversy over using force for humanitarian purposes stemmed from a "critical gap" between the unavoidable reality of mass human suffering and the existing rules and mechanisms for managing world order. To fill this gap, the commission identified an emerging international obligation—the "responsibility to protect"—which requires states to intervene in the affairs of other states to avert or stop humanitarian crises. According to the commission, sovereignty means that "the state authorities are responsible for the functions of protecting the safety and lives of citizens and promotion of their welfare"; that "the national political authorities are responsible to the citizens internally and to the international community through the UN"; and that "the agents of state are responsible for their actions; that is to say they are accountable for their acts of commission and omission."

The commission's boldest contribution, however, was to argue that the responsibility to protect binds both the individual states with respect to their own population and the international community as a whole. The individual state has the primary responsibility to protect the individuals within its jurisdiction, but where a state fails to do so, other responsibilities to protect ensure first falling on the international community acting through the United Nations, even if enforcing it requires infringing on state sovereignty. Thus, "where a population is suffering serious harm, as a result of internal war, insurgency, repression or state failure, and the state in question is unwilling or unable to halt or avert it, the principle of nonintervention yields to the international responsibility to protect."

This has been illustrated, of late, with the globalizing threats to, and the related demand for, human security. This important issue has been raised in Burma, Zimbabwe, and China. In Burma, the junta resisted aid both from the country's own monks and outside humanitarian actors.[66] Given the ambit of security implied within humanity law, this would suggest the possibility of the Security Council's authorizing the delivery of aid extend to forcible means. One could argue that this is in accord with the very purpose of the United Nations, and therefore is not a violation of territorial integrity or of political independence, insofar as it is intended to deliver human security to the population within, and not to change boundaries and so on. Consider, here, China's response to earthquake disaster in exhorting for international aid on behalf of its people.[67] Indeed, similar sorts of arguments have been made regarding advocacy for expanded humanitarian intervention of a political and military nature, aimed more and more at peoples and populations, rather than proceeding along a state-centric basis (discussed in chapter 5 in relation to RtoP). This was illustrated recently in the military response to the crisis in Libya.

Of course, a legitimate limiting principle to humanitarian intervention or RtoP along these lines would be to refrain from granting such aid wherever such aid was itself threatening to humanity rights. This kind of situation might occur either because of the form of the provision—for instance, the actions of personnel (e.g., as in rights-abusing humanitarian workers)—or the nature of the food or medicine at issue, for example in Zambia, or in Latin America, with the Nestlé infant formula scandals. This comprehensive view of the means and ends of humanitarian aid is tied up with humanity law logic. (Indeed, as we have seen, it is raised by all sides of the sanctions regime.)

The present overuse of the term "global justice," as discussed at the outset of this chapter, reflects the point that to some extent, the concept has come to be synonymous with accountability. In other words, the phrase "global justice" has come to include transnational sanctions for bad leadership, reflecting an increasing awareness of the link between issues of social and economic disparities and issues of bad government. (Indeed, this linkage was foreshadowed years ago by Rawls in his view of the minimum regimes that would be sufficient in terms of the necessary political foundations.) In recent attempts to wrestle with the problem of global justice, there have commonly been appeals to criminal justice, such as with the ICC, which is aimed at ensuring a global modicum of the rule of law.[68]

But we so far lack a framework for balancing humanity rights, and this problem reflects a basic difficulty of stating economic needs in "rights" terms—and vice versa.[69] However, if we read the idea of rights through Sen's notion of the pluralism of justice claims, this may pose less of a problem than it seems at first—for after all, almost all rights instruments (domestic, regional, or international) entail some kinds of balancing structures already, via limitations clauses, margins of appreciation, and so on. Here, what one needs is a hermeneutics that is able to reconcile an approach that involves balancing with the intuition that there should also be a universalizable minimum.

The moral intuition of the absolute threshold only really becomes operative where, paradoxically, it turns out that balancing is also required. This minimum is a threshold of human security—not of food, or of health, or of any one element that is absolutized—and we see this in the difficult triage in situations like that of the Haiti earthquake. Indeed, the very concept of human security can illustrate, in a normatively meaningful way, why we can imagine balancing as being required even when we are dealing with what appear to be imperatives to meet the most basic needs of the physical person.

The "right to life" is often deemed to have the status of *jus cogens*— that is, to be a nonderogable value that (as discussed in chapters 3 and 5) has become increasingly protectable, even in conflict situations. Yet this status of the right to life as nonderogable does not answer the question of the responsibility, whether of state or nonstate actors, for respecting, promoting, or fulfilling that right. Moreover, related concepts of privacy, dignity, and so forth will necessarily affect the nature of the responsibility that is imposed or shouldered here. Addressing the challenge of understanding the meaning and interdependency of rights, the UN human rights institutions have developed a complex approach to understanding the responsibility for enforcing and honoring social and economic rights.[70]

THE RISE OF HUMAN SECURITY DISCOURSE: A BASIS FOR A NEW LEGITIMACY BEYOND THE STATE

What is the significance of turning to legal language—and, in particular, to the language of what is defined here as humanity law? First, the turn to international humanitarian law, and to its enforcement via international criminal discourse, adds a level of moral seriousness that does not risk collapsing into mere moral emotion—that is, pious wishes or an indignation at "injustice." Furthermore, the language of humanitarian law is a language of accountability; it offers the promise of holding states to account if and when they depart from the basic protection of their peoples.

On the other hand, another advantage of this discourse is that—unlike the discourses of religion or morality—it is not unbounded. In addition, the humanity law discourse provides a route to non-state-actor responsibility—which is of great importance, given the manner in which nonstate actors may be situated where they have control and the capacity, their actions may affect the fulfillment of human security. Finally, the broader humanity rights language and, in particular, the turn to law beyond interstate law, in the way of chartered commitments, may well offer a way and a space for diverse actors to express a seriousness about their commitments in this area.

A human-centered approach to security connects the concern with the state and its development with the claims and interests of other actors and institutions. This process was already under way, given the pressure on the state in globalization, but it is also under way—and even more so—in the contexts discussed here, of the conditions of global injustice that are often associated with weak and failed states. Here, one can see a form of alternative legitimation that is obtainable through the adherence to, and the protection of, humanity rights.

One might see this development as having roots that go back to early liberalism—that is, most obviously, to Hobbes, but also other pivotal philosophers such as Montesquieu, who wrote that "liberty is the opinion each citizen has of their own security," and of Locke, or of Spinoza, who opined that "the virtue of the State is security."[71] Interestingly, these formulations all focus on the capacity of the state to protect as central to its legitimacy—rather than on democracy, or the state, as an expression of collective will. This understanding of the state, given the existing changes associated with globalization, points to the possibility of a global perspective—since, of course, the threats or vulnerabilities to which "citizens" or "civilians" are exposed are, in many cases, not limited by national boundaries. In this sense, what emerges is that the liberal idea of the human has a global telos.

This notion—which possibly legitimates contemporary institutionalization—may go some way toward supporting a notion of global society.

A NEW GLOBAL AGENDA?

The ascendant humanity-centered norms would, at the very least, seem to
pose the requirement of a global minimum of protection, as discussed
above. Yet the norms are also extraordinarily capacious in their potential
for the protection of persons, peoples, and the state. The new humanism
will undoubtedly have implications for reorienting our perspective on core
debates in human rights over the last decades, such as the debate over the
meaning of universality.

What humanity law comprehends normatively, at this point, are commitments to the basic protection of the survival of humanity—at the
individual and group levels, as well as on a universal basis. The humanity
law framework reflects these two understandings: Indeed, this is how
humanity law reconciles some of the basic tensions posed by the international order (or disorder) that exists today: It pursues a range of normative
aims, traditionally reflected in different international legal regimes—such
as *jus ad bellum, jus in bello,* human rights, and even the regimes related to
sustainable development, trade, and finance—and thus it becomes instilled
in the guiding concept of "human security."

If the law of humanity is, first and foremost, about human survival,
the question that is begged, of course, is what survival means here.
Arguably, survival of the person, of the human, *as such,* means one's being
embodied in a corporeal form, but also being in and of a people (as taken
up in chapter 8). Therefore, even the protection of a threshold humanity
norm to the preservation of peoples opens a space to bring in an array of
political and social, and even cultural rights (as was taken up in the last
chapter). The language of security is very broad-ranging; consider, for
example, the United Nations Human Security Unit and its working definitions,[72] which comprehend many forms of security—economic, environmental, political, and so on—so that one might say that security is
broad-ranging in some respects (that is, in cutting cross-sector) but not in
others. Indeed, the word "security" suggests an absolute, or a minimalist,
requirement, which would at least point to a threshold. However, this is
not necessarily the same; and in any event, ought to be distinguished from
a moral minimum. Indeed, the idea that is raised here is that there may
well be a notion of a *vital core* defensible concept of a threshold, as discussed above.[73]

Historically, the international-humanitarian-law regime had long been conceptualized—and its distinctive provenance had long been organized—around the notion of distinction; that is, in terms of a narrow sphere of protected persons. Now, with the humanity law framework, there is a convergence with, and an injection of, a universalizing human rights discourse and framework.

A thin view might zero in on abject poverty and famine and epidemics as human disasters. Lowering our expectations may be a downside to an approach based on "threshold poverty"—for instance, as is described by Gary King and Christopher Murray, or what one might conceive of as a safety-net approach. Yet this downside is a consequence of trying to conceptualize globally, for "human security is a global issue and a global challenge."[74] Moreover, "rights to food" or medicine[75]—have a pedigree in international humanitarian law, one of the strands informing the humanity law framework. This reminds us that these rights may entail not only some notion of a universal minimum but more far-reaching entitlements specific to the situations. In other words, within the humanity law framework, there is room for both a thin universalist notion of global justice as a minimum threshold of human security as well as a thicker, more contextualized conception of duties beyond borders.

CHAPTER 7

⟡

Humanity Law and the Future of International Law

Debating Sovereignty and Cosmopolitanism

S o far this book has considered the emergence of the humanity law framework in the context of the evolving challenges posed for the regulation of
conflict after the Second World War and especially and above all in the
post-Cold War and post-9/11 eras; the focus has been on the intersecting trajec-
tories of international humanitarian law, the law on the justification of the use
of force (ius ad bellum) and international human rights law, as they engage with
these challenges. However, simultaneous to and interconnected with the rise of
humanity law have been debates about the meaning and future of international
law as such. Many of the features of humanity law—its purporting to apply
beyond the state, its empowerment of nonstate actors even against their own
sovereigns, and its imposition of limits as well as responsibilities on states that
do not appear to be derived, at least not with uncontroversial clarity, from formal
acts of state consent or agreement—have inspired the hopes of some that a
global constitutional or cosmopolitan order is in the making and the fears and
enmity of others, who have commitments to ideals of sovereignty and state-
centric conceptions of democratic or republican legitimacy. This chapter
addresses the interaction of the emergence of humanity law with the debates
over international law between those with opposing cosmopolitan and republican commitments. Humanity law's ascendancy and diffusion has not occurred
through a counter-hegemonic challenge to sovereignty from above, from a
pretended higher or supreme normative order that seeks to impose itself over
and above the state, but rather in large measure through interpretation[1] or

reinterpretation of legal norms by a large range of actors including domestic actors, political and judicial. One of the best illustrations of how humanity law is propagated through interpretation and reinterpretation rather than imposition from above is its use in domestic litigation.[2] The reading of the law of nations by the United States courts in Alien Tort Claims Act cases is an example explored in depth below-one that clearly confounds the idea of a sharp or tragic conflict between the American "republican" constitutional tradition and the deep penetration of international legal normativity. This obviously puts in question the critique of international law by American "sovereigntist" conservatives but it also undermines notions that European conceptions of constitutionalism are inherently more hospitable to international legal order, especially those inspired not by reciprocity of state obligation but a conception of normative legal community at the level of the human.

For cosmopolitans, and increasingly for liberal constitutionalists, the state, is neither the beginning or the end—a position that is held to varying degrees by Jurgen Habermas, David Held, and Mary Kaldor.[3] The cosmopolitans' faith in universal law assumes, or depends on, the truth of the normative substance of that law. The asserted universalism of human rights law is clearly one inspiration for this faith, and underpins the many constitutional analogies that are used to articulate the normative primacy of the new international law. The drive to normalize and generalize the international criminal responsibility of individuals reflects a faith in international law's capacity to embody tenets of foundational social morality. At the same time, we witness articulations of a utopian vision of the law as ensuring that politics is answerable to universal morality. For example, Jurgen Habermas has called for "the normative taming of political power through law."[4] Moreover, David Held interprets the changes in international law as a sign of the entrenchment of "liberal international sovereignty."[5]

But what sort of universalism are we dealing with? As the legal skeptics (or realists) remind us, the cosmopolitan perspective is itself situated in a particular context. Today, this context is Europe, more often than not. Indeed, a European international-law-based vision is often rightly or wrongly juxtaposed to an image of American exceptionalism.[6] So it is that we can see the ways the humanity law debates lie at the core of the current reorganization of the international sphere, contributing the parameters for a new version of global bipolarity. Thus, as Jurgen Habermas has written in *The Divided West*, "the belief and adherence to law and particularly transnational law is depicted as the province of the new Europe, of the new sovereignty."[7] Others, such as Philippe Sands, have argued that the stature and centrality of law is constitutive of a transatlantic divide.[8] Perhaps more important, whether or not the United States employs the same vocabulary that Europe does when it comes to international law issues, these pivotal debates serve to frame both

U.S.-Europe relations and other characterizations of outlaw, or rogue, states.

For cosmopolitans, the proliferation of law is somehow isomorphic to, and representative of, underlying political and social realities—as well as constituting a vindication of the truth of cosmopolitan law's normative substance. Political progress is inferred from the expansion, thickening, and deepening of law. The advent of what are, to date, largely judicially enforced norms is heralded as a sign of the emerging possibility of universal citizenship. However, this claim is perhaps ironic, since the ascendancy of global judicial power has occurred in the absence of political consensus, and even arguably in order to fill the gap created by that absence. This difficulty is finessed or obscured by the recourse to constitutional language. Again, Habermas states: "Following two world wars, the constitutionalization of international law has evolved along the lines prefigured by Kant toward cosmopolitan law and has assumed institutional form in international constitutions, organizations and proceedings." [9]

For Habermas, "cosmopolitan law" is the great hope, offering legitimate governance at the level of the world community. The move toward an ethical-and-human-rights-law discourse is construed as somehow opposite, and superior, to the classic or traditional language of state interest. [10] Thus, Habermas describes "the new dispute . . . over whether law remains an appropriate medium for realizing the declared goals of achieving peace and international security and promoting democracy and human rights throughout the world." [11] Indeed, for some, this is humanity law's main virtue: In a global system, it offers standards that can be used to judge and delimit the state from above (e.g., as in the case of Thomas Pogge). This approach represents one side of the polarized debate over the potential of the law.

The cosmopolitan perspective effectively captures the spirit that animates the proliferation of law. Yet because cosmopolitanism tends to essentialize this spirit as a timeless moral truth, it somehow elides the range of historically contingent factors that *explain* the law's normative direction in the present era. More problematic still is the cosmopolitan position's dependence on the capacity of the law to function effectively as an authoritative ordering of individual rights and duties. This dependence is implied in the cosmopolitan requirement of a universal ground of legitimacy, one that does not depend on political agreement or on compromise between diverse multivariate political and moral claims.

Here, the cosmopolitan perspective cannot but fail to do justice to the complexity of the current situation, which throws up independent and conflicting individual—and group—humanity rights claims, entangled with the state and statehood. The advent of new processes and regimes allows not only for a greater multilateralism but also for a multilateralism marked by the expansion in the representation of diverse state—and nonstate—interests in international affairs, wherever there is conflict over how to reconcile the protection of preservation rights of persons and peoples with other state interests. One thinks of the Balkans, of Libya, and of the dilemmas surrounding the human rights costs of humanitarian intervention.

"Law skeptics"—including realist scholars of international relations—see the post–Cold War moment in terms of a reassessment and realignment of state interests and interstate power relations. For those thinkers who would see law in narrow, state-centric terms, the developments in legalism I discuss here have little or no material effect, because for these thinkers, there would remain only one measure of the basis for legality. It is a measure that is largely postulated in state-centric terms—namely, in terms of the possibility of compelling states' compliance with rules to which states have consented. The analogy is clearly to the positivist account of domestic law, which gives primacy to the efficacy of command as a characteristic of legal order; international law, in this view, is meaningful only to the extent to which it is a set of effective commands to states.[12]

Notwithstanding the changes that have been explored here, for realists, state power remains the fundamental category explaining behavior in the international realm. To realists, the state continues to be the main actor in international relations, and therefore realists question the degree to which there may be significant substantive transformation in the relation that international law bears to the state-citizen relationship (for example, changes relating to the judicialization of the state) or any other citizen-collective relationship.[13]

For much of the last decade, there has been a position, associated with the Bush administration, that is closely aligned with realism or law skepticism; this position is sometimes known as "neo-sovereigntism."[14] Neo-sovereigntists view popular sovereignty as the central or exclusive source of legal legitimacy; translated to the international level, this position is unrelentingly state-centric, since for those who adhere to this school of thought, it is only within states that republican popular sovereignty can be exercised. Thus, to them, state's consent to international legal rules becomes the essential proxy or vehicle for the democratic legitimization of international legal rules. This view of law is reductive and does not recognize the receptivity even of the old common law to customary international law, as did the United States Supreme Court in *Paquete Habana*; it is an arcane originalism that is simply not adequate to the current phenomena we are witnessing around the globe. In its American incarnation, this school of thought espouses a distinctive republican view as to what it is that gives law legitimacy.

Oddly, considering that this school of thought comes close to denying any existence for international law independent from the will of states, neo-sovereigntism has gained support not just among realist theorists of international politics, such as Stephen Krasner, but also among a group of legal scholars, who use it selectively. This group seeks primarily to invoke the neo-sovereigntist view to oppose the reception of international law into domestic law, particularly through adjudication.[15] Therefore, what is at stake here goes beyond ostensible U.S.-European differences, which often seem to be a matter of transient perceptions of political power relations, or quarrels between intellectuals and ideologues; it also has implications for a more pressing debate, regarding the current sources of legitimacy and the law, and the nature of expectations regarding the normative aims of the law.

The realist/cosmopolitan positivism/constructivist debate bears a resemblance to the postwar law/morals debate described earlier. One position embraces law, while the other reflects a morality-tinged political power. In Habermas's words, "the new dispute...is over whether law remains an appropriate medium for realizing the declared goals of achieving peace and international security and promoting democracy and human rights throughout the world."[16] Yet, evidently, this representation is also flawed, as the new role of law in global politics transcends any one particular debate and any one geographical space.

THE INTERPRETIVE TURN

Let us reconsider the debates regarding the meaning of global legalism in light of the paradigm shift just discussed and the salient elements of the humanity law framework. These elements can best be understood to enable an interpretive space and normative direction that may help to defuse several areas of conflict.

Interpretation responds to the proliferation and fragmentation of legal orders, which renders elusive the search for an original context-less "intended" meaning to the "law." Hence, one might say that we are already and always in the mode of interpretation. Judicial interpretation is well suited to making sense of diverse normative sources, under conditions of political conflict and moral disagreement. Courts are inherently in dialogue with other courts and institutions that also play interpretive roles, and their decisions in individual cases can give meaning to law without purporting to give "closure" to normative controversies in politics and morals.[17]

Thinking of humanity law in hermeneutic terms fits well with current legal and political conditions. Given the complexity of globalization (including legal globalization), the messy relationship of these forces to all levels of governance, and the related proliferation and fragmentation of legal regimes that are decentralized (i.e., not ordered hierarchically), the exercise of adjudication or dispute settlement simply cannot be framed in terms of the application of a rule that is based on the divination of the common will of the states that consented to that rule. Rather, the meaning of these norms is significantly deterred by interpretive practices ex post their "original" articulation in positive legal instruments. Or such norms may pose a conflict between regimes, spurring the demand for "confirmatory principles."[18] Particularly since humanity law involves diverse interests and norms, its interpretation occurs in the context of normative pluralism. In the presence of different cultures and traditions, humanity-law-based interpretation offers the possibility of a ground of shared meaning. Humanity law, as an interpretative lens, navigates the narrow strait between the Scylla of difference and the Charybdis of universalism. But since practice arises in real cases of individual rights, steering this path is not about defining a static ideal; rather, it concerns the continuing evolution of a norm that will help to guide and manage conflict.

Moreover, the inquiry is delimited by interpretation as *praxis*—and especially by adjudication, where the parameters of state-citizen, citizen-society, and citizen-citizen relations are regularly contested. The subjects of the law are always linked up to the normative legal regime, with the potential for tension and the demand for the reconciliation of a multiplicity of values to elucidate what one might conceive as a guiding principle of interpretation.

What is at stake is the perception of the meaning, force, and authority of international law today, and the question is how to respond to the demand for a guiding "rule of recognition"—a principle that sets the sources and bases for law's authority and significance and provides some means of managing or resolving normative conflict.[19] This principle must go to the weight of the relevant and diverse legal norms, and is related to the question of whether there is an institution or actor possessing ultimate interpretive authority over the norms in question. Finally, this principle must determine what concerns or values might legitimately guide the decisionmaking that informs the global rule of law.

FROM THE LAW OF NATIONS TO THE COVENANTS BETWEEN STATES—AND BACK AGAIN?

Traditionally, with the very limited exception of *jus cogens*, the set of norms that are thought to be universally valid and hence peremptory, state consent has been understood to be the preeminent source of legitimacy in international law. The theory was that the sovereign could only be constrained by its own will. The object of international law—its core values and interests in the interstate system—had traditionally been seen in this light. Consider, for example, the jurisdiction of the ICJ: Setting to one side the case of advisory jurisdiction that is based on referral of questions by the

UN General Assembly, the ICJ's jurisdiction *over a state* depended on the consent of the state in question (which could take any of several forms).

Humanity law implies a different ordering of the sources of legitimacy. One fundamental ground of legitimacy—derived from a human-centered, not state-centered, perspective—is the expectation of a minimum threshold of decent behavior below which conduct becomes inhuman. This is a notion that actually, in some ways, is anticipated in Grotius. It is informed in part by natural law or justice (a concept of universal morality); in part by practices that are common to the various peoples or nations (jus gentium); and in part by shared intuition or feeling of what is humane. (This last dimension was developed further later on by Rousseau, with his emphasis on compassion, the source of modern humanitarianism.) The sense of a minimum "human" threshold—a notion that is derived from such diverse sources—underpins, explicitly or implicitly, many of the particular constraints on state conduct (and not only on state conduct) in humanitarian and human rights law.

The shift in what constitutes the rule of law normatively connects up to a shift in what we count as legitimate and authoritative sources of law. Changes in legal personality, subjectivization, and judicialization go together here not only with related understandings of responsibility and accountability but also with related shifts in the subjects and sources of lawmaking. Nonstate actors are acquiring new rights and duties with the interlacing of the three doctrinal sources of the humanity law framework. With the addition of new personality and related regulation as a result of the amalgamation of the three sources of the humanity law framework (the law of armed conflict, the law of human rights, and of international criminal responsibility), there is added agency, subjectivity, and responsibility under multiple regimes. This, in turn, is making for a layered approach to rights and duties in a globalizing sphere. Where persons and peoples have humanity rights, one can see that there is an attendant opportunity to shape the law to which they are subject, and to shape the relevant values that are at issue. Of course, insofar as there is already a weakening of state-centric bases for legitimacy, this poses less of a challenge to the current system. This is often seen wherever individuals are helping to shape international law beyond strict expressions of state consent.

There is greater awareness about changes in the meaning of relevant practice informing current international law. The locus classicus for the sources of international law, Article 38 of the ICJ Statute, refers to "international custom" as evidence that a general practice is accepted as law.[20] This means, in turn, that there are two dimensions to the proof of the existence of a customary rule: First, there is the establishment of the "generality" of the practice, and second, there is the practice's acceptance as "law"—*opinio* juris.[21] The traditional understanding of *opinio juris* entails evidence that states see themselves as bound, whereas the more contemporary approach to custom now tends to privilege *opinio juris* over the generality of practice itself. Indeed, some jurists, such as Theodor Meron, have observed that the recognition of *opinio juris* may no longer depend entirely on the actual intentions of state actors, but rather up to the judiciary among others.[22]

As establishing state consent becomes less important in controversies proving customary law, one can see that the basis for legitimacy accordingly has shifted to some notion of a shared humanity-based normativity. That notion is at least somewhat more expansive than the notion that underpins *jus cogens*—that is, the set of norms from which there is no derogation. Notable in this respect are recent opinions in the ICJ on the legality of the use of force— for example, in *Oil Platforms*, *Nuclear Weapons*, and *Yugoslavia v. Belgium*. As discussed in chapter 3, these opinions draw from humanity protection: For example: "The right to live, physical integrity, are these not norms with the status of ius cogens?"[23] As Judge Simma explained, "a great many rules of humanitarian law applicable in armed conflict are ... fundamental to the respect of the human person and 'elementary considerations of humanity.'"[24] Thus, in one way or another, these norms appear to be legitimated beyond state consent. Such a view of legitimacy facilitates the application of norms to situations that represent changes in the nature of international order that were not contemplated when the norms were codified through treaty law. One such change, for instance, would be the application of the Geneva Conventions to terrorism and to noninterstate conflicts.

The debates concerning the reality and status of international law have been sharpest in the United States. The United States' peculiar system of separation of powers and federalism—as well as its layered historical and modern experiences of both colonization and empire, involving often-contested projections of extraterritorial law[25]—have made it at once more sensitive to issues of sovereignty and consent as well as keenly aware of the potential for legal conflict and pluralism. As will be seen, there are a number of instances of judicialization where one can witness decisionmakers wrestling with the issues of the paradigm shift and the reconstitution of the rule of law.

A decade or so ago, legal scholars Jack Goldsmith and Curtis Bradley began to question the aegis, pedigree, and relevance of international law. This attack began with a challenge to the expanded role that human rights advocates, sympathetic pundits, and academics had attributed to custom in international law. This challenge Goldsmith and Bradley labeled, rather oddly, the "modern position." The challenge to international law, while first more particularly aimed at the role of custom, was dramatically extended in a subsequent book by Goldsmith and Eric Posner, *The Limits of International Law*.[26] The crux of the book's argument is that the contemporary developments that manifest themselves as legalization and judicialization distort international law's traditional sources and therefore, along the way, result in the loss of international law's essential rationale and legitimacy. International law is seen, at its core, as legitimate only when it is facilitating mutually self-interested cooperation between states. Traditional rules are interpreted in this light and, therefore, appear as little more than crude default rules that would usually be improved through states' bargaining between and among themselves to reach an agreement. State consent undermines the notion of the force of custom—a force grounded in and legitimated not by democratic process per se but by state practice over time, as interpreted by international tribunals. Goldsmith, Bradley, and Posner's approach at once draws from twentieth-century positivism and a nationalist republicanism ostensibly supported by an originalist view of the constitution.

These scholars do acknowledge the changes in international law and, in particular, in its sources[27]—beginning with the postwar genesis of the human rights revolution, and picking up steam with the end of the Cold War and the transition into the last two decades of the twentieth century. Yet these scholars portray the legal development with respect to the understanding of customary law as a perverse distortion, largely attributable to a handful of academics who were making international pronouncements, the "modern CIL [customary international law] of human rights."[28]

On the opposite side of the debate are human rights scholars and advocates for customary law—the objects of critique by the likes of Goldsmith—who insist on the continuity of the tradition that recognizes and honors the long-standing receptivity of the common law to custom.[29] Yet insofar as this tack (within the human rights movement) is often framed in a timeless way, it may lead to a different kind of denial of present-day complexities. Thus, these opposite positions appear, at some level, to be existentially important, as each independently frames the relevant question at stake as a matter of a core statement—and one might say that these core statements serve as alternative stances regarding the bases for legitimacy in the international realm today.

The heart of the problem is the continued adherence to state consent as the exclusive indispensable source of legitimacy, even when it comes to legal developments in the area of human rights. In the extreme state-centric approach, the authority of international law—whether via customary international law or via treaty—continues to depend on ex ante agreement among states.[30] The legitimizing impact is weaker where the state is nondemocratic, or where executive and expert elites hegemonize the lawmaking process on behalf of the "state," but still, state consent does stand (if often in an attenuated or distorted way) for the principle of democratic self-determination. The persistence and indeed renewal of customary law today reflects in part the increased significance for legitimacy of the normative substance of the law relative to formal acts of state consent; this aspect of humanity law, as has been explained elsewhere in this book, does not indicate a full revival of natural law conceptions of international obligation so much as the effectiveness in practice of multiple and diverse claims based upon appeals to the human in a variety of fora. Thus, increasingly, courts and tribunals have been prepared to "declare" the existence of a customary rule, in order to ensure the law's adequacy to human protection, without paying particular attention to state practice or even the traditional kinds of evidence for opinio juris (foreign office statements, etc). In theory, states can always override custom through subsequent conventions (unless it has become ius cogens). But the urgency of felt demands for adequate regulation, particularly of the newer or transformed types of violent conflict discussed in this book, is at odds with the rather cumbersome processes of collective will formation that underly multilateral lawmaking processes. Ultimately, though, this would be not enough to provide legitimacy, unless the underlying norms of humanity law were themselves not increasingly seen as compelling.

Indeed, the tribunals (and the law they generate) are now wrestling with the problem of the changing legitimacy of law, wherever it may depart from sources other than explicit ex ante state consent—such as custom, and, relatedly, the "principles of law recognized by civilized nations."[31] This dynamic can be seen, in particular, wherever courts have been called on to apply the "law of humanity." I have already alluded to such controversies in prior chapters, which have discussed how to best understand some of the changes in international legality as they appear both procedurally (such as in struggles over personality or jurisdiction) or substantively, includes private actions for violations of the "law of nations"; adjudications of international humanitarian law in a variety of settings beyond traditional state consent; issues arising from the global antiterror campaigns; and instances of the adjudication of individual rights in domestic constitutional law that seek to draw on and reconcile foreign and domestic norms, particularly as concerns humanity-related rights.

Humanity law is neither utopian nor aspirational in content; rather, it is grounded in common practices that imply at least a minimal common, normative ground. Ultimately, the appeal is to a threshold norm of decency, one that is arguably inseparable from the idea of the rule of law itself, as in the writing of David Dyzenhaus and Lon Fuller.[32]

AN EVOLVING LAW OF NATIONS?

Since the very beginning of international law, its contours have been defined through the concept of the "law of nations"; it has thus focused on offenses that were considered to be plainly the concern of the international community, and of justice. Historically, the normative meaning of the phrase "law of nations" extends beyond voluntary state obligation. For Hugo Grotius, violations of the "law of nations" could justify a range of remedial actions, including in some instances punishment of the offending party, even if they were a foreign sovereign: the notion of redress here clearly was based on a substantive notion of justice and its required remedies as well as implying a jurisdictional conception of who had a right, under the law of nations to impose these remedies.

Recently that there has been a revival of the law of nations. This has taken place in a number of areas—in international criminal justice, as discussed earlier, but also litigation involving the law of nations under the United States Alien Torts Claims Act. The ATCA holds liable "an individual who, under actual or apparent authority, or color of law, of any foreign nation—(1) subjects an individual to torture shall, in a civil action, be liable for damages to that individual; or (2) subjects an individual to extrajudicial killing shall, in a civil action...for damages to the individual's legal representative, or to any person who may be a claimant in an action for wrongful death."[33] Indeed, the ATCA cause of action dates back to America's early origins, where jurisdiction was created to allow suits by foreign diplomats in conflicts involving the relation of foreign states vis-à-vis individuals who were brought together by harm.

The ATCA was conceived as a necessary guarantee to insure against the harm perpetrated against individual persons from leaking into interstate conflict and destabilizing the international order.[34] Centuries later, and now more than two decades ago, in the landmark case of *Filartiga v. Pena Irala*, a group of plaintiffs who were foreign nationals and Paraguayan citizens brought suit in U.S. federal court against a fellow Paraguayan for the wrongful death of their relative by torture in that country.[35] There was no conventional law on point; the plaintiffs' claim was not grounded on a specific treaty, as the Convention Against Torture and other Cruel, Inhuman or Degrading Treatment or Punishment had not yet come into existence. Thus the question for the U.S. Court of Appeals for the Second Circuit was whether, under the ATCA, the torture alleged violated the "law of nations."

The Second Circuit reasoned as follows: "Where there is no treaty, and no controlling executive or legislative act or judicial decision, resort must be had to *the customs and usages of civilized nations*; and, as evidence of these, to the works of jurists and commentators, who by years of labor, research and experience, have made themselves peculiarly well acquainted with the subjects of which they treat."[36] The court thus chose a dynamic approach to interpreting the meaning of the law of nations as deployed in the statute. The court concluded that "courts must interpret international law not as it was in 1789, but as it has evolved and exists among the nations of the world today."[37] Furthermore, to count as part of the "law of nations," the court reasoned, a particular rule must be "a settled rule of international law" by "the general assent of civilized nations."[38] After consulting various international law sources, the court held that official torture is prohibited by the law of nations. The court also held that for purposes of civil liability, "the torturer has become—like the pirate and slave trader before him—*hostis humani generis*, an enemy of all mankind. In the twentieth century, the international community has come to recognize the common danger posed by the flagrant disregard of basic human rights and particularly the right to be free of torture... . Among the rights universally proclaimed by all nations, as we have noted, is the right to be free of physical torture."[39]

A humanity law perspective offers a way to understand the law here in terms of the substantive rights at issue. Thus conceived, the ATCA's aim is to avoid conflicts with foreign nationals that could otherwise escalate into diplomatic tensions, even hostilities, between states. In *The Paquete Habana*,[40] the U.S. Supreme Court endorsed the view that "resort must be had to the customs and usages of civilized nations" as reflected in "the works of jurists and commentators" where the norm at issue (there, the norm of respecting humanitarian values against the confiscation of fishing vessels) constituted "an established rule of international law, founded on considerations of humanity."[41] The *Filartiga* Court suggested that this area of law reflects changes in how the law, as defined in Article 38 of the Statute of the ICJ, can be established or proven, especially a greater role for judicial precedent and the views of scholars in establishing what custom is.[42]

This case opened the door to tort claims by nonstate actors against other nonstate actors in relation to violations of that part of international law considered "the law of nations." Indeed, one might understand the case as involving the construction of the global community on the basis of the violation of the law of nations. Twenty years later, in *Sosa v. Alvarez-Machain*,[43] a case involving an ATCA challenge based on arbitrary arrest and detention, the Supreme Court held that these torts did not meet the test for Alien Tort Statute eligibility.[44] Nevertheless, the Court maintained that "the door is still ajar" to such litigation, even though it is "subject to vigilant doorkeeping."[45] Even among those opposed to this decision, the Court's ruling is understood to recognize the viability of judicial interpretations—or an act of "recognition"—of the "law of nations,"[46] where there is "definition" and "acceptance among civilized nations" and, one might say, relatedly, where there is other involvement by jurists and civil society in such adjudicative lawmaking.[47]

The ATCA cause of action has something in common with elements of humanity law (as discussed in previous chapters)—such as the invocation of offenses against humanity as the basis for just war; the "Martens Clause"; the Geneva Conventions, Common Article 3; references to the "inhumane"; and the criminalization of "crimes against humanity." The ATCA cause of action, which is based on the "law of nations," in implying a universally applicable normativity, risks being unbounded in the range of situations to which it applies. In the context of the ATCA, however, actual usages and practices serve an important delimiting function.

But these usages and practices are merely illustrative—they do not create a set of frozen categories that excludes the possibility of the causes of action evolving and expanding. What claims will be eligible for Alien Tort Statute litigation remains open-ended: Indeed, the Supreme Court referred to the congressional intention that the ATCA "remain intact to permit suits based on other norms that already exist or may ripen in the future into rules of customary international law."[48] Accepting that open-endedness is a constant in this area of law, the U.S. Supreme Court both recognized a cognizable cause of action for wrongs parallel to historical violations of the "law of nations" and noted that the definition of that cause of action remains open to interpretation, for the relevant claim "must be gauged against the current state of international law."[49] Federal courts thus retain the ability to "adapt ... the law of nations to private rights" by "recognizing any further international norms as judicially enforceable today."[50]

While *Filartiga* required only that Alien Tort Statute claims be based on a settled rule of international law "by the assent of civilized nations," in *Sosa*, the scope of Alien Tort Statute claims was depicted in terms of three spheres. First, there was the prevailing interstate view—"the general norms governing the behavior of national states with each other"; then, there were two spheres that one might see as reflecting the growing influence of humanity law. One was the "conduct of individuals situated outside domestic boundaries and consequently carrying an international savor."[51] The other was the set of "rules binding individuals for the benefit of other individuals [when that set of rules] overlap[s] with the norms of state relationships."[52] Invoking the cause of action's historical roots, the Court reasoned that "it was this narrow set of violations of the law of nations, admitting of a judicial remedy and, at the same time threatening serious consequences in international affairs, that was probably on minds of the men who drafted the ATS [Alien Tort Statute] with its reference to tort."[53] Offenses against ambassadors, violations of the entitlement to safe conduct, and individual actions arising out of prize captures and piracy were all, according to the Court, "uppermost in the legislative mind."[54] "Any claim based on the present-day law of nations," the Court asserted, should "rest on a norm of international character accepted by the civilized world and defined with a specificity comparable to the features of the eighteenth-century paradigms we have recognized."[55]

Before *Sosa*, the Alien Tort Statute's reach had already been construed to include summary execution, disappearance, genocide, war crimes, crimes against humanity, and instances of cruel, inhuman, or degrading treatment.[56] Post-*Sosa* cases recognize crimes against humanity as actionable, as instances of "cruel, inhuman and degrading treatment."[57] In *Doe v. Saravia*, a U.S. district court relied on sources drawn from international criminal law, from Nuremberg to the Rome Statute, to trace the prohibitory norm of "crimes against humanity," declaring that "the prohibition against crimes against humanity constitutes such a specific, universal and obligatory norm [as the ATCA envisions]."[58] Similarly, in its 2005 affirmance in *Cabello v. Fernandez-Larios*, the U.S. Court of Appeals for the Eleventh Circuit allowed a cause of action for crimes against humanity.[59] Indeed, support for the Alien Tort Statute's rendering crimes against humanity actionable appears in Justice Stephen Breyer's concurrence in *Sosa*, which argues that crimes against humanity and other international crimes could be litigated under the Alien Tort Statute on the basis of "universal jurisdiction."[60] As Breyer argued in his concurrence: "Today international law will sometimes reflect not only *substantive* agreement as to certain universally condemned behavior but also *procedural* agreement that universal jurisdiction exists to prosecute a subset of that behavior. That subset includes torture, genocide, crimes against humanity, and war crimes."[61]

Whatever the current status of the "law of nations" may be, what appears abundantly clear is the recognition of an ongoing space for an evolving normativity in this area of the law, where accountability lies at the nexus of public and private rights. In this regard, the cause of action, tacking a narrow path the U.S. Supreme Court has said, should be "definable" and universalizable.[62] Still, courts diverge on issues such as whether the prohibition on cruel, inhuman, or degrading treatment is sufficiently specific to be actionable under the Alien Tort Statute.[63] In *Doe v. Liu Qi*, the district court asserted that "it is not necessary for every aspect of what might comprise a standard . . . [to] be fully defined and universally agreed before a given action meriting the label is clearly proscribed under international law"[64] and that "conduct sufficiently egregious may be found to constitute cruel, inhuman or degrading treatment under the ATCA."[65] Accordingly, "the question under the ATCA is whether that conduct is universally condemned as cruel, inhuman, or degrading."[66] The district court further noted that "this approach is entirely consistent with *Sosa*."[67]

This jurisprudence reflects the evolving normative space that the ATCA inhabits, which can be seen as an established structural feature of humanity law. Moreover, it indicates the ways an agreement on procedure may be a ground for substantive normative legitimacy. Or rather, perhaps—as Jurgen Habermas, has argued[68]—one can see that there is a reflexive relationship of proceduralism to substantive normativity. This area defines, in an ongoing way, elements of contemporary rule of law, as it creates a space redefining the elements of the egregious sources of conflict in global order, and directs where the remedy should be granted.[69] The U.S. Congress not only has not stepped away from this reading of the law but also has extended its logic in the Torture Victim Protection Act, which provides a private cause of action for victims of torture even where other state-centric nexuses are not present—thus affording the Supreme Court's approach added democratic legitimization.[70]

The dynamic interplay of the procedural and the substantive is evident here, where the revival of this cause of action illustrates not only the growing role of persons and peoples in humanity law as potential subjects of the regime but also their role as lawmakers. Traditionally, only nation-states (and certain intergovernmental organizations) had been seen as the subjects of international law. Hence, in *Filartiga*, the court's analysis under the law of nations was aimed at the responsibility of states and its officials.[71] But the notion of this as a clear line has been challenged regularly in subsequent case law, beginning with a case involving terrorism, *Tel-Oren v. Libyan Arab Republic*. There, in a suit for redress for a terrorist attack, the U.S. Court of Appeals for the D.C. Circuit was confronted with the question as to the extent to which *Filartiga* applied to nonstate actors. Although the decision stopped short of extending liability, the concurring opinion noted the growing support for individual responsibility under the law of nations.[72]

Later, in *Kadic v. Karadzic*, a case arising out of the Balkans atrocities in which victims of the atrocities brought suit against Radovan Karadzic, the self-proclaimed leader of the Republika Srpska (the Bosnian-Serb Republic), seeking damages for "genocide, rape, forced prostitution and impregnation, torture and other cruel, inhuman, and degrading treatment, assault and battery, sex and ethnic inequality, summary execution, and wrongful death."[73] The U.S. Court of Appeals for the Second Circuit, held that genocide, as a violation of the "law of nations," was actionable and attributable to private actors, whether undertaken by persons operating under the auspices of a state or by persons operating as private individuals.[74] This ruling drew from the rise of international responsibility for individuals in international criminal law.

Finally, in *Sosa*, the U.S. Supreme Court appears to connect up the jurisdictional question of its aegis over the private actor to the direction of the substantive issue before it, and of how to interpret the cause of action under the ATCA and its reference to the "law of nations." Specifically, the Court observed that "whether a norm is sufficiently definite to support a cause of action" raises a "related consideration [of] whether international law extends the scope of liability for a violation of a given norm to the perpetrator being sued, if the defendant is a private actor, such as a corporation or individual."[75] The question as to the potential liability of corporations would be narrowed substantially in *Kiobel*.[76]

Yet, as to related individual responsibility, arising in the corporate context in *Khulumani v. Barclay,* which came before the U.S. Court of Appeals for the Second Circuit, the plaintiffs filed multiple actions against over fifty corporate defendants, alleging liability for "actively and willingly collaborating with the government of South Africa" to maintain the system of apartheid. More specifically, the plaintiffs argued for the corporations' indirect liability for claims of egregious human rights violations.[77] In *Khulumani*, a majority of the Second Circuit found such jurisdiction where the case was connected to the most serious violations of humanity law rights, with Judge Katzmann, in his concurrence, bringing to bear the precedents of the international criminal tribunals— in what clearly was an instance of the use of a humanity law framework:[78]

I conclude that the recognition of the individual responsibility of a defendant who aids and abets a violation of international law is one of those rules 'that States universally abide by, or accede to, out of a sense of legal obligation and mutual concern.' ... Recognized as part of the customary law which authorized and was applied by the war crimes trials following the Second World War, it has been frequently invoked in international law instruments as an accepted mode of liability. During the second half of the twentieth century and into this century, it has been repeatedly recognized in numerous international treaties, most notably the Rome Statute of the International Criminal Court, and in the statutes creating the International Criminal Tribunal for the Former Yugoslavia ("ICTY") and the International Criminal Tribunal for Rwanda ("ICTR"). Indeed, the United States concedes, and the defendants do not dispute, that the concept of criminal aiding and abetting liability is 'well established' in international law."[79]

In a further elaboration in *South African Apartheid Litigation v. Daimler*, the U.S. District Court for the Southern District of New York held that for a defendant to be held liable for aiding and abetting a violation of customary international law under the ATCA, "customary international law requires that an aider and abettor know that its actions will substantially assist the perpetrator in the commission of a crime or tort in violation of the law of nations."[80]

Yet a dilemma raised by the exercise of such universal jurisdiction was the extent to which U.S. courts' taking jurisdiction might raise rule-of-law implications for the foreign country's court (a possibility that had been considered to be a risk earlier on in the *Khulumani* litigation). Relatedly, the exercise of universal jurisdiction raises a similar question: To what extent does such jurisdiction send a message about the inadequacy of domestic rule of law, as a matter of the measure of the availability of rights remedies, especially where human-rights-related policy is at stake?[81] Indeed, one might say that the expansion of universal jurisdiction raises challenges similar to those raised by the "complementarity" principle in the international legal system (as discussed in chapter 4). One might conceive the problem in terms of the ramifications that flow from the prevailing state-centric system with respect to expanding the humanity rights framework.

OF STATE CONSENT AND HUMANITY RIGHTS: AN ATTEMPTED RECONCILIATION

Even in areas that may appear to be of traditional interstate concern, such as the interpretation of treaties, humanity law has significant purchase. Here, the point of departure is the prevailing canons of interpretation, as codified in Articles 31–32 of the Vienna Convention on the Law of Treaties. Article 31 has often been interpreted (most notably, in the jurisprudence of the World Trade Organization) along the lines of "plain meaning" as used by domestic courts—and this interpretive approach has been employed despite the fact that Article 31 emphasizes not only the "ordinary meaning" of the words of the treaty text that is being interpreted but also the text's purpose, object, and context, while taking an expansive view of what context encompasses. Moreover, Article 31 itself recognizes that there is a broader normative universe in which the treaty operates; accordingly, Article 31(3c) refers to other relevant rules of international law that are applicable between the parties.[82]

As Joseph Weiler has argued, the Vienna Convention on the Law of Treaties 31.1 should not be read as separating the exercise of discerning

the "ordinary meaning" of the words in a treaty from teleological interpretation; rather, "ordinary meaning" can only be discerned in light of object
and purpose.[83] The potential of teleological interpretation in the evolution
of humanity law is well established in the *Tadic* appeal previously discussed
at chapter 3. Moreover, Article 31(3c) of the Vienna Convention on the
Law of Treaties, in referring to norms "applicable between the parties" does
not *limit* the relevance of the broader universe of humanity law to the interpretation of treaties. For as Judge Simma points out in his separate opinion
in *Armed Activities in the Congo*, there is a "community interest" in humanity
law that transcends the privity of treaty obligations.

According to Judge Simma, "at least the core of the obligations deriving
from the rules of international humanitarian and human rights law are
valid *erga omnes*. . . . Reflecting back, its advisory opinion on *Legality of the
Threat or Use of Nuclear Weapons*, the ICJ stated that "a great many rules of
humanitarian law applicable in armed conflict are so fundamental to the
respect of the human person and 'elementary considerations of humanity'"
that they are "to be observed by all States whether or not they have ratified
the conventions that contain them, because they constitute intransgress-
ible principles of international customary law."[84]

Similarly, in its *Wall* advisory opinion, the ICJ affirmed that the rules of
international humanitarian law "incorporate obligations which are essentially of an *erga omnes* character"[85] As international criminal appeals judge
Theodor Meron, an international law scholar, argues it is the international
law system's broader telos that guides its interpretation beyond the immediately demarcated subjects. Judge Meron writes: "The teleological desire
to solidify the humanizing content of the humanitarian norms clearly
affects the judicial attitudes underlying the 'legislative' character of the
judicial process. Given the scarcity of actual practice, it may well be that,
in reality, tribunals have been guided, and are likely to continue to be
guided, by the degree of offensiveness of certain acts to human dignity;
the more heinous the act, the more the tribunal will assume that it violates not only a moral principle of humanity but also a positive norm of
customary law."[86]

In another forum in deciding the meaning and precedential value of ICJ
decisions adjudicating treaties in cases where individual rights in domestic
courts are at stake, the U.S. Supreme Court has said that the first step is
interpretation. It has proposed an "interpretive approach"[87]—which, as
the Court itself observes, given that the parties making the law are states,
is not simply a matter of self-execution.[88]

Dimensions of this struggle are evident in the interpretation of humanity
law in the context of the so-called global war on terror. Here, humanity law

becomes entangled in controversies concerning the separation of powers—that is, in America, the relationships among the executive, judicial, and legislative branches. These debates are often perceived as rooted in American exceptionalism, in that they involve the peculiarities of the American constitutional system. Yet at the same time there are general questions of legitimacy at stake—which go to the very recognition of legal norms, of legal authority, and the status of international juridical norms as "law." Therefore, my approach here aims to reconceive these as part of a broader problem, as being characteristic of the current fragmentation and amalgamation of humanity law, which often lies outside the context of strict domestic control, calling for guidance in the interpretation of conflict. These conflicts arguably transcend traditional interstate conflict and, therefore, require reconciliation with other areas of law, such as human rights law or constitutional law. As will be seen, here, too, humanity law can serve as interpretive guidance in decisionmaking.

The legal responses to the "global war on terror" (i.e., the counterterror campaign) (discussed in chapter 5) raise the question of the interpretation of humanity law; one example is the interpretive work that is currently done by Geneva Conventions, Common Article 3. Consider once again the decision in *Hamdan v. United States*, in which the U.S. Supreme Court sought to avoid the potential morass of textual or source-based interpretation by simply assuming that the Geneva language meant that jurisdiction existed over the terror-related conflict, and therefore holding that Geneva Common Article 3 applied. This decision made possible a first line of protection of humanity rights.[89] Indeed, the invocation of humanity law here helped to illuminate one way to avoid an essentialized view of the apparent conflict between legal orders that was before the Court, regarding whether the law of war was to apply—and, instead, to reconcile that apparent conflict via an interpretation that was in keeping with humanity law values.

Another body of interpretation that is relevant to humanity law, is the ICJ case law surrounding the application of the Vienna Convention on Consular Relations, in situations where a suspect who is a foreign national faces charges for an offense that may carry the death penalty. In the last decade, domestic and international courts have become enmeshed in issues concerning life and death—issues that are situated between the procedural and the normative; between politics and doctrine; between the international and the domestic; and between the individual and the state. From the perspective of the state, the cases appear to raise the question of what the ICJ's effects are, but they also raise a broader question: Just how is it that international law judgments regarding consular rights get enforced in U.S. courts?

In the U.S. Supreme Court case *Medellin v. Dretke*, Mexican national sentenced to death in US state court claimed that his consular rights had been denied. The Court addressed the question whether the Vienna Convention on Consular Relations gave rise to immediate duties and remedies that could be directly invoked by individuals. Put another way, the Court addressed the question whether the Convention conferred justiciable rights.[90] Yet another issue raised was the relationship of ICJ interpretation to domestic court interpretation of the Vienna Convention on Consular Relations. Here, one might conceive of the challenge as that of horizontal dialogue between domestic and international courts and tribunals, wherever humanity-based normativity is at stake.[91] This could be understood against the context of the International Law Commission's Articles on State Responsibility, which are predicated on state responsibility being engaged by actions and omissions regardless of the "branch" of government at issue, and including the judicial organs.

In the cases under discussion, a majority of the U.S. Supreme Court asserts that the reliance on other judicial interpretations is clearly required—particularly, wherever humanity rights (that is, the norms concerning the right to life and related preservation rights for persons and peoples) are at stake. As the majority in *Sosa* declared, in asserting that it retained the authority to interpret evolving violations of the law of nations, "it would take some explaining to say now that federal courts must avert their gaze entirely from any international norm intended to protect individuals."[92]

As Justice Ruth Bader Ginsburg observed, the U.S. Supreme Court had always enforced those ICJ judgments relating to individual rights.[93] (This raises the question whether the enforcement or the interpretation of international law is at issue in a given case). Once again, this points to the way one might see that human-centered normativity is entangled in the relevant jurisdictional questions. Nevertheless, in this case, the Court ultimately was closely split but decided against the notion of self-execution of American Convention on Human Rights Article 36(1), despite the ICJ's contrary holding. That conclusion, notably, goes toward the general sense of the status of humanity rights as emergent, but not yet consolidated. In *Medellin v. Texas*, the U.S. Supreme Court distinguished between treaties involving directly applicable individual rights (as opposed to states' rights) by seeking to delineate those norms that are amenable directly to domestic judicial remedies.

As the number of obligations imposed by international law is concededly growing, we see that it is in the area where international law generates more than one duty that interpretation is likely to be in greater demand and will likely play a most important role.[94] Indeed, at the heart of the decision in *Medellin* was the question of what law applied to the case—with the decision often blurring the procedural/jurisdictional issues with the substantive merits. Here, again, as in the ATCA litigation, the Court embraced an "interpretive approach," looking for "clarity" as to where international law ought be enforced.

Turning to related case law and interpretation in other tribunals, *Bosnia v. Serbia*,[95] *Tadic*, and *Nicaragua* all address the relationship between state responsibility and the behavior of nonstate actors in conflict situations. Here, we see that state responsibility—rather than shrinking as individual responsibility expands—actually grows as well. That is because, in the first instance, states that are increasingly responsible even for the behavior of private actors, under international treaties (either through rules of attribution of state responsibility or primary obligation to prevent or control non-state behavior)—illustrating precisely the ways humanity law can lead to a pervasive global rule of law. We saw something similar in the relationship between civil actionability in domestic fora and international criminal liability, for example, in *Khulumani*.[96] These kinds of liability are hardly inversely related—if anything, the relationship is the reverse; as one expands, so does the other.

In assessing the existence of responsibility,[97] the ICJ in the *Nicaragua* case deployed a strict standard, invoking an "effective control" test. In the same vein, in the more recent *Tadic* case—involving prosecution in the ICTY (hence, aimed instead at individuals)—the ICTY deployed a lower standard as to the nexus that must be proven to establish responsibility, looking to "de facto control."[98] This decision clearly reflects the ways the guiding interpretive principle draws inevitably from the relevant subject of the interpretive enterprise. *Tadic* involves the prosecution of violations of humanity-related rights, and therefore it guides the interpretation of the understanding of individual responsibility in the service of the greater protection of humanity rights.[99]

Now, consider *Bosnia v. Serbia*, which involved a suit in the ICJ. The conflict was waged by states, but the merits went to an offense regarding violations of human rights including genocide. So the case once again raised the question of what standard of responsibility should apply, but this time in a context where, arguably, we have come full circle from the traditional interstate situation: Here what is at stake is a case of inferring *from* individual responsibility, in order to reconceptualize state or collective responsibility.[100] Hence, now—post-*Nicaragua* and post-*Tadic*—with the advent of tribunalization and its individuation of responsibility in the international realm, a new question emerges: Against whom do human rights obligations run? So far, what is clear is that there is an absence of a clearly judicial hierarchy in terms of substantive doctrinal development.

Moreover, what cases like *Medellin* make clear is that the consular obligations, unlike many of the other prevailing treaties—like the Convention on the Prevention and Punishment of the Crime of Genocide and like much of the international humanitarian law discussed here—do not simply concern obligations between *state* parties. They also imply duties that are owed to individuals, and therefore they posit a teleological value that may well inform the direction of the doctrine. Might this line of interpretation then point to a human right that is implied? Some regional courts have so concluded.[101]

Indeed, in this regard, one might analogize to the extradition of the Chilean dictator Augusto Pinochet (discussed in chapter 3), which raised a conflict between adhering to traditional state-centric immunities and honoring countervailing claims of human rights. In the House of Lords case *Ex Parte Pinochet*, Lord Millett, of the majority, stated that "international law cannot be supposed to have established a crime having the character of a *jus cogens* and at the same time to have provided an immunity which is co-extensive with the obligation it seeks to impose."[102] This case may offer another example of one in which judicial powers—local, regional, and international—may well differ regarding the appropriate standard of individual responsibility but where, ultimately, the normativity transcends and goes to the humanity law subject and values. Indeed, conceding just this point in turn serves to reopen the debate about responsibility at home with global effects, at least in terms of discursive impact, as it opens a dialogue as to what would constitute the rule of law in the contemporary context.

"FOREIGN" LAW IN "DOMESTIC" COURTS? JUDICIAL RECOGNITION OF HUMANITY RIGHTS

A final illustration involves a vivid debate over international and foreign law in domestic courts that squarely reflects some of the dilemmas that are posed by the globalization of humanity law and by its broader normative impact. Once again, these dilemmas bring together the domestic and the international judiciary; the individual and the state; and procedural, jurisdictional, substantive, and normative rights. Particularly where the controversy in question raises humanity rights issues, there now is an evolving interpretive debate regarding the force and authority of foreign law in domestic constitutional law. This last area of debate involves the question of what guides interpretations of international humanity rights where they interface with domestic constitutional law.

From a humanity law perspective, these debates involve areas where there has been a distinct change—as a result of the expansion in, and proliferation of, international humanitarian law—in the overlapping and recombination of legal orders, which, at a minimum, spurs reinterpretation. These judicialized controversies, all deal with rights of humanity. In particular, the controversies at issue concern claims that are made based on widely shared practices regarding the rights to life of humankind, as set out in a variety of human rights conventions, as well as enforced in international-humanitarian-law charters.

As previously discussed, these are rights of a basic sort, such as the right to decent treatment, and the rights of persons and peoples to preservation. Ultimately, the prism of humanity law can help us understand these debates as being related to the ongoing evolution of the law, insofar as they involve the dynamic relationship of the local and the international systems—and particularly as they relate to the protection of basic rights and to the sites of related duties regarding what one might term global humanity rights. Here, the judicial enterprise—particularly its comparativist dimensions— gains a significant new foundation if we assume the common ground of "humanity law" and if there is a horizontal interpretative dialogue between domestic and international tribunals. We now live in a world of multiple legal orders where there is not centralization, or monopoly, or a hierarchy of interpretative authority, and where interpretative legitimacy is a concept that pertains to nonstate actors as well.

In his now classic essay on international law in *The Concept of Law,* H. L. A. Hart describes the nature of international law and explains, in particular, what gives this law its authority.[103] Hart readily concedes that international law lacks many of the features that are thought to be characteristic of legal systems, based on the paradigm of domestic law: a central government, courts with compulsory jurisdiction, and effective sanctions that are imposed by a central authority.[104] Nevertheless, for Hart, these observed differences, instead of putting in question the character of international law as "law," lead to a rethinking of the necessary conditions that have to be present in order to characterize a normative order as "law."[105] For Hart, "the proof that 'binding' rules in any society exist is simply that they are thought of, spoken of, and function as such."[106] In the case of individuals, who voluntarily accept the far more strongly coercive system of municipal law, the motives for supporting such a system may be extremely diverse.

International law has been changing in directions that arguably bring it closer, in its forms and ways of operation, to domestic law. For example, this can be said of international law's development of processes and institutions of judicialization and of the centralization of its sanctions. Even more important, this can be said with regard to the degree to which international law has emergent potential for the kind of applicability and direct effect on individuals that domestic law routinely displays. It follows, therefore, that around the world, courts are engaging more often with foreign sources in their constitutional jurisprudence.[107]

Jeremy Waldron has employed the term "jus gentium"[108] to articulate his notion of a "universal law administered in all civilized countries" that has always been used to solve problems.[109] Historically, there was always an overlap between the law of nations, in this specific sense, and international law. Indeed, already, in Grotius, there is a complex interconnection between natural law (jus gentium as the common practice of "civilized" nations) and voluntary law (treaty law and conventional international law). In fact, insofar as there was always a basis for importing foreign law into the domestic context[110] (for uses that predate the modern state but continue to pertain today) we must ask the question: To what extent does jus gentium reach back to an older tradition in international law, grafting parts of that tradition onto the present time?

One meaning of the jus gentium was the internal "common" law of the Roman Empire. Beyond the common law, historically, the idea of "higher" law was always informed by international and foreign sources.[111] Indeed, the notion of universal rights, as a matter of higher law, underlies the theory of international law. Thus, here we might consider the link between comparative constitutional law and the sources of international law. Indeed, one might see comparative constitutionalism as interrogating foreign mores with a view to tracing the contours of a universal legal normativity. Interestingly, while there are differences in approach, one can see that cosmopolitans such as Waldron and Kwame Anthony Appiah share this problem-solving approach as a basis for their views.

Historically, jus-gentium-like cases raised questions about whether common norms of humanity exist. Indeed, one might argue that the law that has emerged like jus gentium, historically, could be seen as an extension of the law that protected aliens, following them as they traveled, to the extent that this law was undergirded by concepts of justice, and not just by concepts of reciprocity. In today's globalizing world, there are many problems relating to persons and peoples on the move—whether these issues involve the rights of aliens or the rise of the migration of minorities or of entire peoples.[112] That is, if one of the oldest meanings of jus gentium is as a common law meant to regulate dealings with aliens, then, with globalization, one might suppose that this concern gains a renewed significance today. Here we can see that in the global order, something has changed: There is far greater movement and interaction of persons and peoples across state boundaries. But of course there are plain differences today vis-à-vis the historical view of jus gentium, too—as the relevant peoples' rights no longer hang on mere state consent; instead, they are informed by state conventions, and by claims-making by diverse actors, as well as by their recognition and interpretation by courts.

In a number of areas, it is apparent that there are overlapping and recombinant legal orders, with an impact on both international and domestic law—but particularly on domestic constitutional law. This is a movement whose bona fides occur primarily in the area that is defined here in terms of the "law of humanity."

One basis for the judicial recognition of humanity law rights emerges from the overlap between international and constitutional interpretation. Both types of interpretation are increasingly recognized by scholars as relating to public law orders that share affinities, in that they involve the regulation and constraint of the state but are also commonly seen as being justified and legitimated by state consent.[113] This development is best rationalized in terms of practices in conditions analogous to those of constitutional change, primarily involving discrete areas of unsettled law. It informs the interpretation of norms for the resolution of conflict. One might say that the bases for comparativism's revival today go further than the largely functionalist enterprise postulated by Waldron, because what is at stake, at present, is not merely problem-solving. Instead, the uses of humanity law—in and of themselves—help to define our sense of the relevant issues that we perceive as in "common," for example by drawing the line between private causes of action and public rights.

Other scholars, such as Eyal Benvenisti, put the point another way: They comprehend the turn to foreign law in light of checks and balances that are needed as a result of changes in domestic regimes that are occurring due to globalization.[114] Humanity law generates and transforms the meaning of the enterprise, redefining the weight and relevance of the law of the human community and, in this way, helping to shape an alternative rule of law.

For the first half of the twentieth century, in U.S. constitutional jurisprudence, the relevant nexus was a community defined by language—notably, the community of "English-speaking nations." In the words of Justice John M. Harlan II in *Poe v. Ullmann*, the regulation at issue "involves what, by common understanding throughout the English-speaking world, must be granted to be a most fundamental aspect of 'liberty.'"[115] Yet this principle was ultimately abandoned, as it lacked workable parameters, for what is the significance of limiting the principles to those embraced by "English-speaking" peoples?[116] In the modern cases, the relevant constitutional parameters regarding foreign authorities are often derived from the "common law" or "Anglo-American heritage."[117] In the lower courts, one might see the following of Anglo-American jurisprudence as simple adherence to a system of binding authority. However, in the Supreme Court, such common law norms reflect a broader concern for consistency and for a need to remain within the legal tradition over time. These norms perhaps draw from historical inquiry into preconstitutional traditions,[118] or perhaps are grounded in common political cultures that are "democracy based" or of a "civilized nature."

For example, the current invocation by the U.S. Supreme Court of the jurisprudence of the European Court of Human Rights[119] could be seen to hark back to historical understandings of unified law on the continent. In *Lawrence v. Texas*, in discrediting a domestic ruling limiting privacy and humanity rights, the U.S. Supreme Court majority invoked the European Court of Human Rights rulings and "Western tradition."[120] Here, we are dealing with something less narrow than *jus cogens* but also something with a stronger, or more emphatic, normative pull than the notion of "general principles of law of civilized nations." More specifically, we are seeing a threshold rights-centered international legal normativity, reflecting a strong enough sense of universal practice to justify general application (or at least, to justify a strong interpretative presumption that this core is consistent with, and must be respected in, any reading or application of particular treaties and particular domestic legal rules—even, and perhaps especially, constitutional ones).

Substantial common ground on this plane exists among national constitutions, and conformity with international conventions demonstrates a consensus on basic human rights, as well as on the protection of decency[121] and integrity.[122] From these data points, one might infer a bounded universal "law of humanity," the logical peak of the comparativist project. This bounded universalism is limited by the nature of humanity law itself. "Humanity rights" are pivotal in the present globalizing regime, which is, again, distinguished so far by interdependence but not by integration; globalization therefore spurs a related demand for shared rights wherever interdependence is strengthened. One might say that comparative constitutional law's current extension offers an alternative conception of legitimacy, grounded in core human rights and needed to reinforce a nascent global order.

Comparative constitutionalism is now extending its quest for conformity into the sphere of due process, where the phenomenon has been most evident in developments within criminal procedure. Yet the normative desirability of such integration (and, even more so, possible convergence) may well be debatable,[123] given the extant difference in legal cultures and political traditions.[124] Hence, we see here the connection between procedure and normativity.

Comparativism's normative role in constitutional interpretation is evident in current American constitutional jurisprudence in the context of life and death. The U.S. Supreme Court has been willing to turn outward to invoke an understanding of evolving human decency in a global order—an interpretive move that, again, reflects the pervasiveness of humanity rights. In interpreting the Eighth Amendment's protection from "cruel and unusual punishment," through its case law from *Thompson v. Oklahoma*[125] through *Stanford v. Kentucky*[126] and *Atkins v. Virginia*,[127] the U.S. Supreme Court has demonstrated its increasing reliance on foreign sources of law.

In *Stanford*, Justice William Brennan, in dissent, relied on comparative materials to support the view that "contemporary standards of decency" would preclude the execution of juveniles.[128] Over a vigorous dissent challenging foreign law's relevance, a plurality in *Thompson* relied on such experience to inform the meaning of "civilized standards of decency"[129] in relation to the "fundamental beliefs of this [n]ation."[130] In *Atkins*, a majority found that "within the world community," execution of the mentally retarded is "overwhelmingly disapproved."[131] In a recent Supreme Court death penalty case (in which the issue was invoking the death penalty for rape), the Court pointed to an attempted equivalence approach—which would counsel the acceptance of death as a penalty only when life-or-death humanity rights are at stake.[132] In *Lawrence v. Texas*, where the criminalization of sodomy was said to violate a due process "liberty," the Court majority relied on European authority and "values we share with a wider civilization."[133] Whereas here we see comparativism's uses in humanity-rights-expanding decisions, in other related humanity rights areas, such as abortion and euthanasia, these values have pointed in diverse directions. There are marked underlying conflicts among the various views of persons, peoples, and states. Thus, we can see that comparativist practices are similarly being justified by the humanity-centered norms themselves.[134] In other words, comparativism is typically employed when the tribunal or court seeks support or confirmation for its normative choices.

One can see, therefore, that comparativism, when developed by a transnational legal actors, including civil society, offers a strong, independent potential for global solidarity.[135] The concerted turn outward of comparativism enables alternative justifications to form the basis of sometimes shared but always principled decisionmaking.[136] By pluralizing rationales, comparativism in judicial review offers potential cosmopolitan effects that may well transcend the authority of any one state. This view derives some support from the significant contemporary increase in the use of comparative analysis by domestic constitutional courts. This globalizing potential is most evident as it concerns humanity rights. Moreover, insofar as the form of conflict resolution informs judge-made law, it isn't only states but also persons who are more broadly involved in adjudication and interpretation—by judges, scholars, and civil society. Since the judicial arena has become the site of conflict resolution among overlapping and recombinant legal orders, it has spurred the rise of independent principles of interpretation. Indeed, one can see the particular link between conflict resolution, international law, and interpretation—a strand that runs through the three illustrations in this chapter, reflecting the bases for the expansion of jurisdiction in the managing of conflict in global society.

To conclude, this rearticulation of the role of comparativism in areas of humanity law offers new purchase in the prevailing debates about such methods and about the perception of the expansion of judicial power worldwide. This is true, first, because comparativism arises in limited areas involving humanity rights that have always, going back historically, been areas of shared law reflecting issues of common humankind, and second, because insofar as these instances of judicialization increasingly involve areas of diminished democratic consent, they demonstrate that this area of law has long been justified on other, rights-based grounds. Indeed, these observations hark back to a Grotian tradition, as is seen in the regular use of comparativism in his works, as Lauterpacht has observed.[137]

This chapter has traced a number of contemporary debates over the ongoing meaning of international law, and has demonstrated the connections between these debates. It has done so while looking at a variety of adjudicative contexts where the question raised is: What counts as the ultimate sources of the authority of international law? Are these sources simply democratic consent and related agreed upon understandings of justice? What is the relevance to international law of the increasing use of notionally foreign law in domestic courts, in international or constitutional law cases, where human rights are at stake? These questions reflect the growing nexus between transformations in jurisdiction and transformations in the underlying substantive values. The relevant trends reflect the use of humanity law as a dynamic basis for evolving interpretation, across state lines; and as a source of normative values and concerns, for a global system in flux. Humanity law is redefining the rule of law, both at home and on the global stage.

CHAPTER 8

⌒◊⌒

A Humanity Law of Peoples

Normative Directions and Dynamics

GETTING BEYOND THE STATE: HUMANITY AS SUCH

[Grotius] is the first authoritative statement of the principle of humanitarian intervention—the principle that the exclusiveness of domestic jurisdiction stops where outrage upon humanity begins.
    Hersch Lauterpacht, *"The Grotian Tradition in International Law" (1946)*[1]

In the words of Kofi Annan, "there can be no global justice unless the worst of crimes—crimes against humanity—are subject to the law. In this age more than ever do we recognize that the crime of genocide against one people truly is an assault on us all—a crime against humanity."[2]

The ambit of humanity law is intrinsically global. Within domestic jurisdictions, what constitutes the discriminatory treatment of persons and peoples may well depend on the judgment of that political and legal community, concerning what grounds of distinction or differentiation are permissible. This inquiry goes to the very meaning of equality within the polity. But one can see that more and more, that constitutionalism, too, is informed by humanity law considerations, regardless of the constitutional history or tradition of the particular polity.[3] This change is most visible in equality jurisprudence that has conventionally understood discrimination in terms of the comparison of the treatment of individuals, whereas, more and more, equality jurisprudence is now preoccupied with comparative relationships between groups, and particularly with laws or policies that may isolate, subordinate, or marginalize particular groups,[4] or lead to inequality in groups' relation to other groups. The focus is usually (although not always) groups that constitute varying political versus ethnic majorities (as has been explored by Amy Chua,[5] or as in the challenge of affirmative action in South Africa)—thus giving rise to a more nuanced vocabulary. Sometimes these issues arise in transitional contexts—for example, in *Korematsu*, involving the wartime detention of a group of U.S. citizens based on race and ethnicity and holding that such discrimination could only be a matter of last resort.[6]

However, we have seen the way the spread of transitional justice and its concern for past treatment on a group basis risks further stoking identity politics and accentuating divisiveness—as in the Turkey/Armenian relationship. What emerges, ultimately, is a concept of justice as *between* peoples. Perhaps this is most evident wherever the norm is articulated transnationally—for example, in the context of the European Union, in the case of *Sejdic and Finzi v. Bosnia and Herzogovina* in the European Court of Human Rights. Another good example comes from the recently decided advisory opinion of the ICJ ruling on the legality of the declaration of independence of Kosovo.[7]

In cases like these, it is clear that values of stability of statehood and self-determination that had been settled since the postwar period— entrenched in the UN Charter, and so on—are now in play with other values, such as those of the protection of persons and peoples, e.g., self-determination as a remedy for oppression.[8] In its advisory opinion regarding Kosovo, in exploring the question of recognition and the legality of independence, the ICJ explained: "Taking all factors together, the authors of the declaration of independence of February 17, 2008 did not act as one of the Provisional Institutions of Self-Government within the Constitutional Framework, but rather as persons who acted together in their capacity as representatives of the people of Kosovo outside the framework of the interim administration."[9] Indeed, the court explained: "The authors of the declaration of independence emphasize their determination to 'resolve' the status of Kosovo and to give the people of Kosovo 'clarity about their future.'"[10]

Notably, the Supreme Court of Canada, in the *Quebec Secession* case, emphasized that "international recognition is not alone constitutive of Statehood and, critically, does not relate back to the date of secession to serve retroactively as a source of a 'legal' right to secede in the first place."[11] The court continued by noting that "recognition, even if granted, would not, however, provide any retroactive justification for the act of secession, either under the Constitution of Canada or at international law."[12]

From a humanity law perspective, recognition is both individual and collective in character. Habermas argues that protecting the individual's integrity in a liberal constitutional system requires also protecting his or her group affiliations: The guarantee, Habermas argues, should be "of equal treatment, decided on by the citizens themselves, of the life contexts, that safeguard their identities."[13]

But now, with globalization, the claim is for the protection of affiliative rights—rights lying beyond citizen-state relations—at the level of peoples, viewed transnationally—such as rights to be protected, at least, from extreme abuses such as grave violence and annihilation. As Arendt observed, ultimately it is the threat to peoples that "endangers the international order, and mankind in its entirety."[14]

By grounding the protection of persons and peoples in the "association that binds the human race," the "law of humanity" gives persons and peoples a legal and ethical status that is not entirely dependent on their membership in a particular political community. Indeed, one strand of the law of humanity, deriving from international humanitarian law, is aimed at persons and peoples: the conferral of a protected status on certain vulnerable classes or groups—for example, consider the categories of the wounded or the sick, or more broadly, the status of a "protected person" (Geneva Conventions, Article 4)—implicitly transcends original individualist, or hyperliberal conceptions of rights as derivative from the claim of the unsituated self, to adopt Michael Sandel's critical language.[15] Whereas in liberal individualism (expressed in the thought of Hobbes, etc.), the animating value is individual preservation, the fundamental basis for protected status is selfhood, not peoplehood.[16] Yet one might also say that what is ultimately at stake is a redefined peoplehood, one that moves away from state-based political categories, and toward a focus on the collectivities and their humanity.

The protection of humanity is predicated on the protection of individuals in light of their peoplehood. This provides a different ground for a concern with the survival and protective treatment of peoples, for it does not attribute any intrinsic value to the status of particular peoples (unlike, for instance, the communitarianism of Charles Taylor),[17] and thus, it takes us beyond the entrenched and often polarizing liberal/communitarian debate, by understanding the distinctive value of peoplehood in a manner that is more compatible with moral cosmopolitanism, e.g., Jeremy Waldron.[18] The question ultimately is this: What standard of justice can be applied, in the equal treatment of peoples, that could serve as a basis to guide international intervention and the contours of international society?

RE-CENTERING THE INTERNATIONAL SUBJECT:
OF PERSONS AND PEOPLES

In the liberal state, the ultimate subject is said to be the individual, and the aim is to protect and fulfill the individual's rights. Universality is generally framed in terms of the protection of individual autonomy. "Peoples," as such, are not necessarily seen as possessing rights; rights are thought to belong to states, or to derive from the claims of those who belong to particular "peoples" to equal or nondiscriminatory treatment in the liberal polity. But within the humanity law framework, claims by, or on behalf of, peoples—even if only where such claims are invoked and exercised by states and state actors—can still have a constitutive or legitimating effect.

The protection of persons and peoples within the realm of the United Nations began with the adoption of the UN Charter. Article 2 describes one of the purposes behind the United Nations as "develop[ing] friendly relations among nations based on respect for the principle of equal rights and self-determination of peoples, and to take other appropriate measures to strengthen universal peace."[19] Additional rights developed with the signing of the Convention on the Prevention and Punishment of the Crime of Genocide (1948),[20] which declared genocide a "crime under international law" that the parties "undertake to prevent and punish."[21] Simultaneously, the United Nations adopted the Universal Declaration of Human Rights, which stated in its preamble: "Recognition of the inherent dignity and of the equal and inalienable rights of all members of the human family is the foundation of freedom, justice and peace in the world."[22] Additional rights were conferred to stateless persons and refugees in the 1951 Convention Relating to the Status of Refugees and its 1967 Protocol,[23] followed by the 1954 Convention Relating to the Status of Stateless Persons. Under Article 9 of that Convention, a contracting state "may not deprive any person or group of persons of . . . nationality on racial, ethnic, religious or political grounds."[24] With respect to rights, which include freedom of religion, public education, public relief, and social security, the host country must treat the stateless person in the same manner as its own nationals, on equal basis, subsequently, other rights protections would follow, e.g., as set out in the International Convenant on Civil and Political Rights as well as others set out in the regional conventions.

Instantiation of protection along group lines can be seen in the many instances of litigation and decision making that relate to transitional and post-conflict justice.[25] Thus the ICJ decision in *Bosnia v. Serbia*[26] illustrates the complexity of justice in relations between peoples, especially within a system of international law that has conventionally been premised on state responsibility. When the ICJ was confronted with a humanity rights claim for reparations for genocide by a state claiming to represent Bosnian Muslim peoples as the victims, the ICJ struggled with the question of what space ought to be occupied by peoples in this forum.

In this case, the ICJ deftly avoided two undesirable outcomes: On the one hand, it avoided the denial of humanity rights that might have been inferred from dismissing the case entirely for lack of jurisdiction—as the genocide claim was not clearly about the state and its responsibility. On the other hand, the ICJ also avoided a strong statement of collective guilt on the part of the Serbian people. Instead, the court charted out a fertile "third way," or middle ground—by deferring to the ICTY holding that there had been genocide in its iconic site, Srebrenica, and by insisting that the Serbian state, even where it had previously abdicated its responsibility to its peoples, could still change course and honor its duty to protect the ethnic groups by fully discharging its duty to prosecute individuals for these persecutory offenses.[27]

The European Court of Human Rights, in *Sejdic and Finci v. Bosnia and Herzegovina*[28] struggled with the consequences of postwar ethno-partition in the region, and the discriminatory ramifications of the adoption of a constitutional structure that sought to define government along ethnic lines indefinitely. According to the Constitution of Bosnia (originating in the Dayton Accords), the applicants before the European Court of Human Rights, who were of Roma and Jewish origin, were ineligible to stand for election to the House of Peoples of Bosnia (the second chamber of the state parliament) and to the presidency (the collective head of state). Eligibility for either office required affiliation with a "constituent people" of Bosnia (Serb, Croat, or Muslim).

Finding a violation of the equality provisions of the European Convention on Human Rights, the court held: "Racial discrimination is a particularly egregious kind of discrimination and, in view of its perilous consequences, requires from the authorities special vigilance.... It is for this reason that the authorities must use all available means to combat racism, thereby reinforcing democracy's vision of a society in which diversity is not perceived as a threat but as a source of enrichment."[29] The court found that the need for power sharing as part of the political settlement in Bosnia was not "an objective and reasonable justification" for the discriminatory policy because power sharing could be achieved without the "total exclusion of representatives of the other communities."[30]

Likewise, in another case, *Orsus v. Croatia* concerning Croatian schools with Roma-only classes—the court struck down the segregation plan. The court explained that "the Roma have become a... disadvantaged and vulnerable minority."[31] And "notwithstanding that [the policy at issue] is not specifically aimed at that group," the court held that "discrimination means treating differently, without an objective and reasonable justification, persons in relevantly similar situations.... [A] general policy or measure which is apparently neutral but has disproportionately prejudicial effects on persons or groups of persons who, as for instance in the present case, are identifiable only on the basis of an ethnic criterion, may be considered discriminatory."[32] Both instances reflect peoples and their rights as the relevant subject of equal protection.

Vindication of humanity rights often implies a duty of recognition, protection, and preservation of individuals and groups of individuals—that is, of persons and peoples—whether or not they are protected by the state. Hence, in the *Al Jedda* case, while rejecting the particular claims that had been made concerning counterterror detentions in the British zone of Iraq, the House of Lords *in dicta* suggested that states participating in Operation Iraqi Freedom were to abide strictly by their obligation under international law, particularly where "involving those relating to the essential humanitarian needs of the Iraqi people."[33]

Where humanitarian discourse permeates the discussion of claims and counterclaims in these conflicts, the result tends to impasse or paralysis. Humanity law penetrates below the surface of conflict (that is, the obvious claims and polemics of the warring factions or groups) to its roots, where what is revealed is, precisely, the prevalence of situations where persons and or peoples have been left unprotected. Indeed, viewing the situation through a humanity law lens, one might map out the nature of contemporary conflict in terms of either competing group affiliations or sites where—for one reason or another—it has from time to time become, or may be, difficult to reconcile the protections of the individual, the collective, and the state.

This has been seen of late in parts of Africa—for example, Congo—as well as in parts of the Middle East (e.g., in the Occupied Territories and in Lebanon), and in the recent violence involving peoples in the Caucasus of the former Soviet Union; Kurds in Iraq; and Uighurs and Hmong in China and Mongolia.

In many of these instances, the struggle for power is being framed in humanity law terms—with, for example, Hamas and Hezbollah each making claims that they are providing critical humanitarian support[34] to their affected peoples. Meanwhile, Russian and Georgian authorities similarly purport that their true aim in the Caucuses is "to protect life."[35] Of course, these campaigns can equally well be *challenged* on the grounds that they are unable to deliver and, relatedly, on grounds of inconsistency wherever their behavior may not adequately reflect humanitarian regard.[36] At present, the problem of the place of the group and its subjectivity goes to the place of collectives, and of affiliations—whether religious or ethnic—that are being reconceived as part of a broader transnational status. The debate is over the construction and representation of humankind. In other times, the struggle has been framed somewhat simplistically—for instance, it has been depicted as being about groups per se, and their quest for survival, always vis-à-vis the state. After all of decolonization's unfoldings, the current state of foreign affairs reflects that we are in the midst of a long-postponed debate over the status and treatment of collectivities and affiliations.

ON JUDGMENT AND COMMUNITY

Humanity-law-based judgment processes are aimed at establishing normative parameters that regulate the legitimate relation of peoples, and peoplehood, to the state as well as to individuals and other collective affiliations (e.g., gender)—which explains the importance, at present, of prohibiting distinctive bases for violent action, particularly "ethnic cleansing" involving the aim of dissolution of the group (as was discussed, regarding protection, in chapter 5).

Judgment is a way to organize meaning, to sort out a chaotic world. Judgment, as Arendt wrote, is a matter of making intelligible what is often considered incomprehensible.[37] Judgment is an expression of shared values, at least implicitly. As she observes in *Eichmann in Jerusalem*, it is the very nature of criminal law to set the normative boundaries of the community by defining those acts that put the agent outside that community: offenses that are perpetrated not only against the victim but also—and primarily—against the community whose law is violated.[38] Put another way, with respect to the crime against humanity, the adjudged harm is to "the international order, and mankind in its entirety."[39]

In this regard, the turn to this ethico-juridical discourse may well be, in many instances, displacing other premodern forms, such as religion, in performing meaning-making and other related functions (discussed below). At one level, the very enterprise of judgment seems to assume—and indeed is predicated on—a shared realm: a "community," at least, of language, if not of (minimum) shared values.

Yet there is, apparently, no *pregiven* community, constituted by agreed-on common values that transcend group differences. This difficulty takes us back to the beginnings of classic international law and the Grotian view of a fluid international society where there may well be few a priori interests, but where it is judgment or a solidarist enforcement of rules that, in an ongoing way, structures the community.[40] In international criminal law, the otherwise elusive world community comes to recognize itself in the act of judging that someone is outside its bounds, beyond its normative limits. The universalizable recognition or judgment recognition of the offender implies a dynamic basis for evaluation that goes to the human being and his/her/their status and treatment, a shared subject that appeals to common values and, hence, to universality.

Legal judgment is now apparently playing a bigger role in shaping prevailing political discourse and negotiations than in the past. This development has the potential for reconstructing the friend/enemy distinction in legalist terms—that is, as a law/outlaw distinction, as we have seen is occurring in foreign affairs (and as was described in chapters 2 and 3). Law offers a transnational normative language.[41]

International humanitarian law has traditionally been preoccupied with the avoidance of unnecessary suffering, as well as with the preservation of a minimum of human decency and dignity amid the horror of war. International judgment has not been its central concern—at least, not until a conflict's end. In contrast, the human rights tradition has tended to be less adverse to judgment than international humanitarian law has been, with the amalgamation of human rights crimes and crimes against humanity during conflict. At the same time, the just war tradition has provided a strong basis for judgment, as is illustrated by the emphasis on aggression and on the wrongfulness of the conflict itself in the landmark post–World War II trials, drawing, as well, from prior traditions. And, as a general matter, violations of the laws of conflict are punished within domestic criminal justice systems.

The ICC Statute, by contrast, extends to internal, as well as international, conflict with respect to "crimes against humanity." Moreover, the "Court shall exercise jurisdiction over the crime of aggression" and in regard to crimes against humanity, too—where the scope and reach of the offense in its jurisdiction extends to actions perpetrated by private, as well as public, power (as for many of the offenses there is no state-action requirement).[42] In some regard, this feature of the Rome Statute system shares an element of the premodern state—for within the Grotian tradition, society's interest extends to abuses of public and private power—but after the evolution of the modern state, we can more readily see that this development implies a far bigger role for judgment. Thus, for example, human rights law now is overlapping with international humanitarian law, which has traditionally been committed to a kind of neutrality between antagonists in conflict, in the sense of refraining from judging their relative legitimacy in terms of substantive values.[43]

An important dimension of legalism or legocentrism is that it allows for judgment that is not (at least directly) grounded in morality or religion but is constituted through the praxis of law and its defining, bounded normativity—whether the inquiry at issue is the determination of who is an offender in a criminal trial, or what is the entitlement of persons with protected status in humanitarian law. The normative contours of humanity become visible through the legal praxis of humanity law. Here, one can see that humanity law does offer a basis for the exercise of violence—so long as it fits within principles of humanity law regarding intervention; that is, so long as it is an action comporting with such values. Above all, this is how behavior is made intelligible—by creating an epistemic community, one that is organized around a certain shared sense of the rules, yet one that may nevertheless lack the touchstone of other common values. At the same time, there is an open-endedness to this community, by virtue of its implicit jurisdiction over who is staking claims based on the status of the human.

Traditionally, the criminal law operates to define who is an offender against the "community," and the tribunals, through their sanctioning power, have the capacity to isolate and remove the offender from the community. Thus, in the case of crimes against humanity, the effect is to determine who is outside the community, and therewith—reflexively, as it were—to define the boundaries as such of the "international community," or what, in other periods, would have been known as the society or community of "civilized nations." It is in its criminal justice form that we can most clearly see humanity law being directed at, and operating with immediate effect on, persons and peoples. Humanity law becomes a spectacular form of global regulation, a rare area of immediate contact regarding the private agency and subjects, with a public dimension. Wherever humanity rights are pitted or juxtaposed against state sovereignty, there is an evident confrontation, and one where humanity rights often prevail, at least in legal argument.

One place this can be seen is in the ways universality jurisdiction is articulated in various fora. Examples range from high-profile cases such as *Eichmann* and *Pinochet*, as discussed earlier in chapter 3, to cases involving challenges to so-called amnesty laws—for instance, *Barrios Altos*, where traditional state defenses against transitional judgment and human rights claims have been rejected, and humanity law norms requiring judgment and redress have prevailed: "The so-called laws of self amnesty are an aberration, an inadmissible affront to the juridical conscience of humanity."[44] What is evident is the impetus to develop the individuation and privatization of duties and their enforcement.

By limiting self-determination along these lines, humanity law proscribes states from legitimating the identity of the state by invoking the ethnos wherever it comes into conflict with humanity rights. Moreover,

one might expect that this would limit political identity insofar as collectivities claim it, along lines that could, in a complementary fashion,
also stabilize the state. In this way, the humanity law justificatory
regime apparently resolves the supposed paradox that has been set into
play since the postwar constitutional wave. Indeed, what has become
evident is that there are new humanity rights conditions placed on
states' recognition (i.e., after a political breakup), or even earlier, in self-
determination processes held within a broader regional and international context.

Thus, consider, for example, the EC decision to condition the recognition of successor states to the former Yugoslavia on the commitment to
the protections of persons and peoples.[45] The Badinter Commission
stressed the requirement of protections for people and minorities within
these territories, explaining that "the peremptory norms of general international law and, in particular, respect for the fundamental rights of the
individual and the rights of peoples and minorities, are binding on all the
parties to the succession."[46] Or consider Canada's Supreme Court in
Quebec Secession, where protection of minority and aboriginal rights was
held to be a fundamental basis for assessing any claim for succession.
More recently, consider the connection between statehood, recognition
of peoplehood, and self-determination, as it is being relitigated in the
context of Serbia's own judicial challenge to Kosovar independence. There,
the discussion of the *international* legality of secession often turned, in
part, on the state's treatment of its own peoples.[47] Along these lines, the
African Commission on Human and People's Rights, while declaring
Southern Cameroonians "a people," nevertheless stopped short of ruling
on rights to self-determination via secession, given the absence of massive human rights violations and the adequacy of existing forms of
political participation.[48]

Consider, too, the significance of the European Union reaction to
Turkey's demonstrable betterment in its consideration of its (then) political
minorities. Or consider Serbia's accession to the European Union, where a
critical condition of membership in that entity has become evidence of
compliance with humanity law—that is, of the criminal enforcement of
crimes against humanity in tribunalization processes. Referring to the
arrests of alleged war criminals, the EU Council asserted, "this development
illustrates the commitment of the new government...to contribute to
peace and stability in the Balkans region."[49] What these practices reflect is
that—beyond adherence to simple majority rule, by electoral democracy—
today there is an added requirement of an assurance of the protection of
persons and peoples in their humanity rights.

THE GLOBAL UNIVERSAL

The very idea of a global rule of law implies a measure of universalizability across situations and regimes. Yet there is no a priori view of those norms that we all share. This distinguishes humanity law from attempted revivals of natural law. Instead, the universal comes to sight through evolving practice, where the humanity norm comprehends duties and rights relating to the ultimate preservation and protection of persons and peoples. We see recurring instances of recognition across judicial systems, for example in *Hamdan, Kadi, Isayeva,* and *Barrios Altos,* of rights to life and to humane treatment, as well as of the right of judicial access or judicial protection.[50]

While it appeals to universal absolutes, humanity law is also dynamic and contextual, as its sources are responsive to current and past conflict, and the meanings of humanity law rights and duties are shaped by multiple actors, persons, peoples, and states. As I discussed in chapter 7, in Theodor Meron's words, "the teleological desire to solidify the humanizing content of the humanitarian norms clearly affects the judicial attitudes underlying the 'legislative' character of the judicial process. Given the scarcity of actual practice, it may well be that, in reality, tribunals have been guided, and are likely to continue to be guided, by the degree of offensiveness of certain acts to human dignity; the more heinous the act, the more the tribunal will assume that it violates not only a moral principle of humanity but also a positive norm of customary law."[51] This could also be seen as essentially *solidarist* in form, as what is involved are dynamic acts of interpretation against a context of violent struggle. Hence, here, the rule of law appears to be defined as an obligation to a form of resistance to violence and distinct types of criminal behavior, and this, too, constitutes a source of value-based connective structure for the society.

So far, one might say that the preeminent norm of humanity law converges on a rule of law that is aimed at the recognition and preservation of humankind in global politics. But one can also rationalize other actors, and varieties of forms of global engagement, that may well be coercive and involve even military intervention. Nevertheless, as I discussed in chapters 4 and 5, even when such actions are taken, they are situated likewise within a framework of the rule of law, and are understood in terms of its enforcement.

TOWARD A NEW GLOBAL SOLIDARITY

Violations of the integrity of peoples and peoplehood are seen not just as attacks on the particular group but also, more broadly and meaningfully, as attacks also on the idea of humankind. In Arendt's words, "the latter is an attack on human diversity as such, that is, on a characteristic of the 'human status' without which the very words 'mankind' or 'humanity' would be devoid of meaning."[52]

The normative significance for international law of collectivities that are organized along ethnic or religious lines has become ever greater since the last World War, and indeed has taken on an utterly changed relevance.[53] This is because, with globalization, the relevant loyalties and affiliations are no longer subsumed within conceptions of national constitutionalism—that is, they are not exclusively seen in terms of subnational statuses and identities. Rather, peoples have an increasingly transnational status. Thus, in current political conditions "peoples" increasingly compete with the state as the major locus of collective loyalty and allegiance.

For some cosmopolitans, such as Martha Nussbaum, group-identity-based claims are often threatening to human rights. Insofar as these claims depend on a subrational or nonrational basis for human solidarity, that basis would be located in compassion or fellow feeling. Thus, for Nussbaum, the appeal to humanity has its basis in the universal experience of suffering, which is capable of transcending differences.[54] Of course, as I discussed in chapter 5, the norm of "inhuman conduct" is aimed at minimizing suffering;[55] thus, the International Covenant on Civil and Political Rights, Article 7, provides that "no one shall be subject to cruel, inhuman or degrading treatment or punishment." And, the Covenant, likewise, embodies a shareable norm, and indeed informs a strand of thought that gives rise to a basis for humanity law—that is, the strand based on "Geneva Rights," which is seen in the extension of norms associated with the law of armed conflict, particularly Common Article 3, protecting against "inhuman or degrading treatment." For example, illustrative of interpretation of this norm is visible in the modern debate on whether waterboarding as a torture.[56] Yet a greater conceptual difficulty remains constitutes the focus on suffering, for the assurance of "humane" conduct only gets us part of the way there in terms of preserving what is quintessentially human.[57]

Others question whether human suffering or compassion can serve as a basis for common values: In other words, can the removal of a "neutral" normative scheme truly protect human rights?[58] This is a theme of popularized works of moral philosophy, such as Jonathan Glover's book *Humanity*.[59] Consider Costas Douzinas's critique of a specious or empty humanitarianism.[60] According to Richard Rorty, human rights culture is a matter of "hearing sad and sentimental stories," often those associated with past-oriented transitional justice. Consider also Michael Ignatieff's challenge to the notion that there can be a human rights position that is "neutral"[61]—even more telling, one might suppose, when applied to a legal regime that is informed by international humanitarian law as well. Protecting rights, for Ignatieff, irrevocably means taking a position, and proposing that there is no getting around the value of "dignity" and its most inclusive, least particularistic formulation, "dignity as agency."[62] One is reminded of Carl Schmitt's attack on the "false" neutrality of "humanitarian liberalism," or the more contemporary challenge to such presumed or purported impartiality posed by David Kennedy, as in *The Dark Sides of Virtue*, where he calls for a "frank" account.[63]

However, humanity law today moves beyond the natural spectre as it includes elements of the just war traditions and via new criminal justice is operationalized through judgment processes. It does not necessarily aim at historical neutrality; that is, it does not posit an abstract system of hierarchized legal norms, as set out in legal philosopher Hans Kelsen's view, which Schmitt closely identified with legal liberalism.[64] Instead, the premise of humanity law is the shared experiences of the memory of inhumanity, and the claims to rights of situated, affected agents. This is the face of humanity as such—as it presents itself, in a body and of a people. Moreover, humanity law postulates that the very awareness of a particular people occurs within the context of a common humanity—a humanity that transcends the particular persons who are organizing as peoples; goes beyond fixed or "essentialist" racial, ethnic, or religious categories; and possesses a strong subjective element, a matter of a will to live collectively that may well be inherent in what it is to be human.

Humanity law has evolved through demands for justice and judgment, claims concerning legal rights and the responsibility of human agents with intentionality. Its ground therefore is not in the passions, or in sentimentality: Its basis does not lie in mere indignation or sorrow at suffering, however it is caused—whether by natural or manmade disaster, or by intended inequity or cruelty of the worst kinds. Without the possibility of judgment, humanity law would lack much of its normative bite; for it would risk becoming merely a plaint against the woes of the world, or a simple aspiration to paradise. But humanity law means more: It means judgment within the law. As Jacques Derrida has observed, law is by definition bounded—hence it supposes that something is "out of bounds."[65] Here is where criminal jurisdiction becomes central to the legally determinate character of humanity law, differentiating it from moral humanitarianism: Such jurisdiction is increasingly universal, yet at the same time it is a jurisdiction to apply bounded and binding norms through judgments that are legal in all the strong senses of the word, procedurally and substantively.

Humanity law—as a basis for a universal, global rule of law—depends on a discourse and structure of claims-making that has become the lingua franca, surpassing while also encompassing human rights law and norms. Global justice today is denoted by its claims-making, where adjudication has become a central means of vindicating many of these claims. Here, the process—that is, the process that gives access to the judicial protection of recognition—itself constitutes a dimension of the justice that is meted out.

Consider, for example, the last decade's adoption of contemporary conventions such as the Convention on the Elimination of All Forms of Discrimination against Women, which makes the state explicitly responsible for *private*, as well as *public*, discrimination: As a regular matter, this convention is being used in advocacy on behalf of vulnerable populations, whether they are religious groups, ethnic groups, or other collectivities. It has been a force in women's advocacy strategy, as seen in the work of the renowned feminists Catharine MacKinnon and Carol Gould and of NGOs, such as those that came together at Beijing; and of the Global Justice Center, which is deploying similar norms in its advocacy work. This reflects an instance of the express construction of peoplehood that is beyond the state, and that is clearly distinct from historical understandings of collective identity formation.[66] According to MacKinnon, "women are a global group in the sense that the distinctive social definition, treatment, and status of women as a sex relative to men is recognizable in diverse forms all over the world." In landmark litigation, a suit was brought against Balkans henchman Radovan Karadžić for redress on behalf of rape victims in the Balkans, for violation of the "law of nations."[67] In *Are Women Human?* MacKinnon argues for women's "full human status."[68] In her view, women's critical rights problem is that "being a woman is not yet a name for a way of being human." The status of the group is seen as essential to its ability to comprise a part of humanity.

Several critical dimensions of humanity law are revealed in this kind of advocacy. First, this is a framework that has evolved through addressing situations of conflict, and related legal regimes, and is therefore self-consciously attentive to the challenges of regulating violence. In other words, in humanity law, violence is not the exception, nor is it assumed to be; what distinguishes humanity law from the historical conception of the cosmopolitan peace is that its aim is not the final elimination of violence, but rather its humanization. Next, here is a framework that can effectively deal with the increasing role of private agency, and of nonstate actors generally. Aimed and addressed beyond citizens, and beyond the nexus to the state, humanity law can encompass collectivities with strong affiliations— even if those affiliations are defined on a subjective basis (not limited to established bases such as of ethnicity or religion).[69] Here, I take one side of the debate on this question, taken up by the tribunals—for example the ICTR in *Akayesu*—as well as by scholars, such as Larry May.[70] Indeed, there is an element of self-identification or self-construction, in envisioning rooted persons linked up to the diversity of humanity.[71] For ethnic groups and women's groups, it is important that they not be marginalized—and hence not relegated to the private sphere. It is also important for them that there be no thick line between public and private. Lastly, positive rights are definable in, and through, the nexus to the human; we see that humanity rights, in assuring human security, necessarily span political, economic, social, and cultural rights. For this reason, humanity rights are apt to address issues of group preservation and flourishing.

EMERGING HUMANITY NORMS: DIRECTIONS FOR A GLOBAL RULE OF LAW

The notion of a clear divide between the justice of going to war and justice in the waging of war was itself a part of the liberal theory of rule of law. Under that theory, the entitlement of civilians to protection was deemed without regard to the rights and wrongs of the conflict itself; importantly, that right stemmed from the right to self-preservation, which was qualified in liberal theory by the necessity of self-defense.

What exactly might this mean? To what extent is the arch commitment to individual preservation the challenge from legality? Beyond the preservative norm and related basic rights, might there be other rights that follow as a result of the then-expanding system of relevant law?

For humanity law the core here is, of course, the preservation and protection of persons *and* peoples; even in—indeed, especially importantly in—contested sovereignty/occupation contexts. Hence, it makes sense that in the Balkans, and along the post-Soviet Islamic frontier, diverse judiciaries have recognized a "right to life." Unlike a utopian vision, humanity law has as its point of departure the existing legal and political schema. Therefore, it should help us understand a variety of debates that are about human rights, as well as over global values—such as the debate over the relative importance of political versus socioeconomic rights. The animating norm of preservation operates on a number of levels. It begins with the humane treatment of the body, for example, so that the rights are, first and foremost, rights of the existence and protection of the individual, and rights against degrading treatment of any kind. As noted, the International Covenant on Civil and Political Rights Article 7 provides: "No one shall be subject to cruel, inhuman or degrading treatment or punishment." Similarly, the European Covenant of Human Rights, Article 3, states that "No one shall be subjected to torture or to inhuman or degrading treatment or punishment." Converging here with human rights law is Geneva Convention Article 3: "Persons taking no active part in hostilities . . . shall in all circumstances be treated 'humanely.' . . . To this end the following acts are and shall remain prohibited at any time and in any place with respect to the aforementioned persons all violence to life and person . . . outrages on personal dignity, in particular, humiliating and degrading treatment."

There are groups—often, those operating or existing across state boundaries—that find themselves more vulnerable to threats to preservation, individual and collective, that also exist at a global or transboundary level. Woman constitute such a group.[72] Another example is the Roma in Europe, where many controversies are now being legalized—on both sides, for example as seen in the challenge to the recent 2010 French deportation order.[73] Some of the threats to preservation emerge from increased economic interdependence—that is, the threat posed by the competition in the global marketplace even as it also opens up new opportunities at the same time.[74] Others may relate to disease, or environmental problems such as climate change.

Furthermore, while the core norm associated with the humanity rights framework is preservation, actualizing this norm may well imply a related elaboration of law. In other words, actualization of the norm requires enforcement processes and an array of judicial review mechanisms, between international humanitarian law and international human rights law orders. Ensuring just and fair enforcement means that basic guarantees trigger other rule-of-law values, such as the equality of legal protection and the general applicability of the law.[75] Indeed, as I have argued in preceding chapters, much of the legal development of the last years has been dedicated to this normative commitment: The appeal to universality is seen in (among other developments) the focus on the elimination of politically based immunities, and so on, as well as in the protection of Geneva-based humanity rights to access to courts.[76]

The advent of legalization and judicialization gives rise to claims to recognition and other entitlements that sound in the protection of status and equality vis-à-vis others—for example, in terms of the status of persons and peoples. This concept of equality was expanded on in Article 27 of the 1966 International Covenant on Civil and Political Rights: "In those States in which ethnic, religious or linguistic minorities exist, persons belonging to such minorities shall not be denied the right, in community with the other members of their group, to enjoy their own culture, to profess and practice their own religion, or to use their own language, as well as rights to religious freedom and against discrimination on this basis, rights importantly accorded to persons to be enjoyed in community, and protectable beyond nationals.[77] One might see these protections as building on the Convention on the Prevention and Punishment of the Crime of Genocide.

More explicitly, the International Covenant on Economic, Social and Cultural Rights, Art 15(1), recognizes rights to culture; and the later

Declaration on the Rights of Indigenous Peoples, at Article 9, provides: "Indigenous peoples and individuals have the right to belong to an indigenous community or nation, in accordance with the traditions and customs of the community or nation concerned. No discrimination of any kind may arise from the exercise of such a right."[78] In addition, the African Charter on Human and Peoples' Rights sets out rights to existence, as well as to "economic, social and cultural development."[79] One might see these protections as building on its Convention on the Prevention and Punishment of the Crime of Genocide.

Prior to the UN Declaration on the Rights of Indigenous Peoples, the Council of Europe 1995 Framework Convention for the Protection of National Minorities noted that "the upheavals of European history have shown that the protection of national minorities is essential to stability...in this continent," and therefore concluded that a "genuinely democratic society" should "create appropriate conditions enabling them to express, preserve and develop this identity." The 1998 Oslo Recommendations regarding the Linguistic Rights of National Minorities provide for equality of access to resources, inter alia. Still, jurists such as Antonio Cassese have said that, so far, law is not equipped to deal with the postcolonial rise in claims to self-determination.[80] Benedict Kingsbury elaborates conceptual structures to deal with competing views of peoples' claims, whether in domestic or international law. Going further, Kingsbury proposes that the human rights program "be adapted and renovated to take account of distinctive issues raised by indigenous peoples."[81]

Humanity law rights, in their operation, have had an important impact on the reconstruction of the rule of law—since now the offenses themselves go to the very questions of whether there is equal protection of the law; whether, and to what extent, it matters that these protections are being expressed in rights terms; and what might follow from the construction of these claims in these terms. Thus, we return to the Grotian understanding of the core right as that of the right to have rights, as it were. The importance of this foundational right is best illuminated when it is threatened: As Arendt wrote in *The Origins of Totalitarianism*, "we became aware of the existence of a right to have rights...and a right to belong to some kind of organized community, only when millions of people emerged who had lost and could not regain these rights."[82] More recently, Justice Stephen Breyer has written of the nexus between the substantive workings of the law of nations and related procedural rights (as discussed in chapter 7).[83]

Humanity rights discussed here are based on group identity, that is, the individual's greatest affiliations to peoples, and peoples to humankind.

These would seem to owe a debt to transitional justice developments over recent decades. In this sense, humanity law appears to point in a backward-looking direction, insofar as it defines itself in terms of past violations and the related group claims for justice—such as the claims made in *Khulumani* (a U.S. Alien Tort Statute suit) for damages based on corporate complicity with apartheid discussed in chapter 7. On the other hand, we also saw that the broad commitment to universalizability is predicated on a prospective— not retrospective—direction for the law. Nevertheless, such humanity-rights-based framing is not unbounded, and is clearly better than the alternatives: It is less unbounded than the undefined exhortations of past abuses, and collective calls for vindication, that occur outside of the legal and judicial processes. (In any event, this reflects that there is a move away from the identification of the state with its constituent peoples.)

What becomes evident—when one reasons from the ultimate value of preservation, and its logic in relation to sovereignty—is that humanity law may well offer a basis for a more robust protection of group rights, certainly, than that hitherto associated with traditional liberalism, or cosmopolitanism.[84] The protections that humanity law can afford are also more nuanced than the protections proposed by communitarians—which tend to emphasize the promotion of the group and its identity, characterized in somewhat dichotomous and static formulation, over that of individuals. To communitarians, the commitment to the community is seen as an implicit sacrifice of individuality and of individual choice about identity.

Within the humanity law framework, there is an explicit understanding of the significance of the collective identity, for both the human as individual and the group as part of humankind—that is, as seen in terms of the status of humanity. Indeed, here it may be useful to hark back to the observations mentioned earlier (in the reflections, particularly, of postwar philosophers such as Shklar and Arendt) about the significance of the shared norm that is implied in the "crime against humanity," and the ways its normativity always enmeshes the group in its particulars, as well as in the status of humankind in general.

Humanity law also may well afford group protection that is less absolute, or more bounded, than that which is demanded on communitarian principles. While humanity law assures the protection of a variety of group affiliations, nevertheless, as we have already seen, there are inevitably limits to this protection—limits that may also derive from the logic of the humanity law framework itself. Comparing the protection that is afforded to groups under a pluralist scheme with that afforded to groups under the humanity law framework, one can see that humanity law may result in less protection in some instances of cultural (i.e., multicultural) rights wherever those rights come into stark conflict with other competing rights within the humanity law framework.

The most difficult contemporary issues involve reconciling the relevant preservation rights, such as the rights of persons and of peoples. While the humanity law framework does not always yield determinate answers to these questions, it may well help us understand the relevant values at stake and the trade-offs between and within these values. In this regard, consider recent controversies over ethnic and religious expression and practice in the public sphere, particularly in Europe, for example, the so-called head-scarf controversy or *l'affaire du foulard*.

Indeed, the humanity law framework offers an alternative beyond the traditional liberal/communitarian debate—one that is designed to deal with today's number one problem. Such matters involve competing preservation claims—of the individual, the group, and in addressing the state. Under humanity law, such claims are conceived in terms of a dynamic interaction—a feature that is missing in the inherited approaches. Reframing varying claims in terms of those of preservation may help clarify the relevant issues at stake.

Controversies of this sort—once they are understood to pose a problem within humanity law—allow deliberation within a transformed, law-based framework and discourse. This framework and discourse benefit from an implicit change—a reworking, if you will—with respect to the relevant relationships of persons, peoples, and the state. This reworking may facilitate the resolution of a given conflict, though the determination will necessarily be case by case, depending on the plausibility and fixity of the relative claims.

If we approach these issues in terms of humanity protection as the *Grundnorm*, this perspective can be seen to offer a means of understanding and addressing contemporary issues of culture and political identity that transcend the prevailing approaches of liberalism and cosmopolitanism. These two schools of thought can be described, respectively, as being based on individual rights and as being based on a multicultural form of individual rights that tends to protect the value of diversity. Both schools of thought, however, presume a particular (and often static) view of liberty and the state. The "multiculturalism" debate is commonly framed as if the groups at issue somehow remain unaltered by the struggle for recognition.[85] Specific ethical or religious belief systems are not adequate bases for common values under conditions of admitted diversity and value fragmentation. Here, one can see that law becomes crucial as a normative discourse that offers an element of the universal.[86] Humanity law is a continuous, pervasive form of legal ordering that, like postwar constitutionalism, aspires to universality in its rights protection. But humanity law, unlike postwar constitutionalism is relatively open-ended and forward-looking—able to embrace emerging and future threats, such as terrorism, disease, natural disaster, climate change, and so forth.

Accordingly, from a humanity law perspective, a decisionmaker confronting a conflict would need to consider the group's claim to preservation together or with other individual rights (say, against coercion). By the same token, a group's claims to equal protection will depend on its own viable protection of its members' humanity rights. And then, under a humanity law approach, one would need to add to the mix the state's obligations vis-à-vis both persons and peoples, and the extent to which today, the state's legitimacy depends on fulfilling its multiple duties to protection.

In the context of various debates regarding religious identity and liberal citizenship, Ayelet Shachar refers to "transformative accommodation" that is enabled by joint governance by the state and private groups;[87] in some way, this illuminates the sort of interaction that is already producing change in global politics. Or, in this vein, there are the proposals of the Archbishop of Canterbury, which go to the symbolic importance of equal accommodation on a group basis.[88] On a global level, in a transition, the capacity and willingness of a state to protect humanity rights (rather than merely state interests) has become a leading sign of a well-functioning successor regime and of its commitment to international duties to uphold the rule of law, as reflected in the UN Secretary-General 2004 Report. In this regard, consider the recent declaration of the legality of the independence of Kosovo.[89]

Humanity's complex, layered normativity has the capacity to lead the shift away from the long-prevailing state-centric, territorialized rule-of-law values and toward an approach grounded directly in the security of persons and peoples. Here, the primacy of state security is slowly but surely complemented, relativized, and perhaps even transcended by a humanity-centered security. Once this is understood, it inevitably challenges the way state sovereignty is understood: States may be good at protecting their own security, but in light of global threats, they cannot necessarily fully do the same when it comes to human security. Today, the most menacing threats appear to be global in nature: terrorism, weapons of mass destruction, climate change, pandemics. Moreover, many of the most vulnerable groups are not fixed within stable state borders. In these circumstances, sovereignty as the state's monopoly of coercion within its borders, tied to its purported capacity to determine outcomes on that fixed territory, is not enough to guarantee security, unless pooled or shared with other actors, whether nonstate or multistate, that are also operating on the global stage.

THE FATE OF THE POLITICAL AND THE REORDERING OF
INTERNATIONAL SOCIETY

Humanity law's distinctive character as legality reflects the ways the preservation of persons and peoples gives rise to new categories of political legitimacy—categories that are neither state-centric nor premised on the characteristic legitimizing institutions of domestic democracy.

Early on in *The Law of Peoples*, Rawls recognized that—once other collectivities beyond the state are normatively significant (even if there is no "justice" between them in the strict sense)—legitimacy cannot depend simply on the operation of democratic institutions that is characteristic of the fully developed liberal-democratic state. Hence the significance of global rule of law in distinguishing "decent" (i.e., minimally legitimate) states from outlaw states. Rawls viewed a "well ordered society as being peaceful and not expansionist": While not necessarily democratic or liberal, such a society, according to Rawls, has a "legal system which satisfies certain requisite conditions of legitimacy in the eyes of its own people; and as a consequence of this, it honors basic human rights."[90] One might compare this view with Anne-Marie Slaughter's view, as expressed in her article "Law among Liberal States,"[91] which presumes a stable and normatively meaningful distinction between liberal and illiberal states. From a humanity law perspective, the very understanding of what counts as legitimacy and rule of law may well be defined in terms of constituent peoples; for this reason, the humanity law understanding may well conflict with preexisting statist understandings.

Once we concede that democracy is not, in itself, a sufficient basis for legitimation, this conclusion does not merely have implications for legitimacy at the level of the state, and related interstate relations. It also follows that other political collectives may well pose relevant rivals—a reality that complicates the political scene, as it offers, like other aspects of globalization, a new "market" in political choices. This situation has focused attention on the contemporary significance of demarcating the outlaw enemy, so that the new line is no longer drawn "between friend and enemy" (i.e., a political decision à la Schmitt); instead, it is a line drawn by humanity law, distinguishing between a lawful and a nonlawful rivalry for power. As we have seen, for example in chapter 5, law—and, in particular, humanity law—operates as the relevant legitimating line.

This new category of humanity law is turning out to be a very useful mechanism, as it can be used in ways that are far more flexible than other political litmus tests. For, as a normative regime, it is at once more open-ended and more robust than democratic legitimization, as is seen in

many regions of the world where short shrift is given to liberal proceduralism, but humanity law may well displace the priority of other justice-based
legitimation. Indeed, as a shared minimum, the combined law of humanity
and human security may well be a better contender to lay the basis for
international security, but there are contradictions and tensions here, too.

The reconceptualization of the insider/outsider division impacts and
shapes sovereign rights, which a state may lose by the failure (whether by
will or incapacity) to protect its people or treat them according to the
minimum threshold required by humanity law. Moreover, this failure may
well trigger the right, individual or collective, to support other groups—
that is, peoples, or political organizations beyond the state.

In conclusion, humanity law shapes the contemporary role of peoples,
and the complex interaction of persons, peoples, and states; thus, this perspective can offer a way to make sense of current political and legal developments. After all, the phenomena of recent years show that in weak states,
the notion of peoples is not only galvanizing subjects to choose alternative
identities but may also be an agent capable of delivering critical human
security. Such a shift may have important effects for reconceiving the bases
of legitimacy in human security terms, particularly insofar as they redefine
the way the social contract can be understood, moving away from the historical state-based notion of that contract. Indeed, we may well conceive of
several current political conflicts in this light. In the end, humanity law
leads us to conclude that—rather than seeing such affiliations as all
negative—we now can better appreciate that the greatest stability in a
state is achievable precisely where the interests of the state can be aligned
with those of its citizens, viewed as both persons and peoples.

One can see a new standard of political legitimacy emerging, where
across the state/nonstate divide a variety of groups and actors now struggle
for authority. Whether across national borders or within them, nonstate
actors are not mere subjects or recipients of governance; rather, they themselves practice governance, in claiming or framing their rights on the basis
of a shared humanity. In this regard, the concept of humanity-centered
normativity can help us understand today's remarkable contestations
regarding global justice issues—ranging from criminal law to environmen-
talism, to medical treatment—and help us also to see why global justice has
never mattered more.

At this time—of a world politics that is significantly characterized by
heightened interconnection, and dependence, but lacking in political integration—one can see that there is an added critical importance to humanity
law. The parallel application of humanity law's three strands reflects the
chaotic nature of world conditions, marked as they are by pervasive conflict

that is more and more applicable to civilians. What this means is that order can no longer be achieved via a return to foundational delimitations—whether of territory, nationality, and/or power. Yet, given the conditions of conspicuous conflict, the various global threats, and the multiplicity of the actors involved, this is hardly a story of unquestioned progress. Instead, one might make a tentative conclusion that humanity law offers the most plausible basis at present: first, by offering language and processes by which to deal with conflict (i.e., claims-making, adjudication, and resolution), and second, by gesturing at a telos that is aimed at ensuring the protection of the persons and peoples who arguably form a threshold or basis prefiguring global society.

CHAPTER 9

☙

Conclusion

orn at a moment of great uncertainty and flux in global affairs,
humanity law supplies a new discourse for politics. This discourse
goes hand in hand with judicialization and greater reliance generally on legal processes and norms in the ordering of international society,
the regulation of conflict, and the protection of human security. Humanity
law is universalizing enough to offer a new legal and political subjectivity.
This subjectivity is defined and shaped by the humanity concept itself,
and is articulated and achieved through the multiplication of claims in
diverse actors' struggles over access to courts and other institutions of
global law.

In today's world, power is exceptionally fragmented and disorga-
nized—or perhaps, to put it more accurately, very complexly diffused.
Against the context of the prevailing power balance, there has been a
substantial increase in the number of weak and failed states, so that we
see heightened conflict that often plays itself out along multiple axes
(not just between states but also between and among majorities and
minority communities; collectivities defined or self-defined by ethnicity or religion; political factions; gangs; terrorist organizations;
secession movements; and more). We observe greater interdependence
and interconnection of diverse actors across state boundaries, yet we
still lack a well-institutionalized or well-ordered division of authority or
hierarchy of norms. One way to put this is that there is interconnection
without integration. Humanity law affords a language and a framework
that are capable of recognizing the claims and interests of multiple
actors in preservation and security, both individual and collective. It
also contributes a substantive and determinate but open-ended and

contextually applied normativity that is guiding politics today; a basis for legitimacy that is derived from humanitarian values and concepts of humanity rights and human security.

This framework provides a transformed basis for legitimation of foreign policy. Studying the framework can help us understand actions that are taken by diverse agents who appear to be caught in cycles of destructiveness yet, at another level, are seeking ways to attain this. In these ways, a humanity-law-based perspective should elucidate and contribute to a better understanding of current foreign policy controversies, as well as allowing us to make progress in describing and initiating the sort of rethinking that would be required for their resolution.

A NEW NORMATIVITY

Traditionally, the challenges for global law and politics have been framed or posed in terms of the state and the protection of its security and/or sovereignty. Humanity law engages a broader set of interests and values that are now recognized as being at play, and responds to the claims of state and nonstate actors that operate on the global stage (as was elaborated in chapter 3).

LESSONS FOR FOREIGN AFFAIRS

- Law has become central and foundational to the normative discourse of international affairs. We see a revival of the Grotian moment, as it were, in a discourse of international affairs that is increasingly preoccupied by the legality—not just the political bona fides—of global engagements. Insofar as the emergence of an expanded humanity law framework constitutes a discourse of law and ethics, humanity law is also being used in politics, with a variety of results. The pivotal role of law in the discourse of diplomacy has become clear since the end of the Cold War; humanity-centered claims permeate much foreign affairs discourse. What may not be as clear, however, is that this humanity-based judgment is in some sense two-sided: In other words, it is used by international society to denote and stigmatize regimes, yet these justifications have, relatedly, also become the basis for affirmative human rights protection claims, with the potential for more interventionism.

- The institutionalization of the new international law—as exemplified in the creation of courts—entails the challenge of elaborating a doctrine and discourse that can enable the balancing of the interests of persons and peoples, whose protection is at the core of humanity law, with those of states.
- Humanity law, as we have seen, may well constitute not just a basis for constraining the use of force but also a source of justifications for moving to force—and to various forms of interventionism, from judicial to military. (And such engagement may no longer be relegated to the state; consider, for instance, the role of Hezbollah in Lebanon.)
- Yet the increase in the willingness of states to intervene on behalf of distant peoples itself poses risks and dangers—which are framed in terms of the very values of humanity law that underpin the impetus to intervene: To see the nature of this crucial dilemma for foreign policy and strategy, one need only consider Somalia, Lebanon, Iraq, Afghanistan, and most recently Libya. In policymaking regarding contemporary conflicts—from the Balkans to Darfur to the Middle East—while there is an expression of a strong interest in condemning certain conduct, such as ethnic cleansing, at the same time there is also an evident lack of political consensus supporting intervention through the use of force. While this tension regarding enforcement persists, it sheds light on the useful role that trials and judgment can serve in the construction of political understandings of conflict, and of various political actors.
- Humanity law at the same time circumscribes rights-based intervention. The commitment to the protection of persons and peoples requires that just wars be waged justly, in ways that are in keeping with the very humanity rights that inspire the use of force in the first place. Policymakers have to consider whether they can achieve humanity law goals while also using means that are consistent with the normativity of humanity law. One might term this the "anti-Machiavellian principle." The treatment of persons, regardless of their nexus to the state, has become an indispensable part of the calculus of the potential for justice in the use of force. Indeed, the terms of engagement are now at the heart of political strategy, and have become an independent goal of interventions that are justified along humanity law lines—as can be seen, for example, in the reshaping of Coalition policy, in Operation Enduring Freedom, regarding Afghanistan. A

contemporary example is Security Council Resolution 1973 regarding Libya.[1]

- The humanity law framework entails border crossings (in prevailing territorial-state terms) of many kinds, destabilizing the norm of territorial sovereignty. As became manifestly clear with the NATO intervention in Kosovo, such border crossings are not capable of justification according to the letter of the UN Charter, as they are neither instances of the conventional "self-defense" of a "state" under armed attack (Article 51) nor authorized by the Security Council pursuant to Chapter VII. Indeed, the campaign against terror has also led to individual incidents of the use of force across territorial boundaries in Yemen, Pakistan, Sudan, and Georgia—incidents that often occur without the actual or implied consent of the states on the territory of which the incursion occurred. Again and again, states and tribunals are willing to compromise or suspend classic Westphalian norms of territoriality and sovereignty where humanity rights are at stake.

- Where humanity rights are at stake, this may trigger the related duty of "RtoP," as was illuminated in UN Security Council Resolution 1973 with respect to Libya.[2] However, the full implications of the RtoP for the UN Charter security system are not yet clear.

- One can see an evident tension between—and balancing of—*state* interests and interests in *human* security, where the law comes in ex ante in shaping the aims of the conflict, for example, *Tadic*, yet its enforcement generally depends on a certain degree of political exhaustion of other remedies having first occurred.

- Humanity law reaches political leaders—for instance, by removing the sovereign immunities that historically lay at the heart of the law of nations. But the limits remain contested: Examples include the *Case Concerning the Arrest Warrant of 11 April 2000 (Democratic Republic of the Congo v. Belgium)* in the ICJ and *Regina v. Bartle*, the case regarding the potential extradition of Pinochet in the UK House of Lords. So far, as we have seen, neither the ICC prosecutor alone (nor, for that matter, the "universality" prosecutor—Spain's Baltasar Garzon) have alone been able to target state/political leaders except when all else (that is, all hope of political remedies) fails. At that point, for example, the ICC prosecutor can proceed with a Security Council referral, and the targeting can be seen as a matter of political necessity, for example, Bashir and Qaddafi.

- Humanity law's extension of responsibility beyond the state enables it to reach violence that is perpetrated either by the military or by nonstate militia who are in control in a given situation. Here, we can see the growing significance of the enforcement of humanity law rights vis-à-vis private actors. One example is the ICC's involvement in the situation in, and cases out of, Uganda, and involving its long-standing conflict with the Lord's Resistance Army, where the state of Uganda referred private actors to the ICC for the offense of abducting and using child soldiers in the commission of atrocities constituting "crimes-against-humanity." Interestingly, the first state referral is for acts by private actors for offenses not hitherto considered to be the most grave; these referrals may be best understood through a humanity law lens.

- Humanity law exacts accountability from whoever wields public power and therefore deliver human security. Accountability takes the form of criminal and civil (smart, i.e., targeted) sanctions, as well as via the form of suits against state and nonstate actors. Of course, individuation has other costs, such as reliance on this form of accountability, which may elude other, more comprehensive political projects.

- While judicialization would appear to depend on the state and its institutions, as we have seen, these processes also often depend on private actors making claims and operating across state borders, pursuing civil society's interests via a range of justice options. This is reflected in the ongoing pursuit of diverse forms of transitional justice, that is, accountability more and more conceived as a human right, as well as in the emergence of so-called universality jurisdiction, whether the jurisdiction asserted is criminal, as in *Pinochet,* or civil, as in *Karadzic* or *Khulumani* (in the U.S.). The complex dynamic of this evolving understanding of the potential and uses of legal power is well illustrated by the precedents where the impetus for judicialization and legalization generally draws from private actors, and NGOs within civil society. In these instances, tensions between the state's political and judicial branches reflect its ambivalence as to its role in such law enforcement. Here, one can see that states are still present, but often they are acting through forms of judicial accountability where the focus is on the extension of jurisdiction—that is, on an expansion, as it were, of judicial supervision, yet one that may occur with or without the state. One might see this as a way, for a time, to turn over these issues to the base, working with civil society from the bottom up, as it were. Thus, for example, universal jurisdiction could be thought of as a device for localizing accountability below the level of the state, engaging a range of interested parties. That perspective helps explain some of the apparently fragmented or contradictory quality of the amalgamated legal framework—for instance, where multiple sites are in play, as in *Pinochet* and *Khulumani*. This framework ultimately may result in the destabilization of state policymaking on accountability.

• Where human rights are at stake, legal accountability has the appeal of providing a fair resolution to conflict, offering a neutral form of adjudication, ensuring the equality of parties, and so on. Yet legal accountability often abstracts from conflict, in terms of its statement of what is the relevant problem and who are the relevant actors. Consider the ICC referral of Bashir for the atrocities in Darfur. The involvement of the ICC arguably makes some political or diplomatic options for resolving the conflict more difficult to realize, while at the same time affecting what the international community, as well as the antagonists may view as the content or criteria for a legitimate settlement.

• Yet humanity law's concern with accountability may well continue to risk overshadowing and dominating other more state-centric projects, such as nation-building and democratization. As there are multiple and diverse actors (i.e., actors who often are private and nonstate) entangled in human protection, there is a rising demand to find ways of making these actors accountable for what happens on the ground, whether or not doing so is possible through the state itself (i.e., via legal principles of state responsibility). One can see the imperative of a pragmatic, contextual approach to accountability: The bottom line is that there has to be some locus or site of responsibility whenever human security at stake. This regularly comes up in military conflict; for example, dilemmas of responsibility have arisen in the campaign against terror where there are possible international, regional, and local sites of accountability. This prompts a new way of thinking about how ideas of accountability would apply to nonstate actors performing public functions. An example of this issue arises in the *Al Jedda* case before the House of Lords.

• The approach has been to treat some groups, for example, Hamas, Hezbollah, and Al Qaeda, as state proxies for purposes of arms races or conflicts over the use of force, as occurred in Iraq and in fighting in the arenas of terror and counterterror. Pursuing a humanity law logic, one might expose contradictions where these groups may threaten rather than protect human security. That is, one might compete in the arenas of human security. For instance, one might not expressly allow a gap in humanitarian aid but instead might co-opt the issue of aid in terms of human security on the ground in the occupied territories, or in Lebanon. Countering such groups may involve an affirmative policy of offering food, medicine, infrastructure, and other needed commodities in precisely the areas where these groups have become the de facto providers of human security.

- International law has developed quite sophisticated rules on state responsibility, including rules for attributing the behavior of diverse agents to the state (as contained in the International Law Commission's Articles on State Responsibility). The international responsibility of nonstate collectivities (e.g., private militias) in relation to the acts and omissions of individual members of those groups, remains quite unclear. Unresolved issues relate, for instance, to these actors' legal relationship to the acts and omissions of individual agents. Consider *Prosecutor v. Tadic* and *Bosnia v. Serbia*; the particular issues raised by the Serb militia in Bosnia; and the problem of attribution in these settings. The question is clear: How should we assess the principle of responsibility that relates to the varying functions and degrees of control that link up the conduct of nonstate actors to the responsibility of the state? In a departure from the prevailing state-centric international human rights all-or-nothing approach, recent cases point to an emergent pragmatic approach to the threshold question of responsibility, relating to the state's degree of control. A good example of the use of this approach can be found in *Al Skeini*, involving contestation over the meaning of "effective control," and the related allocation of responsibility in the context of accountability in the campaign against terror.

- The proliferation of other nonstate actors, such as courts and prosecutors, creates important effects on the international stage, especially in the context of conflict, where it may have a boomerang effect, in that what is good for humanity, in many instances, results in an ultimate overall increase in state responsibility under international law. Through principles of control and attribution, as well as through emergent duties to prevent and to prosecute in the case of crimes against humanity, states are presented with new burdens and challenges with respect to the control, and the accountability, of nonstate actors. Equally, when one thinks about human security, the responsibilities of states for the realization of economic, cultural, and social rights have become both more keenly felt and more boldly asserted.

- The humanity law framework has led to changes in the status of those injured or killed, and has importantly informed issues relating to the treatment of civilian populations—whether by strengthening protection under a humanity law framework and, where relevant capacity fails, triggering bases for intervention.

- Humanity law aspires to be protective of all; it affirms the universality of global society. Humanity law's emphasis on protecting the interests of persons and peoples has become increasingly well recognized and more deeply entrenched through the multistate enforcement mechanisms and processes, sanctions, remedies, and institutions—for example with related international law applied in domestic courts, for example *Hamdan*—but also with access to regional judicial institutions, for example *Kadi* and *Barrios Altos*, respectively from Europe to the Americas. Notably, all of these are justified not simply in terms of state consent but also in terms of a more elaborated or robust view of accountability, which is capable of articulation by public and private actors alike. Struggles over the nature and degree of engagement and intervention point to an understanding of the core human security right to protection, understood as human security—at least, protection from the worst attacks that go to the survival of persons and/or peoples. And that right, in turn, relates to the ongoing reconceptualization of war that is underway, as well as the reemergence of just war concepts, and the emphasis on the place of judgment in conflict. The universal content of humanity law protection embraces the rights to life, to humane treatment, and to judicial protection. These rights are at issue in a range of humanity-law-influenced proceedings— such as *Hamdan, Kadi, Isayeva, Barrios Altos, Abella*, and *Coard*, a case challenging U.S. detention policies of individuals during a military campaign in Grenada in 1983—that have held that "certain fundamental rights may never be suspended, as is the case, among others, of the right to life, the right to personal safety, or the right to due process....Under no circumstances may governments employ...the denial of certain minimum conditions of justice as the means to restore public order."[3]

• Due process rights are often framed in terms of the humanity law framework. This means that such rights may be *drawn from the multiple strands of law within the law of war*, such as Common Article 3 and Geneva rights. And moreover, these core humanity rights are read in light of human rights to life provided for from the international covenants and similar agreements and laws, and enforced in cases such as *Hamdan, Kadi, Ilascu v. Moldova, Tadic* (ICTY); *Wall* (ICJ); and *Coard*. Interestingly, unlike the twentieth-century formulations, which were framed largely in terms of limits on state power, these rights are now framed in universalizable terms of minimum assurances setting forth the basic norms of human society.

• In the protection of "peoples," the recognition of past wrongs and the related preservation of group histories and culture often appears in terms that transcend the usual nexus to the state and the related understanding of self-determination and self-preservation. One can see the vindication of rights of peoplehood, where, notably, full statehood is no longer the aspiration. Rather, nowadays, group-based claims are made increasingly in humanity rights terms, that is, protection against ethnic cleansing or protection of culture. Indeed, the articulation and vindication of such claims can be seen to jeopardize the humanity rights of other peoples. The new message has not been an easy one for the international society to learn. For example, consider Kosovo, where there has been a push by states for recognition, without a clear solution that would protect the humanity rights of all peoples in the relevant territory—as was illustrated in the *Badinter* case. Here, we can see a dimension of the complementarity that humanity law bears to politics—where the turn to courts appears vis a vis politics. There is a concern that the law may be dealing with apples and oranges, in seeking reconciliation of first, the right to self-preservation of the state within its borders with, the rights of other collectives. How can the reconciliation of these rights be accomplished, exactly? The issue is being raised, for instance, in the Balkans, and in conflicts along the Islamic frontier.

- The appeal of the evolving humanity law framework, as it is applied equally in conflict and in peacetime situations, suggests that the issues at the heart of conflicts today are not being well handled by domestic constitutional systems. (Consider, for example, the controversies taking place over the exercise of religion, particularly Islam, in Europe today—specifically in France, Turkey, and beyond.) Humanity law rights are in principle equally enforceable across countries, as well as across the public/private divide. They posit or offer new limits on the state's treatment of its groups in terms of its political, cultural, religious, or similar identity. Even in the recent past, other states couldn't intervene to protect their diasporic minorities. But now there has been an important normative change: Wherever groups (defined in terms of a basis ethnic affiliation) are moved around with an aim to destroy them—that reality can serve as a basis for intervention beyond the state. Meanwhile, however, the notion of state-building along the lines of group identity, where exclusionary means are deployed, for example in the Balkans, is off the table as a means to resolve conflict (*Seydic*). This last observation has important implications for state-building and democratization projects in the Middle East and elsewhere.

- These new rights may well entail affirmative obligations on the state. The assertion of group-based rights and diverse bases goes beyond the usual politically grounded affiliations as well as the secular/sectarian divide, which is not well captured by an intrastate framework. For example, the protection of cultural rights may transcend national boundaries. These conflicts often display tension within the human rights discourse the critical difficulty is the reconciliation of competing claims to preservation. Hence, consider the Balkans, or the Turkey/Armenian conflict, or Europe/Islam—examples of peoples confronting nationalism, and vice versa. One can better understand this in terms of the dynamic of humanity law, where peoples' claims (1) have status and standing beyond the as-yet-incomplete mapping within the state, and (2) have implications for the state in its protection of persons with affiliations beyond nationality and citizenship. Even some of the issues as to dealing with terrorism can be reconceptualized along these lines. Hence, what we see is the emergence of transnational rights, implying the equal recognition of peoples across borders. Such solidarity exists across state lines and in normative terms, constituting an emergent global human society.

NOTES

CHAPTER 1

1. The sources of the epigraphs to this chapter are as follows. Hugo Grotius, *The Rights of War and Peace*, trans. A. C. Campbell (Westport, Conn.: Hyperion Press, 1979) bk. 2, ch. 25; the Einsatzgruppen case, U.S.N.R., Military Tribunal II, Justice Michael A. Musmanno, Case 9: Opinion and Judgment of the Tribunal, 8 April 1948, 112–116, available at www.einsatzgruppenarchives.com/trials/crimesagainst.html; Kofi A. Annan, "Two Concepts of Sovereignty," *Economist,* 18 Sept. 1999, 49; Barack Obama, Remarks in address to the Nation on Libya (March 28, 2011), available at www.whitehouse.gov/search/site/remarks%20on%20libya (last visited April 6, 2011).
2. Case Concerning Oil Platforms (Iran v. U.S.), Judgment (International Court of Justice, November 6, 2003) (Higgins, Simma, op.).
3. See Ruti Teitel, "Humanity's Law: Rule of Law in a Global Politics," *Cornell International Law Journal* 35 (2002): 355, 356–359.
4. Mary Kaldor, *New and Old Wars: Organized Violence in a Global Era* (Stanford: Stanford University Press, 2007).
5. Translation of Oral Pleadings of Belgium, Legality of the Use of Force (Yugoslavia v. Belgium), CR 1999/14 (International Court of Justice, May 10, 1999).
6. U.N. Security Council Resolution 1973, U.N. Doc. S/RES/1973 (2011).
7. Ruti Teitel and Robert Howse, "Crossjudging: Tribunalization in a Fragmented but Interconnected Global Order," *New York University Journal of International Law and Politics* 41 (2009): 959.
8. Press Release, Secretary-General Reflects on Intervention in Thirty-Fifth Annual Ditchley Foundation Lecture, SG/SM/6613 (June 26, 1998).
9. Kofi A. Annan, "Two Concepts of Sovereignty," *The Economist,* September 18, 1999.
10. United States v. Otto Ohlendorf, reprinted in IV Trials of War Criminals before the Nuremberg Military Tribunals under Control Council Law No. 10411 No. 10 (Washington, D.C.: United States Government Printing Office, 1950), 498 (emphasis added).
11. David Golove, "Treaty-Making and the Nation: The Historical Foundations of the Nationalist Conception of the Treaty Power," *Michigan Law Review* 98 (2000): 1075.
12. Decision on the Defence Motion for Interlocutory Appeal on Jurisdiction (October 2, 1995), Appeals Chamber, International Criminal Tribunal for the Former Yugoslavia, para. 97.
13. See Press Release, U.N. Secretary-General Kofi Annan, Address Before the Commission on Human Rights in Geneva, Switzerland, SG/SM/6949 HR/CN/898 (April 7, 1999).

14. Press Release, Secretary-General Presents His Annual Report to General Assembly, SG/SM/7136, GA9596 (September 5, 1999).
15. Independent International Commission on Kosovo, *Kosovo Report: Conflict, International Response, Lessons Learned* (Oxford: Oxford University Press, 2000), 2: "The Commission concludes that the NATO military intervention was illegal but legitimate. It was illegal because it did not receive prior approval from the UN Security Council. However, the Commission considers that the intervention was justified because all diplomatic avenues had been exhausted and because the intervention had the effect of liberating the majority population of Kosovo from a long period of oppression under Serbian rule."
16. Bill Clinton, Remarks at Harvard University, November 19, 2001, available at www.news.harvard.edu/specials/2001/clinton/clintonspeech.html (last visited March 14, 2011).
17. See Rome Statute of the International Criminal Court, U.N. Doc. A/Conf. 183/9, 2187 U.N.T.S. 90, Article 5(1)(d), 5(2), July 17, 1998.
18. See generally Robert O. Keohane, Andrew Moravcsik, and Anne-Marie Slaughter, "Legalized Dispute Resolution: Interstate and Transnational," *International Organizations* 54 (2000): 457.

CHAPTER 2

1. See Tzvetan Todorov, *Imperfect Garden: The Legacy of Humanism* (Princeton: Princeton University Press, 2002): 160–190 (discussing Montaigne, Constant, Rousseau); Luc Ferry and Alain Renault, *From the Rights of Man to the Republican Idea* (Chicago: Chicago University Press, 1990).
2. See United Nations, Universal Declaration of Human Rights, U.N. General Assembly Resolution 217a (III), U.N. Doc. A/810, December 10, 1948.
3. Hersch Lauterpacht, "The Grotian Tradition in International Law," *British Yearbook of International Law* 23 (1946).
4. See The Nottebohm Case (Liechtenstein v. Guatemala), 1955 I.C.J. 4 (April 6, 1955); Draft Articles on Diplomatic Protection, Report of the International Law Commission on the Work of its Fifty-Sixth Session, UN Doc. A/59/10 (2004).
5. United Nations, General Assembly, Convention on the Elimination of All Forms of Discrimination Against Women, U.N. General Assembly Resolution 34/180, December 18, 1979, Articles 2 and 3.
6. Francisco de Vitoria, *De Indis Relectio*, sec. 3, proof 12 (1532), reprinted in *Classics of International Law*, ed. James Brown Scott (Washington, D.C.: Carnegie Institute, 1917), Vol. 7, 152. "[I]f there were any human law which without any cause took away rights conferred by natural and divine law, it would be inhumane and unreasonable and consequently would not have the force of law." Ibid.
7. Gordon Sherman, "Jus Gentium and International Law," *American Journal of International Law* 12(1) (1918): 56–63; Jeremy Waldron, "Foreign Law and the Modern Ius Gentium," *Harvard Law Review* 119 (2005): 129; Malcolm Shaw, *International Law*, 5th ed. (Cambridge: Cambridge University Press, 2003): 16–17; see also Arthur Nussbaum, *A Concise History of the Law of Nations* (New York: MacMillan, 1962).
8. See Antony Anghie, "Francisco de Vitoria and the Colonial Origins of International Law," *Social and Legal Studies* 5(4) (1996): 321–326.
9. "Quasi medium inter naturale jus, et humanum." Francisco Suarez, *De Legibus*, vol. 2, ch. 17, n. 1, verse 159.

10. See ibid. John P. Doyle, "Francisco Suarez on *The Law of Nations*," in *Religion and International Law*, ed. Mark W. Janis and Carolyn Evans (London: Martinus Nijhoff, 1999): 103–120 (citing Suarez, *De Legibus*).

11. Hersch Lauterpacht, "The Grotian Tradition in International Law," *British Yearbook of International Law* 23 (1946): 31.

12. Hugo Grotius, *De Jure Praedae Commentarius* (Oxford: Clarendon Press, 1950), 12.

13. Hugo Grotius, *De Jure Belli ac Pacis*, trans. Francis W. Kelsey (Oxford: Clarendon Press, 1925), bk. 1, ch. 1, secs. 13–14.

14. See Alberico Gentilli, *De Iure Belli Libri Tres*, trans. William Whewell (Cambridge: John W. Parker; London, 1853): 123–124; Richard Tuck, *The Rights of War and Peace: Political Thought and the International Order from Grotius to Kant* (Oxford: Oxford University Press, 1999): 35.

15. Hugo Grotius, *De Iure Praedae, Commentarius*, trans. Gwladys L. Williams (Oxford: Clarendon Press, 1950), 10–11, commentary 11.

16. See Benedict Kingsbury, "A Grotian Tradition of Theory and Practice? Grotius, Law, and Moral Skepticism in the Thought of Hedley Bull," *Quinnipiac Law Review* 17 (1997): 3, n. 7 (citing Hugo Grotius, *De Jure Belli ac Pacis*).

17. Thomas Hobbes, *Leviathan* (Oxford: Oxford University Press, 1998), ch. 14. See also Benedict de Spinoza, *Ethics* (1677), prop. 22: "No virtue can be conceived as prior to this endeavour to preserve one's own being."

18. See Hugo Grotius, *De Jure Belli ac Pacis*, trans. Francis W. Kelsey (Oxford: Clarendon Press, 1925): book 1, ch. 1, sec. 1.

19. See Martin Van Gelderen, "The Challenge of Colonialism: Grotius and Vitoria on Natural Law and International," *Grotiana*, new ser., 14/15 (1993, 1994): 3–37.

20. Oscar E. Nybakken, "Humanitas Romana," *Transactions and Proceedings of the American Philological Association* 70 (1939): 396–413.

21. Adolf Berger, *Encyclopedic Dictionary of Roman Law* (Transactions of the American Philosophical Society, new ser., 43, pt. 2 (1953): [ii], 333–808.

22. Judith Shklar, *Men and Citizens: A Study of Rousseau's Social Theory* (Cambridge: Cambridge University Press, 1969); see Jean Jacques Rousseau, *Political Writings* (New York: Nelson, 1953).

23. See Grotius, *De Jure Belli ac Pacis*, trans. Francis W. Kelsey (Oxford: Clarendon Press, 1925), bk. 1, ch. 2, secs. 40–41, "to protect humanity and defend justice."

24. Francois Rene de Chateaubriand, *Memoires d'outre-tombe* (Lausanne: Editions Recontre, 1968), vol. 2, ch. 16, 319–322 (my translation).

25. See Jean Henri Dunant, *Un souvenir de Solferino* (Geneva: Jules Fick, 1862).

26. Ibid., 61.

27. See Jean Pictet, *Development and Principles of International Humanitarian Law* (Dordrecht: Martinus Nijhoff, 1983): 62.

28. See Rupert Ticehurst, "The Martens Clause and the Laws of Armed Conflict," *International Review of the Red Cross* 317 (1997): 125–134. See also Ian Brownlie, *Principles of Public International Law* (Oxford: Clarendon Press, 1998).

29. See Rosemary Abi-Saab, "The General Principles of Humanitarian Law according to the International Court of Justice," *International Review of the Red Cross* 259 (1987): 367–375.

30. Hague Convention (II) with Respect to the Laws and Customs of War on Land, and Its Annex: Regulation concerning the Laws and Customs of War on Land: July 29, 1899, 32 Stat. 1803, 1 Bevans 247, 26 Martens Nouveau Recueil (ser. 2) 949. See Hague Convention Preamble

31. See Yves Ternon, *Les Armeniens: Histoire d'un Genocide* (Paris: Seuil, 1996): 125, 248.

32. See Report of the Commission on the Responsibility of the Authors of the War and on Enforcement of Penalties to the Versailles Peace Conference, March 29, 1919, reprinted in *American Journal of International Law* 14 (1920): 95.

33. Quincy Wright, "The Meaning of the Pact of Paris," *American Journal of International Law* 27 (1933): 39.

34. See Minority Schools in Albania, Ser. A/B., no. 64 (Permanent Court of International Justice, April 6, 1935).

35. Ibid.

36. See Milton Leitenberg, *Deaths in Wars and Conflicts in the Twentieth Century* (Ithaca, N.Y.: Cornell University Peace Studies Program, 2003); Security Council, Cross-Cutting Report No. 2, Protection of Civilians, Security Council Report (October 14, 2008), available at www.securitycouncilreport.org/site/c.lKWLeMTIsG /b.4664099/k.1776/CrossCutting_Report_No_2brProtection_of_Civiliansbr14_ October_2008.htm. Mary Kaldor, *New and Old Wars: Organized Violence in a Global Era* (Stanford: Stanford University Press, 1999). See also *New Wars, New Laws: Applying the Laws of War in Twenty-First-Century Conflicts*, ed. David Wippman and Matthew Evangelista (Ardsley, N.Y: Transnational, 2005).

37. Press Release, United Nations, Secretary-General Reflects on "Intervention" in Thirty-Fifth Annual Ditchley Foundation Lecture, U.N. Doc. SG/SM/6613 (June 26, 1998), at 4.

38. See Michael Ignatieff, *The Warrior's Honor: Ethnic War and the Modern Conscience* (New York: Holt, 1997).

39. See Report of the Commission on the Responsibility of the Authors of the War and on Enforcement of Penalties to the Versailles Peace Conference, March 29, 1919, reprinted in *American Journal of International Law* 14 (1920): 95.

40. See ibid. *War Criminals and War Crimes Trials: An Annotated Bibliography and Source Book*, ed. Norman E. Tuterow (New York: Greenwood Press, 1986).

41. See Judith N. Shklar, *Legalism: Law, Morals and Political Trials* (Cambridge, Mass.: Harvard University Press, 1964): 155.

42. Hannah Arendt, *Eichmann in Jerusalem: A Report on the Banality of Evil* (New York: Viking Press, 1964).

43. Geneva Convention I for the Amelioration of the Condition of the Wounded and Sick in the Armed Forces in the Field, 75 U.N.T.S. 31, October 21, 1950; Geneva Convention II for the Amelioration of the Condition of Wounded, Sick and Shipwrecked Members of Armed Forces at Sea, 75 U.N.T.S. 85, October 21, 1950; Geneva Convention III Relative to the Treatment of Prisoners of War, 75 U.N.T.S. 135, October 21, 1950; Geneva Convention IV Relative to the Protection of Civilian Persons in Time of War, 75 U.N.T.S. 287, Article 147, October 21, 1950; Protocol Additional to the Geneva Conventions of August 12, 1949, and Relating to the Protection of Victims of International Armed Conflicts (Protocol I), 1125 U.N.T.S. 3, December 7, 1979; Protocol Additional to the Geneva Conventions of August 12, 1949, and Relating to the Protection of Victims of Non-international Armed Conflicts (Protocol II), 1125 U.N.T.S. 609, December 7, 1978.

44. See Agreement for the Prosecution and Punishment of the Major War Criminals of the European Axis, and Charter of the International Military Tribunal, 82 U.N.T.S. 279 (1945) [hereinafter Nuremberg Charter].

45. Geneva Convention I for the Amelioration of the Condition of the Wounded and Sick in the Armed Forces in the Field, 75 U.N.T.S. 31, Article 3, October 21, 1950; Geneva Convention II for the Amelioration of the Condition of Wounded, Sick

and Shipwrecked Members of Armed Forces at Sea, 75 U.N.T.S. 85, Article 3, October 21, 1950; Geneva Convention III Relative to the Treatment of Prisoners of War, 75 U.N.T.S. 135, Article 3, October 21, 1950; Geneva Convention IV Relative to the Protection of Civilian Persons in Time of War, 75 U.N.T.S. 287, Article 4, October 21, 1950. All reprinted in Adam Roberts and Richard Guelff, *Documents on the Laws of War* (Oxford: Clarendon Press, 1989): 195–369. See generally Geoffrey Best, *War and Law since 1945* (New York: Oxford University Press, 1997).

46. Basic Principles for the Protection of Civilian Population in Armed Conflicts, U.N. General Assembly Resolution 2675 (December 9, 1970).

47. Geneva Convention I for the Amelioration of the Condition of the Wounded and Sick in the Armed Forces in the Field, 75 U.N.T.S. 31, Article 3, October 21, 1950; Geneva Convention II for the Amelioration of the Condition of Wounded, Sick and Shipwrecked Members of Armed Forces at Sea, 75 U.N.T.S. 85, Article 3, October 21, 1950; Geneva Convention 3 Relative to the Treatment of Prisoners of War, 75 U.N.T.S. 135, Article 3, October 21, 1950; Geneva Convention IV Relative to the Protection of Civilian Persons in Time of War, 75 U.N.T.S. 287, Article 3, October 21, 1950.

48. See Geneva Protocol Additional to the Geneva Convention of 12 August 1949, and Relating to the Protection of Victims of Non-international Armed Conflict, 8 June 1977, 1125 U.N.T.S. 609.

49. On the nexus between war and globalization, see Tarak Barkawi, *Globalization and War* (Lanham, Md.: Rowman and Littlefield, 2006); Yves Michaud, *Changements Dans La Violence, Essai sur la Bienveillance Universelle et la Peur* (Paris: Odile Jacob, 2002).

50. See David Kennedy, *The Dark Sides of Virtue: Reassessing International Humanitarianism* (Princeton: Princeton University Press, 2004).

51. See Beth A. Simmons, *Mobilizing for Human Rights: International Law in Domestic Politics* (Cambridge: Cambridge University Press, 2009).

52. See David Held, Anthony McGrew, David Goldblatt, and Jonathan Perraton, *Global Transformations* (Stanford: Stanford University Press, 1999). Rafael Domingo, *The New Global Law* (Cambridge: Cambridge University Press, 2010).

53. See, e.g., Stephen Krasner, *Sovereignty: Organized Hypocrisy* (Princeton: Princeton University Press, 1999); Stephen Krasner, "Structural Causes and Regime Consequences: Regimes as Intervening Variables," *International Organization* 36 (Spring 1982), reprinted in *International Organization: A Reader,* ed. F. Kratochwil and E. Mansfield (New York: HarperCollins, 1993); R. J. Beck, A. C. Arend, and R. D. Vander Lugt, *International Rules: Approaches from International Law and International Relations* (New York: Oxford University Press, 1996).

54. See Joseph H. H. Weiler, "The Rule of Lawyers and the Ethos of Diplomats: Reflections on the Internal and External Legitimacy of WTO Dispute Settlement," *American Review of International Arbitration* 13 (2002): 177; Anne-Marie Slaughter, *A New World Order* (Princeton: Princeton University Press, 2004), 263.

55. See Anne Peters, "Humanity as the A and Ω of Sovereignty," *European Journal of International Law* 20(3) (2009): 513–544.

56. See David Kennedy, "A New Stream of International Law Scholarship," *Wisconsin International Law Journal* 7 (1988): 14–17. See Martti Koskenniemi, "The Politics of International Law," *European Journal of International Law* 1 (1990): 6–10.

57. See Rome Statute of the International Criminal Court, U.N., U.N. Doc. A/Conf. 183/9, 2187 U.N.T.S. 90, July 17, 1998.

58. See, e.g., Jacques Derrida, *Of Grammatology* (Baltimore: Johns Hopkins University Press, 1976); Richard Rorty, *Philosophy and the Mirror of Nature* (Princeton: Princeton University Press, 1979).

CHAPTER 3

1. See Immanuel Kant, *Perpetual Peace* (Upper Saddle River, N.J.: Prentice Hall, 1998); Thomas L. Friedman, *The Lexus and the Olive Tree* (New York: Farrar, Straus and Giroux, 1999); Michael Doyle, "Kant, Liberal Legacies, and Foreign Affairs," *Philosophy and Public Affairs* 12 (1983): 205, 225 n. 23.
2. Compare Edward D. Mansfield and Jack Snyder, *Electing to Fight: Why Emerging Democracies Go to War* (Cambridge, Mass.: Harvard University Press, 2005) (on the correlation between fragile democracies and conflict).
3. Saskia Sassen, *Territory, Authority, Rights: From Medieval to Global Assemblages* (Princeton: Princeton University Press, 2006).
4. *Legalization and World Politics,* ed. Judith L. Goldstein, Miles Kahler, Robert O. Keohane, and Anne-Marie Slaughter (Cambridge: MIT Press, 2001): 1–15.
5. For the argument for norm diffusion, see Martha Finnemore and Kathryn Sikkink, "International Norm Dynamics and Political Change," *International Organization* 52 (1998): 887, 895–896, 901–902, 904.
6. Ruti Teitel with William Vidal, Summary of Findings of Longitudinal Study of Humanity Law Discourse (unpublished survey, Sept. 2006); Tony Blair, Doctrine of the International Community at the Economic Club, April 24, 1999, available at www.number10.gov.uk/Page1297 (last visited March 18, 2011); Bill Clinton, Farewell Address, January 18, 2001, available at http://odur.let.rug.nl/~usa/P/bc42/speeches/farewell.htm (last visited March 18, 2011).
7. Bill Clinton, Speech Announcing the End of the War in Kosovo, June 10, 1999, available at www.australianpolitics.com/usa/clinton/speeches/990610kosovo.shtml (last visited March 18, 2011).
8. See Jack Goldsmith, *The Terror Presidency* (New York: Norton, 2007); Kathryn Sikkink, *Mixed Signals: U.S. Human Rights Policy and Latin America* (New York: Cornell University Press, 2004); Beth Simmons, *Mobilizing for Human Rights: International Law in Domestic Politics* (Cambridge: Cambridge University Press, 2009).
9. Thomas G. Weiss, *Military-Civilian Interactions: Humanitarian Crises and the Responsibility to Protect* (Lanham, Md.: Rowman and Littlefield, 2004).
10. U.N. Security Council Resolution 1973, U.N. Doc. S/RES/1973 (2011).
11. Warren Hoge, "Attacks Qualify as War Crimes, Officials Say," *New York Times,* July 20, 2006, A11 (citing International Red Cross statement documenting both Israeli and Hezbollah violations of international humanitarian law). Press Release, Office of the United Nations High Commissioner for Human Rights, High Commissioner for Human Rights Calls for Protection of Civilians and Accountability in Latest Mideast Crisis (July 19, 2006), available at www.unhchr.ch/huricane/huricane.nsf/view01/5AF0033D13E85EFEC12571B00061BFDE?opendocument.
12. See, e.g., Human Rights Watch, A Face and a Name: Civilian Victims of Insurgent Groups in Iraq (October 2, 2005), available at www.hrw.org/en/reports/2005/10/02/face-and-name-0 (last visited March 18, 2011); Human Rights Watch, Killings in Eastern Rwanda (January 22, 2007), available at www.hrw.org/en/reports/2007/01/22/killings-eastern-rwanda (last visited March 18, 2011).
13. The epigraph to this section is from Michel Foucault, "8 February 1978," in *Security, Territory, Population: Lectures at the Collège de France 1977–1978* (New York: Palgrave Macmillan, 2007): 122.

14. Geneva Convention IV Relative to the Protection of Civilian Persons in Time of War, 75 U.N.T.S. 287, Article 4, October 21, 1950 (setting out terms of protection over grave breaches such as "willful killing, torture or inhuman treatment"); ibid. at Article 147. See U.N. Protection of Civilians in Armed Conflict, Security Council Resolution 1674, U.N. Doc. S/RES/1674 (April 28, 2006).

15. Armed Activities on the Territory of the Congo (Dem. Rep. Congo v. Uganda), Separate Opinion of Judge Simma, I.C.J. Reports 2005, p. 168 (December 19, 2005)) (citing Military and Paramilitary Activities in and against Nicaragua (Nicaragua v. United States of America), Merits, Judgment, I.C.J. Reports 1986, p. 114, para. 218): para. 29. (citing Corfu Channel, Merits, I.C.J. Reports 1949, p. 22.).

16. *Armed Activities on the Territory of the Congo* (Dem. Rep. Congo v. Uganda), Separate Opinion of Judge Simma, para. 27.

17. In the Case of the Prosecutor v. Omar Hassan Al Bashir, Case No. ICC-02/05-01/09, Warrant of Arrest for Omar Hassan Ahmad Al Bashir (International Criminal Court, March 4, 2009).

18. Human Rights Watch, Universal Jurisdiction in Europe: The State of the Art, Vol. 18, No. 5(D) (June 2006): 57.

19. See, e.g., Case Concerning the Arrest Warrant of April 11, 2000 (Dem. Rep.Congo v. Belgium), Judgment of February 14, 2002, 2000 idnumber="I.C.J. 121", 25 para. 60 (2002) ("[R]ules governing the jurisdiction of national courts must be carefully distinguished from those governing jurisdictional immunities: jurisdiction does not imply absence of immunity, while absence of immunity does not imply jurisdiction. Thus, although various international conventions on the prevention and punishment of certain serious crimes impose on States obligations of prosecution or extradition, thereby requiring them to extend their criminal jurisdiction, such extension of jurisdiction in no way affects immunities under customary international law, including those of Ministers for Foreign Affairs. These remain opposable before the courts of a foreign State, even where those courts exercise such a jurisdiction under these conventions.") See Regina v. Bartle, 37 I.L.M. 1302, para. 60 (U.K. House of Lords 1998).

20. R v. Metropolitan Stipendiary Magistrate and others, ex parte Pinochet Ugarte (No. 3), U.K. House of Lords, All ER (D) 325 (March 24, 1999): 203–205.

21. Ibid. 2 WLR at 262 (Lord Hutton).

22. Ibid. 2 WLR at 289–290 (Lord Philips).

23. Prosecutor v. Kallon, Case No. SCSL-2004-15-AR72(E), Decision on Challenge to Jurisdiction: Lomé Accord Amnesty, Appeals Chamber opinion (Special Court for Sierra Leone, March 13, 2004), para. 67.

24. See Hersch Lauterpacht, *Recognition in International Law* (Cambridge: Cambridge University Press, 1947) (on the lifting of state immunities).

25. Geneva Convention Relative to the Protection of Civilian Persons in Time of War, 75 U.N.T.S. 287, August 12, 1949; Geneva Convention Relative to the Treatment of Prisoners of War, 75 U.N.T.S. 135, August 12, 1949; Geneva Convention for the Amelioration of the Condition of the Wounded, Sick and Shipwrecked Members of Armed Forces at Sea, 75 U.N.T.S. 85, August 12, 1949; Geneva Convention for the Amelioration of the Condition of the Wounded and Sick in Armed Forces in the Field, 75 U.N.T.S. 31, August 12, 1949.

26. Emphases added.

27. Ibid. at para. 70; see Prosecutor v. Kordic and Cerkez, Case No. IT-95-14/2, Judgment (Trial Chamber, International Criminal Tribunal for the former Yugoslavia, February 26, 2001): para. 23: "Article 5 vests the International Tribunal

with the capacity to prosecute crimes against humanity 'when committed in armed conflict, whether international or internal in character.'" For the development in regard to armed conflict, see Theodor Meron, "War Crimes in Yugoslavia and the Development of International Law," *American Journal of International Law* 88 (1994): 84 (discussing changes in definition of "crimes against humanity").

28. Legality of the Threat or Use of Nuclear Weapons, Advisory Opinion, 1996 I.C.J. 679, 239 (1996), para. 24 (evaluating the two regimes and construing the relevance of the International Covenant on Civil and Political Rights). See Isayeva v. Russia, Application No. 57950/00, Judgment, European Court of Human Rights (2005); Abella v. Argentina, Case 11.137, Report No. 55/97, Inter-American Court of Human Rights OEA/Ser. L/v1695 Doc. Rev. at 271 (1997): paras. 164–165; Avilan v. Colombia, Case 11.142, Inter-American Court of Human Rights OEA/Ser. L/V/II Doc. 6 Rev. (1998); Fuentes v. Colombia, Case 11.519 Inter-American Court of Human Rights OEA/Ser. L/V/II.95, Doc. 7 Rev. (1998).

29. Legality of the Threat or Use of Nuclear Weapons, Advisory Opinion, 1996 I.C.J. 679, 239 (1996), para. 25 (emphasis added).

30. Inter-American Commission on Human Rights, Report on Terrorism and Human Rights, O.A.S. OEA/Ser. L/V/II.116, Doc. 5 Rev. para. 42, 1 corr. (October. 22, 2002); see Coard v. United States, Case 10.951, Report No. 109/99 (Inter-American Court of Human Rights, September 29, 1999).

31. Case Concerning Armed Activities on the Territory of the Congo (Dem. Rep. Congo v. Uganda), 2005 I.C.J. 116 (2005).

32. Legality of the Threat or Use of Nuclear Weapons, Advisory Opinion, 1996 I.C.J. 679, 239, para. 86, 106 (1996).

33. See Geneva Convention IV Relative to the Protection of Civilian Persons in Time of War, 75 U.N.T.S. 287, Article 2, October 21, 1950; Eyal Benvenisti, *The International Law of Occupation* (Princeton: Princeton University Press, 1993).

34. Legal Consequences of the Construction of a Wall in the Occupied Palestinian Territory, Advisory Opinion 2004 I.C.J. 136, para. 106 (2004). For discussion of the case, see Orna Ben-Naftali and Yuval Shany, "Living in Denial: The Application of Human Rights in the Occupied Territories," *Israel Law Review* 37 (2003–2004): 17, 26. More generally, for discussion of the debate over the question of the treatment of the overlapping regimes, see "Special Issue on Parallel Applicability of IHR and IHL," *Israel Law Review* 40 (2).

35. Ibid. at para. 104.

36. Ibid. at 240, paras. 25 and 106.

37. Here, compare Aeyal Gross, "Human Proportions: Are Human Rights the Emperor's New Clothes of the International Law of Occupation?" *European Journal of International Law* 18(1) (2007): 1–5, 18, 35 (arguing that the application of human rights law in the territories is potentially rights-diminishing), with William Schabas, " *Lex Specialis*? Belt and Suspenders? The Parallel Operation of Human Rights Law and the Law of Armed Conflict, and the Conundrum of *Jus Ad Bellum*," *Israel Law Review* 40 (2007): 592 (arguing against the application of international humanitarian law, as it is predicated on a state of conflict), and Nancy Prud'homme, "*Lex Specialis*: Oversimplifying a More Complex and Multifaceted Relationship," *Israel Law Review* 40 (2007): 356 (on the reductionism of the courts approach). For more information, see the Goldstone Report, Human Rights in Palestine and Other Occupied Arab Territories: Report of the United Nations Fact Finding Mission on the Gaza Conflict, Human Rights Council, U.N. Doc. A/HRC/12/48

(2009) [hereinafter Goldstone Report], para. 85, available at www2.ohchr.org/english/bodies/hrcouncil/specialsession/9/docs/UNFFMGC_Report.pdf (last visited March 15, 2011).

38. See Case Concerning the Application of the Convention on the Prevention and Punishment of the Crime of Genocide (Bosnia and Herzegovina v. Serbia and Montenegro) 2007 I.C.J. 91 (2007); see para. 404 regarding "effective control"; see ibid. at para. 399, citing Nicaragua v. United States, 1986 I.C.J. 520 (1986) ("for this conduct to give rise to legal responsibility of the United States it would in principle have to be proved that that State had effective control of the military or paramilitary operations in the course of which the alleged violations were committed"). See Bankovic v. Belgium, 2001-XII European Court of Human Rights 333 (Grand Chamber) (denying jurisdiction for an aerial bombardment of a radio and TV station in Belgrade for failing to constitute the exercise of territorial control).

39. Al-Skeini v. Secretary of State for Defence, [2007] UKHL 26 ("It is therefore necessary to turn to the facts to see if British troops could be said to have been in *effective control* of Basrah City for the purposes of Strasbourg jurisprudence at the relevant time." (emphases added)). This case is now on appeal at the ECHR. Al-Skeini and others v. United Kingdom (no. 55721/07) (European Court of Human Rights, pending).

40. See, e.g., Armed Activities on the Territory of the Congo (Dem. Rep. Congo v. Uganda), 45 I.L.M. 271, 310 (2005); Application of the Convention on the Prevention and Punishment of the Crime of Genocide (Bosnia and Herzegovina v. Serbia and Montenegro), 46 I.L.M. 188 (2007): 391–392.

41. Armed Activities on the Territory of the Congo (Dem. Rep. Congo v. Uganda), 45 I.L.M. 271, 357–358 (2005) (Kooijmans, J., concurring).

42. Ibid.

43. Armed Activities on the Territory of the Congo (Dem. Rep. Congo v. Uganda), Separate Opinion by Judge Simma, 45 I.L.M. 271, para. 13.

44. Ibid., para. 19 (emphasis added).

45. Ibid. at para. 41.

46. Ibid. at para. 39 (citing Legality of the Threat or Use of Nuclear Weapons, I.C.J. Reports 1996 (I), p. 257, para. 79).

47. See Geneva Conventions, Article 49, 50, 129, 146 respectively providing "each contracting state must ensure that its legislation provides 'effective penal sanctions for persons committing…any of the "grave breaches" defined in the Conventions." It must "bring such persons, regardless of their nationality, before its own courts," or "hand over for trial to another contracting state which has made out a prima facie case." Ibid.

48. Rome Statute of the International Criminal Court [hereinafter "the Rome Statute"], Rome Statute of the International Criminal Court, U.N. Doc. A/Conf. 183/9, 2187 U.N.T.S. 90, Articles 11–9, July 17, 1998 (setting out the court's jurisdiction). See also Geneva Convention I for the Amelioration of the Condition of the Wounded and Sick in the Armed Forces in the Field, 75 U.N.T.S. 31, Article 3, October 21, 1950 (incorporating, for the first time, "armed conflict not of an international character" into the lexicon of the law of war); see Statute of the International Tribunal for the Prosecution of Persons Responsible for Serious Violations of International Humanitarian Law Committed in the Territory of the Former Yugoslavia since 1991, annexed to Report of the Secretary-General Pursuant to Paragraph 2 of Security Council

Resolution 808, U.N. Doc. S/25704/Annexes (1993); Statute of the International Criminal Tribunal for the Former Yugoslavia [hereinafter "ICTY Statute"], U.N. Security Council Resolution 827, U.N. SCOR, annex, 48th Sess., 3217th Mtg., U.N. Doc. S/RES/827 (May 25, 1993), *as amended by* U.N. Security Council Resolution 1166, U.N. SCOR, annex, U.N. Doc. S/RES/1166 (1998); Statute of the International Tribunal for Rwanda, U.N. Security Council Resolution 955, U.N. SCOR, 49th Sess., 3453rd Mtg., U.N. Doc. S/RES/955 (1994), as annexed to U.N. Doc. S/IN-F/50 (1996) [hereinafter "ICTR statute"]. See Theodor Meron, "International Criminalization of Internal Atrocities," *American Journal of International Law* 89 (1995): 554, 554–555. The first case prosecuted by the ICTY dealt with this issue, see Prosecutor v. Tadic, Case No. IT-94-1, Judgment in Sentencing Appeals (Appeals Chamber, International Criminal Tribunal for the former Yugoslavia, January 26, 2000).

49. Prosecutor v. Tadic, Case No. IT-94-1, Decision on the Defence Motion for Interlocutory Appeal on Jurisdiction (International Criminal Tribunal for the former Yugoslavia, October 2, 1995): para. 129. On the other hand, "grave breaches," as defined in the Geneva Convention, applied only to international conflicts (emphasis added). Ibid.

50. Ibid. at para. 119.

51. Ibid. at para. 97.

52. Prosecutor v. Tadic, Case No. IT-94-1, Judgment (Trial Chamber, International Criminal Tribunal for the former Yugoslavia, May 7, 1997): para. 654.

53. Theodor Meron, *The Humanization of International Law* (Boston, Mass.: Martinus Nijhoff, 2006); Noora Arajärvi, "The Role of the International Criminal Judge in the Formation of Customary International Law," *European Journal of Legal Studies* 1 (2007).

54. See Prosecutor v. Tadic, Case No. IT-94-1, Decision on the Defence Motion for Interlocutory Appeal on Jurisdiction (International Criminal Tribunal for the former Yugoslavia, October 2, 1995): paras. 72–78.

55. Prosecutor v. Tadic, Case No. IT-94-1, Decision on the Defence Motion for Interlocutory Appeal on Jurisdiction (International Criminal Tribunal for the former Yugoslavia, October 2, 1995): para. 74.

56. In adopting the ICTY Statute, the Security Council established the International Tribunal with the stated purpose of bringing to justice persons responsible for serious violations of international humanitarian law in the former Yugoslavia, thereby deterring future violations and contributing to peace and security.

57. Prosecutor v. Delalic et al. ("Celibici"), Case No. IT-96-21, Appeal Judgment (International Criminal Tribunal for the former Yugoslavia, February 20, 2001): para. 194 (emphasis added).

58. Statute of the International Criminal Tribunal of Rwanda, annexed to United Nations, General Assembly, Resolution 955, U.N. Doc. S/RES/955 (1994) ICTR Statute. For discussion, see José Alvarez, "Crimes of States/Crimes of Hate: Lessons from Rwanda," *Yale Journal of International Law* 24 (1999): 365, 443 (on the perils of primacy jurisdiction over internal genocide).

59. Prosecutor v. Tadic, Case No. IT-94-1-T, Trial Judgment (International Criminal Tribunal for the former Yugoslavia, May 7, 1997): para. 654 (emphasis added).

60. Case Concerning Military and Paramilitary Activities in and against Nicaragua (Nicaragua v. United States), 1986 I.C.J. 520, 115 (1986). See also Antonio Cassese, "The Nicaragua and *Tadic* Tests Revisited in light of the ICJ Judgment on Genocide in Bosnia," *European Journal of International Law* 18 (2007).

61. See Prosecutor v. Kupreskic et al., Case No. IT-95-16, Trial Judgment (International Criminal Tribunal for the former Yugoslavia, January 14, 2000): paras. 551–555,

"such a policy need not be explicitly formulated, nor need it be the policy of a State." Prosecutor v. Akayesu, Case No. ICTR-96-4, Trial Judgment (International Criminal Tribunal for Rwanda, September 2, 1998): para. 580: "There is no requirement that this policy must be adopted formally as the policy of a state. There must however be some kind of preconceived plan or policy."

62. See Report of the International Law Commission on the Work of Its Forty-Third Session," U.N. Doc. A/46/10 (1991) at 103; relied on in Prosecutor v. Tadic, Case No. IT-94-1-T, Trial Judgment (International Criminal Tribunal for the former Yugoslavia, May 7, 1997): para. 655.

63. See Abella v. Argentina, Case 11.137, Report No. 55/97, OEA/Ser. L/v1695 Doc. Rev. at 271 (Inter-American Court of Human Rights, 1997), paras. 164–165.

64. Coard v. United States, Case 10.951, Report No. 109/99 (Inter-American Court of Human Rights, September 29, 1999), para. 59.

65. Coard et al. v. the United States (Inter-American Commission of Human Rights, September 29, 1999).

66. See Hannah Arendt, "Epilogue," in *Eichmann in Jerusalem: A Report on the Banality of Evil* (New York: Viking Press, 1964): 253–298. The Draft Articles on Diplomatic Protection endeavour to grapple with these difficulties.

67. The Nottebohm Case (Liechtenstein v. Guatemala), 1955 I.C.J. 4 (April 6, 1955).

68. Reservations to the Convention on the Prevention and Punishment of the Crime of Genocide, Advisory Opinion, I.C.J. Reports 1951, p. 15 (International Court of Justice, May 28, 1951): 23 (emphasis added).

69. Eichmann v. Attorney General of Israel, 36 I.L.R. 277 (S. Ct. Isr. 1962).

70. Ibid. (Landau, J., Opinion).

71. Prosecutor v. Anto Furundzija, 38 I.L.M. 317 (International Criminal Tribunal for the Former Yugoslavia, 1999) (quoting Israel v. Eichmann, 26 I.L.R. 277 (S. Ct. Isr. 1962)).

72. See Article 6. See also *Armed Activities* (Joint Sep. Opinion of Judges Higgins, Kooijmans, Elaraby, Owada, and Simma). See Bosnia vs Serbia, 46 I.L.M. 188 (9430).

73. See Carl Schmitt, *The Concept of the Political* (Chicago: University of Chicago Press, 1996).

74. David Luban, "A Theory of Crimes against Humanity," *Yale Journal of International Law* 49 (2004): 86–167, 140.

75. See S.S. Lotus (France v. Turkey), 1927 P.C.I.J. (Ser. A) No. 10 (September 7, 1927).

76. Universal Declaration of Human Rights, U.N. General Assembly Resolution 217a (III), U.N. Doc. A/810 at 71, December 10, 1948.

77. See Judith N. Shklar, *Legalism: Law, Morals and Political Trials* (Cambridge, Mass.: Harvard University Press, 1964): 155.

78. See Hannah Arendt, "Epilogue" in *Eichmann in Jerusalem: A Report on the Banality of Evil* (New York: Viking Press, 1964): 253–298.

79. See U.N. Security Council Resolution 138, U.N. Doc. S/4349 (June 23, 1960).

80. See Prosecutor v. Nikolic, Case No. IT-94-2, Decision on Interlocutory Appeal Concerning Legality of Arrest (International Criminal Tribunal for the Former Yugoslavia, September 5, 2003): Article 13, para. 26.

81. Eichmann v. Attorney General of Israel, 36 I.L.R. 277 (S. Ct. Isr. 1962). For discussion of the ambivalent meaning of prosecuting "the crimes against humanity" offense in these terms, see Hannah Arendt, *Eichmann in Jerusalem: A Report on the Banality of Evil* (New York: Viking Press, 1963).

82. For more, see Guyora Binder, "Comment: Representing Nazism: Advocacy and Identity at the Trial of Klaus Barbie," *Yale Law Journal* 98 (1989): 1321.

83. See Prosecutor v. Kupreskic et al., Case No. IT-95-16, Trial Judgment (International Criminal Tribunal for the Former Yugoslavia, January 14, 2000): paras. 547–548.

84. See Final Report of the United Nations Commission of Experts Established Pursuant to Security Council Resolution 780 (1992), U.N. Doc. S/1994/674, para. 78.

85. See Vukovar Rule 61 Decision, Case No. IT-95-13-R61 (International Criminal Tribunal for the former Yugoslavia, April 3, 1996).

86. See Prosecutor v. Tadic, Case No. IT-94-1, Decision on the Defence Motion for Interlocutory Appeal on Jurisdiction (International Criminal Tribunal for the former Yugoslavia, October 2, 1995): paras. 72–78.

87. See Regina v. Bartle, 37 I.L.M.1302 (U.K. House of Lords 1998) (op. of Lord Hope of Craighead).

88. Paul Kahn, "On Pinochet," *Boston Review* (1999), available at http://bostonreview.net/BR24.1/kahn.html.

89. See Marlise Simmons and Victoria Burnett, "Spanish Prosecutors Formalize Objection to Torture Indictments," *New York Times,* April 18, 2009, available at http://query.nytimes.com/gst/fullpage.html?res=9804E7D81538F93BA25757 C0A96F9C8B63&scp=4&sq=spain%20indictment%20bush&st=cse (last visited May 19, 2009) (Spanish prosecutors objected to the indictment of Bush administration officials for torture, arguing that American courts were the proper forum for criminal action).

90. Decision of the Supreme Court Concerning the Guatemala Genocide Case, 42 I.L.M. 686 (Spain. S. Ct. 2003).

91. Amnesty International, Universal Jurisdiction: The Duty of States to Enact and Implement Legislation, AI Index: IOR 53/002-018/2001 (2001).

92. Ibid. at 358.

93. Naomi Roht-Arriaza, "Guatemala Genocide Case: Spanish Constitutional Tribunal Decision on Universal Jurisdiction over Genocide Claims, *American Journal of International Law* 100 (2006): 207.

94. The 1993 Loi relative à la répression des infractions graves aux Conventions de Genèva du 12 aout 1949 aux Protocoles I et II du 8 juin 1977 ("Anti-Atrocity Law") and 1999 Amendment: Authorized Belgian courts to prosecute individuals accused of genocide, crimes against humanity, or war crimes without any direct link to Belgium. Spain: Article 23(4) of the Organic Law: Provides universal jurisdiction over several crimes, including genocide, terrorism, offenses related to prostitution, crimes related to the corruption of minors and the handicapped, and other crimes that Spain has a duty to prosecute under international treaties. A broad interpretation of Spain's universal jurisdiction statute was upheld in the recent Guatemala Genocide Case, in which, in September 2005, Spain's Constitutional Tribunal (Spain's highest court) reversed the decisions of the Audiencia Nacional and the Supreme Court by issuing "a ringing endorsement of broad universal jurisdiction."

95. See Victoria Burnett, "Jesuit Killings in El Salvador Could Reach Trial in Spain," *New York Times,* November 13, 2008, available at www.nytimes.com/2008/11/14/ world/americas/14salvador.html?n=Top/Reference/Times%20Topics/Subjects/E/ Extradition (last visited March 25, 2009). The querella in the case refers to the priests' Spanish origins: "La querella describe los hechos relacionados con el asesinato de los sacerdotes Jesuitas de origen español y nacionalizados salvadoreños."

96. Scilingo, No. 16/2005, Audiencia Nacional, Penal Chamber, 3d section (April 19, 2005). Antonio Betancourt, "World Briefing Americas: Mexico: Three-Way

Extradition," *New York Times,* June 11, 2003, Foreign Desk, late ed., A8; see also Press Release, Amnesty International, Mexico/Argentina/Spain: Justice One Step Closer Following Landmark Extradition Decision (June 11, 2003), AI Index: AMR 41/025/2003 (Public), News Service No: 139. See also Press Release, Human Rights Watch, Mexico: Court Ruling a Victory for International Justice (New York, June 10, 2003), available at www.hrw.org/en/news/2003/06/10/mexico-court-ruling-victory-international-justice (last visited March 30, 2009).

97. See Loi modifiant la loi du 16 juin 1993 relative a la repression des violations graves du droit international humanitaire et l'article 144ter du Code judiciaire [Act amending the law of June 16, 1993, concerning the prohibition of grave breaches of international humanitarian law and Article 144 of the Judicial Code], April 23, 2003, Moniteur Belge 24846, 24853 Article 7 (Belg.), trans. in 42 I.L.M. 740, 755 (2003).

98. For an excellent history of universal jurisdiction in Belgium, see Luc Walleyn, "Universal Jurisdiction: Lessons From the Belgian Experience," *Yearbook of International Humanitarian Law* 5(2002): 394–406. Similarly, in 2003, the Spanish Supreme Court limited the reach of its universal-jurisdiction law via the same nexus requirement the Belgian amendment had instituted. See Naomi Roht-Arriaza, "Universal Jurisdiction: Steps Forward, Steps Back," *Leiden Journal of International Law* 17 (2004): 375–389.

99. See Press Release, Registrar, European Court of Human Rights, Decision as to the Admissibility of Ould Dah v. France (No. 13113/03) (March 30, 2009), available at European Court of Human Rights Portal (HUDOC) , http://cmiskp.echr.coe.int/tkp197/view.asp?item=1&portal=hbkm&action=html&highlight=Ould%20|%20Dah&sessionid=46911285&skin=hudoc-pr-en (last visited February 18, 2010).

100. See Decision as to the Admissibility of Ould Dah v. France (No. 13113/03) (European Court of Human Rights, March 30, 2009) (decision is only available in French), available at European Court of Human Rights Portal (HUDOC), http://cmiskp.echr.coe.int/tkp197/view.asp?item=1&portal=hbkm&action=html&highlight=13113/03&sessionid=46911116&skin=hudoc-fr (last visited February 18, 2010). Another high-profile conviction for crimes committed in 1990s Tunisia is "France Jails Tunisian Diplomat for Torture," Agence France Presse, December 15, 2008, available at www.google.com/hostednews/afp/article/ALeqM5gTIWQI7cr9uGHdU-0zW5gfr0mjxA (last visited February 18, 2010).

101. See, e.g., Belgium's Amendment to the Law of June 15, 1993 (As Amended by the Law of February 10, 1999 and April 23, 2003) Concerning the Punishment of Grave Breaches of Humanitarian Law, August 7, 2003, reprinted in 42 I.L.M. 1258 (2003). For an overview of the changes, see Luc Reydams, "Belgium Reneges on Universality: The August 5, 2003 Act on Grave Breaches of International Humanitarian Law," *Journal of International Criminal Justice* 1 (2003): 679.

102. Cour de Cassation [Court of Cassation] February 12, 2003, Pasicrisie Belge 2003, Vol. 1, 307, 317–318 (Belg.).

103. Human Rights Watch, The Trial of Hissene Habre: Time Is Running Out for the Victims, January 2007, available at www.hrw.org/en/reports/2007/01/26/trial-hiss-ne-habr (last visited February 18, 2010).

104. African Union, Decision sur le Proces d'Hissene Habre et l'Union Africaine [Decision on the Hissene Habre Case and the African Union], Assembly/AU/Dec.127 (VII) available at www.africa-union.org/root/AU/Documents/Decisions/decisions_fr.htm (last visited February 18, 2010).

105. Case Concerning Questions Related to the Obligation to Prosecute or Extradite (Belgium v. Senegal), Order, I.C.J. 144 (2009): at p. 1.

106. Ibid. at 17: "[T]he Circumstances, as they now present themselves to the Court, are not such as to require the exercise of its power under Article 41 of the Statute to indicate provisional measures."

107. Hissène Habré v. Senegal, Decision No. ECW/CCJ/JUD/06/10, para. 61 (Court of Justice of the Economic Community of West African States, November 18, 2010) [unofficial translation of the French original], available at the website of Human Rights Watch, www.hrw.org/en/habre-case (last visited March 18, 2011).

108. M. Cherif Bassiouni, "Universal Jurisdiction for International Crimes: Historical Perspectives and Contemporary Practice," *Virginia Journal of International Law* 42 (2001): 81, 142. The Crimes against Humanity Act of 2000, Secs. 6 and 8 provide for jurisdiction over genocide, war crimes, and crimes against humanity that are committed outside Canada when such crimes are committed by Canadian citizens, by persons employed by Canada in a civil or military capacity, by citizens of a state with which Canada was in an armed conflict with, and by persons present in Canada after the alleged offense was committed. Jurisdiction is also allowed when the victim is a Canadian citizen. Crimes against Humanity and War Crimes Act, 2000, c. 24, C-45.9, Secs. 6 and 8. Sec. 6 of the German Criminal Code provides that "German criminal law shall further apply, regardless of the law of the place of their commission, to the following acts committed abroad: (1) genocide…" Sec. 6(9) allows for the application of German criminal jurisdiction for acts covered by "an international agreement binding on the Federal Republic of Germany… if they are committed abroad." Italy: Article 7 of Italian Criminal Code. In Switzerland: Code Pénal Militaire, Article 6, extends universal jurisdiction over the crimes of genocide, crimes against humanity, and war crimes.

109. See generally M. Cherif Bassiouni, "Universal Jurisdiction for International Crimes: Historical Perspectives and Contemporary Practice," Virginia Journal of International Law 42 (2001).

110. See Larry May, *Crimes against Humanity: A Normative Account* (New York: Cambridge University Press, 2005).

111. See In the Case of the Prosecutor v. Omar Hassan Al Bashir, Case No. ICC-02/05-01/09, Warrant of Arrest for Omar Hassan Ahmad Al Bashir (International Criminal Court, March 4, 2009).

112. See Loi modifiant la loi du 16 juin 1993 relative à la répression des violations graves du droit international humanitaire et l'article 144 ter du Code judiciaire, April 23, 2003, M.B., May 7, 2003, translated in 42 I.L.M. 749 (2003). Belgium: Act Concerning the Punishment of Grave Breaches of International Humanitarian Law, 38 I.L.M. 918 (February 10, 1999).

113. See Prosecutor v. Tadic, Case No. IT-94-1-T, Trial Judgment (International Criminal Tribunal for the former Yugoslavia, May 7, 1997): para. 654.

114. Prosecutor v. Furundzija, Case No. IT-95-17/1, Judgment (International Criminal Tribunal for the former Yugoslavia, December 10, 1998): para. 156.

115. Ibid.

116. See Kunarac, Case No. IT-96-23 and 23/1, Trial Judgment (International Criminal Tribunal for the former Yugoslavia, February 22, 2001): para. 470.

117. Ibid. Compare International Covenant on Civil and Political Rights, U.N. General Assembly Resolution 2200A (XXI), Article 7, March 23, 1976 (regarding relevant

humanitarian law) with Second Optional Protocol to the International Covenant on Civil and Political Rights, U.N. General Assembly Resolution 2200A (XXI), March 23, 1976 (regarding the prohibition against violence to the life, health, and physical or mental well-being of persons, "in particular murder, torture or cruel treatment.").

118. See "Spain Rejects US 'Torture' Probe," BBC News, April 16, 2009, available at http://news.bbc.co.uk/2/hi/8002262.stm (last visited February 18, 2010).

119. Ibid.

120. See Giles Tremleett and Justin Webster, "Judge Baltasar Garzon Suspended over Franco Investigation," *Guardian*, May 14, 2010.

121. Raphael Minder, "Spanish Judge Says His Fight for Human Rights Will Endure," *New York Times*, June 8, 2010.

122. International Federation for Human Rights, Universal Jurisdiction Developments: January 2006–May 2009, available at www.unhcr.org/refworld/publisher, IFHR,,TUR,4a26393f2,0.html (last visited March 18, 2011).

123. Ibid. Recently, Finland also invoked the concept, as Francois Bazaramba, a Rwandan pastor, was sentenced to life on charges of genocide. "Finnish Court Sentences Rwandan Pastor to Life," Reuters Africa, June 11, 2010, available at http://af.reuters.com/article/topNews/idAFJOE65A0JD20100611 (last visited March 18, 2011).

124. Prosecutor v. Tadic, Case No. IT-94-1, Appeal Judgment (Appeals Chamber, International Criminal Tribunal for the former Yugoslavia, July 15, 1999).

125. Statute of the Iraqi Special Tribunal, reprinted in 43 I.L.M. 231 (2004): Article 1(b): "The Tribunal shall have jurisdiction over any Iraqi national or resident of Iraq accused of the crimes listed in Articles 11 to 14 below, committed since July 17, 1968 and up until and including May 1, 2003, in the territory of the Republic of Iraq or elsewhere, including crimes committed in connection with Iraq's wars against the Islamic Republic of Iran and the State of Kuwait. This includes jurisdiction over crimes listed in Articles 12 and 13 committed against the people of Iraq (including its Arabs, Kurds, Turcomans, Assyrians and other ethnic groups, and its Shi'ites and Sunnis) whether or not committed in armed conflict." Article 10: "The Tribunal shall have jurisdiction over any Iraqi national or resident of Iraq accused of the crimes listed in Articles 11–14, committed since July 17, 1968 and up and until May 1, 2003, in the territory of Iraq or elsewhere, namely: (1) The crime of genocide; (2) Crimes against humanity; (3) War crimes; or (4) Violations of certain Iraqi laws listed in Article 14 below."

126. U.N. Security Council Resolution 1973, U.N. Doc. S/RES/1973 (2011).

127. See Margaret E. Keck and Kathryn Sikkink, *Activists beyond Borders: Advocacy Networks in International Politics* (Ithaca: Cornell University Press, 1998).

128. H. L. A. Hart, *The Concept of Law* (Oxford: Oxford University Press, 1961): 208–231.

129. See ibid. at 212–225, 222–226. See also Louis Henkin, *How Nations Behave: Law and Foreign Policy*, 2d ed. (New York: Columbia University Press, 1979): 42–44, 88–90, 93.

130. See, e.g., The Ambrose Light, 25 F. 408, 415–416 (D.C.N.Y. 1885) (explaining that piracy is a "violation of the common right of nations, punishable under the common law of nations by the seizure and condemnation of the vessel."). See Beth Van Schaack, "Justice without Borders: Universal Civil jurisdiction," *Proceedings of the Annual Meeting—American Society of International Law* 99 (2005): 120–122.

131. Filartiga v. Pena-Irala, 630 F.2d 876, 884 (2d Cir. 1980).

132. Kadic v. Karadzic, 70 F.3d 232 (2d Cir. 1995). See also Khulumani v. Barclay National Bank Ltd., 504 F.3d 254 (2d Cir. 2007) (vacating lower court decision holding that aiding and abetting violations of customary international law could not form the basis for ATCA jurisdiction); see also Chavez v. Carranza, 559 F.3d 486, *cert. denied* (6th Cir. 2009) (affirming 2005 jury verdict holding Colonel Nicolas Carranza, former vice-minister of defense of El Salvador, civilly liable for crimes against humanity).

133. See Sosa v. Alvarez-Machain, 542 U.S. 692, 762 (2004) (Justice Breyer's concurring opinion concerns the relation civil tort sanctions bear to the universalization of criminal jurisdiction for torture, piracy, and genocide as *jus cogens*): Sosa, 124 U.S. at 2765–2766; see also Rasul v. Myers, 512 F.3d 644 (D.C. Cir. 2008); vacated and remanded, Rasul v. Myers, 129 S.Ct. 763 (2008). See generally Basic Principles and Guidelines on the Right to a Remedy and Reparation for Victims of Gross Violations of International Human Rights Law and Serious Violations of International Humanitarian Law, U.N. General Assembly Resolution 60/147, March 21, 2006.

134. See Al Maqalah v. Gates, 605 F.3d 84 (D.C. Cir. 2010).

135. See Statute of the International Court of Justice, Article 38, as annexed to the Charter of the United Nations, 59 Stat. 1031, 33 U.N.T.S. 993; T.S. No. 993; 3 Bevans 1153 (signed at San Francisco, June 26, 1945).

136. See Rome Statute at Article 126.

137. See Jack Snyder and Leslie Vinjamuri, "Trials and Errors: Principle and Pragmatism in Strategies of International Justice," *International Security* 28(3) (Winter 2003–4): 5–44.

138. UN Mission in Kosovo Regulations 1999/24, 1999/25, and 2000/64. The resulting "Regulation 64 Panels" apply the law in force in Kosovo prior to March 1989 to the extent that it is compatible with international human rights norms.

139. See Tom Perriello and Marieke Wierda, Lessons from the Deployment of International Judges and Prosecutors in Kosovo, Prosecutions Case Studies Series (International Center for Transitional Justice, March 2006): 28, available at www.ictj.org/static/Prosecutions/Kosovo.study.pdf#search=%22ictj%2C%20 prosecution%20case%20study%2C%20kosovo%22, last visited March 30, 2009.

140. See United Nations Transitional Administration in East Timor (UNTAET), On the Establishment of Panels with Exclusive Jurisdiction over Serious Criminal Offences, U.N. Doc. UNTAET/REG/2000/15, Sec. 2.2. Agreement between the United Nations and the Government of Sierra Leone on the Establishment of a Special Court for Sierra Leone (January 16, 2002). U.N. Doc. UNTAET/REG/2000/15 (June 6, 2000); UNTAET, On the Organization of Courts in East Timor, U.N. Doc. UNTAET/REG/2000/11 (March 6, 2000); As amended by UNTAET, On the Amendment of UNTAET Regulation No. 2000/11 on the Organization of Courts in East Timor and UNTAET Regulation No. 2000/30 on the Transitional Rules of Criminal Procedure, U.N. Doc. UNTAET/REG/2001/25 (September 14, 2001).

141. See Statute of the Special Court for Sierra Leone, Article 2.4.

142. Statute of the Special Court for Sierra Leone (January 16, 2002), Article 1(1).

143. See ibid.

144. For more information, visit the website of the Special Court for Sierra Leone, at www.sc-sl.org/CASES/ProsecutorvsCharlesTaylor/tabid/107/Default.aspx (last visited March 30, 2009).

145. Agreement between the United Nations and the Royal Government of Cambodia Concerning the Prosecution under Cambodian Law of Crimes Committed during

the Period of Democratic Kampuchea, June 6, 2003, entered into force April 29, 2005, UN Doc. A/RES57/228B (Annex) (May 13, 2003).

146. Law on the Establishment of the Extraordinary Chambers, NS/RKM/1004/006 (October 27, 2004), Article 4, available at www.cambodiatribunal.org/tribunal-background/eccc-law-a-procedure.html, last visited March 18, 2011 [hereinafter "Law on the Establishment"].

147. Law on the Establishment, Article 5.6–7.

148. "Scarred, Not Healed," *Economist*, July 29, 2010, available at www.economist.com/node/16703385 (last visited March 29, 2011); see also Seth Mydans, "Khmer Rouge Hearing Ends," *New York Times*, November 21, 2007, available at www.nytimes.com/2007/11/21/world/asia/22cambo.html, last visited March 25, 2009.

149. See Laura A. Dickinson, "The Promise of Hybrid Courts," *American Journal of International Law* 97 (2003): 295, for a comprehensive discussion of the current hybrid tribunals.

150. Armed Activities on the Territory of the Congo (Democratic Republic of the Congo v. Rwanda) (Feb. 3, 2006) No. (International Court of Justice) (joint separate opinions of Higgins, Simma, and others). On the role of international law in socialization of states, see Ryan Goodman and Derek Jinks, *Socializing States: Promoting Human Rights through International Law* (Oxford: Oxford University Press, forthcoming).

151. Decision as to the Admissibility of Behrami v. France, Case No. 71412/01, and Saramati v. France, Norway and Germany, Case No. 78166/01 (European Court of Human Rights, May 2, 2007): paras. 148–149.

152. See ibid., para. 148.

153. Yassin Abdullah Kadi and Al Barakaat International Foundation v. Council and Commission, Judgment in Joined Cases C-402/05 P and C-415/05 P (European Court of Justice, September 3, 2008).

154. See Supplement to an Agenda for Peace: Position Paper of the Secretary General on the Occasion of the Fiftieth Anniversary of the UN, GA 50/60 at 70, UN Doc. a/50/60-S/1995/1 (January 3, 1995).

155. For a critical assessment of the case, see Joseph Weiler, "Kadi—Europe's Medellin," *European Journal of International Law* 19 (2008): 895.

156. See Isayeva v. Russia, Application No. 57950/00, Judgment, European Court of Human Rights (2005).

157. Ibid. at paras. 174, 175–176.

158. Ibid. at para. 176.

159. Ibid. at para. 209.

160. See Jeremy Waldron, "Minority Cultures and the Cosmopolitan Alternative," *University of Michigan Journal of Law Reform* 25 (1992): 751; Tzvetan Todorov, *On Human Diversity: Nationalism, Racism, and Exoticism in French Thought* (Cambridge, Mass.: Harvard University Press, 1993).

161. See Harold J. Berman, *Law and Revolution: The Formation of the Western Legal Tradition* (Cambridge, Mass.: Harvard University Press, 1983); Kenneth L. Karst and Keith S. Rosen, *Law and Development in Latin America: A Case Book* (Berkeley: University of California Press, 1975) (colonial courts). For a comparative analysis of the role of courts, see Martin Shapiro, *Courts: A Comparative and Political Analysis* (Chicago: University of Chicago Press, 1986): 23. On extraterritoriality, see Ralph Wilde, "R (on the application of Al-Skeini) v. Secretary of State for Defence (Redress Trust Intervening)," *American Journal of International Law*

102(3) (2008): 628. Ralph Wilde, "Complementing Occupation Law? Selective Judicial Treatment of the. Suitability of Human Rights Norms," *Israel Law Review* 42(3) (2009).

162. On globalization generally, see David Held and Anthony McGrew, *Globalization/ Anti-globalization: Beyond the Great Divide* (Cambridge: Polity Press, 2007): 62–87; *Transnational Legal Processes: Globalisation and Power Disparities*, ed. Michael Likosky (Boston: Butterworths, 2002), 385–389. For the historical articulation of the "law of nations" see discussion at chapter 2 and see William Blackstone, *Four Commentaries on the Laws of England*, 1st ed. (1765–1769), 67. See also Hugo Grotius, *De Jure Belli ac Pacis*, trans. Francis W. Kelsey (Oxford: Clarendon Press, 1925), 16.

163. See Decision of the Supreme Court Concerning the Guatemala Genocide Case, 42 I.L.M. 686 (Spain. S. Ct. 2003).

164. See U.N. Security Council Resolution 1593, U.N. Doc. S/RES/1593 (2005).

165. See U.N. Security Council Resolution 1970, U.N. Doc. S/RES/1970 (2011).

166. See Agreement on Accountability and Reconciliation between the Government of Uganda and the Lord's Resistance Army/Movement (June 29, 2007), and Annexure to the Agreement on Accountability and Reconciliation (February 19, 2008).

167. Pursuing International Justice: A Conversation with Luis Moreno-Ocampo, Prosecutor, International Criminal Court, Council on Foreign Relations (February 5, 2010), available at www.cfr.org/human-rights/pursuing-international-justice-conversation-luis-moreno-ocampo/p21418; see also Luncheon Dialogue with Fatou Bensouda, Deputy Prosecutor, Office of the Prosecutor, International Criminal Court, Annual Meeting of the American Society of International Law (March 24, 2011).

168. See ibid.

169. See Jack Snyder and Leslie Vinjamuri, "Trials and Errors: Principle and Pragmatism in Strategies of International Justice," *International Security* 28(3) (winter 2003–4): 5–44.

170. See Mark Tushnet, *Taking the Constitution away from the Courts* (Princeton: Princeton University Press, 1999).

171. See Jeffrey Dunoff and Joel Trachtman, "The Law and Economics of Humanitarian Law Violations in Internal Conflict," *American Journal of International Law* 93 (1999): 402–403 (focusing chiefly on state compliance).

CHAPTER 4

1. The quotation in the epigraph is from Barack Obama, Remarks by the President at the Acceptance of the Nobel Peace Prize, Oslo, Norway (December 10, 2009), available at www.whitehouse.gov/the-press-office/remarks-president-acceptance -nobel-peace-prize (last visited March 30, 2011).

2. Compare Hugo Grotius, *The Rights of War and Peace,* ed. Richard Tuck (Indianapolis: Liberty Fund, 2005) with Richard Tuck, *The Rights of War and Peace: Political Thought and the International Order from Grotius to Kant* (Oxford: Oxford University Press, 1999). See also Michael Walzer, *Arguing about War* (New Haven: Yale University Press, 2005): 4.

3. Hugo Grotius, *De Jure Belli ac Pacis*, trans. Francis W. Kelsey (Oxford: Clarendon Press, 1925): bk. 2, ch. 20, 40. See also ch. 2 at 16: "Now as public war can never take place, but where judicial remedies cease to exist..." (Hugo Grotius, *The Rights of War and Peace,* ed. Richard Tuck [Indianapolis: Liberty Fund, 2005]: at 83).

4. Emer de Vattel, *Le droit des gens; Ou, Principes de la loi naturelle appliqués à la conduite et aux affaires des nations et des souverains* (1758).

5. Ibid. at ch. 3, 12, sec. 188.

6. See Protocol I, Preamble, whereby the High Contracting Parties provide as follows: "Reaffirming that the provisions of the Geneva Conventions of 12 august 1949 and of this Protocol must be fully applied,…without any adverse distinction based on the nature or origin of the armed conflict, or on the causes espoused by or attributed to the Parties to the conflict."

7. See William Blackstone, *Commentaries on the Laws of England (A Facsimile of the First Edition of 1765–1769)* (Chicago: University of Chicago Press, 2002), vol. 2, 66–67 (discussing the existing application of international law to individuals).

8. See Richard Tuck, *The Rights of War and Peace: Political Thought and the International Order from Grotius to Kant* (Oxford: Oxford University Press, 1999).

9. See Regina v. Bartle and the Comm'r of Police, Ex Parte Pinochet (U.K. House of Lords, 1999), I.L.M. 38 (1999): 644.

10. Justice Jackson, Opening Address by the United States, November 21, 1945, available at the website of the Avalon Project, Yale Law School, http://avalon.law.yale.edu/imt/11-21-45.asp (last visited July 17, 2010).

11. Justice Jackson, Report to the President on Atrocities and War Crimes, June 7, 1945, available at the website of the Avalon Project, Yale Law School, http://avalon.law.yale.edu/imt/imt_jack01.asp (last visited March 30, 2009).

12. See Telford Taylor, *The Anatomy of the Nuremberg Trials: A Personal Memoir* (New York: Knopf, 1992): 41.

13. Compare the principle of individual responsibility as set forth in the Agreement for the Prosecution and Punishment of the Major War Criminals of the European Axis and the Charter of the International Military Tribunal, 82 U.N.T.S. 279 (1945) [hereinafter IMT Charter]: Article 6 with the Rome Statute, at Article 25.

14. See Rene Provost, *International Human Rights and Humanitarian law* (Cambridge: Cambridge University Press 2002).

15. See United States v. Ohlendorf (The Einsatzgruppen Case), reprinted in 4 Trials of War Criminals before the Nuremberg Military Tribunals under Control Council Law No. 10, 411 (1946–1953), 112 (emphasis added).

16. See IMT Charter, at Article 6(c).

17. United States v. Ohlendorf (The Einsatzgruppen Case), reprinted in 4 Trials of War Criminals before the Nuremberg Military Tribunals under Control Council Law No. 10, 411 (1946–1953), 112. (emphasis added).

18. IMT Charter, Article 6.

19. "Persons charged with genocide or any of the other acts enumerated in Article III shall be tried by a competent tribunal of the State in the territory of which the act was committed, or by such international penal tribunal as may have jurisdiction with respect to those Contracting Parties which shall have accepted its jurisdiction." Convention on the Prevention and Punishment of the Crime of Genocide (1948), entered into force January 12, 1951, 78 U.N.T.S. 277.

20. See Nottebohm Case (Liechtenstein v. Guatemala), Judgment, 1955 I.C.J. 4 (April 6) (holding that Liechtenstein is not entitled to extend its protection to Nottebohm vis-à-vis Guatemala based on the principle of effective nationality: the national must prove a meaningful connection to the state in question).

21. Prosecutor v. Tadic, Case No. IT-94-1, Decision on the Defence Motion for Interlocutory Appeal on Jurisdiction (International Criminal Tribunal for the former Yugoslavia, October 2, 1995): para. 58.

22. See, e.g., Statute of the International Criminal Tribunal for Rwanda, U.N. Security Council Resolution 955, U.N. Doc. S/RES/955 (1994).

23. U.N. Security Council Resolution 827 on Establishing an International Military Tribunal for the Prosecution of Persons Responsible for Serious Violations of International Humanitarian Law in the Territory of the former Yugoslavia since 1991, U.N. Doc. S/RES/827 (May 25, 1993).

24. See U.N. Security Council Resolution 764, U.N. Doc. S/RES/764 (1992), I.L.M. 31 (1992): 1465; U.N. Security Council Resolution 771, S/RES/771 (1992), I.L.M. 21 (1992): 1470.

25. See United Nations, Secretary-General, Final Report of the Commission of Experts Established Pursuant to Security Council Resolution 780 (1994), Available in Letter Dated May 24, 1994 from the Secretary-General to the President of the Security Council, Annex I, S/1994/674 [hereinafter Final Report of the Commission of Experts].

26. See and compare Interim Report of the Commission of Experts, U.N. Doc. S/25274 (February 10, 1993): para. 55 ("The expression ethnic cleansing is relatively new").

27. Ibid.

28. See Jacques Dumas, *Les Sanctions Penales des Crimes Allemandes* (Paris: Librairie Arthur Rousseau, 1916).

29. See Declaration of German Atrocities, November 1, 1943, 3 Bevans 816, 834, Dep't St. Bull. (November 6, 1943): 310–311.

30. Although this might change, ten years later. See Diane F. Orentlicher, Shrinking the Space for Denial: The Impact of the ICTY in Serbia," Open Society Institute Report (May 2008). But see Laurel E. Fletcher and Harvey M. Weinstein, "Violence and Social Repair: Rethinking the Contribution of Justice to Reconciliation," *Human Rights Quarterly* 24 (2002): 573.

31. See Prosecutor v. Nikolic, Case No. IT-94-2-I, Rule 61 Hearing: Opening Statement by Justice Richard Goldstone (Trial Chamber, International Criminal Tribunal for the former Yugoslavia, October 9, 1995).

32. See, e.g., Bulletin, International Criminal Tribunal for the former Yugoslavia, No. 15/16 10-III-1997 (referring to the Celebici trial as the first where Bosnian Serbs are victims of crimes charged), available at www.un.org/icty/BL/15art1e.htm (last visited March 30, 2009).

33. Ibid.

34. See United Nations, Secretary-General, Statute of the International Tribunal for the Prosecution of Persons Responsible for Serious Violations of International Humanitarian Law in the Territory of the former Yugoslavia, Article 5, Annex to Report of Secretary-General, Article 5(g) citing "rape" as a "crime against humanity."

35. See Prosecutor v. Akayesu, Case No. ICTR-96-4-T, Trial Judgment (International Criminal Tribunal for Rwanda, September 2, 1998): para. 597 ("Like torture, rape is a violation of personal dignity"); Prosecutor v. Kvocka, Case No. IT-98-30/1, Judgment (Trial Chamber, International Criminal Tribunal for the former Yugoslavia, November 2, 2001): para. 180 ("Sexual violence is broader than rape and includes such crimes as sexual slavery or molestation. Moreover, the *Akayesu* Trial Chamber emphasized that sexual violence need not necessarily involve physical contact and cited forced public nudity as an example").

36. See Human Rights Watch, Justice at Risk: War Crimes Trials in Croatia, Bosnia and Herzegovina, and Serbia and Montenegro, 16 Human Rights Watch Report

No. 7(D), at 9 (2004), available at www.hrw.org/en/reports/2004/10/13/justice-risk (last visited March 30, 2009).

37. For discussion, see Theodor Meron, "Comments: War Crimes in Yugoslavia and the Development of International Law," *American Journal of International Law* 88 (1994): 78.

38. See Immanuel Kant, *The Metaphysics of Morals*, trans. Mary Gregor (New York: Cambridge University Press, 1991): 183.

39. See Prosecutor v. Tadic, Case No. IT-94-T, Prosecutor's Response to the Defense's Motions (International Criminal Tribunal for the former Yugoslavia, filed on June 23, 1995): 23.

40. See Final Report of the Commission of Experts, at Annex 4, "The Policy of Ethnic Cleansing," at 21. See, e.g., Prosecutor v. Jelisic, Case No. IT-95-19-A, Prosecutor v. Nikolic, Case No. IT-94-2-R61.

41. See Convention on the Prevention and Punishment of the Crime of Genocide (1948), entered into force January 12, 1951, 78 U.N.T.S. 277 (defining "genocide" in terms of acts committed "with intent to destroy, in whole or in part, a national, ethnical, racial or religious group, as such"). Regarding the recognition of crimes against humanity, see IMT Charter, at Article 6(c).

42. See Prosecutor v. Kupreskic, Case No. IT-95-16, Judgment (Trial Chamber, International Criminal Tribunal for the former Yugoslavia, January 14, 2000): para. 543. In the 1987 prosecution of Klaus Barbie, a Nazi chief in occupied Lyon, France's High Court defined persecution as being committed in a systematic manner in the name of a "[s]tate practicing a policy of ideological supremacy," Federation Nationale des Deportes et Internes Resistants et Patriotes and Others v. Barbie, 78 I.L.R. 125, 128 (Criminal Chamber, Fr. Court of Cassation, 1985).

43. See United Nations, Security Council, Report of the Secretary-General Pursuant to Paragraph 2 of the Security Council Resolution 808 (1993).

44. For a critique, see George Fletcher, *Defending Humanity: When Force Is Justified and Why* (Oxford: Oxford University Press, 2008).

45. See U.N. Charter, at Article 69(c).

46. United Nations, Secretary-General, Statute of the International Tribunal (For the Prosecution of Persons Responsible for Serious Violations of International Humanitarian Law in the Territory of the former Yugoslavia), Article 5, Annex to Report of Secretary-General. See U.N. Security Council Resolution 955 Establishing the International Tribunal for Rwanda, S/RES/955 (1994) I.L.M. 33 (1994): 1598.

47. See Prosecutor v. Kupreskic, at para. 548 (citing *Barbie*). For discussion of the grey area between combatants and noncombatants, see *Tadic* discussion at chapter 3 (counterterror campaign now turning away from this binary opposition).

48. See Paul J. Magnarella, "Recent Developments in the International Law of Genocide: An Anthropological Perspective on the International Criminal Tribunal for Rwanda," in *Annihilating Difference: The Anthropology of Genocide* (Berkeley: University of California Press, 2002): 310–24.

49. See Legality of the Use of Force (Serbia and Montenegro v. Belgium), 2004 I.C.J. 279 (December 15, 2004); See also Ruti Teitel, "The Wages of Just War," *Cornell International Law Journal* 39 (2006): 689–698.

50. On the customary bases for international criminal law, see Theodor Meron, "War Crimes in Yugoslavia and the Development of International Law," *American Journal of International Law* 88 (1994): 79; Prosecutor v. Semanza, Case No. ICTR-97-20-T, Judgment and Sentence (Trial Chamber, International Criminal Tribunal for Rwanda, May 15, 2003): paras. 348–349: "Persecution may take diverse forms

and does not necessarily require a physical act.... Persecution may include acts enumerated under other sub-headings of crimes against humanity, such as murder or deportation, when they are committed on discriminatory grounds. Persecution may also involve a variety of different acts, not enumerated elsewhere in the Statute, involving serious deprivations of human rights."

51. Statute of the International Criminal Tribunal for the former Yugoslavia, UN Doc. S/25704 (1993), Article 5.

52. See Press Release, International Criminal Tribunal for the former Yugoslavia, Tribunal Welcomes the Arrest of Radovan Karadžić, NJ/MOW/PR1275e (July 21, 2008); Dan Bilefsky, "Karadzic Arrest Is Big Step for a Land Tired of Being Europe's Pariah," *New York Times*, July 23, 2008; and Prosecutor v. Karadžić and Mladić, Case No. IT-95-5/18, Amended Indictment of Radovan Karadžić (International Criminal Tribunal for the former Yugoslavia, May 31, 2000).

53. See Jenia Ioncheva Turner, "Nationalizing International Criminal Law," *Stanford Journal of International Law* 41 (2005): 1.

54. See Human Rights Watch, Unfinished Business: Serbia's War Crimes Chamber, Human Rights Watch Report (June 2007), available at http://hrw.org/backgrounder/eca/serbia0607/index.htm (last visited April 16, 2009). See Diane Orentlicher, *Shrinking Space for Denial: The Impact of the ICTY in Serbia* (OSI Report, 2008).

55. See Dayton Accords, Annex 4 (1995), referring to the constitution of Bosnia and Herzegovina, Article 9: "1. No person who is serving a sentence imposed by the International Tribunal and who has failed to comply with an order to appear before the Tribunal, may stand as candidate or hold any appointive, elective, or other public office in the territory of Bosnia and Herzegovina."

56. Press Release, Council of the European Union, 8/207 (July 22, 2008), regarding the Karadzic arrest: "This development illustrates the commitment of the new government in Belgrade to contribute to peace and stability in the Balkans regions. It is a significant step on Serbia's path toward the EU." See EurActive, EU Hails Arrest of Serbian War Criminal Karadzic, July 22, 2008, available at www.euractiv. com/en/enlargement/eu-hails-arrest-serbian-war-criminal-karadzic/article-174402 (last visited April 16, 2009).

57. Press Release, Council of the European Union, Joint Statement by EU HR Ashton and EU Commissioner Füle on Serbian Declaration on Srebrenica (March 31, 2010), available at www.europa-eu-un.org/articles/en/article_9644_en.htm (last visited April 17, 2011).

58. "Reactions to Arrest of Fugitive Karadzic," Reuters, July 21, 2008, available at www.reuters.com/article/idUSL2197077320080721.

59. Press Release, Council of the European Union, Joint Statement by EU HR Ashton and EU Commissioner Füle on Serbian Declaration on Srebrenica (March 31, 2010), available at www.europa-eu-un.org/articles/en/article_9644_en.htm (last visited July 17, 2010).

60. "Reactions to Arrest of Fugitive Karadzic," Reuters, July 21, 2008, available at www.reuters.com/article/idUSL2197077320080721.

61. "While recalling the European Parliament's resolution on Srebrenica of January 2009, the European Union notes the reaffirmation to fully co-operate with the International Criminal Tribunal for the former Yugoslavia (ICTY), in particular the arrest and handing over of the remaining fugitives, and to continue the domestic processing of war crimes." Joint Statement by High Representative Catherine Ashton and Commissioner Štefan Füle on the Serbian Declaration on

Srebrenica Brussels (31 March 2010), available at www.consilium.europa.eu/
uedocs/cms_data/docs/pressdata/EN/foraff/113647.pdf (last visited March 17,
2011); Olli Rehn, the EU Enlargement Commissioner, has said: "Serbia must show
that nobody is above the law and that anybody indicted for serious crimes will
face justice"; quoted in Dusan Stojanovic, "EU Suspends Talks with Serbia over
Mladic," *Washington Post*, May 3, 2006, available at www.washingtonpost.com/
wp-dyn/content/article/2006/05/03/AR2006050300697_pf.html; The E.U.
foreign policy chief, Catherine Ashton, explained that "Serbia's pledge to cooperate fully with the International Criminal Tribunal in The Hague was 'crucial' for
completing an agreement that is a steppingstone to talks on Serbian membership
in the European Union"; quoted in Dan Bilefsky, "E.U. Finds Serbia Censure
Lacking," *New York Times,* March 31, 2010, available at www.nytimes.
com/2010/04/01/world/europe/01iht-serbia.html (last visited March 17, 2011).

62. As of 12 October 2010, there are 114 States Parties to the Rome Statute The States
Parties to the Rome Statute, International Criminal Court, available at http://
www.icc-cpi.int/Menus/ASP/states+parties/ (last visited April 17, 2011). There
are currently fifteen cases pending in five Situations: (Situation in the Democratic
Republic of Congo, Situation in the Central African Republic, Situation in Uganda,
Situation in Darfur, and Situation in Kenya). Situations and Cases, International
Criminal Court, available at http://www.icc-cpi.int/Menus/ICC/Situations
+and+Cases/ (last visited April 17, 2011).

63. Prosecutor v. Tadic, Case No. IT-94-I, Decision on the Defence Motion For
Interlocutory Appeal on Jurisdiction (International Criminal Tribunal for the
former Yugoslavia, October 5, 1995): para. 97; see Prosecutor v. Tadic, Case No.
IT-94-1, Appeal Judgment (International Criminal Tribunal for the former
Yugoslavia, July 15, 1999). See also Ruti Teitel, "Nuremberg and Its Legacy, Fifty
Years Later," in *War Crimes: The Legacy of Nuremberg,* ed. Belinda Cooper (New
York: TV Books, 1999).

64. See Stephen Krasner, *Sovereignty: Organized Hypocrisy* (Princeton: Princeton
University Press, 1999), 182–183.

65. See United Nations 2005 World Summit Outcome Document, U.N. Doc. A/60/
L.1(2005): paras. 138–140.

66. For a classification on the various perspectives on the use of force under the UN
Charter, see Matthew C. Waxman, *Regulating Resort to Force: Form and Substance
of the UN Charter Regime* (forthcoming) (on file with the author).

67. See UN Charter, at Articles 51, 52, 53 in light of UN Charter at Article 2, para. 4.
See Louis Henkin, Editorial Comment, "NATO's Kosovo Intervention: Kosovo and
the Law of "Humanitarian Intervention," *American Journal of International Law* 93
(1999): 824, 827–828 (a "living Charter" would support an interpretation of the
law and an adaptation of UN procedures). Contra, see *International Law and the
Use of Force,* ed. Christine Gray (New York: Oxford University Press, 2008):
26–31.

68. Rome Statute at Article 17. For an argument that the ICC is intended to play a
secondary role to national governments, see Jenia Turner, "Nationalizing
International Criminal Law," *Stanford Journal of International Law* 41 (2005): 5–6.
See also William Burke White, "Proactive Complementary: The International
Criminal Court and National Courts in the Rome System of International Justice,"
Harvard International Law Journal 49 (2008): 56. ("ICC would step in to undertake
its own prosecutions only where national governments fail to prosecute and
where the Court has jurisdiction.")

69. See George Bermann, "Taking Subsidiarity Seriously," *Columbia Law Review* 94 (1994): 331. See also Robert Howse and Kalypso Nicolaidis, "Enhancing WTO Legitimacy: Constitutionalization or Global Subsidiarity?," Governance 16 (2003): 73.

70. Minimum Humanitarian Standards: Analytical Report of the Secretary-General Submitted Pursuant to Commission on Human Rights Resolution 1997/21, U.N. Doc. E/CN.4/1998/87 (1998): para. 74.

71. Rome Statute at Articles 25, 3(a); (b).

72. Rome Statute at Article 5(2); see The Crime of Aggression, Resolution RC/Res.6, Kampala (Uganda), 31 May–June 11, 2010, available at www.icc-cpi.int/Menus/ ASP/ReviewConference/Resolutions+and+Declarations/"Rome Statute Amendment Proposals," in Review Conference of the Rome Statute, Kampala, Uganda 31 May– June 11, 2010, available at www.icc-cpi.int/NetApp/App/MCMSTemplates/Content. aspx?NRMODE=Published&NRNODEGUID={10B31AA2-326E-498B-B270- 5924F98D7937}&NRORIGINALURL=/Menus/ASP/ReviewConference&NRCACHE HINT=Guest#proposals (last visited March 17, 2011).

73. While Article 1 of the Resolution sets out a general definition of aggression, Article 3 includes a nonexhaustive list of acts constituting aggression. The current proposal before the Special Working Group on the Crime of Aggression references Resolution 3314 in its entirety, defining an "act of aggression" with the same general language contained in Article 1 of the Resolution, followed by the list of acts. See Official Records of the Assembly of the States Parties, Seventh Session (second resumption), 9–13 February 2009, Report of the Special Working Group on the Crime of Aggression, Seventh Session (second resumption), ICC-ASP/7/ SWGCA/2, February 20, 2009, at Annex I, Proposals for a Provision on Aggression Elaborated by the Special Working Group on the Crime of Aggression, Article 8 *bis* (hereinafter "SWGCA Report").

74. The Crime of Aggression, Resolution RC/Res. 6, Kampala (Uganda), 31 May–June 11, 2010, available at www.icc-cpi.int/iccdocs/asp_docs/Resolutions/RC-Res.6- ENG.pdf (last visited April 17, 2011); Rome Statute Amendment Proposals, Review Conference of the Rome Statute, Kampala, Uganda 31 May–June 11, 2010, available at www.icc-cpi.int/NetApp/App/MCMSTemplates/Content.aspx ?NRMODE=Published&NRNODEGUID={10B31AA2-326E-498B-B270-5924 F98D7937}&NRORIGINALURL=/Menus/ASP/ReviewConference&NRCACHE HINT=Guest#proposals (last visited March 17, 2011).

75. "ICC States Reach Compromise on Crime of Aggression," Reuters, June 11, 2010, available at www.reuters.com/article/idUSTRE65A6SE20100611 (last visited March 17, 2011).

76. Ibid.

77. SWGCA Report, Annex I, Article 8 *bis*, para. 1.

78. The general principles of individual criminal responsibility contained in Article 25(3) of the Rome Statute remain applicable to the crime of aggression. See SWGCA Report, Annex I, Article 8(1) and draft Article 25(3 *bis*).

79. A further proposal would add a new paragraph 3 *bis* to Article 25, the provision of the Statute on individual criminal responsibility: "In respect of the crime of aggression, the provisions of the present article shall *only apply to persons being in a position effectively to exercise control over* or to direct the political or military action of a State." See SWGCA Report, Annex I, Article 25(3 *bis*) (emphasis added.)

80. The Crime of Aggression, Resolution RC/Res. 6, Kampala (Uganda), 31 May–June 11, 2010, available at www.icc-cpi.int/Menus/ASP/ReviewConference/Resolutions +and+Declarations/ (last visited March 17, 2011).

81. Ibid.
82. Judith N. Shklar, *Legalism: Law, Morals, and Political Trials* (Cambridge, Mass.: Harvard University Press, 1964): 155–156.
83. Rome Statute at Article 17.
84. Press Release, Office of the Prosecutor, Prosecutor's Statement on the Prosecutor's Application for a warrant of Arrest under Article 58 Against Omar Hassan Ahmad Al Bashir, July 14, 2008, available at www.icc-cpi.int/Menus/ICC/Situations +and+Cases/Situations/Situation+ICC+0205/Background+information/Prosecutor _s+Statement+on+the+Prosecutor_s+Application+for+a+warrant.htm (last visited August 3, 2010); see also Security Council Resolution 1593, U.N. Doc. S/RES/1593 (adopted on March 31, 2005).
85. Human Rights Watch, Sudan: National Courts Have Done Nothing on Darfur, June 11, 2007, available at www.hrw.org/en/news/2007/06/11/sudan-national-courts-have-done-nothing-darfur (last visited March 30, 2009).
86. Luis Moreno-Ocampo, "Now End This Darfur Denial," *Guardian*, July 15, 2010, available at www.guardian.co.uk/commentisfree/libertycentral/2010/jul/15/world-cannot-ignore-darfur (last visited March 17, 2011).
87. International Crisis Group, New ICC Prosecution: Opportunities and Risks for Peace in Sudan (July 14, 2008), available at www.crisisgroup.org/en/publication-type/media-releases/2008/new-icc-prosecution-opportunities-and-risks-for-peace-in-sudan.aspx (last visited March 20, 2011).
88. UN News Centre, International Criminal Court Prosecutor Says First Darfur Cases Are Almost Ready, December 14, 2006, available at www.un.org/apps/news/story.asp?NewsID=20989&Cr=sudan&Cr1 (last visited March 30, 2009).
89. See "Uganda Asks Sudan to Arrest Rebel Leader Accused of Atrocities," *New York Times*, October 8, 2005, A7; Evelyn Leopold, "Global Court Targets Uganda Cult in First Case," Reuters, October 6, 2005.
90. See Palestinian authority referral to the ICC. See Letter to the UN High Commissioner on Human Rights from the Office of the Prosecutor of the International Criminal Court, January 12, 2010, available at www.icc-cpi.int/menus/icc/structure%20of%20the%20court/office%20of%20the%20prosecutor /comm%20and%20ref/palestine/12%20january%202010%20_%20letter%20 to%20the%20un%20high%20commissioner%20on%20human%20rights (last visited March 17, 2011).
91. In January 2007, the ICC confirmed the charges for the court's first trial in the case The Prosecutor v. Thomas Lubanga Dyilo, for the Situation in the Democratic Republic of the Congo. However, the case has been wracked by conflict. After a trial began on January 26, 2009, the trial court ordered Lubanga's trial halted on July 8, stating that prosecutors had not complied with an order to turn over certain information to his defense. Prosecutors have appealed against the court's decision to release Lubanga, and the court subsequently suspended his release on July 23, 2010. See "Court Suspends Release of Congo's Lubanga," Reuters, July 23, 2010, available at www.reuters.com/article/idUSLDE66M1PT (last visited March 17, 2011). In addition, the ICC has issued five arrest warrants for senior leaders of the Lord's Resistance Army for the Situation in Uganda. On May 1, 2007, the ICC issued arrest warrants for a Sudanese minister, a militia leader, and the chairman and general coordinator of military operations of the United Resistance Front for the situation in Darfur, Sudan. On March 4, 2009, the court issued a warrant for the current sitting president of Sudan, Omar Hassan Ahmad Al Bashir, on charges of crimes against humanity, war crimes, and genocide. A

second warrant for Bashir's arrest was issued by the Trial Part on July 15, 2010. On May 23, 2008, the ICC issued an arrest warrant for ex–vice president Jean-Pierre Bemba for crimes committed on the territory of the Central African Republic. Bemba was surrendered to the court on July 3, 2008, and is currently facing five counts of war crimes. The trial is set to commence this year. For a current update on the ICC docket, see www.icc-cpi.int/Menus/ICC/Situations +and+Cases/Situations/ (last visited August 3, 2010).

92. See Skye Wheeler, "Uganda Rebels, Government Sign 'Permanent' Ceasefire," Reuters, February 23, 2008, available at http://uk.reuters.com/article/2008/02/23/idUKL23150811._CH_.242020080223 (last visited March 20, 2011).

93. See Human Rights Watch, Sudan: National Courts Have Done Nothing on Darfur, June 11, 2007, available at www.hrw.org/en/news/2007/06/11/sudan-national-courts-have-done-nothing-darfur (last visited March 30, 2009).

94. The Prosecutor v. Omar Hassan Ahmad Al Bashir, Warrant of Arrest for Omar Hassan Ahmad Al Bashir, Case No. ICC-02/05-01/09 (International Criminal Court, Pre-Trial Chamber I, March 4, 2009) (appeal of denial of grounds for jurisdiction over genocide on evidentiary grounds).

95. See Seventh Report of the Prosecutor of the International Criminal Court to the UN Security Council Pursuant to UNSCR 1593 (2005), paras. 105 and 106, available at www.icc-cpi.int/NR/rdonlyres/C4584AF2-6A72-4BB0-94E6-45F43CE18F68/277787/UNSC_2008_En.pdf (last visited March 30, 2009).

96. International Crisis Group, The ICC Indictment of Bashir: A Turning Point for Sudan? available at www.crisisgroup.org/home/index.cfm?id=5959&l=1 (last visited May 21, 2009); Reed Brody, Playing It Firm, Fair and Smart: The EU and the ICC's Indictment of Bashir, Human Rights Watch, March 19, 2009, available at www.hrw.org/en/news/2009/03/19/playing-it-firm-fair-and-smart-eu-and-iccs-indictment-bashir (last visited May 21, 2009).

97. U.N. Security Council Resolution 1973, U.N. Doc. S/RES/1973 (2011).

98. According to the Rome Statute, "crimes against humanity" will include the crimes of "apartheid" and the "disappearance" policies of Latin American and African military regimes; "rape" is also codified at several places in the new statute, including as a "crime against humanity." See "rape, sexual slavery, enforced prostitution, forced pregnancy . . . or any other form of sexual violence of war crime," ibid. at Article 8, para. 2(b)(xxii), and potentially a form of genocide. See ibid. at Article 6 (b)–(d).

99. The Whitney R. Harris World Law Institute of Washington University in St. Louis Law School launched a project in the spring of 2008 to draft a multilateral treaty condemning and prohibiting crimes against humanity. The Institute has released a draft treaty for comments, gearing up for an international conference in March 2010. The initiative's website is available at: http://law.wustl.edu/crimesagainst-humanity/ (last visited May 21, 2009). See also "Work Begins on Specialized Convention on Crimes against Humanity," Washington University in St. Louis School of Law, available at http://law.wustl.edu/news/index.asp?id=7194 (last visited May 21, 2009), and "Crimes against Humanity Treaty Draft Released for Comments," Washington University in St. Louis School of Law, available at http://law.wustl.edu/news/index.asp?id=7650 (last visited February 10, 2010).

100. See "Prosecutors of International Criminal Tribunals Call for Full Cooperation," International Criminal Tribunal for Rwanda Press Release, ICTR/INFO-9-2-662. EN (November 19, 2009). For additional information, see Patricia M. Wald, "Genocide and Crimes against Humanity," Washington University Global Studies Law Review 6 (2007): 621.

101. Judith N. Shklar, *Legalism: Law, Morals, and Political Trials* (Cambridge, Mass.: Harvard University Press, 1964): 165.
102. Ibid. at 162.
103. See generally H. L. A. Hart, *The Concept of Law*, 2d ed. (Oxford: Clarendon Press, 1994) (on the uses of sanctions for norm-strengthening functions in domestic law); Judith N. Shklar, *Legalism: Law, Morals, and Political Trials* (Cambridge, Mass.: Harvard University Press, 1964); Ruti Teitel, *Transitional Justice* (New York: Oxford University Press, 2000): 216–230.
104. See Prosecutor v. Kupreskic, Case No. IT-95-16, Judgment (Trial Chamber, International Criminal Court for the former Yugoslavia, January 14, 2000): para. 543 (citing Prosecutor v. Nikolic, Case No. IT-94-2, Rule 61 Decision (Trial Chamber, International Criminal Tribunal for the former Yugoslavia, October 20, 1995): para. 26).
105. See Hugo Grotius, *The Rights of War and Peace*, ed. Richard Tuck (Indianapolis: Liberty Fund, 2005), bk. 2, chs. 1, 2, 5, and 16.
106. Immanuel Kant, *The Philosophy of Law*, trans. W. Hastie (Edinburgh: T. and T. Clark, 1887): 198.
107. Dan Kahan, "Social Influence, Social Meaning, and Deterrence," *Virginia Law Review* 83 (1997): 349 (law plays a role in shaping perception through its expressive and normative regulatory effects).
108. Joel Feinberg, *Doing and Deserving* (Princeton: Princeton University Press, 1970); See Dan Kahan, "Social Influence, Social Meaning, and Deterrence," *Virginia Law Review* 83 (1997): 349. See also Elizabeth Anderson and Richard Pildes, "The Expressive Theories of the Law, a General Restatement," *University of Pennsylvania Law Review* 148 (2000): 1503.
109. See Martha Finnemore and Kathryn Sikkink, "International Norm Dynamics and Political Change," *International Organization* 52 (1998): 887, 895–896, 901–902, 904. See also Kathryn Sikkink, "From State Responsibility to International Criminal Accountability: A New Regulatory Model for Core Human Rights Violations" (2008), paper presented at the Annual Meeting of the American Political Science Association, Boston, August 28, 2008.
110. Press Release, International Criminal Tribunal of the former Yugoslavia, Tadic Case: The Verdict (May 7, 1997), CC/PIO/190-E, available at www.icty.org/sid/7537 (last visited March 17, 2011).
111. Prosecutor v. Rutaganda, Judgment and Sentence, Case No. ICTR-96-3-T (International Criminal Tribunal of Rwanda, December 6, 1999): para. 385.
112. See Press Release, The Hague, President of Uganda Refers Situation Concerning the Lord's Resistance Army (LRA) to the ICC, January 29, 2004, available at www.icc-cpi.int/menus/icc/press%20and%20media/press%20releases/2004/president%20of%20uganda%20refers%20situation%20concerning%20the%20lord_s%20resistance%20army%20_lra_%20to%20the%20icc (last visited April 6, 2011).
113. Statute of the International Criminal Tribunal for the former Yugoslavia, UN Doc. S/25704 (1993), Article 7(1); see also Statute of the International Criminal Tribunal for Rwanda, SC Res. 955 (November 8, 1994), Article 6(1).
114. Rome Statute at Article 25(3).
115. See Kiobel v. Royal Dutch Petroleum, 621 F. 3d 111 (2d Cir. 2011).
116. Khulumani v. Barclay Nat'l Bank Ltd., 504 F.3d 254, 281 (2d Cir. 2007) (Katzmann, J., concurring).
117. See U.N. Security Council Resolution 827, U.N. Doc. S/RES/827 (May 25, 1993), and U.N. Security Council Resolution 955, U.N. Doc. S/RES/955 (November 8,

1994) (establishing ad hoc international criminal tribunals for the former
Yugoslavia and Rwanda; noting "that the establishment of an international tribunal and the prosecution of persons responsible for the above-mentioned violations of international humanitarian law will contribute to ensuring that such
violations are halted and effectively redressed"). See Agreement between the
United Nations and the Government of Sierra Leone on the Establishment of a
Special Court for Sierra Leone (January 16, 2002); United Nations Transitional
Administration in East Timor, Regulation No. 2000/15 on the Establishment
of Panels with Exclusive Jurisdiction over Serious Criminal Offences (June 6,
2002). On the Sierra Leone Tribunal and other hybrid tribunals, see Jack
Snyder and Leslie Vinjamuri, "Trials and Errors: Principles and Pragmatism in
Strategies of International Justice," *International Security* 28 (Winter 2003–4).
See also Laura Dickenson, The Promise of Hybrid Tribunals, Vol. 97, No. 2.,
April 2003.

118. United Nations, Security Council, Report of the Secretary-General on the
Establishment of a Special Tribunal for Lebanon, S/2006/893 (2006). See also U.N.
Security Council Resolution 1757 Establishing the Special Tribunal for Lebanon, S/
RES/1757 (2007), available at www.stl-tsl.org/sid/49 (last visited March 17, 2011).

119. Mariam Karouny, "The Prosecutor of the U.N.-backed Tribunal Issued on Monday
a Draft Indictment over the 2005 Killing of Statesman Rafik al-Hariri, a Long-
Anticipated Move That Has Touched Off a Lebanese Political Crisis," *Reuters*,
January 17, 2011, available at www.reuters.com/article/2011/01/17/us-lebanon
-tribunal-idUSTRE70G4EH20110117 (March 20, 2011).

120. And yet the tribunal is already facing setbacks. Lebanese general Jamil el-Sayed,
who was detained from 2005 to 2009, filed a request in March 2010 for access to
court investigation files in order to establish, he claimed, that he was the victim
of slander and arbitrary detention. "General to Challenge UN Hariri Court in
Public Hearing," Agence France Presse, June 31, 2010, available at www.google.
com/hostednews/afp/article/ALeqM5jGLK37VSQAaPl7Fpn1Fd3PJgztMA (last
visited July 4, 2010). In 2010, Sayyed Hassan Nasrallah, the leader of Lebanon's
Hezbollah movement, said he anticipated several indictments of members of
Hezbollah by the United Nations prosecutor investigating the 2005 killing of
former Lebanon prime minister Rafik Hariri. "The leader of Lebanon's powerful
Hezbollah group said Sunday he expected many members of his group would be
indicted by a U.N. investigation into the killing of former prime minister Rafik
al-Hariri"; Laila Bassam, "Hezbollah Expects Many Indicted over Hariri Killing,"
Reuters (July 25, 2010), available at www.reuters.com/article/idUSTRE66O1O
220100725 (last visited March 17, 2011).

121. See H. L. A. Hart, *The Concept of Law* (Oxford: Oxford University Press).

122. See Hugo Grotius, *The Rights of War and Peace,* ed. Richard Tuck (Indianapolis:
Liberty Fund, 2005), bk. 2, 20, XK, 247; William Blackstone, *Commentaries on the
Laws of England (A Facsimile of the First Edition of 1765–1769)* (Chicago: University
of Chicago Press, 2002): 66–67 (discussing the then-existing application of international law to individuals).

123. See Hugo Grotius, *The Rights of War and Peace*, ed. Richard Tuck (Indianapolis:
Liberty Fund, 2005).

124. Ibid.

125. See Richard Arneson, "Just Warfare and Noncombatant Immunity," *Cornell
International Law Journal* 39 (2006): 663; David Rodin, "How Rights Move: Losing
and Acquiring Rights in the International Domain," Carnegie Council
Presentation, New York, N.Y., November 11, 2009.

126. See Arneson, "Just Warfare Theory and Noncombatant Immunity," *Cornell International Law Journal* 39 (2006): 663.

127. See Rome Statute at Articles 5, 8.

128. UN Security Council Resolution 1973, U.N. Doc S/RES/1973 (2011). See also Press Release, UN Press Centre, Security Council Approves "No-Fly Zone" over Libya, Authorizing "All Necessary Measures" to Protect Civilians, by Vote of 10 in Favour with 5 Abstentions, available at www.un.org/News/Press/docs/2011/sc10200.doc.htm (last visited March 20, 2011).

129. Press Release, the White House, Remarks by the President on the Situation in Libya (March 18, 2011), available at www.whitehouse.gov/the-press-office/2011/03/18/remarks-president-situation-libya (last visited March 20, 2011); see also Press Release, the White House, Remarks by the President in Address to the Nation on Libya (March 28, 2011), available at www.whitehouse.gov/the-press-office/2011/03/28/remarks-president-address-nation-libya (last visited March 29, 2011).

130. See U.N. Protection of Civilians in Armed Conflict, Security Council Resolution 1674, U.N. Doc. S/RES/1674 (April 28, 2006).

131. Armed Activities on the Territory of the Congo (Democratic Republic of the Congo v. Uganda), Simma Separate Opinion, 2000 I.C.J. 111, (19 December 2005) (citing Military and Paramilitary Activities in and against Nicaragua (Nicaragua v. United States of America), Merits, Judgment, I.C.J. Reports 1986, p. 114, para. 218): para. 29.

132. See UN Charter, at Articles 2, 51.

133. See Report of the International Commission on Kosovo (2000), 3.

134. Michael Walzer, *Just and Unjust Wars: A Moral Argument With Historical Illustrations* (New York: Basic Books, 2000); Ariel Colonomos, *La Pari de la Guerre* (Paris: Noel, 2009).

135. See H. L. A. Hart, *The Concept of Law* (Oxford: Oxford University Press), 213–232.

136. For more on targeted killings, see Dapo Akande, Clearing the Fog of War? The ICRC's Interpretive Guidance on Direct Participation in Hostilities, EJIL Analysis, EJIL: Talk!/Blog of the *European Journal of International Law,* available at www.ejiltalk.org/clearing-the-fog-of-war-the-icrcs-interpretive-guidance-on-direct-participation-in-hostilities/ (last visited March 17, 2011); Eben Kaplan, "Targeted Killings," Council on Foreign Relations (March 2, 2006), available at www.cfr.org/publication/9627/ (last visited March 17, 2011); Nils Melsner, *Targeted Killing in International Law* (New York: Oxford University Press, 2008); Mary Ellen O'Connell, "Unlawful Killing with Combat Drones: A Case Study of Pakistan, 2004–2009," in *Shooting to Kill: The Law Governing Lethal Force in Context,* ed. Simon Bronitt, Forthcoming Notre Dame Legal Studies Paper No. 09-43, available at SSRN: http://ssrn.com/abstract=1501144 (last visited March 17, 2011); Program on Humanitarian Policy and Conflict Research, Harvard University, On the Legal Aspects of "Targeted Killings": Review of the Judgment of the Israeli Supreme Court, Policy Brief, May 2007, available at http://opt.ihlresearch.org/index.cfm?fuseaction=Page.viewPage&pageId=707 (last visited March 17, 2011).

137. See Independent International Commission on Kosovo, *The Kosovo Report: Conflict, International Response, Lessons Learned* (Oxford: Oxford University Press, 2000).

138. Samantha Power, "Our War on Terror," *New York Times,* July 29, 2007, available at www.nytimes.com/2007/07/29/books/review/Power-t.html (last visited April 18, 2009). See Stephen Holmes, "Looking Away," *London Review of Books,*

November 13, 2002, available at www.lrb.co.uk/v24/n22/holm01_.html (last visited April 18, 2009).

139. President Barack Obama, Remarks by the President at the Acceptance of the Nobel Peace Prize, Oslo, Norway (December 10, 2009), available at www .whitehouse.gov/the-press-office/remarks-president-acceptance-nobel-peace-prize (last March 17, 2011).

140. U.N. Security Council Resolution 1973, U.N. Doc. S/RES/1973 (2011).

141. Letter dated October 7, 2001, from the Permanent Representative of the United States of America to the United Nations Addressed to the President of the Security Council, UN Doc. S/2001/946.

142. See Michael Walzer, *Arguing about War* (New Haven: Yale University Press, 2005): 9.

143. See Carlotta Gall, "British Criticize Air Attacks in Afghan Region," *New York Times*, August 9, 2007, A1. Richard Norton-Taylor, "Division in NATO after US Doubts Afghanistan Tactics," *Guardian*, January 16, 2008, available at www. guardian.co.uk/world/2008/jan/16/usa.afghanistan (last visited May 21, 2009); Peter Graff, "New Tactic for U.S., NATO in Afghanistan: Say Sorry," Reuters UK, April 17, 2009, available at http://uk.reuters.com/article/usTopNews/idUK-TRE53G3L620090417 (last visited May 21, 2009); Carlotta Gall and David E. Sanger, "Civilian Deaths Undermine Allies' War on Taliban," *New York Times*, May 13, 2007, available at www.nytimes.com/2007/05/13/world/asia/13AFGHAN. html?_r=1&pagewanted=1 (last visited May 21, 2009); Carlotta Gall, "From Hospital, Afghans Rebut U.S. Account," *New York Times*, January 25, 2009, available at www.nytimes.com/2009/01/26/world/asia/26afghan.html?scp=5&sq=af ghanistan+civil+death&st=nyt (last visited May 21, 2009).

144. Carlotta Gall, "British Criticize Air Attacks in Afghan Region," *New York Times*, August 9, 2007, A1 ("but one reliable count puts the number killed in Helmand this year at close to 300. British officers on the ground in Helmand, speaking on condition of anonymity, said the Americans had caused the lion's share of the civilian casualties in their area. They expressed concerns that the Americans' extensive use of air power was turning the people against the foreign presence.") For a related report on civilian losses in the region, see Human Rights Watch, The Human Cost: The Consequences of Insurgent Attacks in Afghanistan (2007).

145. See David Wippman, "Introduction," in *New Wars, New Laws? Applying the Laws of War in Twenty-First Century Conflicts* (Ardsley, N.Y.: Transnational, 2005); see also U.N. Security Council, Cross-Cutting Report: Protection of Civilians, 2008 No. 2, October 14, 2008, available at www.securitycouncilreport.org/atf/ cf/%7B65BFCF9B-6D27-4E9C-8CD3-CF6E4FF96FF9%7D/XCuttingPOC2008. pdf (last visited March 30, 2009).

146. Ibid.

147. See Jennifer Glasse, "General McChrystal: Success in Afghanistan Is Not Assured," Voice of America, October 1, 2009.

148. Matt Robinson, "Targeted Civilian Killings Spiral in Afghan War: U.N.," *Reuters*, March 9, 2011, available at www.reuters.com/article/2011/03/09/us-afghanistan -civilians-idUSTRE7224WJ20110309 (last visited March 20, 2011).

149. Laura King, "Afghan Leader Urges Coalition Troops to Curb Civilian Deaths," *Los Angeles Times*, February 21, 2010 (emphasis added).

150. See John F. Burns, "British Court Rejects European Rights Laws for Nation's Troops," *New York Times*, A11, July 1, 2010 (comparing the bases for UK and U.S. policies in Afghanistan).

151. Kofi Annan, "An Illegal War," *New York Review of Books*, October 21, 2004, 16.
152. Estimates of the Iraqi civilian death toll from the beginning of the war through June 2006 range from fifty thousand to six hundred fifty thousand deaths. The World Health Organization estimates 151,000 civilian deaths during this period. See Lawrence Altman and Richard Oppel, "W.H.O. Says Iraq Civilian Death Toll Higher Than Cited," *New York Times*, January 10, 2008, A14.
153. Case of Isayeva v. Russia, No. 57950/00 (European Court of Human Rights, February 24, 2005): 173.
154. Ibid.
155. Ibid., para. 175.
156. Ibid., para. 176.
157. Ibid., para. 191.
158. For discussion of justifications made for NATO intervention in Kosovo, see Antonio Cassese, "A Follow-Up: Forcible Humanitarian Countermeasures and Opinio Necessitatis," *European Journal of International Law* 10 (1999) 791–799 (referring to a number of states' making arguments in terms of human rights, rather than the UN Charter: e.g., the Netherlands argued that "a gradual shift is occurring in international law" whereby respect for human rights is more mandatory (than in the Charter) and respect for sovereignty less absolute (citing statement in the Security Council of the delegates of Netherlands, 4011th meeting S/PV.4011 at 12)).

CHAPTER 5

1. See, e.g., Universal Declaration of Human Rights, U.N. General Assembly Resolution 217 (III), Article 20, December 10, 1948.
2. See The Effect of Reservations on the Entry into Force of the American Convention on Human Rights (Articles 74 and 75), Advisory Opinion OC-2/82, Inter-American Court of Human Rights, Ser. A, No. 2, para. 30 (1982), I.L.M. 22 (1982): 37.
3. E.g., Helsinki Watch, War Crimes in Bosnia-Hercegovina, vols. 1–2, 5, New York: Human Rights Watch, 1992; Theodor Meron, "Humanization of Humanitarian Law," *American Journal of International Law* 94(2) (2000): 239–278.
4. See Geneva Convention Relative to the Treatment of Prisoners of War, 75 U.N.T.S. 135 (August 12, 1949) (on the treatment of combatants). See Yoram Dinstein, "Human Rights in Armed Conflict: International Humanitarian Law," in *Human Rights in International Law*, ed. Theodor Meron (Oxford: Oxford University Press, 1984): 345, 347.
5. On human rights theory, see Jeremy Waldron, *Theories of Rights* (New York: Oxford University Press, 1984); Maurice Cranston, *What Are Human Rights* (New York: Taplinger, 1973); *Human Rights*, ed. Ellen Frankel Paul, Fred D. Miller, Jr., and Jeffrey Paul (Oxford: Blackwell, 1984).
6. See Coard et al. v. the United States (Inter-American Commission of Human Rights, September 29, 1999) (involving rights claims regarding the United States in Grenada; looking to whether State observed the rights of a person subject to its authority and control).
7. See, e.g., Minority Schools in Albania, Ser. A/B., No. 64 (Permanent Court of International Justice, April 6, 1935).
8. International Covenant on Economic, Social and Cultural Rights, U.N. General Assembly Resolution 2200A (XXI), 993 U.N.T.S. 3, December 16, 1966 (entered into force January 3, 1976). See also Convention on the Prevention and

Punishment of the Crime of Genocide, 78 U.N.T.S. 277, December 9, 1948 (entered into force January 12, 1951). See Prosecutor v. Akayesu, Case No. ICTR-96-4-T, Judgment (International Criminal Tribunal for Rwanda, September 2, 1998), I.L.M. 37 (1998): 1399 (applying the Genocide Convention, Article 2, to all "stable and permanent" groups); Prosecutor v. Kayishema and Ruzindana, Case No. ICTR -95-1-T, Judgment (International Criminal Tribunal for Rwanda, May 21, 1999), para. 98. For discussion of these precedents, see William A. Schabas, "International Law Weekend Proceedings: Groups Protected by the Genocide Convention: Conflicting Interpretations from the International Criminal Tribunal for Rwanda," *ILSA Journal of International and Comparative Law* 6 (2000): 375.

9. See Hannah Arendt, "Epilogue," in *Eichmann in Jerusalem: A Report on the Banality of Evil* (New York: Viking Press, 1963): 268.

10. See Prosecutor v. Akayesu, Case No. ICTR-96-4-T, Judgment (International Criminal Tribunal for Rwanda, September 2, 1998): 511, 516.

11. Annex 4, The Policy of Ethnic Cleansing, Final Report of the United Nations Commission of Experts Established Pursuant to Security Council Resolution 780 (1992); U.N. Doc. S/1994/674 at 33 [hereinafter Annex, Final Report]. See Statute of the International Criminal Tribunal for the Former Yugoslavia, Article 48 at 1173, U.N. Doc. S/RES/827 (May 25, 1993); Ruti Teitel, "Bringing the Messiah through the Law," in *Human Rights in Political Transitions: Gettysburg to Bosnia*, ed. Carla Hesse and Robert Post (New York: Zone Books, 1999), 178.

12. International Covenant on Civil and Political Rights, U.N. General Assembly Resolution 2200A, December 16, 1966 (entered into force March 23, 1976); Geneva Conventions, Common Article 3.

13. See Statute of the International Criminal Tribunal for the former Yugoslavia, Article 48, U.N. Doc. S/RES/827 (May 25, 1993).

14. Rome Statute of the International Criminal Court [hereinafter "Rome Statute"], U.N. Doc. A/Conf. 183/9, 2187 U.N.T.S. 90, Article 7, July 17, 1998.

15. Ibid. at Article 7(2)(g).

16. Application of the International Convention on the Elimination of All Forms of Racial Discrimination (Georgia v. Russian Federation), No. 140, Judgment (International Court of Justice, April 1, 2011).

17. For the historical conceptualization, see Agreement for the Prosecution and Punishment of the Major War Criminals of the European Axis ("Nuremberg Charter"), Article 6(c), 82 U.N.T.C. 280 (August 8, 1945) (applied only to the persecution during the war). For the contemporary view, see Ruti Teitel, "The Universal and the Particular in International Criminal Justice," *Columbia Human Rights Law Review* 30 (1999): 285. See also Beth Van Schaack, "The Definition of Crimes against Humanity: Resolving the Incoherence," *Columbia Journal of Transnational Law* 37 (1999): 787.

18. For example, consider the definition and prosecution of "ethnic cleansing"; see Annex, Final Report, 33.

19. See Rome Statute at Article 7, regarding "Crimes against Humanity."

20. Prosecutor v. Tadic, Case No. IT-94-1, Decision on the Defence Motion for Interlocutory Appeal on Jurisdiction (International Criminal Tribunal for the Former Yugoslavia, October 2, 1995): para. 91.

21. Armed Activities on the Territory of the Congo (Dem. Rep. of Congo v. Uganda), Separate Opinion by Judge Simma, 45 I.L.M. 271 (December 19, 2005), para. 19.

22. See Georgia v. Russia (Joint dissenting opinion of President Owada, Judges Simma, Abraham and Donoghue and Judge ad hoc Gaja).

23. U.N. Doc. A/59/565 (December 2, 2004): 12.

24. In Larger Freedom: Towards Development, Security and Human Rights for All: Report of the Secretary-General, U.N. Doc. A/59/2005 (March 21, 2005): para. 78.

25. See Rome Statute at Article 5 (codifications of genocide and other offenses as the most serious offenses to the international community. Article 6 provides "genocide means the following acts committed with intent to destroy, in whole or in part, a national, ethnical, racial or religious group, *as such.*") (emphasis added).

26. See Human Rights Watch, Up in Flames: Humanitarian Law Violations and Civilian Victims in the Conflict over South Ossetia (January 23, 2009), available at www.hrw.org/en/reports/2009/01/22/flames-0 (last visited March 25, 2011).

27. Compare David Kennedy, *The Darker Side of Virtue: Reassessing International Humanitarianism* (Princeton: Princeton University Press, 2004), 111.

28. Kofi A. Annan, Speech of December 11, 2006 at Truman Presidential Museum and Library, available at www.un.org/News/ossg/sg/stories/statments_full.asp ?statID=40 (last visited September 6, 2007); see Secretary-General Calls for Renewed Commitment in New Century to Protect Rights of Man, Woman, Child—Regardless of Ethnic, National Belonging, U.N. Doc. HR/CN/898, reprinted in Press Release, SG/SM/6949 (April 7, 1999); Press Release, U.N., Secretary-General Kofi Annan, The Effectiveness of the International Rule of Law in Maintaining International Peace and Security, Address Before the Centennial of the First International Peace Conference in the Hague, *reprinted in* SG/SM/6997 (May 18, 1999). The Grotius quotation in the epigraph is from *De Jure Belli ac Pacis,* bk. 2, ch. 25, 8, 2.

29. See Ibid. (Annan stating to the Security Council, "In the face of massive and ongoing abuses, consider the imposition of appropriate enforcement action.")

30. See U.N. Security Council Resolution 1160, U.N. Doc. S/RES/1160 (March 31, 1998); U.N. Security Council Resolution 1199, U.N. Doc. S/RES/1199 (September 23, 1998); U.N. Security Council Resolution 1203, U.N. Doc. S/RES/1203 (October 24, 1998).

31. For the debate regarding the legality of unauthorized intervention on humanitarian grounds, compare W. Michael Reisman, "Unilateral Action and the Transformations of the World Constitutive Process: The Special Problem of Humanitarian Intervention," *European Journal of International Law* 11 (2000): 3; Thomas M. Franck, "Sidelined in Kosovo: The United Nations' Demise Has Been Exaggerated; Break it, Don't Fake it," *Foreign Affairs* 78 (1999); Jonathan I. Charney, "Editorial Comments: NATO's Kosovo Intervention: Anticipatory Humanitarian Intervention in Kosovo," *American Journal of International Law* 93 (1999): 834. See Antonio Cassese, "A Followup: Forcible Humanitarian Countermeasures and Opinio Necessitatis," *European Journal of International Law* 10 (1999): 791–799 (arguing that, to date, there is an absence of international law authorization for intervention).

32. See Antonio Cassese, "A Followup: Forcible Humanitarian Countermeasures and Opinio Necessitatis," *European Journal of International Law* 10 (1999): 791, 795 (citing Statement in the Security Council of the Delegates of Netherlands, 4011th meeting, S/PV.4011, at 12).

33. See speeches of Bush, Blair, author's compilation (2006) (on file with the author).

34. See, e.g., Samantha Power, "Our War on Terror," *New York Times*, July 29, 2007, available at www.nytimes.com/2007/07/29/books/review/Power-t.html (last visited April 18, 2009); see chapter 4, text at n. 128.

35. See U.N. Security Council Resolution 808, U.N. Doc. S/RES/808 (May 25, 1993).
36. See Immanuel Kant, "Toward Perpetual Peace: A Philosophical Sketch," in *Kant: Political Writings*, ed. H. Reiss (Cambridge: Cambridge University Press, 1970): 105. Richard Tuck, *The Rights of War and Peace: Political Thought and the International Order from Grotius to Kant* (New York: Oxford University Press, 2000). See also Michael Doyle, "Liberalism and World Politics," *American Political Science Review* 80 (1986): 1151–1169 (on Kant, liberal states, and war).
37. Judith Shklar, *Legalism: Law, Morals and Political Trials* (Cambridge, Mass.: Harvard University Press, 1964): 129.
38. See Hugo Grotius, *The Rights of War and Peace*, ed. Richard Tuck (Indianapolis: Liberty Fund, 2005), bk. 2, ch. 25, paras. 7–8.
39. See, e.g., U.N. Security Council Resolution 827, U.N. Doc. S/RES/827 (May 25, 1993) (stating that "the prosecution of persons responsible for serious violations of international humanitarian law...would contribute to the restoration and maintenance of peace"). See Rome Statute at Preamble; Statute of the International Criminal Tribunal for Rwanda, Preamble, U.N. Doc. S/RES/955 (1994).
40. See Ruti Teitel, "Bringing the Messiah through the Law," in *Human Rights in Political Transitions: Gettysburg to Bosnia, ed.* Carla Hesse and Robert Post (New York: Zone Books, 1999), 178. See also Press Release, U.N., Security Council Strongly Condemns Humanitarian Law Violations by Bosnian Serbs, Paramilitary Forces; Cites Summary Executions, Mass Expulsions, SC/6149 (December 21, 1995).
41. See generally José Alvarez, "Crimes of States/Crimes of Hate: Lessons from Rwanda," *Yale Journal of International Law* 24 (1999): 365.
42. See Independent International Commission on Kosovo, *Kosovo Report: Conflict, International Response, Lessons Learned* (New York: Oxford University Press, 2000): 186. For a critique, see Alfred P. Rubin, *Review Article, The Independent International Commission on Kosovo, Kosovo Report* (Oxford: Oxford University Press, 2000).
43. See Hugo Grotius, *The Rights of War and Peace*, ed. Richard Tuck (Indianapolis: Liberty Fund, 2005), Book 3, ch. 3: 552, 633.
44. Press Release, The White House, Remarks by the President on Libya (March 19, 2011), available at http://m.whitehouse.gov/the-press-office/2011/03/19/remarks-president-libya.
45. Independent International Commission on Kosovo, *Kosovo Report: Conflict, International Response, Lessons Learned* (New York: Oxford University Press, 2000): 186.
46. See United Nations 2005 World Summit Outcome Document, U.N. Doc. A/60/L.1 (2005). See also Although World Summit Outcome "Disappointing," UN Reform Efforts Must Continue, U.N. Doc. GA/10392, September 21, 2005, available at www.un.org/News/Press/docs/2005/ga10392.doc.htm (last visited March 19, 2011).
47. For discussion of accountability problems in the UN Security Council, see Robert Keohane, "The Concept of Accountability in World Politics and the Use of Force," *Michigan Journal of International Law* 24 (2003): 1121.
48. See Tony Blair, Statement on Iraq Following UN Security Council Resolution, available at www.number-10.gov.uk/output/Page3206.asp (last visited September 18, 2007).
49. Security Council Resolution 1970, U.N. Doc. S/RES/1970 (2011); Security Council Resolution 1973, U.N. Doc. S/RES/1973 (2011).

50. See United Nations 2005 World Summit Outcome Document, U.N. Doc. A/60/L.1 (2005): paras. 138–140.

51. See Security Council Resolution 1674, U.N. Doc. S/RES/1674 (April 28, 2006) (reaffirming "state's responsibility to protect populations from genocide, war crimes, ethnic cleansing and crimes against humanity"). See Carsten Stahn, "Responsibility to Protect: Political Rhetoric or Emerging Legal Norm?" *American Journal of International Law* 101 (2007): 99 (arguing that where the Security Council doesn't act, there is room for states to intervene, particularly where they would have a claim to self-defense). For a discussion of the anxiety that this will become an illegitimate basis for unilateral intervention, see also Jose Alvarez, The Schizophrenias of R2P, Panel Presentation, 2007 Hague Joint Conference on Contemporary Issues of International Law: Criminal Jurisdiction 100 Years after the 1907 Hague Peace Conference, The Hague, June 30, 2007.

52. UN Security Council Resolution 1674, U.N. Doc S/RES/1674 (2006).

53. UN Security Council Resolution 1973, U.N. Doc S/RES/1973 (2011). With respect to the use of force in the conflict in Libya, see Harold Koh, Statement Regarding Use of Force in Libya, American Society of International Law Annual Meeting, Washington, D.C. (March 26, 2011), available at www.state.gov/s/l/releases/remarks/159201.htm.

54. David Chandler, "The Responsibility to Protect: Imposing the 'Liberal Peace,'" *International Peacekeeping* 11 (2004): 59.

55. See Press Release, Security Council Debate: If State Unable, Unwilling to Protect Citizens against Extreme Violence, Security Council Must Assume Responsibility, Secretary-General Tells Council, U.N. Doc. SG/SM/1000-SC/8444 (July 12, 2005).

56. Secretary-General's address to the General Assembly, New York (September 19, 2006), available at www.un.org/apps/sg/sgstats.asp?nid=2209 (last visited March 11, 2009).

57. See Secretary-General's address at dinner on the 50th Anniversary of the Korea Society (May 15, 2007), available at www.un.org/apps/sg/sgstats.asp?nid=2569 (last visited March 11, 2009).

58. See Secretary-General's Message on United Nations Day (October 24, 2007), available at www.un.org/events/unday/2007/sgmessage.shtml (last visited March 19, 2011); see Press Release, UN News Centre, Appointment Confirmed of UN Special Advisor on the Responsibility to Protect (December 11, 2007).

59. See U.N. Security Council Resolution 1769, U.N. Doc. S/RES/1769 (2007).

60. See U.N. Security Council Resolution 1674, U.N. Doc. S/RES/1674 (2006) (citing United Nations 2005 World Summit Outcome Document, U.N. Doc. A/60/L.1 (2005): paras. 138, 139).

61. Press Release, U.N. Secretary-General Defends, Clarifies "Responsibility to Protect" at Berlin Event (July 15, 2008), U.N. Doc. SG/SM/11701 (emphases added).

62. Ibid.

63. Implementing the Responsibility to Protect: Report of the Secretary-General, U.N. Doc. A/63/677; Early Warning, Assessment and the Responsibility to Protect: Report of the Secretary-General, U.N. Doc. A/64/864 (July 14, 2010).

64. See Implementing the Responsibility to Protect: Report of the Secretary-General, U.N. Doc. A/63/677 (January 12, 2009).

65. See Situation of Human Rights in Myanmar, Note by the Secretary-General, U.N. Doc. A/60/221 (August 12, 2005): para. 106.

66. Compare Gareth Evans and Mohamed Sahnoun, "The Responsibility to Protect," *Foreign Affairs* 81(6) (2002): 110, with Mahmood Mamdani, "The Politics of Naming, Genocide, Civil War, Insurgency," *London Review of Books*, March 8, 2007: 5–8.

67. Rome Statute, Preamble.

68. Rome Statute at Article 5. See Report of the Special Working Group on the Crime of Aggression, Resumed fifth session, ICC-ASP/5/SWGCA/3 (January 31, 2007). See Rome Statute at Article 51(d). On the crime of aggression, see Non-paper by the Chairman on the Elements of Crimes, Informal Inter-sessional Meeting on the Crime of Aggression June 8–10, 2009 (May 28, 2009), available at www.icc-cpi.int/Menus/ASP/Crime+of+Aggression/. The definition will incorporate prior understandings set out by the General Assembly. For more discussion of areas of controversy, see chapter 4.

69. See Rome Statute, at Articles 25, 27 (on individual responsibility and the irrelevance of official capacity); but consider the ICJ: Case Concerning the Arrest Warrant of April 11, 2000 (Democratic Republic of Congo v. Belgium), Provisional Measures, 2000 I.C.J. 121 (2000).

70. See "Alberto Gonzales, January 25, 2002, Draft Memorandum from the White House Counsel to President Bush," in *The Torture Papers: The Road to Abu Ghraib*, ed. Karen Greenberg and Joshua Dratel (Cambridge: Cambridge University Press, 2005).

71. Compare Almog v. Arab Bank, PLC, 471 F. Supp. 2d 257, 285 (E.D.N.Y. 2007) (organized systematic suicide bombings and other murderous attacks against innocent civilians for the purpose of intimidating a civilian population are violations of the "law of nations") with Saperstein v. Palestinian Authority, 2006 WL 3804718, 7 (S.D. Fla. 2006).

72. See Katharine Q. Seelye and Michael Falcone, "Obama Says Clinton Is 'Bush-Cheney Lite,'" *New York Times*, July 27, 2007, Sec. A19 (on the debate between presidential candidates on the placing of a priori conditions on diplomatic meetings with the leaders of Syria, Cuba, and Venezuela).

73. On Al Qaeda's broader social justice identity, see *What Does Al Qaeda Want: Unedited Communiques*, ed. Robert Marlin (Berkeley: North Atlantic Books, 2004); Brad K. Berner, *The World According to Al Qaeda* (New Delhi: Peacock Book, 2007). John Kifner, "Hezbollah Leads Work to Rebuild, Gaining Stature," *New York Times*, August 16, 2006, available at www.nytimes.com/2006/08/16/world/middleeast/16hezbollah.html?ex=1313380800&en=c016b6007fee4b3a&ei=5088&partner=rssnyt&emc=rss (last visited September 18, 2007). Ninety percent of Hamas's work is social welfare related. See Council on Foreign Relations, Backgrounder on Hamas, available at www.cfr.org/publication/8968/#6 (last visited January 8, 2008).

74. "Excerpts: Bin Laden Video," *BBC News*, October 29, 2004, available at http://news.bbc.co.uk/2/hi/middle_east/3966817.stm (last visited April 13, 2010); Osama bin Laden has also purportedly said: "Justice is the right thing to do; injustice is suffering." "Purported bin Laden Message to Europe: Leave Afghanistan," CNN, November 29, 2007, *available at* http://edition.cnn.com/2007/WORLD/meast/11/29/bin.laden.message/index.html (last visited April 13, 2010).

75. Ismail Haniyeh, "1967: Our Rights Have To Be Recognized," *Guardian*, June 6, 2007, available at www.guardian.co.uk/commentisfree/2007/jun/06/israel.comment (last visited April 15, 2010).

76. See Nicolas Sarkozy, "Address at the Opening of the Fifteenth Ambassadors' Conference" (August 27, 2007), available at www.elysee.fr/elysee/elysee.fr/

anglais/speeches_and_documents/2007/speech_at_the_opening_of_the_
fifteenth_ambassadors_conference.79296.html (last visited September 18,
2007).

77. On the legitimacy of preventive war, see Ariel Colonomos, *La Pari de la Guerre*
(Paris: Noel 2009). See John Yoo, "Using Force," *University of Chicago Law Review*
71 (2004): 729 (arguing "anticipatory self-defence"); John Yoo, "Why Iraq's
Weapons Don't Matter," *Legal Times*, August 4, 2003, available at www.aei.org/
article/18962 (last visited March 20, 2011); but see Michael Walzer, *Just and
Unjust Wars: A Moral Argument with Historical Illustrations* (New York: Basic Books,
1977): 76–77. See also Michael Walzer, *Arguing about War* (New Haven: Yale
College, 2004): 146–147. See Henry Shue and David Rodin, *Preemption: Military
Action and Moral Justification* (New York: Oxford University Press, 2007). See also
David Rodin, "The Ethics of Asymmetric War," in *The Ethics of War: Shared Problems
in Different Traditions*, ed. Richard Sorabji and David Rodin (Burlington, Vt.:
Ashgate, 2006), 153. See Ariel Colonomos, *Moralizing International Relations:
Called to Account* (New York: Palgrave MacMillan, 2009).

78. For example, Lt. Col. Avital Leibovich, a spokeswoman for the Israeli military,
said: "What is foremost in our minds is protection of our civilians who live within
range of the border"; Ethan Bronner, "Report Criticizes Gaza Restrictions," *New
York Times,* August 19, 2010, available at www.nytimes.com/2010/08/20/world/
middleeast/20gaza.html (last visited March 20, 2011); see also Ismail Haniyeh,
"1967: Our Rights Have To Be Recognized," *The Guardian*, June 6, 2007, available
at www.guardian.co.uk/commentisfree/2007/jun/06/israel.comment (last visited April 15, 2010).

79. U.N. Human Rights Council, Fact-Finding Mission on the Gaza Conflict, Human
Rights in Palestine and Other Occupied Arab Territories, paras. 1624–1628, 1629,
U.N. Doc. A/HRC/12/48 (September 25, 2009) [hereinafter Goldstone Report].

80. See Goldstone Report.

81. See International Criminal Court, Fifteenth Diplomatic Briefing: Compilation of
Statements (The Hague, April 7, 2009): 8 (discussing the Palestinian National
Authority's acceptance of ICC jurisdiction).

82. See Kenneth Roth, "The Law of War in the War on Terror," *Foreign Affairs* (January/
February 2004), available at www.foreignaffairs.com/articles/59524/kenneth-
roth/the-law-of-war-in-the-war-on-terror (last visited March 20, 2011).

83. On the characterization of the war, see John Yoo, "Using Force," *University of
Chicago Law Review* 71 (2004): 729; see "Alberto Gonzales, January 25, 2002,
Draft Memorandum from the White House Counsel to President Bush," in *The
Torture Papers: The Road to Abu Ghraib*, ed. Karen Greenberg and Joshua Dratel
(Cambridge: Cambridge University Press, 2005): 118–121.

84. See Rasul v. Bush, 542 U.S. 466 (2004) (jurisdiction exists over aliens asserting
habeas corpus rights in custody at Guantánamo).

85. See "Jay Bybee, January 22, 2002, OLC Memorandum for Alberto Gonzales," in
Karen Greenberg and Joshua Dratel, *The Torture Papers: The Road to Abu Ghraib*
(Cambridge: Cambridge University Press, 2005): 81–117. See "Alberto Gonzales,
January 25, 2002, Draft Memorandum from the White House Counsel to
President Bush," in ibid., 118–121.

86. Harold Koh, Legal Advisor, U.S. Dept of State, The Obama Administration and
International Law, Address to Annual Meeting of the American Society of
International Law (March 25, 2010), available at www.state.gov/s/l/releases/
remarks/139119.htm.

87. 'Ralph Wilde, "Legal "Black Hole"?: Extraterritorial State Action and International Treaty Law on Civil and Political Rights,'" *Michigan Journal of International Law* 26 (2005): 739–806.

88. Barrio Altos Case, Inter-American Court of Human Right (Judgment of March 14, 2001), paras. 14–15.

89. See Boumediene v. Bush, 128 S. Ct. 2229, 2277 (2008) (Kennedy Op.).

90. While the administration's strategy may have been one of isolating aliens, the trend toward judicialization has led in another leveling direction. On the issue of the rights of aliens in the war on terror, see David Cole, *Enemy Aliens* (New York: New Press, 2003). But see Munaf v. Geren, 128 S. Ct. 2207 (2008) (in case of American in custody in Iraq, holding that United States courts have jurisdiction over habeas corpus petitions filed on behalf of American citizens detained overseas in camps operated by the multinational force in Iraq).

91. See Hamdi v. Rumsfeld, 542 U.S. 507, 531 (O'Connor op.).

92. See A (FC) & Others (FC) v. Secretary of State for the Home Department, (2004) UKHL 56 (December 16, 2004), paras. 54–73 (holding law incompatible with the European Convention on Human Rights because it discriminated between British and foreign nationals in not providing for the potential detention of British terror suspects).

93. See Hamdi v. Rumsfeld, 542 U.S. 507, 519 (2004) (there is "no bar to this Nation's holding one of its own citizens as an enemy combatant"). See also Neal Katyal and Laurence Tribe, "Waging War, Deciding Guilt: Trying the Military Tribunals," *Yale Law Journal* 111 (2002): 1259, 1300–1301; James B. Anderson, "*Hamdi v. Rumsfeld*: Judicious Balancing at the Intersection of the Executive's Power to Detain and the Citizen-Detainee's Right to Due Process," *Journal of Criminal Law and Criminology* 95 (2005): 689.

94. Rasul v. Bush, 124 S. Ct. 2686, 2698 (2004) (holding that United States courts have jurisdiction to consider challenges to the legality of the detention of foreign nationals captured abroad in connection with hostilities and incarcerated at Guantánamo Bay).

95. See Boumediene v. Bush, 128 S. Ct. 2229, 2277 (2008).

96. See Maqaleh v. Obama, 620 F. Supp. 2d 51 (D.D.C. 2009) ("United States citizenship plainly not a litmus test...otherwise *Boumediene* would not have come out the way it did") (Slip Op. at 9), overturned in Maqaleh v. Gates 605 F. 2d 84, 94 ("(c)learly the alien citizenship of the petitioners in this case does not weigh against their claim to protection of the rights of habeas corpus...").

97. See Boumediene v. Bush, cert. denied, 549 U.S. 1328 (April 2, 2007). But consider the appeals in the U.S. Supreme Court regarding the Guantánamo detainee policy (June 30, 2007) (agreeing to review enemy combatant policy of detention without habeas corpus); Boumediene v. Bush and Al Odah v. U.S., cert. granted, 127 S. Ct. 3067 (June 29, 2007). See William Glaberson, "In Shift, Justices Agree to Review Detainees Case," *New York Times*, June 30, 2007, A1.

98. Press Release, Periodic Review of Individuals Detained at Guantánamo Bay Naval Station Pursuant to the Authorization for Use of Military Force, Executive Order No. 13567 (March 7, 2011).

99. See Linda Greenhouse, "Americans Held in Iraq Draw Justices' Attention," *New York Times*, December 8, 2007, A15. So far, no lower court has reached a holding restricting access by detainees in Iraq along citizenship grounds. See Stephen Vladec, "Deconstructing Hirota: Habeas Corpus, Citizenship, and Article III," *Georgetown Law Journal* 95 (2007): 1497 (arguing against citizenship-based distinctions regarding access to courts under Article 3).

100. For another opposite view, see David Frum and Richard Perle, *An End to Evil: How to Win the War on Terror* (New York: Random House, 2003) (arguing for dirty war against foreign suspects).

101. For the congressional response to *Hamdan* via the Military Commissions Act, see Curtis Bradley, "The Military Commissions Act of 2006: The Military Commissions Act, Habeas Corpus, and the Geneva Conventions," *American Journal of International Law* 101 (2007): 322.

102. See Military Commissions Act, Pub. L. 109–306 (2006). In October 2009, Congress approved revisions to the MCA. The new Military Commissions Act of 2009 was enacted as part of the massive National Defense Authorization Act for 2010. See Military Commissions Act, Pub. L. No. 111–84, 123 Stat. 2190 (2009) [hereinafter "the MCA"].

103. Hamdan v. Rumsfeld, 548 U.S. 557 (2006).

104. Hamdi v. Rumsfeld, 542 U.S. 507, 535 (2004).

105. Ibid. Hamdan v. Rumsfeld, 548 U.S. 557, 642 (2006) (Stevens, J., op.) (insisting on a "regularly constituted court, affording all the judicial guarantees which are recognized as indispensable by civilized peoples").

106. Beyond the state consent view of its authority, and the broader transformation regarding the relevant normative balance, consider the shift away from the assumption of jurisdiction controlled by states. Might they still retain discretion to prosecute within certain limits—i.e., as implied in the duty to prosecute? In this way, for example, one can better understand the acceptance of the ICC, which relies in great part on states' consent to allow international jurisdiction over the prosecution of their nationals, and even state leaders. Still, the ICC seems to take a traditional state-centric view when it participates in a broader way that is comity-centered. In addition, consider that while there are generally elements of state consent, this hasn't always been true—for instance, wherever there is a Security Council referral, such as in Darfur. All of this suggests that the main question isn't who is a signatory. Rather, the key requirement is that there be a normative driver here. Hence, the consensus on this norm means that it allows, in some instances, for political leaders—even of nonstate signatories—to end up in the dock. See Geneva Conventions, Common Article 3. See also European Convention for the Protection of Human Rights and Fundamental Freedoms, November 4, 1950, at Article 3.

107. Kadi v. Council of the European Union and Commission of the European Communities, European Court of Justice (September 3, 2008): paras. 284, 344. In such a case, it is nonetheless the task of the European Community judicature to apply, in the course of the judicial review it carries out, techniques that accommodate on the one hand legitimate security concerns about the nature and sources of information taken into account in the adoption of the act concerned and on the other the need to accord the individual a sufficient measure of procedural justice. (See, to that effect, the judgment of the European Court of Human Rights in Chahal v. United Kingdom, Reports of Judgments and Decisions 1996-V, Sec. 131 (November 15, 1996).) Kadi v. Council of the European Union and Commission of the European Communities, European Court of Justice (September 3, 2008): para. 351 ("The Court cannot, therefore, do other than find that... the fundamental right to an effective legal remedy which they enjoy has not, in the circumstances, been observed.").

108. Kadi v. Council of the European Union and Commission of the European Communities, European Court of Justice (September 3, 2008): para. 281.

109. Her Majesty's Treasury v. Ahmed and Others, The Supreme Court Hilary Term, UKSC2 (2010). On appeal from (2008) EWCA Civ 1187 (January 27, 2010).
110. See R (on the application of Al Jedda) (FC) v. Secretary of State for Defence, UKHL 58(2007) (currently on appeal with the European Court of Human Rights as case number 27021/08).
111. Al-Skeini v. Secretary of State for Defence, EWCA Civ 1609 (2005); Al-Skeini v. Secretary of State for Defence, UKHL 26 (2007) (on appeal to the ECHR) FIX.
112. Ibid., para. 10 (since September 3, 1953, the United Kingdom has been bound under international law to comply with the obligations undertaken in the European Convention on Human Rights, and in later protocols to the Convention that it has formally ratified).
113. See Loizidou v. Turkey, 15318/89 (European Court of Human Rights, December 18, 1996); Cyprus v. Turkey, 25781/94 (European Court of Human Rights, May 10, 2001): paras. 129–130; Ilascu v. Moldova and Russian Federation, 48787/99 (European Court of Human Rights, July 8, 2004) (as to Russia, de facto control was sufficient).
114. Case of Isayeva v. Russia, No. 57950/00 (European Court of Human Rights, February 24, 2005).
115. Ibid., paras. 19–23, 42, 69.
116. Ibid., para. 172 (court "held unanimously that there has been a violation of Article 2 of the Convention in respect of the respondent State's obligation to protect the right to life of the applicant, her son and three nieces").
117. Ibid., para. 173.
118. See Coard et al. v. the United States (Inter-American Commission of Human Rights, September 29, 1999) (depended on whether "under the specific circumstances the State observed the rights of a person subject to its authority and control.").
119. Ibid. at paras. 10–12.
120. Al-Skeini v. Secretary of State for Defence, [2005] EWCA Civ. 1609; Al-Skeini v. Secretary of State for Defence, [2007] UKHL 26. (The House of Lords gave judgment on June 13, 2007 [2007] UKHL 26). The majority of the House of Lords (Lord Rodger, Baroness Hale, Lord Carswell, and Lord Brown, with Lord Bingham dissenting) held that the general purpose of the Human Rights Act of 1998 was to provide a remedial structure in domestic law for the rights guaranteed by the European Convention on Human Rights, and that the 1998 Act should therefore be interpreted as applying wherever the United Kingdom had jurisdiction under Article 1 of the European Convention on Human Rights.
121. Ibid., para. 24.
122. Ibid., paras, 145, 148.
123. See R (on the application of Al Jedda) (FC) v. Secretary of State for Defence, UKHL 58(2007): para. 39 (Lord Bingham).
124. Case of Isayeva v. Russia, No. 57950/00 (European Court of Human Rights, February 24, 2005): para. 172.
125. Ibid., para. 173. For a critique of such decisions, see, e.g., Yuval Shany, "Human Rights and Humanitarian Law as Competing Legal Paradigms for Fighting Terror," in *International Humanitarian Law and International Human Rights Law*, ed. Orna Ben-Naftali (Oxford: Oxford University Press, 2011) (in part for the absences of state practice, but also, again, to evaluate on the basis of the old jurisprudence approach, i.e., the role of state practice). For military operations in practice, see Colonel Richard Kemp, International Law and Military Operations in Practice, Address to Jerusalem Center for Public Affairs Joint International

Conference on Hamas, the Gaza War and Accountability under International Law (June 18, 2009).

126. See Rome Statute, at Articles 5–8.

127. See "McCain Amendment," Detainee Treatment Act of 2005, H.R. 2863, Div. A, Titl. X, Sec. 1003 (2005). See MCA of 2006, Pub. L. 109–306 (2006): Sec. 6(c)(1), providing that "no individual in the custody or under the physical control of the United States Government, regardless of nationality or physical location, shall be subject to cruel, inhuman, or degrading treatment or punishment." But other sections of the MCA make it more difficult for detainees to obtain relief for such abuses.

128. See, e.g., Michael Ignatieff, *The Lesser Evil: Political Ethics in an Age of Terror* (Princeton: Princeton University Press, 2004). See also Gabriella Blum, The Laws of War and the "Lesser Evil" (unpublished paper, 2009), *available at* http://papers.ssrn.com/sol3/papers.cfm?abstract_id=1315334 (last visited March 9, 2009).

129. See David Kretzmer, *The Occupation of Justice: The Supreme Court of Israel and the Occupied Territories* (Albany: State University of New York Press, 2002). See Alan M. Dershowitz, *Why Terrorism Works: Understanding the Threat, Responding to the Challenge* (New Haven: Yale University Press, 2002) (arguing that torture, if it is to be used, should be regulated by Congress through applications for torture warrants). For relevant case law, see Judgment Concerning the Legality of the General Security Service's Interrogation Methods, Judgment of the Supreme Court of Israel (1999).

130. For a comprehensive account, see *The Torture Papers: The Road to Abu Ghraib*, ed. Karen Greenberg and Joshua Dratel (Cambridge: Cambridge University Press, 2005); *Torture: A Collection*, ed. Sanford Levinson (Oxford: Oxford University Press, 2004). See Jack Goldsmith, *The Terror Presidency: Law and Judgment inside the Bush Administration* (New York: Norton, 2007). See also Mark Mazzetti, "Letters Give C.I.A. Tactics a Legal Rationale," *New York Times*, April 27, 2008, available at www.nytimes.com/2008/04/27/washington/27intel.html?pagewanted=all (last visited March 9, 2009).

131. See President George W. Bush, Memo: Humane Treatment of Al Qaeda and Taliban Detainees (February 7, 2002); see Confirmation Hearing on the Nomination of Timothy Elliott Flanigan to be Deputy Attorney General, S. Hrg. 109-750 (July 26, 2005).

132. Ibid.

133. A (FC) and Others (FC) v. Secretary of State for the Home Department, [2004] UKHL 56 (December 16, 2004).

134. See MCA, Pub. L. No. 109-366 (2006).

135. The MCA aims to address the debate over the treatment of detainees, particularly over the parameters of interrogation; see Pub. L. No. 109-366, sec 6(d)(1), Implementation of Treaty Obligations (2006).

136. See Interpretation of the Geneva Conventions Common Article 3 as Applied to a Program of Detention and Interrogation Operated by the Central Intelligence Agency, Executive Order 13440 (July 20, 2007).

137. See Mark Mazzetti, "Rules Lay Out C.I.A.'s Tactics in Questioning," *New York Times*, July 21, 2007, A1. In October 2009, Congress approved revisions to the MCA. The new Military Commissions Act of 2009 was enacted as part of the massive National Defense Authorization Act for 2010. See Military Commissions Act, Pub. L. No. 111–84, 123 Stat. 2190 (2009).

138. Common Article 3 requires that persons taking no active part in the hostilities "shall in all circumstances be treated humanely." See also Hamdan v. Rumsfeld, 548 U.S. 557 (2006).

139. Hamdan v. Rumsfeld, 548 U.S. 557, 631 (2006) (Stevens op emphasis added).

140. Id.

141. The court determined that the Geneva Conventions were incorporated by Article 21 of the Uniform Code of Military Justice into U.S. law, but it did not reference the source or basis. Thus, it did not resolve whether Common Article 3 constituted customary international law and hence bound Congress and the president, with consequences for the nature of the ensuing obligations in a transnational context. See Hamdan v. Rumsfeld, 548 U.S. 557, 630–631 (2006).

142. Prosecutor v. Tadic, Case No. IT-94-1, Decision on the Defence Motion for Interlocutory Appeal on Jurisdiction (International Criminal Tribunal for the former Yugoslavia, October 2, 1995): para. 102 (citing Nicaragua v. United States, 1986 I.C.J. 520 (1986): para. 218).

143. See Harold Koh, Obama Administration and International Law Address, at the annual meeting of the American Society of International Law, March 25, 2010.

144. Coard et al. v. the United States (Inter-American Commission of Human Rights, September 29, 1999): para. 42.

145. Ibid., para. 60.

CHAPTER 6

1. See Marco Sassòli and Antoine A. Bouvier, *How Does Law Protect in War? Cases, Documents, and Teaching Material in International Humanitarian Law*, Vol. 1 (Geneva: International Committee of the Red Cross, 2006), 54, 347 (including the right to life, right to medicine, right to food, and right against inhuman and degrading treatment). For examples, see Protocol 1, Article 41, on the right to life of enemies hors de combat; Article 56 of Convention 4 protects the right to health of inhabitants of occupied territories; Article 56 of Protocol 1 protects the right to a healthy environment.

2. United Nations Development Programme, *Human Development Report 1994: New Dimensions of Human Security* (New York: Oxford University Press, 1994), ch. 2, pp. 22–40.

3. Joseph E. Stiglitz, *Globalization and Its Discontents: Making Globalization Work* (New York: Norton, 2006). Dani Rodrik, Globalization As If Development Really Mattered, Office of the Chairman of the Group of 77 (New York: UNCTAD, September 2001); see also Simon Teitel, "Globalization and Its Disconnects," *Journal of Socio-Economics* 34 (2005): 444–470.

4. See Robert Howse and Ruti Teitel, *Beyond the Divide: The Covenant on Economic, Social and Cultural Rights and the WTO*, Dialogue on Globalization Occasional Papers, No. 30 (Geneva: Friedrich-Ebert-Stiftung, 2007).

5. For references to "global justice" as distributive justice, see, e.g., *NOMOS 41: Global Justice*, ed. Ian Shapiro and Lea Brilmayer (New York: New York University Press, 1999); *Global Justice*, ed. Thomas Pogge (Oxford: Blackwell Publishing, 2001); *Current Debates in Global Justice*, ed. Gillian Brock and Darrel Moellendorf (Dordrecht: Springer, 2005); Thomas Nagel, "The Problem of Global Justice," *Philosophy and Public Affairs* 33(2) (2005): 113; *Globalization and the Global Politics of Justice*, ed. Barry Gills (Abingdon, England: Routledge, 2008); Pablo De Greiff and Ciaran Cronin, *Global Justice and Transnational Politics* (Cambridge: MIT Press, 2002); and Frank J. Garcia, "Global Justice and the Bretton Woods Institutions," *Journal of International Economic Law* 10 (2007): 461; Christian Barry and Thomas W. Pogge, *Global Institutions and Responsibilities: Achieving Global Justice* (Malden, Mass.: Blackwell Publishing, 2005); *Current Debates in Global Justice, ed.* Gillian Brock and Darrel Moellendorf (Dordrecht: Springer, 2005). For references interpreting global justice to mean criminal justice, see note 20.

6. For the debate, see *NOMOS 41: Global Justice*, ed. Ian Shapiro and Lea Brilmayer (New York: New York University Press, 1999); Stanley Hoffmann, *Duties beyond Borders: On the Limits and Possibilities of Ethical International Politics* (Syracuse, N.Y.: Syracuse University Press 1981): 141–187.

7. See Thomas Nagel, *Ethics* (Oxford: Oxford University Press, 1997).

8. For the cosmopolitan demand as rationalized as a projection that always derives from the perspective of the state, see Charles Beitz, "Cosmopolitan Ideals and National Sentiment," *Journal of Philosophy* 80 (1983): 591.

9. Amartya Sen, *The Idea of Justice* (Cambridge, Mass.: Harvard University Press, 2009): 233.

10. See, in this regard, the reply of Joshua Cohen and Charles Sabel to Nagel: "Extra Rempublicam Nulla Justitia?" *Philosophy and Public Affairs* 34(2) (March 2006): 147–175.

11. Thomas Nagel, "The Problem of Global Justice," *Philosophy and Public Affairs* 33(2) (2005): 131, 126, referring to "this minimal humanitarian morality governs our relation to all other persons... it does require us to pursue our ends,... and to relieve them from extreme threats and obstacles to such freedom if we can do so without serious sacrifice of our own ends." See also ibid., 113, 126.

12. Ibid. Amartya Sen, *The Idea of Justice* (Cambridge, Mass.: Harvard University Press, 2009): 233.

13. See Brian Barry, "Statism and Nationalism: A Cosmopolitan Critique," in *NOMOS 41: Global Justice*, ed. Ian Shapiro and Lea Brilmayer (New York: New York University Press, 1999): 12–66.

14. Report of the World Conference against Racism, Racial Discrimination, Xenophobia and Related Intolerance, Durban, 31 August–8 September 2001, U.N. Office of the High Commissioner for Human Rights, U.N. Doc. A/Conf.189/12 (January 25, 2002) [hereinafter Report of the World Conference against Racism], available at www.unhchr.ch/huridocda/huridoca.nsf/(Symbol)/A.conf.189.12.EN?Opendocument (last visited March 21, 2011).

15. See Peter Singer, "Famine, Affluence and Morality," *Philosophy and Public Affairs* 1 (1972): 229–243; Peter Singer, *Writings on an Ethical Life* (New York: Ecco Press, 2000): xvi.

16. Thomas Pogge, "Introduction," in *Real World Justice: Grounds, Principles, Human Rights, and Social Institutions*, ed. Andreas Follesdal and Thomas Pogge (Dordrecht: Springer, 2005): 8.

17. Ibid., 2.

18. Ibid.

19. Robert Howse and Ruti Teitel, "Global Justice, Poverty and International Economic Order," in *The Philosophy of International Law*, ed. Samantha Besson and John Tasioulas (Oxford: Oxford University Press, 2010), ch. 21.

20. For references interpreting global justice to mean criminal justice, see, e.g., Hans Köchler, *Global Justice or Global Revenge? International Criminal Justice at the Crossroads* (New York: Springer Publishing, 2003); Geoffrey Robertson, *Crimes against Humanity: The Struggle for Global Justice* (New York: New Press, 1999); Kingsley Chiedu Moghalu, *Global Justice: The Politics of War Crimes Trials* (Westport, Conn.: Praeger Security International, 2006); Aryeh Neier, *War Crimes: Brutality, Genocide, Terror and the Struggle for Justice* (New York: Times Books, 1998); Jeremy Rabkin, "Global Criminal Justice: An Idea Whose Time Has Passed," *Cornell International Law Journal* 38 (2005): 753; and International Justice, section on Human Rights Watch website, available at www.hrw.org/doc/?t=justice.

21. See Rome Statute of the International Criminal Court, U.N. Doc. A/Conf. 183/9, 2187 U.N.T.S. 90, Preamble, Articles 1, 5–8, July 17, 1998.
22. See Immanuel Maurice Wallerstein, *The Politics of the World-Economy: The States, the Movements, and the Civilizations* (Cambridge: Cambridge University Press, 1984).
23. Human Security Unit, UN Office for the Coordination of Humanitarian Affairs, Human Security in Theory and Practice, 9 (2002), available at ochaonline.un.org/OchaLinkClick.aspx?link=ocha&docId=1117675.
24. U.N. Millennium Declaration, General Assembly Resolution 55/2, 8th plen. mtg., U.N. Doc. A/55/L.2 (2000).
25. See Paul Collier, *The Bottom Billion: Why the Poorest Countries Are Failing and What Can Be Done about It* (Oxford: Oxford University Press 2007).
26. See John Rawls, "The Law of Peoples," in *On Human Rights: The Oxford Amnesty Lectures 1993*, ed. Stephen Shute and Susan Hurley (New York: Basic Books, 1993), 42.
27. Ibid.
28. See Charles R. Beitz, *Political Equality: An Essay in Democratic Theory* (Princeton: Princeton University Press, 1989); see generally Thomas Pogge, "Introduction," in *Real World Justice: Grounds, Principles, Human Rights, and Social Institutions*, ed. Andreas Follesdal and Thomas Pogge (Dordrecht: Springer, 2005): 2–8.
29. Amartya Sen, *The Idea of Justice* (Cambridge, Mass.: Harvard University Press, 2009): 367.
30. Press Release, Kofi Annan, Secretary-General Salutes International Workshop on Human Security in Mongolia, Two-Day Session in Ulaanbaatar, U.N. Doc. No. SG/SM/7382 (May 8–10, 2000). See also Kofi Annan, "We the Peoples": The Role of the United Nations in the Twenty-First Century, Report of the Secretary-General, U.N. Doc. A/54/2000, March 27, 2000, paras. 66–188; In Larger Freedom: Towards Development, Security and Human Rights for All, Report of the Secretary-General, U.N. Doc. A/59/2005, March 21, 2005, paras. 25–73 (proposing strategies for "making the right to development a reality for everyone and to freeing the entire human race from want," para. 27); Kofi Annan, "In Larger Freedom: Decision Time at the UN," *Foreign Affairs* 84(3) (May/June 2005): 63–74 ("When the UN Charter speaks of 'larger freedom,' it includes the basic political freedoms to which all human beings are entitled. But it also goes beyond them, encompassing what President Franklin Roosevelt called 'freedom from want' and 'freedom from fear.' Both our security and our principles have long demanded that we push forward all these frontiers of freedom, conscious that progress on one depends on and reinforces progress on the others.").
31. See "Burma Shuns Foreign Aid Workers," *BBC News*, May 9, 2008, available at http://news.bbc.co.uk/2/hi/7391535.stm (last visited March 21, 2011); for an interesting discussion regarding the debate relating to forced intervention after Cyclone Nargis in Burma, see Jayshree Bajoria, The Dilemma of Humanitarian Intervention, *Council on Foreign Relations*, June 12, 2008, available at www.cfr.org/publication/16524/dilemma_of_humanitarian_intervention.html (last visited March 21, 2011).
32. U.N. Economic and Social Council, The Millennium Development Goals Report 2008, U.N. Doc. E.08.1.18, 12–19 (August 2008). Secretary-General Ban Ki-Moon made a reference to RtoP in his speech for UN Day. He stated: "If security and development are two pillars of the United Nations work, human rights is the third. I will work with Member States and civil society to translate the concept of the responsibility to protect from word to deed, so as to ensure timely action

when populations face genocide, ethnic cleansing or crimes against humanity." See Press Release, Secretary-General Expresses Determination "To Ensure We Make Progress on Pressing Issues of Our Time, Step by Step," in Message for United Nations Day, U.N. Doc. SG/SM/11203 (October 3, 2007), available at www.un.org/News/Press/docs/2007/sgsm11203.doc.htm (last visited March 21, 2011). See also Kofi Annan, In Larger Freedom: Towards Development, Security and Human Rights for All, U.N. Doc. A/59/2005 (March 21, 2005), at para. 135 ("I believe that we must embrace the responsibility to protect, and, when necessary, we must act on it.").

33. Kofi Annan, "We the Peoples": The Role of the United Nations in the Twenty-First Century, Report of the Secretary-General, U.N. Doc. A/54/2000, March 27, 2000, para. 74 ("History will judge political leaders in the developing countries by what they did to eradicate the extreme poverty of their people—by whether they enabled their people to board the train of a transforming global economy, and made sure that everyone had at least standing room, if not a comfortable seat. By the same token, history will judge the rest of us by what we did to help the world's poor board that train in good order.")

34. World Economic and Social Survey 2008: Overcoming Economic Insecurity, United Nations Department of Economic and Social Affairs, U.N. Doc. E/2008/50/Rev.1, July 1, 2008, at iii (relating health pandemics, such as HIV/AIDS, to economic insecurity).

35. Amartya Sen, *The Idea of Justice* (Cambridge, Mass.: Harvard University Press, 2009): 234.

36. Paul Collier, *The Bottom Billion: Why the Poorest Countries Are Failing and What Can Be Done about It* (Oxford: Oxford University Press 2007).

37. See United Nations, The Millennium Development Goals Report (2007), 7, available at www.un.org/millenniumgoals/pdf/mdg2007.pdf.

38. See UN Development Programme, Human Development Report (Oxford: Oxford University Press, 1994): 23.

39. Prosecutor v. Tadic, Case No. IT-94-1, Decision on Defence Motion for Interlocutory Appeal on Jurisdiction, October 2, 1995, para. 97.

40. See Amartya Sen, "Equality of What?" in *Tanner Lectures on Human Values* 1, ed. Sterling McMurrin (Salt Lake City: University of Utah Press, 1980): 197, reprinted in Amartya Sen, *Choice, Welfare, and Measurement* (Cambridge: Harvard University Press, 1982): 353–369; see Amartya Sen, *Commodities and Capabilities* (New Delhi: Oxford University Press, 1985); see also Judith N. Shklar, *The Faces of Injustice* (New Haven: Yale University Press, 1992).

41. These three offenses are the crime of genocide, crimes against humanity, and war crimes. Rome Statute of the International Criminal Court, U.N. Doc. A/Conf. 183/9, 2187 U.N.T.S. 90, Preamble, Article 5. July 17, 1998.

42. Regarding the Democratic Republic of Congo sanctions, see U.N. Security Council Resolution 1820, U.N. Doc. S/RES/1820 (June 19, 2008), which indicated the council's intention to consider the "appropriateness of targeted and graduated measures" against parties who committed acts of violence toward women and girls in situations of conflict. The Democratic Republic of Congo Sanctions Committee appears to be agreed on the ongoing relevance of the sanctions regime until the situation further stabilizes. Members such as Belgium, France, the United Kingdom, and the United States have broached the idea that sanctions would incentivize better behavior from those responsible for attacks on civilians. See U.N. Security Council Resolution 1799, U.N. Doc. S/Res/1799 (February 15,

2008), which renewed the sanctions regime and the mandate of the Group of Experts until March 31, 2008. See U.N. Security Council Resolution 1698, U.N. Doc. S/RES/1698 July 31, 2006), U.N. Doc. S/RES/1649 (December 21, 2005) and U.N. Security Council Resolution 1596, U.N. Doc. S/RES/1596 (April 18, 2005), which strengthened sanctions including, in Resolution 1698, provisions against actors recruiting and using children in armed conflict; regarding Zimbabwe, see Gideon Gono, "Sanctions Are 'More Deadly Than Warfare,'" *New African*, May 2007, available at http://findarticles.com/p/articles/mi_qa5391/is_200705/ai_n21288061/pg_1?tag=artBody;col1 (last visited March 21, 2011) (describing the "debilitating" effect of current sanctions on the Zimbabwean economy). In July 2008, a U.S.-sponsored resolution in the Security Council to impose new sanctions on Zimbabwe was vetoed by Russia and China. See Press Release, Security Council Fails to Adopt Sanctions against Zimbabwe Leadership as Two Permanent Members Cast Negative Votes, UN Doc. No. SC/9396 (July 11, 2008). In response, both the United States and the European Union tightened up their own sanctions regimes on Zimbabwe, with the European Union focusing on targeted sanctions in order "to avoid anything which would harm the population." See "Zimbabwe Faces New EU Sanctions," *BBC News*, July 17, 2008, available at http://news.bbc.co.uk/2/hi/africa/7512270.stm (last visited March 21, 2011).

43. Press Release, Secretary-General, in Address to International Rescue Committee, Reflects on Humanitarian Impact of Economic Sanctions, U.N. Doc. SG/SM/7625 (November 15, 2000).

44. See "Zimbabwe Faces New EU Sanctions," *BBC News*, July 17, 2008, available at http://news.bbc.co.uk/2/hi/africa/7512270.stm. Regarding Zimbabwe, see Gideon Gono, "Sanctions Are 'More Deadly Than Warfare,'" *New African*, May 2007, available at http://findarticles.com/p/articles/mi_qa5391/is_200705/ai_n21288061/pg_1?tag=artBody;col1 (last visited March 21, 2011) (describing the "debilitating" effect of current sanctions on the Zimbabwean economy). In July 2008, a U.S.-sponsored resolution in the Security Council to impose new sanctions on Zimbabwe was vetoed by Russia and China. See Press Release, Security Council Fails to Adopt Sanctions against Zimbabwe Leadership as Two Permanent Members Cast Negative Votes, UN Doc. No. SC/9396 (July 11, 2008).

45. See August Reinisch, "Developing Human Rights and Humanitarian Law Accountability of the Security Council for the Imposition of Economic Sanctions," *American Journal of International Law* 95 (2001): 851; see, e.g., Security Council Fails to Adopt Sanctions against Zimbabwe Leadership as Two Permanent Members Cast Negative Votes, U.N. Doc. SC/9396 (July 11, 2008); see also Evelyn Leopold and Paul Taylor, "West Seeks U.N. Sanctions on Myanmar," Reuters, September 26, 2007.

46. Press Release, Secretary-General, in Address to International Rescue Committee, Reflects on Humanitarian Impact of Economic Sanctions, U.N. Doc. UNIS/SG/2719 (November 16, 2000).

47. See Robert Howse, "The Concept of Odious Debt in Public International Law No. 185 (2007)," Discussion Paper at the United Nations Conference on Trade and Development Geneva, Switzerland, July 2007.

48. For an articulation of why that debate has become anachronistic, see Robert Howse, "The End of the Globalization Debate: A Review Essay," *Harvard Law Review* 121 (2008): 1528.

49. See generally, Amartya Sen, *The Idea of Justice* (Cambridge, Mass.: Harvard University Press, 2009). In 2001, Sen was appointed to the Commission on Human Security of the United Nations.

50. See Amartya Sen, *Development as Freedom* (New York: Knopf, 2000): 3.
51. Instructive here is the work of the World Bank on the relationship between good governance and development, e.g., Daniel Kaufman, Aart Kraay, and Massimo Mastruzzi, Governance Matters 7: Aggregate and Individual Governance Indicators, 1996–2007, World Bank Policy Research Working Paper No. 4654, June 24, 2008; Daniel Kaufman and Aart Kraay, "Growth without Governance," *Economia* 3 (2002): 1 (demonstrating a positive causal effect running from better governance to higher per-capita income); Daniel Kaufman, Human Rights and Development: Towards Mutual Reinforcement, paper prepared for the Ethics Globalization Initiative and the New York University Center for Human Rights and Global Injustice (2004) (linking human rights, governance, and development), available at http://siteresources.worldbank.org/INTWBIGOVANTCOR/Resources/humanrights.pdf.
52. Kofi Annan, "We the Peoples": The Role of the United Nations in the Twenty-First Century, Report of the Secretary-General, U.N. Doc. A/54/2000, March 27, 2000; see also Franklin Delano Roosevelt, Annual Address to Congress, January 6, 1941, available at http://docs.fdrlibrary.marist.edu/OD4FREES.HTML (last visited March 21, 2011).
53. See Amartya Sen, "Democracy as a Universal Value," *Journal of Democracy* 10 (1999): 3–17.
54. See Martha C. Nussbaum, Disability, Nationality, Species Membership (Cambridge, Mass.: Harvard University Press, 2007): ch. 1.
55. See the 1907 Hague Conventions, the Fourth Geneva Convention of 1949, and the 1977 Additional Protocol 1, which were designed to protect civilians by forbidding the intentional destruction of items that were essential for their survival. See also Jelena Pejic, "The Right to Food in Situations of Armed Conflict: The Legal Framework," *International Review of the Red Cross* 83 (2001): 1097–1109.
56. See, e.g., Geneva Convention Relative to the Protection of Civilian Persons in Time of War (Fourth Convention), August 12, 1949, Article 49, which states: "The Occupying Power undertaking such transfers or evacuations shall ensure, to the greatest practicable extent, that proper accommodation is provided to receive the protected persons, that the removals are effected in satisfactory conditions of hygiene, health, safety and nutrition, and that members of the same family are not separated."
57. See Paul Collier, *The Bottom Billion: Why the Poorest Countries Are Failing and What Can Be Done About It* (Oxford: Oxford University Press 2007): 64–79; Paul Collier, *Wars, Guns, and Violence: Democracy in Dangerous Places* (New York: Harper, 2009). See Susan Marks, "*Human Rights and the Bottom Billion,*" *EHR Law Review* 7 (2009): 37–49.
58. Sabina Alkire, A Conceptual Framework for Human Security, Center for Research on Inequality, Human Security, and Ethnicity, Working Paper 2 (London: University of Oxford, 2003): 3.
59. Ibid., 2. See Commission on Human Security, Human Security Now (2003): 4 (referring to human security "to protect the vital core of all human lives in ways that enhance human freedoms and human fulfillment"), available at www.humansecurity-chs.org/finalreport/index.html.
60. Robert Howse and Ruti Teitel, *Beyond the Divide: The Covenant on Economic, Social and Cultural Rights and the WTO,* Dialogue on Globalization: Occasional Papers, No. 30 (Geneva: Friedrich-Ebert-Stiftung, 2007).
61. Martha Nussbaum, "Compassion and Terror," *Daedalus* 132 (Winter 2003): 10.
62. See Philippe Sands, *The Torture Team: Rumsfeld's Memo and the Betrayal of American Values* (New York: Palgrave Macmillan, 2008); see chapter 5 here for further discussion.

63. See Jeremy Waldron, "Torture and Positive Law: Jurisprudence for the White House," *Columbia Law Review* 110 (2008): 2; "Security and Liberty: The Image of Balance," *Journal of Political Philosophy* 11 (2003): 191.

64. Giorgio Agamben, *Homo Sacer, Sovereign Power and Bare Life* (Stanford: Stanford University Press 1998).

65. See United Nations, Security Council, The Rule of Law and Transitional Justice in Conflict and Post Conflict Societies, Report of the Secretary General, U.N. Doc. No. S/2004/616 (2004) (calling for a comprehensive strategy to "pay special attention to abuses committed against groups most affected by conflict, such as minorities, the elderly, children, women, prisoners, displaced persons, and refugees and establish particular measures for their protection and redress in judicial and reconciliation processes.") UN Security Council, Resolution 1325, U.N. Doc. No. S/RES/1325 (2000). This resolution expressed the "concern that civilians, particularly women and children, account for the vast majority of those adversely affected by armed conflict"; available at www.un.org/events/res_1325e.pdf (last visited March 21, 2011).

66. See "Weeks after Cyclone in Myanmar, Even Farmers Wait for Food," *New York Times*, May 26, 2008, A1; see also Seth Mydans, "Donors Press Myanmar to Let Aid Workers In," *New York Times*, May 26, 2008, A6.

67. See David Barboza, "China Pleads for Help for Millions of Homeless," *New York Times*, May 26, 2008, A5.

68. See United Nations, Security Council, The Rule of Law and Transitional Justice in Conflict and Post Conflict Societies, Report of the Secretary General, U.N. Doc. No. S/2004/616 (2004).

69. See, e.g., Stephen Holmes and Cass R. Sunstein, *The Cost of Rights: Why Liberty Depends on Taxes* (New York: Norton, 1999).

70. See Margo Salomon, *Global Responsibility for Human Rights: World Poverty and the Development of International Law* (Oxford: Oxford University Press, 2008).

71. Benedict de Spinoza, *The Chief Works of Benedict de Spinoza*, vol. 1, *Introduction, Tractatus Theologico-Politicus, Tractus Politicus* (London: George Bell and Sons, 1887): 290. See also John Locke, *The Second Treatise of Civil Government* (Oxford: Blackwell, 1946).

72. United Nations Commission on Human Security, Human Security Now (2003): 4, available at www.humansecurity-chs.org/; United Nations Development Programme, *Human Development Report 1994* (New York: Oxford University Press), 23, available at http://hdr.undp.org/en/reports/global/hdr1994 (last visited March 21, 2011).

73. The Commission on Human Security was established in January 2001 in response to the UN Secretary-General's call at the 2000 Millennium Summit for a world "free from want" and "free from fear." See United Nations Commission on Human Security, Human Security Now (2003): 4, available at www.humansecurity-chs.org/.

74. See Gary King and Christopher J. L. Murray, proposing an optimal definition of security in terms of the concept of "well-being." Human security is measured in terms of expectations of living without experiencing states of "generalized poverty based on falling below critical thresholds in any domain of well-being." Gary King and Christopher J. L. Murray, "Rethinking Human Security," *Political Science Quarterly* 116(4) (2002): 592. They propose a measure: Years of Individual Human Security, i.e., expected number of years of life outside the state of generalized poverty; 595. In their view, the set of thresholds used to define generalized poverty in order to measure human security should be general.

75. E.g., Robert Howse and Ruti Teitel, *Beyond the Divide: The Covenant on Economic, Social and Cultural Rights and the WTO*, Dialogue on Globalization Occasional Papers, No. 30 (Geneva: Friedrich-Ebert-Stiftung, 2007).

CHAPTER 7

1. On interpretation generally, see Michael Walzer, *Interpretation and Social Criticism* (Cambridge, Mass.: Harvard University Press, 1987). For discussion of the potential role of interpretation in the ongoing conceptualization of justice, see Georgia Warnke, *Justice and Interpretation* (Cambridge, Mass.: MIT Press, 1992).
2. See generally Robert O. Keohane, Andrew Moravcsik, and Anne-Marie Slaughter, "Legalized Dispute Resolution: Interstate and Transnational," *International Organizations* 54 (2000): 457.
3. For an exploration of the challenges of cosmopolitanism in the contemporary moment, see Kwame Anthony Appiah, *Cosmopolitanism: Ethics in a World of Strangers:* (New York: Norton, 2007).
4. Jurgen Habermas, *The Divided West*, ed. and trans. Ciaran Cronin (Cambridge: Polity Press, 2006): 116.
5. David Held, "Law of States; Law of Peoples: Three Models of Sovereignty," *Legal Theory* 8 (2001–2): 23.
6. See Bruce Ackerman, "Rooted Cosmopolitanism," *Ethics* 104 (1994): 516, 524.
7. See generally Jurgen Habermas, *The Divided West*, ed. and trans. Ciaran Cronin (Cambridge: Polity Press, 2006).
8. See Philippe Sands, *Lawless World: America and Making and Breaking of Global Rules from FDR's Atlantic Charter to George W. Bush's Illegal War* (New York: Penguin Group, 2005): xii (referring to the Bush administration's "full scale assault, a war on law"). Compare Joseph S. Nye, Jr., *Soft Power: The Means to Success in World Politics* (New York: Perseus Book Group, 2004), with Suzanne Nossel, "Smart Power," *Foreign Affairs* (March/April 2004): 131.
9. See Jurgen Habermas, *The Divided West*, ed. and trans. Ciaran Cronin (Cambridge: Polity Press, 2006): 15.
10. Ibid., 116.
11. Ibid.
12. See Jack L. Goldsmith and Eric A. Posner, *The Limits of International Law* (New York: Oxford University Press, 2005): 192. (For discussion of the drift toward compliance as a central preoccupation, see generally Robert Howse and Ruti Teitel, "Beyond Compliance: Rethinking Why International Law Really Matters," *Global Policy* 1 (2010): 126–36.
13. See generally *Neorealism and Its Critics*, ed. Robert O. Keohane (New York: Columbia University Press, 1986).
14. For discussion of this phenomenon, see generally Peter Spiro, "The New Sovereigntists: American Exceptionalism and Its False Prophets," *Foreign Affairs* (November/December 2004); Jeremy Rabkin, *The Case for Sovereignty: Why the World Should Welcome American Independence* (Washington, D.C.: AEI Press, 2004).
15. See Robert Dahl, "Can International Organizations Be Democratic? A Skeptic's View," in *Democracy's Edges*, ed. Ian Shapiro and Casiano Hacker-Cordón (New York: Cambridge University Press, 1999): 19; Jack Goldsmith and Stephen D. Krasner, "The Limits of Idealism," *Daedalus* 132(1) (Winter 2003): 47.
16. See Jurgen Habermas, *The Divided West*, ed. and trans. Ciaran Cronin (Cambridge: Polity Press, 2006): 116.

17. See generally Cass Sunstein, *One Case at a Time: Judicial Minimalism on the Supreme Court* (Cambridge, Mass.: Harvard University Press, 1999); Cass Sunstein, *Legal Reasoning and Political Conflict* (New York: Oxford University Press, 1996).

18. See Lawrence v. Texas, 539 US 558, 574–577 (2003).

19. See H. L. A. Hart, *The Concept of Law* (New York: Oxford University Press, 1961), 228–2231.

20. See Statute of the International Court of Justice, Article 38, 59 Stat. 1055, 1060 (1945).

21. See Martti Koskenniemi, *From Apology to Utopia: The Structure of International Legal Argument* (New York: Cambridge University Press, 2005): 394–395, 405–407; see generally Martti Koskenniemi, Report of the Study Group on Fragmentation of International Law: Difficulties Arising From the Diversification and Expansion of International Law, A/CN.4/L.663/Rev.1 (2004).

22. See Theodor Meron, "Revival of Customary Humanitarian Law," *American Journal of International Law* 99 (2005): 817 (noting that the "modern approach to customary law, it is said, relies principally on loosely defined *opinio juris*"). See also Anthea Roberts, "Traditional and Modern Approaches to Customary Law," *American Journal of International Law* 95 (2001): 757.

23. See Case Concerning Legality of the Use of Force (Yugoslavia v. Belgium), Provisional Measures, Order (International Court of Justice, June 2, 1999): 124 (thrown out on jurisdictional grounds).

24. Case Concerning Oil Platforms (Iran v. U.S.), Judgment (International Court of Justice, November 6, 2003) (Higgins, Simma, op.).

25. See Sarah Cleveland, "Our International Constitution," *Yale Journal of International Law* 31 (2006): 1.

26. See generally Jack L. Goldsmith and Eric A. Posner, *The Limits of International Law* (New York: Oxford University Press, 2005).

27. Curtis A. Bradley and Jack L. Goldsmith, "Federal Courts and the Incorporation of International Law," *Harvard Law Review* 111 (1998): 2260, 2264.

28. Ibid.; see also Khulumani v. Barclay Nat'l Bank Ltd., 504 F.3d 254, 279 (2d Cir. 2007) ("where there is no treaty, and no controlling executive or legislative act or judicial decision, resort must be had to the customs and usages of civilized nations; and as evidence of these to the works of jurists and commentators") (quoting Sosa v. Alvarez-Machain, 542 U.S. 692, 734 (2004)), aff'd Am. Isuzu Motors, Inc. v. Ntsebeza, 128 S. Ct. 2424 (2008).

29. See, e.g., Harold Hongju Koh, "Why Do Nations Obey International Law?" *Yale Law Journal* 106 (1997): 2599.

30. See, e.g., Goldsmith and Posner, *The Limits of International Law* (New York: Oxford University Press, 2005).

31. See Statute of the International Court of Justice, Article 38, 59 Stat. 1055, 1060 (1945). For a recent illustration, see Sosa v. Alvarez-Machain, 542 U.S. at 734 (referring to works of jurists and commentators "as evidence" of "the customs and usages of civilized nations") (quoting The Paquete Habana, 175 U.S. 677, 700 (1900)). See also Khulumani v. Barclay Nat'l Bank Ltd., 504 F.3d 254, 268–277 (2d Cir. 2007), aff'd Am. Isuzu Motors, Inc. v. Ntsebeza, 128 S. Ct. 2424 (2008) (discussing whether aiding and abetting international law violations constitutes violation of law of nations).

32. David Dyzenhaus, "The Hart-Fuller Debate at Fifty: The Grudge Informer Case Revisited," *New York University Law Review* 83 (2008): 993–99. Lon Fuller, "Positivism and Fidelity to Law—A Reply to Professor Hart," *Harvard Law Review* 71 (4): 630–672.

33. 28 U.S.C.S. Sec. 1350.
34. See Anne-Marie Burley, "The Alien Tort Statute and the Judiciary Act of 1789: A Badge of Honor," *American Journal of International Law* 83 (1989): 461, 481–493 (distinguishing Burley's concept of the purposes of the ATCA from the "denial of justice" view of the original purpose—to avoid conflict; citing Casto).
35. 630 F.2d 876, 878 (2d Cir. 1980).
36. Ibid., 880 (emphasis added) (quoting The Paquete Habana, 175 U.S. 677, 700 (1900)).
37. Ibid., 881.
38. Ibid., 881.
39. Ibid.
40. 175 U.S. 677, 686 (1900) (referring to "ancient usage among civilized nations").
41. Ibid., 700, 708.
42. See generally Curtis A. Bradley and Jack L. Goldsmith, "Federal Courts and the Incorporation of International Law," *Harvard Law Review* 111 (1998); Jack L. Goldsmith and Eric A. Posner, "Understanding the Resemblance between Modern and Traditional Customary International Law," *Virginia Journal of International Law* 40 (2000): 639, 666–667.
43. 542 U.S. 692 (2004).
44. Ibid., 763 (Breyer, J., concurring).
45. Ibid., 729.
46. See generally Julian Ku and John Yoo, "Beyond Formalism in Foreign Affairs: A Functional Approach to the Alien Tort Statute," *Supreme Court Review* 2004 (2004): 153.
47. Sosa v. Alvarez-Machain, 542 U.S. 692, 728 (2004) (quoting Torture Victim Protection Act, 106 Stat. 73 (1992)): 732.
48. Sosa, 542 U.S. at 725 (citing H.R. Rep. No. 102-367, pt. 4 (1991) (articulating the standard for courts hearing "any claim based on the present-day law of nations").
49. Ibid., 733.
50. Ibid., 728, 729.
51. Ibid., 714–715.
52. Ibid., 715.
53. Ibid., 715.
54. Ibid., 720.
55. Ibid., 725.
56. See, e.g., Mehinovic v. Vuckovic, 19 8 F. Supp. 2d 1322 (N.D. Ga. 2002) (cruel, inhuman, or degrading treatment); Estate of Cabello v. Fernandez-Larios, 157 F. Supp. 2d 1345, 1360–1361 (S.D. Fla. 2001), aff'd, 402 F.3d 1148 (11th Cir. 2005) (crimes against humanity); Kadic v. Karadzic, 70 F.3d 232, 241–244 (2d Cir. 1995) reh'g denied, 74 F.3d 377 (2d Cir. 1996), cert. denied, 518 U.S. 1005 (1996) (genocide, war crimes, summary execution, torture); In re Estate of Ferdinand Marcos, Human Rights Litigation, 25 F.3d 1467, 1475–1476 (9th Cir. 1994) (summary execution, disappearance). In Mehinovic v. Vuckovic, the U.S. District Court for Georgia found bases for action under the Alien Tort Statute for cruel, inhuman, or degrading treatment; arbitrary detention; war crimes; crimes against humanity; and genocide, noting: "The United States has explicitly endorsed the approach of the ICTY Statute and the convening of the Tribunal." Mehinovic, 198 F. Supp. 2d at 1344. In laying out the standard, the court invoked Judge Edwards's concurrence in Tel-Oren v. Libyan Arab Republic, 726 F.2d 744, 778 (D.C. Cir. 1984), which looked to the Restatement of the Law of Foreign Relations to identify its claims, including but not limited to state-practiced, state-encouraged, or state-

condoned genocide; slavery or the slave trade; murder or disappearance; torture or other cruel, inhuman, or degrading treatment or punishment; prolonged arbitrary detention; systematic racial discrimination; and consistent patterns of gross violations of internationally recognized human rights.

57. See Cabello v. Fernandez-Larios, 157 F. Supp. 2d 1345 (S.D. Fla. 2001) (conspiracy and accomplice liability for crimes against humanity); Doe v. Liu Qi, 349 F. Supp. 2d 1258, 1306 (N.D. Cal. 2004) (torture; cruel, inhuman, and degrading treatment or punishment; and prolonged arbitrary detention for twenty days) and command responsibility); Doe v. Saravia, 348 F. Supp. 2d 1112 (E.D. Cal. 2004) (liability found for extrajudicial killing and crimes against humanity for single act of assassinating Archbishop Óscar Romero; aiding and abetting liability also imposed); Abdullahi v. Pfizer, Inc. 562 F.3d 163, 184 (2d Cir. 2009) (holding that as international customary law recognizes a norm forbidding nonconsensual human medical experimentation as cruel, inhuman, or degrading treatment, such experimentation may constitute grounds for an ATCA action).

58. 348 F. Supp. 2d at 1154–1157.

59. Cabello v. Fernandez-Larios, 402 F.3d 1148 (11th Cir. 2005).

60. Sosa v. Alvarez-Machain, 542 U.S. 692, 761 (2004) (Breyer, J., concurring).

61. Ibid. (emphasis added).

62. See Sosa at 733 ("determination whether a norm is sufficiently definite to support a cause of action should... involve an element of judgment about the practical consequences of making that cause available to litigants in the federal courts.")

63. Doe v. Liu Qi, 349 F. Supp. 2d 1258, 1321.

64. Ibid., 1321–1322 (quoting Xuncax v. Gramajo, 886 F.Supp. 162, 187 (D. Mass. 1995)).

65. Ibid., 1322; see also Mehinovic v. Vuckovic, 198 F.Supp. 2d 1322, 1348 (N.D. Ga. 2002) (noting that "generally, cruel, inhuman, or degrading treatment includes acts which inflict mental or physical suffering, anguish, humiliation, fear and debasement, which do not rise to the level of 'torture' or do not have the same purposes as 'torture'").

66. Doe v. Liu Qi, 349 F. Supp. 2d 1258 1322.

67. Ibid. However, the Eleventh Circuit Court of Appeals rejected this approach in 2005 in Aldana v. Del Monte Fresh Produce, N.A., 416 F.3d 1242, 1247 (11th Cir. 2005). The court interpreted Sosa narrowly, holding that there is no basis in law for recognizing an Alien Tort Statute claim for cruel, inhuman, or degrading treatment or punishment. The court noted that previous courts upholding such claims had relied on the International Covenant on Civil and Political Rights but ruled that under Sosa, the Covenant did not "create obligations enforceable in the federal courts." Ibid. In November 2006, certiorari was denied. The approach of the District Court in Doe v. Liu Qi has nevertheless been followed in subsequent cases. See, e.g., Bowett v. Chevron Corp., 557 F. Supp. 2d 1080 (N.D. Cal. 2008).

68. See generally, Jurgen Habermas, The Divided West, ed. and trans. Ciaran Cronin (Cambridge: Polity Press, 2006).

69. The Paquete Habana, 175 U.S. 677, 700 (1900) ("resort must be had to the customs and usages of civilized nations").

70. See Torture Victim Protection Act of 1991, 28 U.S.C. Sec. 1350 (1991).

71. Filartiga v. Pena Irala, 630 F.2d 876, 889 (2d Cir. 1980).

72. Tel-Oren v. Libyan Arab Republic, 726 F.2d 774, 792 (1984) (Edwards, J., concurring).

73. Kadic v. Karadzic, 70 F.3d 232, 237 (2d Cir. 1995), cert. denied, 518 U.S. 1005 (1996).
74. Ibid., at 239–224.
75. Sosa v. Avarez-Machain, 542 U.S. 692, 732, n.20 (2004).
76. Kiobel v. Royal Dutch Petroleum, 621 F. 3d 111 (2d Cir. 2011).
77. Khulumani v. Barclay Nat'l Bank Ltd., 504 F.3d 254, 258 (2d Cir. 2007), aff'd Am.Isuzu Motors, Inc. v. Ntsebeza, 128 S. Ct. 2424 (2008).
78. See Khulumani v. Barclay Nat'l Bank Ltd., 504 F.3d 254, 270–281 (2d Cir. 2007) (Katzmann, J., concurring), aff'd Am. Isuzu Motors, Inc. v. Ntsebeza, 128 S. Ct. 2424 (2008).
79. See *Khulumani v. Barclay Nat'l Bank*, 504 F 3d 254 at 269 (Katzmann, J., concurring (citing Brief for the US as Amicus Curiae at 21)).
80. *South African Apartheid Litigation v. Daimler*, 2009 U.S. Dist. Lexis 34572, 70 (S.D.N.Y. 2009).
81. See Ginger Thompson, "South Africa to Pay $3,900 to Each Family of Apartheid Victims," *New York Times,* April 16, 2003, available at http://www.nytimes. com/2003/04/16/world/south-africa-to-pay-3900-to-each-family-of-apartheid-victims.html?scp=1&sq=www.nytimes.com/%222003/04/16%22/world/south-af-rica-to-pay-3900-to-each-family%20of-apartheid-victims.html&st=cse (last visited March 21, 2011) (referencing South African President Mbeke's speech to Parliament, in which he criticized lawsuits filed in U.S. courts for apartheid damages). See Khulumani v. Barclay Nat'l Bank Ltd., 504 F.3d 254 (2d Cir. 2007) (Korman, J., concurring in part and dissenting in part, citing U.S. and South African officials—"worst sort of judicial imperialism"), aff'd Am. Isuzu Motors, Inc. v. Ntsebeza, 128 S. Ct. 2424 (2008).
82. See Case Concerning Oil Platforms (Iran v. U.S.), Judgment (International Court of Justice, November 6, 2003) (Higgins, Simma, Separate Opinion).
83. See generally Henrik Horn and Joseph H. H. Weiler, "European Communities—Trade Description of Sardines: Textualism and Its Discontent," in *The WTO Case Law of 2002,* ed. Henrik Horn and Petros C. Mavroidis (New York: Cambridge University Press, 2005).
84. Case Concerning Legality of the Use of Force (Yugoslavia v. Belgium), Provisional Measures, Order (International Court of Justice, June 2, 1999): para. 79.
85. Legal Consequences of the Construction of a Wall in the Occupied Palestinian Territory, Advisory Opinion 2004 I.C.J. 136 (2004): para. 157.
86. Theodor Meron, "The Geneva Conventions as Customary Law," *American Journal of International Law* 81 (1987): 348, 361.
87. See Medellin v. Texas, 128 S. Ct. 1346, 1361–1363 (2008).
88. Ibid.
89. 548 U.S. 557, 557 (2006).
90. Medellin v. Dretke, 544 U.S. 660 (2005). See Medellin v. Texas, 129 S.Ct. 360 (2008).
91. See Ruti Teitel, "Comparative Constitutional Law in a Global Age," *Harvard Law Review* 117 (2004): 2570, 2584–2587 (on the role of comparativism and dialogue).
92. Sosa, 542 U.S. at 752.
93. See Medellin v. Dretke, 544 U.S. 660, 670 (Ginsburg, J., concurring). Justice Stephen Breyer observed that there is weight to the ICJ judgment. Ibid. at 693–694 (Breyer, J., dissenting).

94. See Tom Ginsburg, Svitlana Chernykh, and Zachary Elkins, "Commitment and Diffusion: How and Why National Constitutions Incorporate International Law," *University of Illinois Law Review* 2008 (2008): 201.

95. See Case Concerning the Application of the Convention on the Prevention and Punishment of the Crime of Genocide (Bosnia and Herzegovina v. Serbia and Montenegro), 2007 I.C.J. 91 (2007): paras. 396–407 (application of the Genocide Convention on the Prevention and Punishment of the Crime of Genocide) [hereinafter Bosnia v. Serbia].

96. See Khulumani v. Barclay Nat'l Bank Ltd., 504 F.3d 254, n. 5 (2d Cir. 2007) (Katzmann, J., concurring, recognizing the principle of individual liability to aid and abet international law violations as a matter of customary law), aff'd Am. Isuzu Motors, Inc. v. Ntsebeza, 128 S. Ct. 2424 (2008).

97. Case Concerning Military and Paramilitary Activities in and against Nicaragua (Nicaragua v. United States), 1986 I.C.J. 520, 115 (1986).

98. Prosecutor v. Tadic, Case No. IT-94-1, Judgment (Appeals Chamber, International Criminal Tribunal for the Former Yugoslavia, July 15, 1999): paras. 115–145.

99. R (On the Application of Al-Skeini and Others) v. Secretary of State for Defence, [2007] UKHL 26, para. 129 (Lord Brown) ("except where a state really does have effective control of territory, it cannot hope to secure Convention rights within that territory").

100. Bosnia v. Serbia, 2007 I.C.J. 91, paras. 396–413.

101. See The Right to Information on Consular Assistance in the Framework of the Guarantees of the Due Process of Law, Inter-American Court of Human Rights, Advisory Opinion No. OC-16/99 (October 1, 1999). See Bruno Simma and Carsten Hoppe, "From LaGrand and Avena to Medellin: A Rocky Road toward Implementation," *Tulane Journal of International and Comparative Law* 14 (2005).

102. See Regina v. Bartle and the Comm'r of Police, Ex Parte Pinochet, 2 WLR 827 (U.K. House of Lords, 1999). Lord Hutton also stated, "My Lords, the position taken by the democratically elected Government of Chile that it desires to defend Chilean national sovereignty and considers that any investigation and trial of Senator Pinochet should take place in Chile is understandable. But in my opinion that is not the issue which is before your Lordships; the issue is whether the commission of acts of torture taking place after September 29, 1988 was a function of the head of state of Chile under international law. For the reasons which I have given I consider that it was not." Ibid.

103. H. L. A. Hart, *The Concept of Law* (New York: Oxford University Press, 1961), 208–231.

104. Ibid., 208–209.

105. Ibid., 212, 222.

106. Ibid. at 226.

107. See Eyal Benvenisti, "Reclaiming Democracy: The Strategic Uses of Foreign and International Law by National Courts," *American Journal of International Law* 102 (2008): 241.

108. See generally Jeremy Waldron, "Foreign Law and the Modern Ius Gentium," *Harvard Law Review* 119 (2005): 129.

109. Riggs v. Palmer, 22 N.E. 188, 190 (N.Y. 1889).

110. See generally Jeremy Waldron, "Foreign Law and the Modern Ius Gentium," *Harvard Law Review* 119 (2005): 129.

111. See K. Zweigert and H. Kötz, *Introduction to Comparative Law* (Oxford: Oxford University Press, 1998); Statute of the International Court of Justice, Article

38(1)(b), 59 Stat. 1055, 1060 (1945) (providing international custom offers evidence of a general practice accepted as law).

112. See Sabino Cassese, "Globalization of Law," *Journal of International Law and Politics* 37 (2005): 663–694.

113. See Darryl Levinson and Jack Goldsmith, "Law for States: International Law, Constitutional Law, Public Law," *Harvard Law Review* 122 (2009): 1791.

114. Eyal Benvenisti, "Reclaiming Democracy: The Strategic Uses of Foreign and International Law by National Courts," *American Journal of International Law* 102 (2008): 241.

115. See, e.g., Poe v. Ullman, 367 U.S. 497, 548 (1961) (Harlan, J., dissenting); Wolf v. Colorado, 338 U.S. 25, 28 (1949) (referring to "the history and the basic constitutional documents of English-speaking peoples"); Malinski v. New York, 324 U.S. 401, 413–414 (1945) (interpreting due process in light of "the history of freedom of English-speaking peoples").

116. See Rochin v. California, 342 U.S. 165, 175–176 (1952) (Black, J., concurring).

117. See Knight v. Florida, 528 U.S. 990, 995–997 (1990) (Breyer, J., dissenting); Thompson v. Oklahoma, 487 U.S. 815, 830 (1988) (plurality opinion) (relying on "nations that share our Anglo-American heritage"); Adamson v. California, 332 U.S. 46, 54 (1947) ("Anglo-American legal tradition" as the basis for the relevant connection).

118. See, e.g., Planned Parenthood of Southeastern Pa. v. Casey, 505 U.S. 833, 952–953 (1992) (Rehnquist, C. J., concurring in the judgment in part and dissenting in part) (noting that "the historical traditions of the American people" began with "the common law which we inherited from England"); Stanford v. Kentucky, 492 U.S. 361, 368 (1989) (justifying American law as in "accordance with the standards of this common-law tradition"); Duncan v. Louisiana, 391 U.S. 145, 149–150 n.14 (1968) (questioning "whether…a procedure is necessary to an Anglo-American regime of ordered liberty"); Trop v. Dulles, 356 U.S. 86, 99–100 (1958) (noting that the constitutional idea of "due process" began with the English Declaration of Rights of 1688 and the Magna Carta).

119. See Lawrence v. Texas, 123 S. Ct. 2472, 2481, 2483 (2003) (citing decisions of the European Court of Human Rights).

120. 123 S. Ct. 2472.

121. See, e.g., Knight, 528 U.S. at 995 (Breyer, J., dissenting) (citing the Privy Council regarding the "inhumanity" of death penalty delays).

122. See Lawrence, 123 S. Ct. at 2472 (describing Fourteenth Amendment "due process" rights understanding); Atkins v. Virginia, 536 U.S. 304, 311–317 (2002) (analyzing Eighth Amendment jurisprudence); Washington v. Glucksberg, 521 U.S. 702, 785–787 (1997) (Souter, J., concurring) (referring to the law of the Netherlands when discussing the right to assisted suicide); Thompson, 487 U.S. at 830 (plurality opinion) (holding that the execution of juveniles violates norms of the western European community); see also United States v. Stanley, 483 U.S. 669, 710 (1987) (O'Connor, J., concurring in part and dissenting in part) (noting the relevance of Nuremberg Trials procedures regarding consent standards for medical experimentalism); Trop v. Dulles, 356 U.S. 86, 101 (1958) (plurality opinion) (inquiring into "evolving standards of decency").

123. On convergence in criminal law, compare George P. Fletcher, *Basic Concepts of Criminal Law* (New York: Oxford University Press, 1998) (arguing for convergence) with James Q. Whitman, *Harsh Justice: Criminal Punishment and the*

Widening Divide between America and Europe (New York: Oxford University Press, 2003) (discussing divergence among American, German, and French criminal justice policies). On the risks of comparativism's misinterpreting similarities, see William P. Alford, "On the Limits of 'Grand Theory' in Comparative Law," *Washington Law Review* 61 (1986): 945, 955.

124. See Mirjan Damaska, "The Uncertain Fate of Evidentiary Transplants: Anglo-American and Continental Experiments," *American Journal of Comparative Law* 45 (1997): 839, 844–847, 851 ("transplantation of fact finding arrangements between common law and civil law systems would give rise to serious strains in the recipient justice system").

125. 487 U.S. 815 (1988).

126. 492 U.S. 361 (1989).

127. 536 U.S. 304 (2002).

128. Stanford, 492 U.S. at 389–390 (Brennan, J., dissenting).

129. Thompson, 487 U.S. at 830–831 (plurality opinion).

130. Ibid., 868 n.4 (Scalia, J., dissenting).

131. Atkins, 536 U.S. at 316–317 n.21 (2002); see ibid. at 324–325 (Rehnquist, C. J., dissenting) (refusing to find other countries' views relevant to the judicial ascertaining of "contemporary American conceptions of decency").

132. See generally, Kennedy v. Louisiana, 128 S. Ct. 2641 (2008) (prohibiting the death penalty for the rape of a child where the crime did not result, and was not intended to result, in death of the victim).

133. See Lawrence v. Texas, 123 S. Ct. 2472, 2483 (2003) (describing the right at issue "as an integral part of human freedom in many other countries").

134. See Washington v. Glucksberg, 521 U.S. 702, 710 n.8, 718 n.16 (1997) (citing Rodriguez v. British Columbia, 107 D.L.R. (4th) 342, 404 (Can. 1993)) (discussing assisted-suicide laws in Austria, Spain, Italy, the United Kingdom, the Netherlands, Denmark, Switzerland, and France); Planned Parenthood of Southeastern Pa. v. Casey, 505 U.S. 833, 945 n.1 (1992) (Rehnquist, C. J., concurring in part and dissenting in part).

135. See Anne-Marie Slaughter, "A Global Community of Courts," *Harvard International Law Review* 44 (2003): 191, 218–219 (demonstrating that transnational adjudication can contribute to a "global community of courts").

136. For example, consider reliance on cosmopolitan law, defined as "those elements of law—albeit created by states—which create powers and constraints, and rights and duties, which transcend the claims of nation-states and which have far-reaching national consequences." David Held et al., "Rethinking Globalization," in *The Global Transformations Reader: An Introduction to the Globalization Debate*, ed. David Held and Anthony McGrew (Cambridge: Polity Press, 2000): 70. The cosmopolitan project attempts to specify the principles and institutions for making sites and forms of power that presently lie beyond the scope of state democratic processes. See generally Jeremy Waldron, "Minority Cultures and the Cosmopolitan Alternative," *University of Michigan Journal of Law Reform* 25 (1992): 751. For a related claim that proposes judicial review modeling democratic self-determination, see Frank I. Michelman, "The Supreme Court, 1985 Term—Foreword: Traces of Self-Government," *Harvard Law Review* 100 (1986): 4, 74–77; see also Eyal Benvenisti, "Reclaiming Democracy: The Strategic Uses of Foreign and International Law by National Courts," *American Journal of International Law* 102 (2008): 241–274 .

137. Hersch Lauterpacht, "The Grotian Tradition in International Law," *British Yearbook of International Law* 23 (1946).

CHAPTER 8

1. The quotation in the epigraph is from Hersch Lauterpacht, "The Grotian Tradition in International Law," *British Yearbook of International Law* 23 (1946): 46.
2. Press Release, United Nations, Establishing International Criminal Court Will Be Fitting Way to Inaugurate New Millennium, Secretary-General Tells Court's Preparatory Commission, UN Doc. No. SG/SM/6895 (February 16, 1999), available at www.un.org/News/Press/docs/1999/19990216.sgsm6895.html.
3. See Ruti Teitel, "Comparative Constitutionalism in a Global Age," *Harvard Law Review* 111 (2004): 2570–2596.
4. See, e.g., "Racism Summit Seeks Breakthrough," *BBC*, September 5, 2001, available at http://news.bbc.co.uk/2/hi/africa/1525981.stm (last visited June 24, 2009). There are many examples. One attempt to theorize this issue in the context of American constitutionalism is Cass Sunstein's anticaste notion of equality jurisprudence. See, e.g., Cass R. Sunstein, "The Anti-caste Principle," *Michigan Law Review* 92 (1994): 2410–2455 (1994).
5. Amy Chua, *World on Fire: How Exporting Free Market Democracy Breeds Ethnic Hatred and Global Instability* (New York: Doubleday, 2003).
6. See Korematsu v. United States, 323 U.S. 214 (1944).
7. Accordance with International Law of the Unilateral Declaration of Independence in Respect of Kosovo, Advisory Opinion (International Court of Justice, July 22, 2010).
8. Ibid.
9. Ibid. at para. 109.
10. Ibid. at para. 105.
11. Reference re Secession of Quebec, 2 S.C.R. 217 (1998): para. 155.
12. Ibid.
13. See Jurgen Habermas, "Struggles for Recognition in the Democratic Constitutional State," in *Multiculturalism: Examining the Politics of Recognition,* ed. Charles Taylor and Amy Guttman (Princeton: Princeton University Press, 1994): 107–148.
14. Hannah Arendt, *Eichmann in Jerusalem* (New York: Penguin, 1963): 276.
15. See Michael Sandel, *Liberalism and the Limits of Justice,* 2nd ed. (Cambridge: Cambridge University Press, 1998).
16. See Geneva Convention IV Relative to the Protection of Civilian Persons in Time of War, 75 U.N.T.S. 287, Article 56, October 21, 1950, Article 56 (regarding "right to health"); or Protocol I Additional to the Geneva Conventions of August 12, 1949, and Relating to the Protection of Victims of International Armed Conflicts (Protocol I), 1125 U.N.T.S. 3, Article 56, December 7, 1979 (regarding the right to a healthy environment).
17. See Charles Taylor, "The Politics of Recognition," in *Multiculturalism: Examining the Politics of Recognition* (Princeton: Princeton University Press, 1994): 25–74.
18. Jeremy Waldron, "Minority Cultures and the Cosmopolitan Alternative," in *The Rights of Minority Cultures,* ed. Will Kymlicka, (Oxford: Oxford University Press, 1995), 93–119.
19. UN Charter, at Article 1(2).
20. Convention on the Prevention and Punishment of the Crime of Genocide, U.N. Doc. A/810 (adopted December 9, 1948; entered into force January 12, 1951).
21. Ibid., Article 1.
22. The Universal Declaration of Human Rights, U.N. General Assembly Resolution 217A, U.N. Doc. A/810 (December 10, 1948), Preamble.
23. Convention Relating to the Status of Refugees, 189 U.N.T.S. 150 (adopted July 28, 1951; entered into force April 22, 1954); see also Protocol Relating to the

Status of Refugees, 606 U.N.T.S. 267 (adopted January 31, 1967; entered into force October 4, 1967).

24. Convention Relating to the Status of Stateless Persons, 360 U.N.T.S. 117 (adopted on September 28, 1954; entered into force June 6, 1960).

25. See United Nations, Security Council, The Rule of Law and Transitional Justice in Conflict and Post Conflict Societies, Report of the Secretary General, U.N. Doc. No. S/2004/616 (2004).

26. Case Concerning the Application of the Convention on the Prevention and Punishment of the Crime of Genocide (Bosnia and Herzegovina v. Serbia and Montenegro) 2007 I.C.J. 91 (2007).

27. Ibid. at paras. 284–285.

28. Case of Sejdic and Finci v. Bosnia and Herzegovina, European Court of Human Rights Applications Nos. 27996/06 and 34836/06, Judgment (December 22, 2009).

29. Ibid. at paras. 43–44.

30. Ibid. at para. 45.

31. Case of Orsus and Others v. Croatia, App. No. 15766/03 (European Court of Human Rights, July 17, 2008): para. 147.

32. Ibid. at paras. 149–150.

33. R (on the application of Al-Jedda) (FC) (Appellant) v. Secretary of State for Defence (Respondent) (2007) UKHL 58 (House of Lords, December 12, 2007); Behrami and Behrami v. France; Saramati v. France, Germany, and Norway, Joint Apps. Nos. 71412/01 and 78166/01, Admissibility Decision (European Court of Human Rights, May 31, 2007): paras. 104, 108.

34. "Hamas says it will oversee Gaza relief efforts," Agence France Presse, January 24, 2009, available at www.google.com/hostednews/afp/article/ALeqM5h3ZqUi VRrrfI7eCUNl3OeI7CIc5A (last visited March 25, 2011).

35. See "Russian Tanks Enter South Ossetia," BBC, August 8, 2008, available at http://news.bbc.co.uk/2/hi/7548715.stm (last visited March 25, 2011). See also Application of the International Convention on the Elimination of All Forms of Racial Discrimination (Georgia v. Russian Federation), No. 140, judgment (International Court of Justice, April 1, 2011).

36. See Human Rights Watch, Up in Flames: Humanitarian Law Violations and Civilian Victims in the Conflict over South Ossetia (January 23, 2009), available at www.hrw.org/en/reports/2009/01/22/flames-0 (last visited March 25, 2011).

37. Ronald Beiner, Hannah Arendt's Lectures on Kant's Political Philosophy (Chicago: University of Chicago Press, 1992), 101.

38. Hannah Arendt, Eichmann in Jerusalem: A Report on the Banality of Evil (New York: Penguin, 1963), 268–269, 276.

39. Ibid., 276.

40. Hedley Bull, Benedict Kingsbury, and Adam Roberts, Hugo Grotius and International Relations (Oxford: Clarendon Press, 1992), 7, 12–13 (on Grotian view of society of states existing when a group of states forms a society, in the sense that the states conceive themselves to be bound by a common set of rules). See Hugo Grotius, De Jure Belli ac Pacis, trans. Francis W. Kelsey (Oxford: Clarendon Press, 1925).

41. In its most expansive version, this claim for law is presaged in Alexandre Kojeve, Outline of a Phenomenology of Right (Lanham, Md.: Rowman and Littlefield, 2007), where Kojeve argues that a universal, global legal normativity will spell the end of politics, at least in Schmittean terms; there is no need to resort to political and, implicitly, violent struggle to resolve any controversy.

42. The preamble of the ICC Statute affirms "that the most serious crimes of concern to the international community as a whole must not go unpunished and that their

effective prosecution must be ensured by taking measures at the national level and by enhancing international cooperation." As provided under Article 5 of the Statute, these crimes are genocide, crimes against humanity, war crimes, and the crime of aggression. Under Article 5, para. 2, "The Court shall exercise jurisdiction over the crime of aggression once a provision is adopted in accordance with articles 121 and 123 defining the crime and setting out the conditions under which the Court shall exercise jurisdiction with respect to this crime. Such a provision shall be consistent with the relevant provisions of the Charter of the United Nations." See also Article 6, defining genocide; Article 7, defining crimes against humanity; and Article 8, defining war crimes.

43. *Humanitarianism and Suffering: The Mobilization of Empathy*, ed. Richard Wilson and Richard Brown (New York: Cambridge University Press, 2008).
44. Barrios Altos Case, Judgment of March 14, 2001, Inter-American Court of Human Rights (Ser. C) No. 75 (2001) (concurring opinion of Judge Trindade, at para. 26).
45. Conference on Peace in Yugoslavia, Arbitration Commission, Opinion No. 1, January 11, 1991, 31 I.L.M 1494 (1992).
46. Ibid.
47. See Accordance with International Law of the Unilateral Declaration of Independence by the Provisional Institutions of Self-Government of Kosovo, Further Written Contribution of the Republic of Kosovo (International Court of Justice, July 17, 2009).
48. See African Commission on Human and Peoples' Rights (May 27, 2009) (citing Katangese Peoples Congress v. Zaire, Comm. No. 75/92 (1995)).
49. Press Release, Council of the European Union, 8/207 (July 22, 2008): "The Council welcomes the arrest of Radovan Karadzic, who is indicted by the ICTY for genocide, crimes against humanity and war crimes. This development illustrates the commitment of the new government in Belgrade to contribute to peace and stability in the Balkans regions. It is a significant step on Serbia's path towards the EU. The Council encourages the Serbian government to continue along that path."
50. Hamdan v. Rumsfeld, 548 U.S. 557 (2006) ("The military commission was not born of a desire to dispense a more summary form of justice than is afforded by courts-martial; it developed, rather, as a tribunal of necessity to be employed when courts-martial lacked jurisdiction over either the accused or the subject matter. See Winthrop 831. Exigency lent the commission its legitimacy, but did not further justify the wholesale jettisoning of procedural protections."): 624; Kadi v. Council of the European Union and the Commission of the European Communities, Case T-315/01, 2008 ECJ EUR-Lex LEXIS 1954 (European Court of Justice, September 3, 2008) (finding a breach of fundamental rights of the European Union); Case of Isayeva, Yusupova, and Bazayeva v. Russia, Nos. 57947-9/00, 57948/00, and 57949/00 (European Court of Human Rights, February 24, 2005) (holding "that there has been a violation of Article 2 of the Convention in respect of the respondent State's obligation to protect the right to life of the three applicants and of the two children of the first applicant); Case of Barrios Altos v. Peru (Inter-American Court of Human Rights, March 14, 2001) (holding that Peru violated "the right to life embodied in Article 4 of the American Convention on Human Rights: para. 51.
51. Theodor Meron, "The Geneva Conventions as Customary Law," *American Journal of International Law* 81 (1987): 348, 361.
52. See Hannah Arendt, *Eichmann in Jerusalem: A Report on the Banality of Evil* (New York: Penguin, 1963), 268–269.

53. See Jerry Z. Muller, "Us and Them: The Enduring Power of Ethnic Nationalism," *Foreign Affairs* 18 (2008): 18.
54. See Martha Nussbaum, "Compassion and Terror," *Daedalus* 132(1) (Winter 2003): 10, 15.
55. E.g., the International Covenant on Civil and Political Rights, Article 7.
56. See Daniel Kanstroom, "On 'Waterboarding': Legal Interpretation and the Continuing Struggle for Human Rights," *Boston College Third World Law Journal* 28 (2008): 269; see chapter 5.
57. See Peter Singer, *One World: The Ethics of Globalization* (New Haven: Yale University Press, 2004): 60–70 (on mistreatment of animals). See also Jeremy Waldron, *Torture, Terror, and Trade-Offs: Philosophy for the White House* (Oxford: Oxford University Press, 2010).
58. See Richard Rorty, *Contingency, Irony, and Solidarity* (New York: Cambridge University Press, 1989).
59. See Jonathan Glover, *Humanity: A Moral History of the Twentieth Century* (New Haven: Yale University Press, 2000).
60. See Costas Douzinas, *Human Rights and Empire: The Political Philosophy of Cosmopolitanism* (New York: Routledge, 2007). See also David Rieff, *A Bed for the Night* (New York: Simon and Schuster, 2002).
61. Michael Ignatieff, *Human Rights as Politics and Idolatry* (Princeton: Princeton University Press, 2001): 9.
62. Ibid., 165.
63. David Kennedy, *The Dark Sides of Virtue: Reassessing International Humanitarianism* (Princeton: Princeton University Press 2004).
64. On Schmitt and Kelson, see David Dyzenhaus, *Legality and Legitimacy: Carl Schmitt, Hans Kelsen and Hermann Heller in Weimar* (Oxford: Oxford University Press, 1997).
65. See Jacques Derrida, *Cosmopolitanism and Forgiveness* (New York: Routledge, 2001).
66. See Benedict Anderson, *Imagined Communities: Reflections on the Origin and Spread of Nationalism* (London: Verso, 1991).
67. See Catherine A. MacKinnon, "Women's September 11th: Rethinking the International Law of Conflict," *Harvard International Law Journal* 47 (2006): 1, 8, n.30.
68. Catherine MacKinnon, *Are Women Human? And Other International Dialogues* (Cambridge, Mass.: Harvard University Press, 2006): 43.
69. See Genocide Convention, Article II (ethnicity seen as a community of people bound together by the same customs, language, and/or race). See William Schabas, *Genocide in International Law: The Crime of Crimes* (Cambridge: Cambridge University Press, 2000): 111–112.
70. Prosecutor v. Akayesu, Case No. ICTR-96-4-T, Trial Judgment (International Criminal Tribunal for Rwanda, September 2, 1998).
71. In Kayishema and Ruzindana, the ICTR stated that "an ethnic group is ones whose members share a common language or culture, or a group which distinguishes itself, as such –self identification; or a group identified by others" (ICTR-95-1-T Trial chamber, May 21, 1999), para. 98.
72. See United Nations, Security Council, The Rule of Law and Transitional Justice in Conflict and Post Conflict Societies, Report of the Secretary General, U.N. Doc. No. S/2004/616 (2004) (calling for a comprehensive strategy to "pay special attention to abuses committed against groups most affected by conflict, such as minorities,

the elderly, children, women, prisoners, displaced persons, and refugees and establish particular measures for their protection and redress in judicial and reconciliation processes.") United Nations, Security Council, Resolution 1325, UN Doc. No S/RES/1325 (2000) (expressed the "concern that civilians, particularly women and children, account for the vast majority of those adversely affected by armed conflict," available at www.un.org/events/res_1325e.pdf (last visited March 25, 2011).

73. The French government issued a press release in July 2010 justifying the deportation order as follows: "The President of the Republic, also found totally unacceptable [the] situation of lawlessness that characterized the Roma people"; Press Release, Communiqué faisant suite à la réunion ministérielle de ce jour sur la situation des gens du voyage et des Roms (July 2010), available at www.elysee.fr/president/les-actualites/communiques-de-presse/2010/juillet/communique-faisant-suite-a-la-reunion.9381.html (last visited March 25, 2011); see also Case of Sejdic and Finci v. Bosnia and Herzegovina, European Court of Human Rights Applications Nos. 27996/06 and 34836/06, Judgment (December 22, 2009). In response to the French order, the European Union has threatened to take legal action. "EU May Take Legal Action against France over Roma," *BBC News*, September 14, 2010, available at www.bbc.co.uk/news/world-europe-11301307 (last visited March 25, 2011).

74. David Held, *Global Transformations, Politics, Economics and Culture* (Stanford: Stanford University Press 1999).

75. The Universal Declaration of Human Rights, U.N. General Assembly Resolution 217A, U.N. Doc. A/810 (December 10, 1948).

76. The Universal Declaration of the Rights of Peoples, The Unrepresented Nations and Peoples Organization (UNPO), Tartu Coordination Office, on 29 August–30 August 1998, 31 October–1 November 1998, and 16 April–17 April 1999 in Tartu and Otepää, Estonia, available at www.unpo.org/article/105 (last visited March 25, 2011).

77. International Covenant on Civil and Political Rights, U.N. General Assembly Resolution 2200A, December 16, 1966 (entered into force March 23, 1976), Article 27. See also Article 1 (protecting all peoples' "right of self-determination.").

78. Declaration on the Rights of Indigenous Peoples, U.N. General Assembly Resolution 61/295, September 13, 2007), Article 9.

79. See African Charter on Human and Peoples' Rights, Articles 20, 22 (entered into force October 21, 1986).

80. See Antonio Cassese, *Self-Determination of Peoples: A Legal Reappraisal* (New York: Cambridge University Press, 1995): 328–329.

81. See Benedict Kingsbury, Nico Krisch, Richard B. Stewart, and Jonathan B. Wiener, "The Emergence of Global Administrative Law," *Law and Contemporary Problems* 68 (2005); Benedict Kingsbury, "Reconciling Five Competing Conceptual Structures of Indigenous Peoples' Claims in International and Comparative Law," *New York University Journal on International Law and Politics* 34 (2001–2): 189. See also James Crawford, The Rights of Peoples (Oxford: Oxford University Press, 1988).

82. Hannah Arendt, *The Origins of Totalitarianism* (New York: Schocken, 1968), 295–296.

83. Sosa v. Alvarez-Machain, 542 U.S. 692, 762 (2004).

84. See Jeremy Waldron, "Minority Cultures and the Cosmopolitan Alternative," *University of Michigan Journal of Law Reform* 25 (1992): 751.

85. See John Rawls, *The Law of Peoples* (Cambridge, Mass.: Harvard University Press, 2001).

86. Interestingly, the U.N. has passed a multitude of resolutions aimed at combating the defamation of groups and, in particular, the defamation of religion. For example, the General Assembly has passed resolutions on combating the defamation of religion in 2006, 2007, and 2008: U.N. General Assembly Resolution 61/164, U.N. Doc. A/RES/61/164 (December 19, 2006); U.N. General Assembly Resolution 62/154, U.N. Doc. A/RES/62/154 (December 18, 2007); U.N. General Assembly Resolution 63/171, U.N. Doc. A/RES/63/171 (December 18, 2008); see also United Nations Economic and Social Council (ECOSOC), Sub-Committee on Human Rights, Racism, Racial Discrimination, Xenophobia and All Forms of Discrimination, P 4, U.N. Doc. E/CN.4/2005/18/Add.4 (December 13, 2004).

87. See Ayelet Shachar, *Multicultural Jurisdictions: Cultural Differences and Women's Rights* (New York: Cambridge University Press, 2001): 146–150.

88. Archbishop of Canterbury, Civil and Religious Law in England: A Religious Perspective (February 7, 2008), available at www.archbishopofcanterbury.org/1575. See also Ian Buruma, *Murder in Amsterdam: The Death of Theo van Gogh and the Limits of Tolerance* (New York: Penguin Group, 2006) (proposing equal treatment across religious group lines).

89. Accordance with International Law of the Unilateral Declaration of Independence in Respect of Kosovo (International Court of Justice, July 22, 2010).

90. John Rawls, *The Law of Peoples* (Cambridge, Mass.: Harvard University Press, 2001), 43, 49.

91. Anne-Marie Slaughter, "Law among Liberal States: Liberal Internationalism and the Act of State Doctrine," *Columbia Law Review* 92 (1992): 1907.

CHAPTER 9

1. UN Security Council Resolution 1973, U.N. Doc S/RES/1973 (2011).
2. Ibid.
3. Coard et al. v. United States, Case No. 10.951, Report No. 109/99, OEA/Ser. L/V/II.106, Doc. 6 Rev. (Inter-American Court of Human Rights, September 29, 1999): para. 59 (holding that both human rights and humanitarian law are applicable in "the protection of the individual").

INDEX